Dedicated to The Whole Earth Catalog

A Sentry Guide to

The 70's Self-Help Revolution

ISBN Paperback 978-1-989647-26-4

A Byrd Press Publication
Toronto
www.byrdpress.com
publisher@byrdpress.com

cover design R.H. Mason
interior art Felipe Silva

A Sentry Guide to

The 70's Self-Help Revolution

Table of Contents

Introduction

This Guide, to the self-help movements that occurred in the 1970s in the United States, like all Sentry Guides, is a study guide and catalog of ideas.

Within, we explore the psychological, wellness, and self-help movements that emerged in the 1970s. This book provides an in-depth analysis of the various self-help books and authors that gained popularity during this time, and examines the cultural and social factors that contributed to the movement's rise. Some topics and personalities are covered in-depth, some are not.

The psychological, wellness, and self-help movements of the 1970s had both positive and negative aspects. On the one hand, these movements encouraged people to take control of their lives and to seek out ways to improve their mental and physical health. They also helped to destigmatize mental health issues and encouraged people to seek out therapy and other forms of treatment.

On the other hand, some critics argue that these movements promoted a culture of narcissism and self-absorption, and that they encouraged people to focus too much on their own individual needs and desires at the expense of others. Additionally, some self-help books and programs were criticized for promoting unrealistic expectations and for oversimplifying complex issues.

The topics covered are presented as they pertained to the general public of the 70s. The assumption is the self-help movement was directed to relatively average people without serious mental illness.

Notes:

This Guide is not a narrative or comprehensive history of the psychological, wellness, and self-help movements of the 1970s. Rather, it is a point of entry into this fascinating and complex topic. Readers are encouraged to flip through the book as they see fit, using it as a study guide and catalog of ideas that they can apply to their own lives. Whether you are a student of cultural history, a self-help enthusiast, or simply curious about the 70s self-help revolution, we hope this book provides some insight, guidance and friendship in your search for the Inner Divine. Wonky formatting is in homage to the DIY publications and underground spirit of the 70s and the acknowledgment that this is a field guide, and a report from the field, and we chose to retain that spirit in the format of this Book.

Part I: Classical Thought to American Pop: Psychology and the Quest for Personal Growth

1. *Eudaimonia* and 'Substantial Happiness': Aristotle and Benjamin Franklin

This section of the book may seem out of place since it is discussing how to define and create happiness, which may not appear to be directly related to the 1970s. However, it is important to note that the pursuit of happiness and self-improvement were key themes during this time. The section will explore the following questions that are relevant to both the 1970s and the pursuit of happiness:

- How does a person define happiness?
- Once defined, how does a person seek to create inner and outer circumstances in which happiness is invited in and is enticed to stay?

Is happiness an ambivalent cat? Is it a dog that can be made loyal through thoughtful, firm and loving attentions? Is it a wild bird visiting curiously, while it is about it's own business?

I do want to take a moment to explore the different views of Aristotle and Ben Franklin on the pursuit of happiness and self-improvement. Both philosophers believed that happiness is the ultimate goal of human life, but they had different ideas about how to achieve it. Aristotle believed that happiness is achieved through virtuous activity, while Franklin believed that happiness is achieved through self-improvement and personal responsibility.

In light of this, let's take a quick look at the similarities and differences of each philosopher's approach to happiness and self-improvement. Aristotle's emphasis on virtuous activity promotes a sense of purpose and meaning in life, but it can also be seen as rigid and inflexible. Franklin's emphasis on self-improvement and personal responsibility promotes a sense of agency and control over one's life, but it can also be seen as individualistic and self-centered. Both informed the American seeker-of-happiness entering the 1970s.

Aristotle's *Eudaimonia*

- Aristotle's theory of *eudaimonia* stems from his understanding of what makes a human being.

- Aristotle's "happiness" means a life of reason and identity as a human being.

- *Eudaimonia* is a way of living that involves virtuous activity and the pursuit of excellence.

Ben Franklin's Idea of Happiness

- Franklin believed that everyone naturally seeks happiness.

- For Franklin, happiness meant lifelong learning in the marketplace of ideas, or self-improvement.

- Franklin's conception of happiness encompasses the great contradiction in American culture: individualistic in the focus on the self, yet communitarian in the reliance on a cooperative marketplace.

- Importantly, Franklin's approach to happiness emphasizes self-discipline, moral virtues, and the pursuit of meaningful goals.

But, Why Aristotle and Ben Franklin?

The late 1960s and 1970s witnessed a cultural shift and a proliferation of self-help philosophies and personal development movements that were influenced by various philosophical traditions, including Aristotle's concept of *eudaimonia* and Ben Franklin's philosophy of self-improvement.

These philosophies played a significant role in shaping the mindset and aspirations of American individuals during that time, particularly in the context of personal growth, self-worth, and happiness. Specifically:

1. Emphasis on Personal Growth and Fulfillment:

The ideas of *eudaimonia* and self-improvement from Aristotle and Ben Franklin resonated with the generation of the late 60s and 70s, as they sought personal growth and fulfillment outside traditional societal norms. There was a growing interest in exploring individual potential and self-actualization, often encouraged by the belief that personal development could lead to a more meaningful and fulfilling life.

2. Focus on Self-Discovery and Authenticity:

Influenced by these philosophical traditions, the self-help movements of the 60s and 70s emphasized the importance of self-discovery and authenticity. This period witnessed an increased interest in introspection, self-exploration, and the pursuit of one's true identity and purpose, reflecting the influence of *eudaimonia* and the idea of living in accordance with one's inherent values and virtues.

3. Cultivation of Personal Agency and Empowerment:

Eudaimonia and Franklin's philosophy of self-improvement fostered the belief in personal agency and the idea that individuals have the power to shape their own destinies. This notion of empowerment fueled the self-help culture of the 60s and 70s, encouraging people to take control of their lives, set goals, and actively pursue paths that would lead to personal fulfillment and happiness.

4. Community and Social Engagement:

Both *eudaimonia* and Franklin's philosophy emphasize the importance of community and social engagement. This emphasis on communal well-being and the idea of contributing to society's betterment influenced the generation of the late 60s and 70s to actively participate in various social and cultural movements aimed at fostering positive societal change, such as the civil rights movement, the feminist movement, and environmental activism.

In summary, the ideas of *eudaimonia* and Franklin's philosophy of self-improvement provided a philosophical framework for the self-help movements and personal development trends that emerged in the late 60s and 70s. These philosophies contributed to a broader cultural shift towards self-exploration, empowerment, and social engagement, emphasizing the pursuit of personal growth and fulfillment within the context of societal well-being.

Why Not Plato and Sartre? Or, Marcus Aurelius and Thomas Jefferson?

Ben Franklin

The 1970s self-help movement drew inspiration from various philosophical traditions, but the focus on Benjamin Franklin's principles over those of philosophers like Plato and Jean-Paul Sartre can be attributed to several key reasons:

1. Practical Approach and Individual Agency: Benjamin Franklin's philosophy emphasizes practical self-improvement through daily habits and personal agency. His emphasis on virtues like industry, frugality, and humility resonated with the practical-minded individuals of the 1970s seeking tangible strategies for self-improvement and success.

2. American Ideals and Pragmatism: Franklin, being one of the founding fathers of the United States, embodied American ideals of pragmatism, entrepreneurship, and self-reliance. His values aligned closely with the American cultural ethos of the 1970s, making his principles particularly appealing to individuals seeking guidance within the context of American values and aspirations.

3. Accessible and Actionable Wisdom: Franklin's aphorisms and writings provided accessible and actionable wisdom that could be readily applied to everyday life. His emphasis on virtues and practical advice on self-discipline, time management, and personal development were easily comprehensible and applicable for individuals looking for immediate ways to improve their lives.

4. Cultural Context of the 1970s: The 1970s marked a period of self-exploration and individualism, with an increasing focus on personal growth and fulfillment. Franklin's pragmatic approach aligned with the spirit of self-empowerment and personal development that defined the cultural landscape of the 1970s.

While Plato and Sartre have made significant contributions to philosophy, their ideas were more abstract and focused on broader existential and metaphysical concerns. In contrast, Franklin's principles provided practical guidance for individuals seeking self-improvement, aligning more closely with the concrete goals and aspirations of the self-help movement of the 1970s.

Aristotle

Aristotle's influence on the 1970s self-help movement can be attributed to several key factors:

1. Emphasis on Virtue and Personal Development: Aristotle's philosophy revolves around the cultivation of virtues and the development of one's character. His emphasis on virtues such as courage, temperance, and wisdom provided a framework for individuals seeking self-improvement and personal development during the 1970s.

2. Focus on Human Flourishing: Aristotle's concept of *eudaimonia*, or human flourishing, resonated with individuals in the self-help movement who were searching for a more meaningful and fulfilling life. His ideas encouraged people to seek a balanced and purposeful existence, aligning with the aspirations of individuals in the 1970s striving for personal growth and fulfillment.

3. Practical Application: While Aristotle's philosophical ideas are profound and theoretical, they also offer practical guidance for leading a virtuous and meaningful life. His teachings on ethics and practical wisdom provided a philosophical basis for individuals seeking actionable advice and guidance for self-improvement.

4. Enduring Philosophical Influence: Aristotle's works have had a lasting impact on Western thought and philosophy. His ideas have been studied and interpreted by countless scholars and thinkers over the centuries, making his philosophy a significant source of inspiration for various intellectual and cultural movements, including the 1970s self-help movement.

Considering these factors, Aristotle's emphasis on personal development, virtue ethics, and human flourishing provided a philosophical basis that aligned with the aspirations and goals of individuals participating in the self-help movement of the 1970s.

His enduring influence on Western thought and his practical insights into ethical living made his philosophy particularly relevant and appealing to individuals seeking guidance for personal growth and fulfillment during that time.

Why Not Plato and Sartre?

Abstract and Complex Philosophies:
Sartre's existentialism and Plato's idealism are complex philosophical systems that deal with abstract concepts and metaphysical inquiries. Their ideas are often more suited for intellectual exploration and academic study rather than practical application in daily life or the self-help context of the 1970s.

Emphasis on Existential Angst and Abstract Ideals:
Sartre's existentialism often focuses on themes of existential angst, freedom, and the absurdity of existence. Plato's philosophical ideas revolve around the forms, the nature of reality, and the pursuit of abstract ideals. While these ideas are intellectually stimulating, they may not provide the immediate practical guidance that individuals in the 1970s sought for personal development and self-improvement.

Why Not Thomas Jefferson and Marcus Aurelius?

This one comes down to personal preference and just finding Ben Franklin and Aristotle a better fit for the purposes of this Book.

Thomas Jefferson and Marcus Aurelius could indeed be relevant figures to consider in the context of the self-help movements of the 1970s. Both individuals have made notable contributions to philosophy and personal development, with their ideas and writings offering valuable insights for individuals seeking guidance and inspiration during that time. HA few observations on that point:

1. Thomas Jefferson:
 - Jefferson's emphasis on individual liberty, democracy, and the pursuit of happiness aligns closely with the values and aspirations of the self-help movements of the 1970s. His advocacy for personal freedom and the pursuit of one's own path resonated with individuals seeking self-empowerment and fulfillment during that period.

2. Marcus Aurelius:
 - Marcus Aurelius, a Roman emperor and Stoic philosopher, has provided timeless wisdom on personal growth, resilience, and ethical living through his "Meditations." His Stoic teachings on the importance of self-discipline, moral virtue, and acceptance of the natural order have offered guidance to individuals seeking inner strength and tranquility during challenging times, which could have been relevant to the cultural context of the 1970s.

Considering the resonance of their ideas with the values and goals of the 1970s self-help movements, the works and philosophies of Jefferson and Marcus Aurelius could have been influential and inspirational for individuals seeking personal development and self-improvement during that period. Their emphasis on personal agency, ethical conduct, and the pursuit of a meaningful life would have been valuable resources for individuals looking for guidance on self-fulfillment and well-being.

How Aristotle and Ben Franklin Differed

Benjamin Franklin's path to happiness and Aristotle's approach to *eudaimonia* share some similarities, such as the emphasis on virtue and the cultivation of a well-rounded character. However, they also differ in their specific philosophical underpinnings and the methods they propose for achieving happiness. Here's a comparison between the two:

1. Virtue and Self-Improvement:

Benjamin Franklin: Franklin emphasized the cultivation of specific virtues such as industry, frugality, and humility. He believed in the importance of self-discipline and personal development as key components of a happy and successful life. His approach was practical and focused on daily habits and behaviors that contribute to a well-lived life.

Aristotle: Aristotle's concept of *eudaimonia* is closely tied to the development of moral and intellectual virtues. He believed that achieving *eudaimonia* requires cultivating virtues such as courage, justice, temperance, and wisdom. Virtuous actions and the exercise of reason were central to Aristotle's understanding of human flourishing.

2. Purpose and Fulfillment:

Benjamin Franklin: Franklin's approach to happiness involved setting clear goals and working towards their achievement. He stressed the importance of a purposeful life, dedicated to self-improvement and the betterment of society. His emphasis on hard work and the pursuit of excellence was in line with his belief in the practical application of one's skills and talents.

Aristotle: Aristotle believed that *eudaimonia* was the ultimate human goal, achievable through the realization of one's potential and the fulfillment of one's unique function or purpose. He emphasized the importance of leading a life in accordance with reason and in pursuit of virtue, aiming for the development of one's intellectual and moral capacities.

3. Community and Social Dimension:

Benjamin Franklin: Franklin emphasized the importance of contributing to the well-being of society and fostering communal harmony. He advocated for civic engagement, philanthropy, and the promotion of the common good as essential elements of a fulfilling life.

Aristotle: Aristotle also underscored the significance of community and social relationships in the pursuit of *eudaimonia*. He believed that human flourishing is intimately connected to the cultivation of meaningful friendships and participation in a just and flourishing society.

While both Franklin and Aristotle share an appreciation for the importance of virtue and personal development in the pursuit of happiness, their approaches differ in their emphasis on specific virtues, methods of self-improvement, and the role of the community in achieving a fulfilling life. Franklin's approach tends to be more practical and focused on individual habits, whereas Aristotle's philosophy encompasses a broader theoretical framework that emphasizes the development of the whole person within the context of society.

Ben Franklin Differing with the 70s

In his autobiography, Benjamin Franklin discusses various personal virtues that he considered essential for individual development and success. These virtues were part of his self-improvement project, and he outlined a system to cultivate them.

The thirteen virtues he identified are as follows:

> **1. Temperance:** Eat not to dullness; drink not to elevation.

> **2. Silence:** Speak not but what may benefit others or yourself; avoid trifling conversation.

> **3. Order:** Let all your things have their places; let each part of your business have its time.

> **4. Resolution:** Resolve to perform what you ought; per form without fail what you resolve.

> **5. Frugality:** Make no expense but to do good to others or yourself; i.e., waste nothing.

> **6. Industry:** Lose no time; be always employed in some thing useful; cut off all unnecessary actions.

7. Sincerity: Use no hurtful deceit; think innocently and justly, and, if you speak, speak accordingly.

8. Justice: Wrong none by doing injuries or omitting the benefits that are your duty.

9. Moderation: Avoid extremes; forbear resenting injuries so much as you think they deserve.

10. Cleanliness: Tolerate no uncleanliness in body, clothes, or habitation.

11. Tranquility: Be not disturbed at trifles or at accidents common or unavoidable.

12. Chastity: Rarely use venery but for health or offspring, never to dullness, weakness, or the injury of your own or another's peace or reputation.

13. Humility: Imitate Jesus and Socrates.

Franklin believed that consistently practicing these virtues would lead to personal improvement and a more virtuous and successful life. He strived to incorporate these principles into his daily routine and encouraged others to do the same.

These virtues outlined by Benjamin Franklin in his autobiography reflect a set of moral and practical guidelines aimed at fostering personal improvement and success. While some of these virtues align with the advice given by psychologists and self-help experts in the 1970s, there are notable differences between Franklin's virtues and the prevailing psychological and self-help guidance of that era, as well as the way some individuals chose to live their lives during the 1970s.

Franklin's Differences with 1970s Psychological Advice

1. Emphasis on Morality: Franklin's virtues are deeply rooted in moral principles and ethical conduct, emphasizing personal integrity, honesty, and justice. While psychological advice in the 1970s may have also emphasized personal growth and well-being, it often focused more on self-actualization, self-expression, and individual fulfillment rather than explicitly moral conduct.

2. Focus on Discipline and Self-Restraint: Franklin's virtues emphasize the importance of self-discipline, restraint, and moderation in various aspects of life. In contrast, 1970s psychological advice often encouraged self-expression, liberation, and exploration of personal desires, advocating for individuals to embrace their impulses and express themselves freely.

Franklin's Differences with Some Individuals' Lifestyles in the 1970s Self-Help Movement

1. Emphasis on Materialism and Self-Indulgence: Some individuals in the 1970s self-help movement embraced a more hedonistic and indulgent lifestyle, focusing on the pursuit of personal pleasure, freedom, and material gratification, which diverges from Franklin's emphasis on frugality, temperance, and humility.

2. Focus on Nonconformity and Counter-Culture Ideals: Certain segments of the 1970s self-help movement promoted nonconformity and counter-culture ideals, advocating for radical social change, experimentation with alternative lifestyles, and rejection of traditional societal norms. This contrasts with Franklin's emphasis on order, industry, and adherence to societal and personal responsibilities.

While there may be differences between Franklin's virtues and the prevailing psychological advice and lifestyles of some individuals in the 1970s self-help movement, it is essential to recognize that each of these perspectives reflects a particular approach to personal development, moral conduct, and individual fulfillment, shaped by diverse cultural, social, and philosophical influences of their respective times.

And, to be fair and honest with the contemporary Reader, Benjamin Franklin, like many historical figures, was a complex individual with both admirable qualities and human flaws. While he espoused the virtues outlined in his autobiography, he was not immune to personal failings or contradictions. His involvement with the Hellfire Club, a rumored secret society known for its libertine and irreverent activities, has been a subject of historical debate and speculation. Some scholars suggest that Franklin's purported association with the club may have been exaggerated or misrepresented over time.

Regarding Franklin's acknowledgment of visiting prostitutes, it is true that he made such a confession in his autobiography. However, it is essential to consider the cultural and historical context in which he lived. Eighteenth-century society often held different moral standards compared to contemporary times, and behaviors that are considered morally unacceptable today were sometimes viewed differently in the past.

While Franklin might not have consistently adhered to all the virtues he preached, it is crucial to assess his character and contributions within the context of his time. Franklin's legacy as a Founding Father, diplomat, inventor, and author remains significant, and his contributions to American history and society are widely acknowledged.

His virtues and achievements have had a lasting impact, and he is still celebrated for his intellectual prowess, diplomacy, and contributions to the development of the United States. However, it is important to acknowledge the complexities of his character and the context in which he lived when evaluating his adherence to his professed virtues.

Aristotle's Arguments with the 70s

Aristotle's philosophical ideas, particularly those related to *eudaimonia* (human flourishing) and virtue ethics, would likely have certain differences with the professionals and seekers involved in the self-help movements of the 1970s. These differences may include the following:

1. Emphasis on Virtue and Character Development:
Aristotle's emphasis on cultivating moral virtues and developing a well-rounded character as a means to achieve *eudaimonia* differs from the self-help movements of the 1970s, which often focused on immediate self-fulfillment, personal expression, and individual happiness rather than the development of a virtuous character as a long-term goal.

2. Community and Social Responsibility:
Aristotle's philosophy stresses the importance of communal well-being and ethical conduct within society. His emphasis on the role of the community and one's responsibilities to others contrasts with some aspects of the 1970s self-help movements, which were often more focused on individual empowerment and self-realization without the same level of emphasis on communal or societal responsibilities.

3. Practical Wisdom and Intellectual Pursuits:
Aristotle highlighted the significance of practical wisdom (phronesis) and intellectual pursuits in the pursuit of *eudaimonia*. His belief in the importance of intellectual contemplation and the development of practical wisdom may differ from the emphasis on immediate gratification and self-expression prevalent in some segments of the 1970s self-help movements.

4. Temporal Perspective and Long-Term Goals:
Aristotle's concept of *eudaimonia* is characterized by a more comprehensive and long-term perspective on human flourishing, which involves the development of one's potential over time. This contrasts with certain trends within the 1970s self-help movements that may have focused more on immediate self-fulfillment, personal liberation, and the pursuit of instant gratification without the same emphasis on the gradual development of one's character and ethical conduct over the long term.

These differences highlight the varying philosophical and cultural contexts between Aristotle's ethical framework and the self-help movements of the 1970s. While both aim at personal development and fulfillment, they differ in their approaches to virtue, community, wisdom, and the temporal perspective on achieving human flourishing.

Hedonism: Ancient and Colonial

Hedonism is a philosophical position that places pleasure and happiness as the ultimate or primary intrinsic good. The classical, colonial, and modern interpretations of hedonism have evolved over time:

1. Classical Hedonism:

In classical philosophy, hedonism originated with the Cyrenaic school of thought in ancient Greece, founded by Aristippus.

It held that pleasure and the absence of pain were the highest good, emphasizing immediate sensual gratification as the primary goal of life.

2. Colonial Era Perspectives:

During the colonial era, hedonism was often viewed in a negative light, associated with indulgence, decadence, and moral degeneracy.

Puritan influences during this time emphasized the dangers of hedonistic pursuits and the importance of self-discipline and moral restraint.

3. Modern and 1970s Context:

In modern times, particularly during the 1970s, hedonism took on a broader cultural significance, reflecting a societal shift toward individualism, personal freedom, and the pursuit of pleasure and self-gratification.

This era saw an emphasis on self-expression, liberation, and the exploration of personal desires, often associated with the counter-cultural movements of the time.

Aristotle and Benjamin Franklin, although differing in their respective historical contexts, both advocated for a more tempered and balanced approach to life that prioritized the development of virtues and the pursuit of long-term fulfillment over immediate gratification.

They veered away from the temptations, arguments, and entrapments of hedonism through the following means:

1. Emphasis on Virtue and Moral Development:

Aristotle and Franklin both emphasized the cultivation of virtues and moral character as a means to achieve a fulfilling and meaningful life, prioritizing qualities such as self-discipline, temperance, and humility over the pursuit of immediate pleasure or self-indulgence.

2. Focus on Purposeful Living and Community Values:

Both Aristotle and Franklin emphasized the importance of purposeful living and contributing to the well-being of society. Their philosophies highlighted the significance of communal harmony, ethical conduct, and the pursuit of the common good, promoting a sense of responsibility and contribution to the greater good.

3. Long-Term Fulfillment and Personal Growth:

Aristotle and Franklin's philosophies centered on the pursuit of long-term fulfillment and personal growth through the development of virtues, wisdom, and practical skills. They emphasized the importance of setting meaningful goals, practicing self-improvement, and contributing to society, encouraging a balanced and purposeful approach to life.

By prioritizing virtues, ethical living, and the long-term pursuit of personal growth and communal well-being, Aristotle and Franklin steered clear of the immediate gratification and self-indulgence associated with classical, colonial, and modern interpretations of hedonism.

Other Thinkers, Other Paths

In addition to the paths to happiness outlined by Benjamin Franklin, Aristotle, and hedonism, the Western tradition has encompassed various other philosophical and cultural approaches to achieving happiness. Some notable paths include:

1. Stoicism:
The Stoic philosophers, such as Seneca, Epictetus, and Marcus Aurelius, advocated for cultivating inner resilience, virtue, and moral strength in the face of life's challenges. They emphasized the importance of accepting the things we cannot change and

focusing on personal virtue and ethical living as the key to achieving inner tranquility and happiness.

2. Epicureanism:
Although it shares some similarities with hedonism, Epicureanism, as articulated by philosophers like Epicurus, promotes the pursuit of pleasure but emphasizes moderation and the avoidance of unnecessary desires and fears. It advocates for the cultivation of simple pleasures, friendship, and the avoidance of pain, fostering a state of tranquility and *ataraxia* (freedom from disturbance).

3. Existentialism:
Existentialist philosophers such as Jean-Paul Sartre and Albert Camus considered the search for personal meaning and authenticity as central to the human experience. They emphasized the importance of individual freedom and responsibility in creating one's own sense of purpose and happiness, often by confronting the inherent absurdity and uncertainties of life.

4. Aesthetics:
Certain Western philosophical traditions, particularly in the 18th century, emphasized the pursuit of beauty, harmony, and artistic experiences as avenues to happiness. Philosophers like Immanuel Kant and Friedrich Schiller highlighted the role of aesthetic appreciation, creativity, and the experience of beauty as essential components of a fulfilling life.

5. Utilitarianism:
Developed by philosophers such as Jeremy Bentham and John Stuart Mill, utilitarianism focuses on the maximization of overall happiness or pleasure for the greatest number of people. It posits that actions should be judged based on their capacity to produce the greatest overall happiness or well-being, emphasizing the importance of promoting the common good and social welfare.

Each of these philosophical traditions offers a unique perspective on the nature of happiness and the paths to achieving it, reflecting diverse approaches to the complexities of human existence and the pursuit of a meaningful and fulfilling life.

How Ben Franklin and Aristotle Paved the Way for Americans as They Approached the Self-Help 70s

Benjamin Franklin and Aristotle have had a profound influence on the American idea of self-invention, self-help, rags-to-riches narratives, self-determination, and individual freedom. Their ideas have shaped the origins of American positive thought and have had a lasting impact on the human potential movement. Here is a summary of their influence:

Benjamin Franklin's Influence:

Franklin's emphasis on virtues, self-improvement, and industriousness contributed to the American ethos of hard work, self-reliance, and upward mobility.

His rags-to-riches story, from humble beginnings to success through diligence and self-discipline, became emblematic of the American dream.

His practical advice on personal development, as outlined in his autobiography, resonated with the American spirit of self-help and individual achievement.

Aristotle's Influence:

Aristotle's ideas about virtue ethics, *eudaimonia*, and human flourishing have influenced the American notion of personal fulfillment and moral character.

His emphasis on the pursuit of excellence, the development of virtues, and the realization of one's potential has contributed to the American belief in self-determination and the cultivation of one's talents and abilities.

Aristotle's philosophy has underscored the importance of living a purposeful and virtuous life, which aligns with the American ideals of personal freedom and self-realization.

Hegge and *Gemütlichkeit*

Hegge and *Gemütlichkeit* are terms that relate to feelings of coziness, comfort, and conviviality in Norwegian and German culture, respectively. *Hegge* being, as of this writing, currently in vogue.

Hegge and *Gemütlichkeit* share certain thematic overlaps with American values from the colonial era up until the 1970s, as well as with the 1970s self-help movement, particularly in reaction to increasing commercialization and the pursuit of traditional sources of happiness beyond material success:

1. Emphasis on Community and Social Connection:
Hegge and *Gemütlichkeit*, along with traditional American values, emphasize the importance of community, social connection, and fostering meaningful relationships. The colonial era in America also valued communal support and the idea of a closely-knit community.

In the 1970s, the self-help movement reacted against materialism by emphasizing the importance of interpersonal relationships and communal well-being.

2. Focus on Comfort and Simple Living:
Both *hegge*, *Gemütlichkeit*, and certain historical American values prioritize comfort, simplicity, and a cozy lifestyle. The colonial era, marked by a focus on basic necessities and communal living, reflected a similar inclination towards a simpler way of life.

In the 1970s, the self-help movement advocated for a return to simpler living, emphasizing the pursuit of inner fulfillment over material possessions.

3. Interest in Traditional and Cultural Practices:
Hegge and *Gemütlichkeit*, deeply rooted in Norwegian and German cultural traditions, align with the American value of preserving cultural heritage and traditional practices.

The 1970s self-help movement, in reaction to increasing commercialization, also sought alternative, more traditional paths to happiness, often drawing from cultural and historical practices that emphasized spiritual well-being and personal fulfillment beyond material success.

Hegge and *Gemütlichkeit*, along with traditional American values and the 1970s self-help movement, all reflect a shared inclination towards community, simple living, and a rejection of excessive materialism.

They emphasize the importance of interpersonal connections, cultural heritage, and the pursuit of personal fulfillment beyond material wealth, aligning with a broader sentiment of seeking happiness through communal well-being and a return to more traditional and authentic ways of living.

I am presenting these concepts now because we will soon examine how the decline of a nurturing culture in an increasingly modernized and fragmented American society, where people are isolated, disconnected, and have weak social connections or community bonds, leads to a longing for wholeness and connection. We will explore how this longing intersects with the American ideals of self-invention.

For now...

Onwards and Upwards to the Early Success Stories

The evolution of the rags-to-riches trope and the early success literature is deeply intertwined with the philosophical underpinnings of Benjamin Franklin and Aristotle, two influential thinkers known for their emphasis on personal development and virtue ethics.

The rags-to-riches narrative, a recurring theme in American literature, often portrays the journey of individuals overcoming adversity and rising from humble beginnings to achieve prosperity and success. This narrative aligns with Franklin's belief in the transformative power of hard work, perseverance, and self-improvement, as well as Aristotle's emphasis on resilience and the pursuit of excellence as integral components of human flourishing.

Franklin's advocacy for self-discipline and moral virtues, as reflected in his renowned autobiography and his foundational role in shaping the American ethos of self-reliance and industriousness, echoes the values portrayed in the rags-to-riches trope. Similarly, Aristotle's philosophy of *eudaimonia*, emphasizing the importance of ethical conduct, personal growth, and the pursuit of a meaningful life, resonates with the notion that success is not solely about material wealth but also about achieving one's full potential and leading a virtuous life.

The early success literature, drawing inspiration from these philosophical ideals, often promoted narratives of resilience, perseverance, and the pursuit of personal excellence. These narratives reinforced the idea that success is attainable through dedication, moral conduct, and the willingness to overcome challenges.

The alignment between the philosophical teachings of Franklin and Aristotle and the thematic elements of the rags-to-riches trope and early success literature underscores the enduring influence of their ideas on the American narrative of achievement and personal development.

Suggested Reading On Aristotle's *Eudaimonia*

"*Eudaimonia*" is a concept rooted in ancient Greek philosophy, particularly associated with Aristotle, and it refers to a state of human flourishing or well-being achieved through living a virtuous and meaningful life. If you're interested in exploring this concept further, here are some books that delve into the idea of *eudaimonia* and its philosophical implications:

1. "Nicomachean Ethics" by Aristotle: This foundational work by Aristotle is where the concept of *eudaimonia* is explored in depth. Aristotle discusses the nature of the good life, ethics, and virtue as essential components of *eudaimonia*.

2. "Eudaimonic Ethics: The Philosophy and Psychology of Living Well" by Daniel D. Pekarsky: This book offers a contemporary perspective on *eudaimonia*, examining its relevance to ethics and psychology.

3. "A Life Worthy of the Gods: The Materialist Psychology of Epicurus" by David Konstan: While Epicureanism and Aristotle's philosophy differ in some respects, both touch on ideas related to *eudaimonia*. This book explores Epicurus's approach to the good life and well-being.

4. "Eudaimonia: The Greatest Gift" by Elliott D. Cohen: This book delves into the concept of *eudaimonia* and its significance in ethics, psychology, and personal development.

5. "Virtue Ethics: A Pluralistic View" by Christine Swanton: Virtue ethics, which includes the concept of *eudaimoni*a, is discussed in this book, which explores different perspectives within virtue ethics.

6. "Virtue and Psychology: Pursuing Excellence in Ordinary Practices" edited by Blaine J. Fowers and Ivan D. Yuen: This collection of essays examines the relationship between virtue ethics, psychology, and well-being, touching on the concept of *eudaimonia*.

7. "Eudaimonic Turn: Well-Being in Literary Studies" edited by James O. Pawelski and D.J. Moores: This book explores the concept of *eudaimonia* as it relates to literature and literary analysis, offering insights into its presence in storytelling and narrative.

These books provide a range of perspectives on *eudaimonia*, from its historical origins in ancient philosophy to its contemporary relevance in ethics, psychology, and personal development. Depending on your specific interests and focus, you can choose the one that aligns best with your exploration of this concept.

Suggested Reading On Benjamin Franklin's
Theories, Works and Practices on Happiness

Benjamin Franklin, known for his multifaceted contributions to American history and thought, provided insightful advice on various aspects of life, including health, wealth, and personal development. For a deeper understanding of Franklin's suggestions on how to live long and prosper, the following books offer comprehensive insights into his life, philosophy, and practical wisdom:

1. "The Autobiography of Benjamin Franklin": Franklin's own autobiography provides valuable firsthand accounts of his life, achievements, and the principles he followed for personal development.

2. "Benjamin Franklin: An American Life" by Walter Isaacson: This biography offers a comprehensive exploration of Franklin's life, highlighting his key contributions to American history, as well as his practical wisdom and insights into successful living.

3. "Benjamin Franklin: An American Life" by J.A. Leo Lemay: Another biography that delves into Franklin's life and provides a detailed analysis of his thoughts on various aspects of life, including health, wealth, and personal success.

4. "The Way to Wealth: Advice, Hints, and Tips on Business, Money, and Finance" by Benjamin Franklin: This compilation presents Franklin's timeless insights and aphorisms on financial success and wealth accumulation, offering valuable lessons for contemporary readers.

By engaging with these books, readers can gain a comprehensive understanding of Benjamin Franklin's life and philosophy, as well as his valuable suggestions on how to lead a prosperous and fulfilling life.

2. Rags to Riches and the Origins of American Positive Thought: Horatio Alger, Walden and Self-Love

In exploring the rich tapestry of the American Dream, the concept of 'Rags to Riches' stands as a resolute emblem of the nation's ethos. This narrative of upward social mobility, resilience, and self-made success has not only shaped the American cultural landscape but has also deeply influenced the trajectory of American positive thought.

Delving into the intricate interplay of individual determination and societal transformation, this chapter seeks to unravel the profound linkages between the 'Rags to Riches' trope and the burgeoning consciousness of self-empowerment in American intellectual history.

Within this context, the pioneering works of Horatio Alger, with their compelling narratives of perseverance and triumph over adversity, serve as pivotal touchstones.

Moreover, this chapter endeavors to illuminate the resonance between Alger's literary legacy and the transcendentalist movement, particularly the philosophical currents espoused by the likes of Thoreau and Emerson.

In this exploration, the echoes of transcendentalist ideals, epitomized in the poetic cadence of Walt Whitman's verses, reverberate alongside the 'Rags to Riches' narrative, underscoring the profound influence of self-love and introspection on the American psyche. By traversing the nuanced landscapes of self-invention and spiritual awakening, this chapter sheds light on the intricate web of influences that have shaped the evolution of American positive thought.

(Proto)Positive Psychology

While the formal field of positive psychology as we understand it today did not emerge until the late 20th century, some elements of positive psychology can be identified in 19th-century popular culture.

These elements were often intertwined with broader cultural and philosophical movements of the time. Here are a few ways in which positive psychology-related ideas appeared in 19th-century popular culture:

1. Transcendentalism:

The Transcendentalist movement, which gained prominence in the United States during the 1830s and 1840s, emphasized the value of self-reliance, individualism, and a deep connection with nature. Figures like Ralph Waldo Emerson and Henry David Thoreau promoted ideas related to self-improvement, personal growth, and the pursuit of a fulfilling life. These themes can be seen as precursors to positive psychology concepts.

2. Self-Help Literature:

The 19th century saw the rise of self-help literature, including books like Samuel Smiles' "Self-Help" (1859) and Orison Swett Marden's "Pushing to the Front" (1894). These books encouraged individuals to take control of their lives, cultivate positive habits, and strive for self-improvement.

One of the most influential figures in popularizing the rags to riches theme in American literature was Horatio Alger Jr. He was a prolific writer of juvenile fiction in the late 19th century, and his books often featured young, disadvantaged protagonists who, through hard work, honesty, and perseverance, achieved success and financial stability. His most famous work, "Ragged Dick," published in 1868, is a quintessential example of this genre.

3. Spiritual Movements:

The New Thought movement, which emerged in the late 19th century, emphasized the power of positive thinking, affirmation, and belief in shaping one's reality. This movement had a significant impact on popular culture, promoting the idea that a positive mental attitude could lead to personal success and well-being.

4. Literary Characters:
19th-century literature often featured characters who embodied positive psychological traits. For example, characters like Pollyanna from Eleanor H. Porter's novel "Pollyanna" (1913) were known for their unwavering optimism and ability to find joy in challenging circumstances.

5. Personal Development:
The 19th century witnessed the proliferation of personal development movements and organizations. People were encouraged to develop their character, cultivate positive virtues, and strive for moral and emotional well-being.

Self-empowerment and self-reliance were central themes in the writings of several influential American thinkers and writers, including Henry David Thoreau, Ralph Waldo Emerson, and Walt Whitman. These transcendentalist thinkers and poets played a significant role in shaping American literature and philosophy, emphasizing individualism, self-discovery, and self-expression. Their ideas influenced not only their contemporaries but also subsequent generations of writers and thinkers.

Horatio Alger: Perseverance and the American Dream

Horatio Alger, renowned for his impactful contributions to American literature, played a pivotal role in shaping the genre of 'success' literature through his major works. Alger's narratives, marked by their portrayal of protagonists overcoming adversity to achieve success through hard work and moral integrity, directly influenced the development and popularization of the 'success' literature genre in the United States.

Alger's major works, such as "Ragged Dick" and "Strive and Succeed," depicted the journey of underprivileged youth striving to improve their socioeconomic status through diligence and ethical conduct. These narratives not only resonated with readers of the time but also laid the foundation for a literary tradition that emphasized the values of perseverance, honesty, and ambition. Alger's portrayal of characters navigating the complexities of urban life and striving for upward mobility provided a template for subsequent authors seeking to inspire readers with tales of personal achievement and self-improvement.

The direct influence of Alger's works on the 'success' literature genre is evident in the proliferation of similar narratives in the late 19th and early 20th centuries. Authors and publishers sought to emulate Alger's storytelling style, incorporating themes of determination, moral rectitude, and the attainment of the American Dream. The genre flourished with the publication of numerous 'rags to riches' stories and motivational tales that echoed Alger's emphasis on the transformative power of hard work and integrity.

Alger's legacy in the genre of 'success' literature remains enduring and significant, as his narratives continue to inspire readers and serve as a cultural touchstone for the enduring belief in the possibility of social mobility and personal advancement. Alger's influence on subsequent generations of writers within the genre highlights the lasting impact of his works on the American literary landscape and the collective imagination of the nation.

Transcendentalist Influences: Self-Reliance and Spiritual Awakening

The transcendentalist movement, a philosophical and literary movement prominent in 19th-century America, left an indelible mark on the nation's intellectual landscape. At its core, transcendentalism emphasized the significance of individualism, introspection, and the innate goodness of humanity.

The transcendentalist movement's philosophical tenets intersected with the 'rags to riches' narrative in several key ways, particularly through the shared emphasis on individualism, self-reliance, and the pursuit of personal growth.

Transcendentalist thinkers, such as Ralph Waldo Emerson and Henry David Thoreau, advocated for the primacy of the individual experience and the cultivation of a harmonious relationship with nature. Their philosophical focus on self-discovery and spiritual awakening resonated with the 'rags to riches' narrative, which often portrayed protagonists overcoming adversity through determination and moral fortitude.

The transcendentalist emphasis on introspection and the belief in the inherent goodness of humanity found common ground with the themes of personal transformation and the pursuit of the American Dream depicted in 'rags to riches' stories.

Key Tenets of Transcendentalism

Transcendentalism was a philosophical and literary movement that emerged in the mid-19th century in the United States. It emphasized the inherent goodness of people and nature, as well as the importance of individual intuition and spiritual exploration. At its core, Transcendentalism was characterized by the following core principles and key beliefs:

1. Intuition and Individual Experience: Transcendentalists believed in the importance of trusting one's intuition and personal experience as sources of truth and knowledge, rather than relying solely on established authorities or traditional institutions.

2. Divinity in Nature: Transcendentalists revered nature and believed that it contained spiritual and moral truths. They saw nature as a direct manifestation of the divine and as a source of inspiration and spiritual insight.

3. Self-Reliance and Nonconformity: Transcendentalists emphasized the value of individualism, self-reliance, and nonconformity. They encouraged people to trust in their own instincts and beliefs and to resist societal pressures and conventions that stifled individual freedom and expression.

4. Skepticism of Materialism: Transcendentalists were critical of the growing materialistic values of society, advocating instead for a focus on spiritual and ethical concerns. They believed that an excessive preoccupation with material wealth and possessions detracted from genuine spiritual fulfillment and human connection.

5. Optimism and Idealism: Transcendentalists maintained an optimistic view of humanity's potential for moral and spiritual growth. They believed in the inherent goodness of people and the possibility of personal transformation and social progress through self-examination and the cultivation of virtuous character.

Biographies of Key Figures

1. Ralph Waldo Emerson (1803-1882):
A leading figure of the transcendentalist movement, Emerson was a renowned essayist, lecturer, and poet.

Emerson's influential essay "Self-Reliance" advocated for the empowerment of the individual and the significance of trusting one's intuition and beliefs. His philosophical currents, emphasizing nonconformity and the celebration of the individual spirit, find resonance with the themes of self-determination and moral integrity inherent in the 'rags to riches' narrative. Emerson's emphasis on the value of personal growth and the realization of one's potential aligns with the transformative journeys of characters striving for success despite challenging circumstances.

2. Henry David Thoreau (1817-1862):
Thoreau, a prominent transcendentalist philosopher, is best known for his book "Walden," which chronicles his experiences living a simple life in nature. Thoreau's emphasis on simplicity, self-reliance, and the significance of introspection in his seminal work "Walden" exemplified the transcendentalist commitment

to spiritual awakening and individual transformation. His philosophical currents, emphasizing the pursuit of a meaningful and deliberate existence, echo the perseverance and self-improvement central to the 'rags to riches' narrative.

Thoreau's call to live deliberately and to confront life's essential facts correlates with the protagonists' determination and resilience in their pursuit of success.

Thoreau's "Walden" serves as a profound reflection of self-reliance and spiritual awakening, encapsulating his philosophical ideals and reverence for a life of simplicity and introspection. Thoreau's retreat to Walden Pond exemplifies his commitment to self-reliance, as he sought to live deliberately and confront life's essential truths.

Through his experiences in nature and deliberate isolation, Thoreau found spiritual awakening and a deeper connection with the natural world, which underscored his belief in the intrinsic link between self-reliance and personal fulfillment. "Walden" embodies Thoreau's call for individuals to cultivate a life of authenticity and self-sufficiency, encouraging readers to discover their own truths and embrace the simplicity found in a life of purposeful reflection and spiritual communion.

Thoreau's ideas on simplicity, introspection, and the importance of self-love further underscore his vision of personal fulfillment. He advocated for a deliberate simplification of one's life, emphasizing the importance of focusing on the essential aspects of existence and detaching oneself from materialistic pursuits.

Thoreau's emphasis on introspection highlighted the significance of self-examination and inner reflection, encouraging individuals to delve into their innermost thoughts and emotions to achieve a deeper understanding of themselves and their place in the world.

Moreover, Thoreau's advocacy for self-love underscored the importance of nurturing one's well-being and cultivating a sense of inner contentment and peace. Through these principles, Thoreau espoused a philosophy that resonated with the quest for personal fulfillment and the attainment of a meaningful and purposeful life.

Returning to Aristotle and Franklin

With this in mind, we return for a moment to the Heroes of our previous section. We find that while the emphasis on introspection and the belief in the inherent goodness of humanity was more pronounced in the transcendentalist movement, traces of these themes can be found in the philosophical perspectives of Benjamin Franklin and Aristotle, albeit in different forms.

1. Benjamin Franklin:

Franklin, known for his practical approach to self-improvement and moral development, advocated for introspection and self-examination as essential tools for personal growth. In his autobiography, he reflected on his own character flaws and outlined methods for cultivating virtues. While his approach was more pragmatic and focused on self-discipline, it still encompassed elements of introspection and self-awareness.

2. Aristotle:

Aristotle, in his ethical philosophy, emphasized the cultivation of virtues and the pursuit of *eudaimonia*, or human flourishing. His belief in the potential for human excellence and the development of moral character implies a fundamental trust in the inherent capacity for goodness within individuals. While his emphasis was more on the cultivation of virtuous behavior within societal contexts, it aligns with the idea of recognizing the inherent potential for goodness in humanity.

Though the dedication to introspection and the belief in the inherent goodness of humanity were more explicitly emphasized within the transcendentalist movement, elements of these concepts can be traced in the philosophical frameworks of Benjamin Franklin and Aristotle, reflecting their respective perspectives on personal development and moral conduct.

Returning to Alger

Alger's literary works, characterized by themes of self-invention and resilience, share a striking resonance with transcendentalist philosophy, which emphasizes individualism and the pursuit of spiritual and personal growth. Alger's protagonists, often depicted as overcoming adversity through self-determination and moral integrity, mirror the transcendentalist ideal of self-reliance and the transformative power of the individual spirit. Alger's emphasis on the capacity for personal transformation and the cultivation of virtues aligns with the transcendentalist belief in the innate goodness of humanity and the potential for spiritual awakening through self-examination and introspection.

Furthermore, the 'rags to riches' narrative, popularized through Alger's works, left a lasting impact on American positive thought, influencing the collective consciousness with its portrayal of perseverance, self-reliance, and the triumph of the human spirit over adversity. The ideals of self-love, inherent in Alger's narratives and reflective of the transcendentalist emphasis on the cultivation of inner fulfillment and authenticity, became integral to American positive thought. The 'rags to riches' narrative not only inspired readers to believe in the possibility of personal achievement but also fostered a cultural ethos of resilience and self-determination that continues to resonate within the broader framework of American optimism and aspiration.

Social Support Networks

Both Benjamin Franklin and Aristotle recognized the importance of social support networks, the library, and the university, although their perspectives and experiences varied.

Benjamin Franklin, known for his emphasis on self-improvement and community engagement, saw the value of social support networks in fostering collective growth and development. Franklin believed in the power of communal collaboration and the sharing of knowledge, which was reflected in his establishment of the Library Company of Philadelphia, one of the first subscription libraries in the American colonies. Franklin understood that access to information and the opportunity for intellectual exchange were critical for personal and societal advancement.

He actively promoted the concept of mutual aid and community development, recognizing the role of social networks in facilitating the sharing of resources and ideas for the greater benefit of society.

On the other hand, Aristotle, in his philosophical works, emphasized the significance of social bonds and communal relationships in fostering the development of virtuous individuals and a flourishing society. Aristotle recognized the importance of the community in providing a nurturing environment for intellectual and moral growth. His advocacy for the role of education, as outlined in his work "Politics," highlighted the importance of the university as a space for the cultivation of knowledge and the promotion of civic engagement. Aristotle's belief in the integral role of the polis, or city-state, in shaping the character and values of its citizens underscores his recognition of the societal framework as essential for individual development and the pursuit of the common good.

So, yes. Both Franklin and Aristotle underscored the importance of social support networks, the library, and the university in promoting personal and communal growth, albeit within different contexts. Their respective contributions to the promotion of education and community engagement reflect their shared belief in the transformative power of knowledge and social interaction in fostering individual and societal well-being.

Alexis de Tocqueville's Observations Regarding Social Support Networks in the United States of America

Alexis de Tocqueville, a French political thinker and historian, observed the significant role of American social support networks and mutual aid societies during his travels to the United States in the 1830s. In his renowned work "Democracy in America," de Tocqueville documented the robust presence of voluntary associations and communal organizations that operated outside the government's purview. He noted that Americans were actively engaged in various voluntary associations, including religious organizations, community groups, and charitable societies, which played a vital role in providing support and assistance to individuals and communities.

De Tocqueville highlighted the importance of these social networks in fostering a sense of civic responsibility and communal solidarity. He observed that Americans, driven by a shared spirit of cooperation and mutual aid, organized themselves into voluntary associations to address social, economic, and cultural needs within their communities. These associations served as critical pillars of support, providing assistance to those in need and fostering a sense of belonging and interconnectedness among citizens.

Moreover, de Tocqueville recognized that these voluntary associations contributed to the maintenance of social order and the preservation of democratic values. They promoted active citizen participation and civic engagement, allowing individuals to collaborate in the pursuit of common goals and interests. De Tocqueville's observations emphasized the significance of these social support networks in reinforcing the fabric of American society, highlighting their role in promoting social cohesion, democratic engagement, and the cultivation of a vibrant civil society outside the realm of formal government institutions.

Social Capital and 'Bowling Alone'

"Bowling Alone: The Collapse and Revival of American Community" is a book by Robert D. Putnam, a political scientist and professor, which examines the decline of social capital and community engagement in the United States. Putnam's work highlights the diminishing trend of participation in voluntary associations, such as clubs, community groups, and social organizations, after the Second World War. He observed a significant decrease in social involvement and civic participation, with individuals becoming increasingly disengaged from communal activities and interpersonal relationships.

Putnam attributed this decline in social support networks to various factors, including the rise of suburbanization, which led to increased isolation and decreased face-to-face interactions among community members. He also pointed to the impact of technological advancements, such as the rise of television and later the internet, which reduced the time individuals spent on communal activities and increased their time spent in isolation. Furthermore, he highlighted the effects of busy work schedules and long commutes, which limited the opportunities for social interaction and community engagement.

The consequences of this decline in social capital, as outlined by Putnam, included a weakened sense of trust and reciprocity among citizens, decreased political participation, and a diminished sense of collective responsibility. He argued that the breakdown of social support networks had implications for the overall health of American democracy and community well-being, as it weakened the bonds of solidarity and cooperation that underpin a thriving civil society. Putnam's work underscored the need for revitalizing communal engagement and promoting active citizenship to foster a sense of shared responsibility and strengthen the social fabric of American communities.

The slowing advancing decline of social integration and common bonds in American daily life, alongside the decline of communal engagement and social support networks, would run counter to the recommendations and ideals put forth by Benjamin Franklin and Aristotle.

Both Franklin and Aristotle emphasized the significance of communal bonds, social cooperation, and the cultivation of virtuous character within a supportive community. Their philosophies underscored the importance of collective well-being, civic participation, and the pursuit of the common good, reflecting a belief in the transformative power of shared values and mutual aid.

The rise of methods of 'self-help' within such a social context can be seen as a response to the challenges posed by the erosion of communal ties and the fragmentation of societal cohesion. 'Self-help' philosophies, rooted in the ethos of individual agency and personal empowerment, have sought to provide individuals with tools for navigating the complexities of an increasingly fragmented and isolating social landscape. These philosophies aim to instill a sense of self-reliance and resilience in the face of societal challenges, offering guidance for personal development and growth within a context of diminishing communal support.

While 'self-help' methodologies serve as a means for individuals to navigate the challenges posed by the decline of communal engagement, they also reflect a broader societal shift towards an emphasis on individual autonomy and self-improvement in the absence of strong communal ties. This shift highlights the evolving dynamics of social cohesion and the changing nature of communal relationships, underscoring the need for adaptive strategies that promote personal development and well-being within an increasingly individualistic social milieu.

What Stayed and What Was Left Behind

Throughout the 18th century to the 1970s, the United States witnessed the emergence of a diverse range of voluntary associations that played crucial roles in various aspects of American society. While some associations continued to thrive beyond the 1960s, others experienced a decline in membership and engagement. The following is a list of some of these notable associations:

1. Religious organizations and churches: Many religious organizations, such as churches, synagogues, and mosques, maintained their significance and continued to play integral roles in communities throughout this period.

2. Civic groups and community organizations: Various civic groups, including local community organizations, neighborhood associations, and homeowners' associations, remained active in fostering community engagement and addressing local concerns while others, such as The Neighborhood Improvement Association, The Citizens for Community Development, The Urban Planning League, The Community Action Council, The Civic Betterment Society saw decline or disappearance reflecting the evolving landscape of community activism and local governance during the late 1970s in the United States.

3. Labor unions and trade organizations: Labor unions and trade organizations, representing workers across different industries, continued to advocate for labor rights and fair working conditions, with some experiencing periods of decline in the latter half of the 20th century.

4. Fraternal societies and lodges: Fraternal organizations and lodges, such as the Freemasons, The Knights of Pythias, The Woodmen of the World, The Independent Order of Odd Fellows, The Grand United Order of Odd Fellows, The Improved Order of Red Men, The Order of United American Mechanics, and Elks Club, retained their influence in fostering social bonds and providing mutual support among their members.

5. Charitable organizations and philanthropic groups: Various charitable organizations, including the Red Cross, The Clara White Mission, The Federation for Community Planning, The Henry Street Settlement, The Russell Sage Foundation United Way, and Salvation Army, remained active in providing social services and humanitarian aid.

6. Social and recreational clubs: Social clubs, country clubs, and recreational organizations, such as The Cotillion Club, The Civic Club, The Rosewood Club, The Country Squires Club and The Green Hills Club continued to offer opportunities for social interaction and leisure activities.

While many of these voluntary associations managed to survive the societal changes of the 1960s, some experienced a decline in membership and influence as a result of shifting societal values, changes in lifestyle patterns, and evolving modes of social interaction. Nonetheless, certain organizations, particularly religious groups, charitable organizations, and some social and recreational clubs, maintained their relevance and continued to serve their respective communities during and after the 1960s.

While some voluntary associations retained their importance in American life during the 1970s, the social landscape of the era also saw the emergence of new forms of community engagement and advocacy.

Amidst the societal changes and cultural shifts of the 1970s, certain organizations managed to maintain their relevance and continued to play significant roles in addressing societal needs and fostering community connections, albeit in different forms which we will touch upon throughout this work. These included:

1. Religious organizations and churches: Religious institutions continued to serve as important pillars of communal support and spiritual guidance for many Americans during the 1970s. Though not touched upon in this work, the Calvary Chapel, Vineyard Churches, Christian Cultural Center, Lakewood Church, and The Potter's House were founded at the same time Rolfing and Biofeedback Therapy were introduced; the same time when Kundalini, Bikram Iyengar Yoga studios were being set up in Los Angeles, New York City, San Francisco and Miami.

2. Charitable organizations and philanthropic groups: Various charitable organizations, responding to the social challenges of the time, remained active in providing assistance and support to individuals and communities in need.

3. Community advocacy groups: New community advocacy groups, arising in response to societal issues such as civil rights, environmental concerns, and gender equality, gained prominence during the 1970s, highlighting the emergence of new forms of grassroots activism and social engagement.

4. Social and recreational clubs: Certain social and recreational clubs continued to offer avenues for leisure activities and social interaction, serving as hubs for community networking and cultural exchange.

The 1970s also marked a period of societal transition, characterized by a growing emphasis on individualism, anti-establishment, anti-traditional attitudes and life choices and the reconfiguration of traditional communal structures.

This shift created a space for the development of new social movements, advocacy groups, and community-based initiatives, reflecting the changing dynamics of American social life and the evolving priorities of the era.

The decade witnessed a growing recognition of the need for innovative approaches to community building and social support, paving the way for the emergence of diverse forms of civic engagement and communal empowerment in the years to come.

Left Behind in the 70s

The rapid social changes that unfolded in the United States during the 1970s, including shifts in religious beliefs, family structures, gender roles, and cultural norms, as well as the impact of civil rights movements, drug culture, and anti-war activism, indeed contributed to a sense of societal upheaval and dislocation. These transformations challenged traditional beliefs and institutions, leading to a period of cultural and ideological flux that left many Americans grappling with uncertainty and searching for new sources of meaning and identity.

Amidst this atmosphere of change and uncertainty, some individuals became more susceptible to charismatic figures, half-baked ideas, and questionable ideologies that promised quick solutions or simplistic explanations for complex societal issues. The vulnerability to manipulation and poor decision-making arose from a combination of factors, including a desire for stability and meaning in a rapidly changing world, a sense of disillusionment with established authorities and institutions, and a longing for belonging and purpose in the face of social fragmentation.

The cultural and social dislocation of the 1970s created fertile ground for the proliferation of charismatic leaders, ideological movements, and fringe groups that preyed on the vulnerabilities of individuals seeking certainty and guidance. Some individuals, in their search for answers and a sense of belonging, were drawn to unscrupulous figures and radical ideologies, leading to instances of poor reasoning and decision-making that had far-reaching consequences for both individuals and society as a whole.

Nevertheless, it is important to note that amidst the turbulence of the era, there were also movements and initiatives that sought to promote social justice, equality, and the exploration of new ideas, contributing to the shaping of a more inclusive and diverse societal landscape in the decades that followed.

Left for the 70s

Between 1900 and 1970, various groups and movements in the United States embodied the wisdom of Benjamin Franklin, the philosophy of Aristotle, the insights of the transcendentalists, and the bootstrap approach of Horatio Alger, each contributing to the development of a diverse and dynamic social landscape. These included:

1. **Progressive activists and social reformers:** Drawing inspiration from Franklin's emphasis on civic engagement and social responsibility, as well as Aristotle's advocacy for a just and equitable society, progressive activists and social reformers sought to address social and economic injustices, promote labor rights, and advocate for political reforms, laying the groundwork for future movements centered on social justice and equality.

2. **Civil rights advocates and anti-segregationists:** Building on the ideals of the transcendentalists and their emphasis on the inherent dignity and equality of all individuals, civil rights advocates and anti-segregationists fought against racial discrimination and segregation, promoting the values of tolerance, inclusivity, and respect for human rights.

3. Environmentalists and conservationists: Reflecting the transcendentalist reverence for nature and the interconnectedness of all life, environmentalists and conservationists worked to protect natural resources, preserve biodiversity, and promote sustainable environmental practices, laying the foundation for the modern environmental movement and the promotion of ecological consciousness.

4. Entrepreneurs and self-made business leaders: Exemplifying the bootstrap approach of Horatio Alger and Franklin's emphasis on industriousness and self-reliance, entrepreneurs and self-made business leaders played a pivotal role in driving economic innovation, fostering job creation, and promoting the spirit of enterprise, shaping the trajectory of the American economy and paving the way for the development of the self-help and personal development movements that would emerge in the decades to come.

This amalgamation of thinkers and movements set the stage for the self-help movements by fostering a cultural climate that emphasized the importance of individual agency, social responsibility, and the pursuit of personal fulfillment.

Their collective influence underscored the significance of self-improvement, social justice, and community engagement, providing the philosophical and ideological underpinnings that would shape the ethos of self-help and personal development in the latter half of the 20th century and beyond.

Suggested Reading

Transcendentalism:

1. Richardson, R. D., Jr. (1995). Emerson: The Mind on Fire. University of California Press.
- This biography offers a comprehensive exploration of Ralph Waldo Emerson's life and intellectual contributions, providing insights into the philosophical underpinnings of Transcendentalist thought and Emerson's role in shaping the movement.

2. Gura, P. F. (2007). American Transcendentalism: A History. Hill and Wang.
- This historical account of Transcendentalism provides a nuanced understanding of the movement's origins, development, and impact on American intellectual and cultural history, offering a comprehensive analysis of its key figures and philosophical tenets.

3. Buell, L. (2004). The Environmental Imagination: Thoreau, Nature Writing, and the Formation of American Culture. Belknap Press.
- Focusing on the relationship between Transcendentalist thought, nature writing, and the broader cultural landscape, this book contextualizes Thoreau's environmental philosophy within the larger framework of American cultural and literary history.

'Walden':

1. Thoreau, H. D., & Walls, L. D. (2004). Walden: A Fully Annotated Edition. Yale University Press.
- This annotated edition of "Walden" provides readers with comprehensive annotations and critical insights into Thoreau's seminal work, offering a deeper understanding of its themes, literary context, and philosophical significance.

2. Myerson, J., & Walls, L. D. (Eds.). (2004). The Cambridge Companion to Henry David Thoreau. Cambridge University Press.
- This collection of essays serves as a valuable companion to Thoreau's works, providing critical analyses and scholarly perspectives on his life, writings, and the enduring influence of his ideas on American literature and philosophy.

3. Fullerton, T. (Developer), & USC Game Innovation Lab. (Windows, 2017). Walden, a game.
- Walden, a game is a first-person open-world video game developed by Tracy Fullerton and the USC Game Innovation Lab

'Bowling Alone':

"Bowling Alone: The Collapse and Revival of American Community" by Robert D. Putnam

In "Bowling Alone," Robert D. Putnam explores the decline of social capital in the United States, delving into the waning engagement in traditional social networks and the diminishing participation in voluntary associations that had once fostered a sense of community and civic engagement.

The concept of 'social capital' elucidates the value embedded in social networks and shared norms of reciprocity and trust, which contribute to the overall well-being of a society. Putnam discusses how the diminishing presence of these social networks and associations has led to a decline in social trust and cooperation, as well as the emergence of new, untested forms of association that may lack the robustness and long-established communal support characteristic of traditional social networks.

This absence of established social capital has created a space in which new groups, including various self-help movements, have proliferated, bringing both opportunities and potential challenges to the fabric of American society.

Voluntary Associations and Community Help Groups in the U.S. from the 19th century to 1970:

1. Johnson, B. H. (2011). *A Nation of Joiners: Freedom of Association and American Political History*. Philadelphia: University of Pennsylvania Press.

- Johnson's book delves into the history of American political and social life, exploring the significance of freedom of association and the role of voluntary associations in shaping American society. It examines the rise and development of voluntary associations and provides insights into how they influenced the political landscape, shedding light on their impact during the 19th century and beyond.

2. Storti, C. (1992). *Americans at Work: A Guide to the Can-Do People*. Boston, MA: Nicholas Brealey Publishing.
- Storti's book provides a comprehensive overview of the American workforce and the key organizations that influenced the U.S. labor scene. Although not directly focused on the rise and fall of voluntary associations, it offers crucial insights into the spirit of community engagement and activism among American workers, providing valuable context for understanding the societal backdrop within which these associations operated during the relevant historical period.

Horatio Alger:

1. Matthews, W. (2007). *American Dreams and Horatio Alger*. University of Massachusetts Press.
- This book provides an insightful analysis of Horatio Alger's works within the broader context of the American Dream, exploring the cultural, social, and economic factors that shaped the 'rags to riches' narrative during his era.

2. Daniels, T. (1995). *When the New Deal Came to Town: A Snapshot of a Place and Time with Lessons for Today*. University of Illinois Press.
- While not solely focused on Horatio Alger, this book offers valuable insights into the historical backdrop of the 'rags to riches' narrative, examining the socioeconomic challenges and opportunities that characterized the era in which Alger's works gained prominence.

Part II: Pioneers of Personal Success

Early Individualism and Success Literature in U.S. Culture

Early individualism and success literature in U.S. culture emerged during the 19th century, reflecting the nation's burgeoning sense of self-reliance, entrepreneurship, and upward mobility. This literary genre underscored the American Dream, emphasizing the idea that through hard work, perseverance, and determination, individuals could achieve personal success and material prosperity.

Key dates and developments in the context of early individualism and success literature in the U.S. include:

- **1776:** Publication of Adam Smith's "The Wealth of Nations," which emphasized the role of individual initiative and free-market capitalism in driving economic growth and prosperity.

- **1828:** Publication of Lydia Maria Child's "The Frugal Housewife," which provided practical advice on household management, frugality, and self-reliance, catering to a growing readership interested in practical strategies for personal success.

- **1859:** Publication of Samuel Smiles' "Self-Help," a seminal work that emphasized the importance of self-reliance, perseverance, and character development in achieving personal and professional success. Smiles' book became a foundational text in the genre of success literature, influencing generations of readers with its emphasis on industriousness and self-improvement.

These early works laid the groundwork for the development of a distinct literary tradition centered on individualism, self-reliance, and the pursuit of success. They provided readers with practical advice, inspirational anecdotes, and moral guidance, fostering a cultural ethos that celebrated the virtues of hard work, determination, and resilience.

Key personalities associated with early success literature in the U.S. include Benjamin Franklin, known for his aphorisms and practical wisdom, and Horatio Alger, whose rags-to-riches stories captivated the imagination of readers with their tales of perseverance and moral rectitude leading to personal triumph.

The historic context surrounding this literary tradition is marked by the expansion of industrialization, the rise of capitalism, and the spirit of manifest destiny that characterized the 19th-century American experience. The literature of this period reflects the optimism and confidence prevalent in the American consciousness, emphasizing the potential for individual agency and upward mobility within the context of a rapidly changing society and evolving economy.

The Emergence of Positive Thinking: Early American Perspectives on Optimism and Resilience

In the tapestry of American intellectual history, the emergence of positive thinking stands as a vibrant thread, woven into the fabric of early American literature and philosophy. Rooted in the burgeoning optimism of the 18th and 19th centuries, positive thinking found fertile ground in the rich soil of a nation seeking to define its identity and purpose. As the United States navigated its formative years, a chorus of voices emerged, promoting the ethos of positivity and resilience in the face of adversity. This essay delves into the historical context of early American thought, exploring the concept of positive thinking, and examining key texts and figures that championed the power of optimism during this foundational period.

Contextualizing Early American Thought
The intellectual landscape of early America was a tapestry of diverse influences, intertwining Puritan ethics, Enlightenment

ideals, and the transcendentalist spirit. Amidst this backdrop, positive thinking emerged as a philosophical current that emphasized the importance of cultivating a resilient mindset, rooted in hope and faith in the face of life's challenges. This outlook was deeply shaped by the Puritan emphasis on perseverance and divine providence, as well as the Enlightenment's focus on human reason and progress. Within this dynamic intellectual milieu, the seeds of positive thinking were sown, germinating into a distinct philosophy of optimism that would resonate throughout American history.

Exploration of Positive Thinking in Early American Literature

Early American literature reflected the burgeoning sentiment of optimism and self-reliance, highlighting the transformative power of positive thought. One notable example is Benjamin Franklin's "Poor Richard's Almanack," a compendium of aphorisms and proverbs that extolled the virtues of industry, frugality, and a positive outlook. Franklin's pithy sayings, such as "Early to bed and early to rise, makes a man healthy, wealthy, and wise," encapsulated the essence of positive thinking, emphasizing the importance of diligence and a proactive mindset in achieving success and well-being.

Similarly, the works of transcendentalist writers, including Ralph Waldo Emerson and Henry David Thoreau, echoed the sentiments of positivity and self-empowerment. Emerson's essays, such as "Self-Reliance" and "Nature," celebrated the inherent goodness of humanity and the transformative potential of individual agency. Thoreau's "Walden" further underscored the power of positive thinking through its exploration of simplicity, self-reliance, and communion with nature, advocating for a life of purpose and mindful contemplation.

Key Figures Promoting the Ethos of Positivity

Beyond literary works, key figures in early American history championed the ethos of positivity and optimism, leaving an indelible mark on the cultural consciousness of the nation. One such figure was Mary Baker Eddy, the founder of Christian Science, whose teachings emphasized the power of positive thought and spiritual healing. Eddy's seminal work, "Science and Health with

Key to the Scriptures," expounded upon the idea that the mind has a profound influence on physical well-being, underscoring the transformative potential of positive thinking in achieving holistic health and spiritual harmony.

Additionally, the influence of Quaker thought, with its emphasis on inner light and the inherent goodness of all individuals, permeated the cultural landscape, nurturing a climate of optimism and egalitarianism. Quaker principles encouraged a positive outlook on human nature, emphasizing the potential for personal growth and spiritual enlightenment. Prominent Quaker figures, such as William Penn and Lucretia Mott, embodied the spirit of positivity through their advocacy for social justice, equality, and the inherent dignity of all individuals, laying the groundwork for a more inclusive and compassionate society.

The emergence of positive thinking in early American thought serves as a testament to the resilience and optimism that permeated the nation's cultural and intellectual fabric. From the aphorisms of Benjamin Franklin to the transcendentalist musings of Emerson and Thoreau, early American literature and philosophy reflected a collective belief in the transformative power of positive thought.

Influential figures, including Mary Baker Eddy and Quaker advocates, further reinforced the ethos of positivity, underscoring the enduring impact of optimism on personal well-being and societal progress. In navigating the complexities of a young nation and shaping the contours of American identity, the spirit of positive thinking illuminated a path toward individual empowerment, resilience, and collective flourishing.

New Thought

New Thought and positive thinking, while sharing some common philosophical threads, represent distinct movements within the broader landscape of American intellectual history.

New Thought, emerging in the late 19th century, was a spiritual and philosophical movement that emphasized the interconnectedness of mind, body, and spirit, advocating for the power of spiritual consciousness and metaphysical principles in shaping one's reality. It incorporated elements of spiritual healing, affirmative prayer, and the idea of the divine potential within each individual. New Thought placed a strong emphasis on the idea that individuals could transform their lives through aligning their thoughts with spiritual truths, and it often incorporated elements of various religious traditions, mystical teachings, and metaphysical concepts. One highly influential theme that will consistently thread through the various methods, techniques, practices, and beliefs shaping the self-help revolution of the 1970s is found in New Thought.

On the other hand, positive thinking, although influenced by New Thought, evolved as a broader cultural and intellectual phenomenon, particularly in the 20th century, emphasizing the practical applications of optimism and resilience in daily life.

Positive thinking, as a psychological and self-help concept, focused on the power of optimism, perseverance, and a constructive mindset in achieving personal success, happiness, and well-being. It drew from psychological research and popular literature, advocating for the practical benefits of maintaining a positive attitude and outlook in navigating life's challenges and pursuing one's goals.

While New Thought encompassed a comprehensive metaphysical worldview that addressed spiritual and existential questions, positive thinking primarily emphasized the psychological and pragmatic aspects of cultivating a constructive mindset for personal growth and achievement.

Despite their distinct emphases, both New Thought and positive thinking contributed to the broader cultural currents promoting the transformative power of the mind and the potential for individuals to shape their realities through the power of thought and belief.

Positive Thinking and New Thought in Literature

The incorporation of positive thinking and New Thought themes in American literary works and philosophical discourse reflects a cultural fascination with the power of the mind and the potential for personal transformation. Throughout American literary history, these themes have influenced the narratives of resilience, personal growth, and spiritual awakening, shaping the perspectives of key authors and thinkers.

In literary works, authors have often explored the transformative power of positive thinking and the principles of New Thought through characters who embody resilience and perseverance. One notable example is the character of Hester Prynne in Nathaniel Hawthorne's "The Scarlet Letter." Hester's inner strength and determination in the face of societal condemnation exemplify the New Thought emphasis on personal agency and the pursuit of spiritual redemption.

Similarly, in the works of F. Scott Fitzgerald, such as "The Great Gatsby," themes of optimism and the pursuit of the American Dream reflect the influence of positive thinking on the portrayal of characters striving for personal fulfillment and social success.

Philosophical discourse in American intellectual history has also been shaped by the principles of positive thinking and New Thought. Thinkers such as William James, through his pragmatic philosophy, emphasized the practical applications of positive thinking and the significance of adopting a constructive mindset in navigating life's complexities. James' exploration of the power of belief and the will to believe underscored the transformative potential of positive thinking in shaping one's experiences and perceptions of reality.

Additionally, the works of pragmatist philosophers, including John Dewey and Charles Sanders Peirce, reflect the influence of New Thought principles in their emphasis on the role of human agency and the power of thought in the quest for personal and societal progress.

The integration of positive thinking and New Thought themes in American literary works and philosophical discourse has contributed to a broader cultural exploration of the human psyche, personal empowerment, and the pursuit of existential fulfillment. By examining the influence of these themes on the works of key American authors and thinkers, it becomes evident that the concepts of optimism, resilience, and the transformative power of the mind have played a significant role in shaping the narrative of the American experience and the quest for individual and collective flourishing.

Influence on the 70s

The principles of positive thinking and New Thought significantly influenced the proliferation of self-help methods, groups, and practices during the 1970s, leading to the adoption of new and unconventional beliefs within popular culture. These ideologies provided a framework for individuals to seek personal transformation and empowerment through various alternative practices and spiritual beliefs.

One notable example is the rise of the human potential movement, which integrated principles of positive thinking and New Thought into its teachings and practices. Organizations such as the Esalen Institute in California fostered a culture of self-exploration and personal growth, emphasizing the potential for individuals to achieve heightened states of consciousness and self-actualization through various psychological and spiritual techniques. This movement popularized practices such as encounter groups, gestalt therapy, and primal scream therapy, encouraging participants to delve into their subconscious minds and confront repressed emotions as a means of achieving psychological liberation and personal transformation.

Additionally, the proliferation of New Age spirituality during the 1970s reflected the widespread adoption of alternative beliefs and practices rooted in positive thinking and New Thought principles. The growing interest in Eastern philosophies, meditation, and holistic healing modalities, such as crystal healing and aura cleansing, exemplified the influence of positive thinking on the exploration of spiritual and metaphysical dimensions of human existence. This period saw the emergence of various New Age groups and communities that embraced a syncretic approach to spirituality, integrating elements of Eastern mysticism, astrology, and metaphysical teachings into their belief systems.

Moreover, the self-help literature of the 1970s drew heavily from the tenets of positive thinking and New Thought, promoting the idea that individuals could manifest their desired outcomes through the power of intention and belief. Authors such as Louise Hay, with her seminal work "Heal Your Body," popularized the idea that positive affirmations and mental attitudes could influence physical health and well-being, leading readers to adopt new beliefs about the mind-body connection and the role of consciousness in healing.

Overall, the integration of positive thinking and New Thought principles into the self-help methods, groups, practices, and adoption of new and unconventional beliefs during the 1970s reflected a cultural shift towards a more holistic and introspective approach to personal growth and spiritual exploration, emphasizing the transformative potential of the mind and the interconnectedness of body, mind, and spirit.

Criticisms of Positive Thinking and New Thought

Criticism of positive thinking and New Thought often centers around the perception that these philosophies promote an overly simplistic and idealistic view of the world, which may overlook the complexities and challenges inherent in human existence. One criticism is that proponents of positive thinking may downplay the importance of acknowledging and addressing negative emotions, experiences, and societal injustices, advocating for a "mind over matter" approach that fails to account for systemic issues and structural inequalities.

Critics also argue that the emphasis on the power of positive thinking may lead to a tendency to blame individuals for their circumstances, suggesting that personal mindset alone determines one's success or failure, while disregarding the broader socioeconomic and cultural factors that shape people's lives. This critique suggests that positive thinking may perpetuate a culture of victim-blaming and oversimplify the complexities of human behavior and societal challenges.

Moreover, some critics perceive New Thought as promoting a passive acceptance of external circumstances, fostering a belief in a deterministic "law of attraction" that suggests individuals can simply manifest their desires through positive thoughts, without taking necessary action or acknowledging the role of external forces in shaping their lives. This criticism highlights the potential danger of promoting a worldview that undermines the importance of critical thinking, social responsibility, and collective action in addressing larger societal issues and promoting systemic change.

Furthermore, the critique of these philosophies often points to the potential for a "mushy-headed" approach that neglects the critical examination of evidence-based practices and the rigorous evaluation of claims. Critics argue that an over-reliance on positive thinking may discourage individuals from engaging in constructive self-reflection and may lead to the dismissal of legitimate concerns and challenges as mere products of negative thinking, potentially hindering personal growth and the pursuit of meaningful change.

While positive thinking and New Thought have garnered popularity and have undoubtedly offered valuable insights for many individuals seeking personal development and spiritual growth, it is essential to approach these philosophies with a critical and discerning mindset, acknowledging their potential limitations and the need for a nuanced understanding of the complexities of human experience and societal dynamics.

Dale Carnegie

Dale Carnegie, known for his influential self-help and interpersonal skills development courses and books, played a significant role in shaping the self-help movement, particularly during the early 20th century. His work reflected the broader cultural zeitgeist characterized by a growing interest in personal development, self-improvement, and the cultivation of effective communication and leadership skills. Carnegie's teachings aligned closely with the principles of positive thinking and New Thought, emphasizing the transformative power of self-confidence, interpersonal skills, and a positive mindset in achieving success and personal fulfillment.

Carnegie's most renowned work, "How to Win Friends and Influence People," published in 1936, emphasized the importance of empathy, active listening, and the cultivation of positive relationships as key drivers of personal and professional success. The book's practical advice on effective communication and human relations resonated with a wide audience, reflecting the societal emphasis on the power of interpersonal skills and emotional intelligence in navigating social and professional interactions.

Furthermore, Carnegie's courses and writings promoted the idea that individuals could achieve their goals through the cultivation of a winning attitude, assertiveness, and the ability to inspire and influence others. His teachings emphasized the importance of self-confidence, the art of persuasion, and the ability to adapt to different social contexts, reflecting the broader cultural fascination with personal agency and the pursuit of success in an increasingly competitive and interconnected world.

Dale Carnegie's contributions to the self-help movement exemplify the convergence of positive thinking, interpersonal skills development, and the pursuit of personal effectiveness within the broader context of the 20th-century American zeitgeist. His emphasis on the power of optimism, effective communication, and interpersonal relationships resonated with a diverse audience, reflecting the enduring appeal of his teachings in the realms of personal development, business leadership, and social interaction.

What Was America like During Carnegie's Time?

During Dale Carnegie's era, spanning the early to mid-20th century, the societal and cultural context was marked by profound changes and challenges. The period witnessed the aftermath of World War I, the Great Depression, and the lead-up to World War II, which significantly impacted the global geopolitical landscape. In the United States, the era was characterized by rapid industrialization, urbanization, and the rise of consumer culture, leading to significant shifts in social norms and values.

1. Post-War Recovery: The aftermath of World War I brought about a sense of disillusionment and a collective desire for economic recovery and stability. This context fostered a heightened focus on self-improvement and personal success, as individuals sought to rebuild their lives and careers amidst the challenges of a post-war society.

2. Economic Challenges: The Great Depression of the 1930s created widespread economic hardship, unemployment, and social upheaval. This period of financial instability fostered a growing interest in effective communication, leadership skills, and interpersonal relationships as individuals sought to navigate the complexities of a rapidly changing job market and business environment.

3. Rise of Industrialization: The era witnessed significant advancements in industrialization, leading to the rise of corporate culture and the increasing importance of interpersonal skills in the workplace. As organizations sought to maximize productivity and efficiency, the demand for effective communication and leadership skills became increasingly pronounced, prompting individuals to seek guidance on how to succeed in a competitive business environment.

4. Shifting Social Dynamics: The early to mid-20th century also witnessed significant shifts in social dynamics, including changing gender roles, evolving family structures, and the emergence of new communication technologies. These changes contributed to an evolving cultural landscape that emphasized the importance of adaptability, resilience, and effective interpersonal connections in both personal and professional spheres.

In this societal and cultural context, Dale Carnegie's teachings gained prominence as individuals and organizations sought guidance on how to navigate the challenges of a rapidly evolving world. Carnegie's emphasis on effective communication, self-confidence, and the cultivation of interpersonal relationships resonated with a society undergoing significant transformation, offering practical strategies for personal and professional success during a time of profound social, economic, and technological change.

Carnegie's Philosophy

Dale Carnegie's influential work, "How to Win Friends and Influence People," emphasizes several key principles that have had a lasting impact on the fields of personal development and interpersonal communication.

1. Principle of Empathy: Carnegie underscores the significance of empathy as a foundational component of effective communication and relationship-building. By encouraging individuals to understand the perspectives and emotions of others, Carnegie highlights the importance of cultivating genuine empathy as a means of fostering trust, understanding, and meaningful connections in both personal and professional interactions.

2. Active Listening: Carnegie's philosophy emphasizes the value of active listening as a critical skill for effective communication. By promoting the practice of attentive listening and genuine engagement with others, Carnegie emphasizes the role of active listening in building rapport, demonstrating respect, and fostering mutual understanding. Active listening, according to Carnegie, serves as a catalyst for fostering meaningful dialogue and cultivating harmonious relationships based on mutual respect and consideration.

3. Interpersonal Skills: Carnegie advocates for the development of strong interpersonal skills as essential tools for successful communication and relationship management. By emphasizing the significance of effective communication, conflict resolution, and negotiation, Carnegie highlights the role of interpersonal skills in navigating complex social dynamics and achieving mutually beneficial outcomes in various interpersonal contexts. Carnegie's philosophy also underscores the transformative power of positive thinking and self-confidence in achieving personal and professional success. By promoting the cultivation of a positive mindset and self-assurance, Carnegie encourages individuals to harness the power of optimism, resilience, and self-belief in overcoming obstacles and pursuing their goals with determination and confidence. Through his emphasis on the role of positive thinking and self-confidence, Carnegie underscores the significance of a proactive and optimistic approach to life and work, highlighting the potential for personal growth, fulfillment, and interpersonal effectiveness.

Carnegie Compared

Dale Carnegie's philosophy shares common threads with the teachings of Ben Franklin, Aristotle, the Transcendentalists, and the New Thought/positive thinking movement in certain aspects, but it also exhibits distinct differences in emphasis and approach.

1. Similarities

Interpersonal Skills: Carnegie's emphasis on effective interpersonal skills aligns with Aristotle's virtue ethics, which highlight the importance of virtues such as patience, kindness, and empathy in fostering harmonious relationships and ethical conduct.

Positive Thinking: Carnegie's focus on the power of positive thinking resonates with the New Thought movement's belief in the role of optimism and self-confidence in shaping personal outcomes.

Self-Improvement: Like Ben Franklin's pursuit of self-improvement through his virtues and daily schedule, Carnegie's teachings encourage personal development and growth, albeit with a focus on communication and relationship skills.

2. Differences:

Practical Application: Carnegie's philosophy is highly practical, emphasizing specific techniques for effective communication and relationship-building. This pragmatic approach differs from Aristotle's philosophical exploration of virtue and the transcendentalists' emphasis on philosophical and spiritual introspection.

Goal-Oriented: Carnegie's philosophy often centers on achieving practical goals, such as winning friends and influencing people, in contrast to the broader philosophical and ethical inquiries of Aristotle, the transcendentalists, and New Thought thinkers.

Interpersonal Focus: While Carnegie's teachings prioritize effective interpersonal skills, Aristotle, the Transcendentalists, and New Thought thinkers may emphasize a broader spectrum of personal development, including moral and spiritual aspects.

In summary, Dale Carnegie's philosophy aligns with earlier and contemporary philosophical and self-help traditions in its focus on positive thinking and interpersonal skills. However, its practical and goal-oriented approach sets it apart from the more comprehensive and philosophical exploration of ethics, virtues, and personal development found in the works of Aristotle, the Transcendentalists, and New Thought thinkers. Carnegie's teachings are geared toward achieving specific outcomes in personal and professional relationships, reflecting the practical and results-oriented nature of his approach.

Where Carnegie Contributed to the Self-Help Revolution of the 70s

Carnegie's groundbreaking contributions to the self-help revolution primarily centered on effective interpersonal communication, public speaking, and leadership development.

His teachings revolutionized the approach to building positive relationships and mastering the art of persuasion, thus laying a solid foundation for the self-help movement's emphasis on interpersonal skills and personal empowerment.

Furthermore, Carnegie's influence extended beyond his lifetime, inspiring a multitude of authors and speakers in the self-help domain. One such figure, Napoleon Hill, built upon Carnegie's principles and introduced the concept of the power of positive thinking and personal initiative in achieving success, as demonstrated in his seminal work "Think and Grow Rich." Similarly, contemporary authors like Rhonda Byrne, the mind behind "The Secret," draw upon Carnegie's legacy, emphasizing the transformative potential of positive thoughts and the law of attraction in shaping one's destiny.

Through his timeless teachings on effective communication and self-confidence, Dale Carnegie continues to inspire a generation of self-help enthusiasts and authors, leaving an indelible mark on the landscape of personal development and achievement.

Criticisms

While Dale Carnegie's teachings have been influential in the realm of personal development and interpersonal communication, they have also faced criticism on several fronts.

1. Superficiality: Some critics argue that Carnegie's approach to building relationships and influencing others can be overly simplistic and focused on surface-level interactions, neglecting the complexities of human emotions and the importance of deeper, more meaningful connections.

2. Manipulation Concerns: There are concerns that Carnegie's emphasis on persuasive techniques and winning friends may be perceived as manipulative, potentially encouraging individuals to prioritize personal gain over genuine, authentic relationships.

3. Limited Cultural Context: Critics suggest that Carnegie's strategies may not adequately consider cultural diversity and the nuances of communication across different social and cultural contexts, potentially leading to misunderstandings or misinterpretations in interpersonal interactions.

4. Lack of Focus on Structural Issues: Some critics argue that Carnegie's teachings place excessive emphasis on individual behavior and fail to address broader societal issues and structural inequalities, potentially downplaying the role of systemic factors in shaping interpersonal dynamics and success.

5. Skepticism of Self-Help Industry: Carnegie's work is sometimes criticized in the broader context of the self-help industry, which has faced scrutiny for promoting simplistic solutions to complex life challenges and for potentially fostering a culture of consumerism around personal development.

While Carnegie's teachings have undoubtedly provided valuable guidance to many individuals seeking to improve their interpersonal skills, these criticisms highlight the need for a nuanced understanding of human relationships and the importance of addressing broader social and cultural dynamics in the pursuit of genuine and meaningful personal growth.

Suggested Reading for This Section

Here is a list of suggested readings for New Thought, the early history of Positive Thinking, and Dale Carnegie, along with cultural histories that contextualize the prominence of these forces:

Certainly, here is a sample bibliography in APA format for the suggested readings on New Thought, the early history of Positive Thinking, and Dale Carnegie:

New Thought:
1. Dresser, H. W. (2007). The Philosophy of New Thought. Cosimo Classics.

2. Haller, J. S. (2012). The History of New Thought. Forgotten Books.

Early History of Positive Thinking:
1. Kennard, A. (2013). The Positive Thinking Secret. Positive Thinking Publishing.

2. Horowitz, M. (2014). One Simple Idea: How Positive Thinking Reshaped Modern Life. Crown Archetype.

Dale Carnegie:
1. Carnegie, D. (1998). How to Win Friends and Influence People. Pocket Books.

2. Kemp, G. (2001). Dale Carnegie: The Man Who Influenced Millions. St Martins Pr.

These suggested readings provide valuable insights into the philosophical foundations of New Thought, the historical development of Positive Thinking, the influence of Dale Carnegie's teachings, and the broader cultural contexts that shaped their prominence within American society.

They offer a comprehensive understanding of these influential forces and their impact on the broader cultural and intellectual landscape of their respective eras.

Books on the Quakers:

Six books on the Quakers, along with descriptions that highlight their relevance to a chapter on New Thought and positive thinking in the U.S.:

1. Frost, J. W. (2010). The Quaker Family in Colonial America: A Portrait of the Society of Friends. New York, NY: St. Martin's Press.

Description: This book offers a comprehensive exploration of the Quaker community during colonial America, providing insights into their religious beliefs and practices, which emphasized the power of inner light and direct spiritual experience, aligning with the core principles of self-discovery and individual spiritual connection prevalent in New Thought philosophy.

2. Hamm, T. D. (2003). The Transformation of American Quakerism: Orthodox Friends, 1800-1907. Bloomington, IN: Indiana University Press.

Description: Hamm's work delves into the evolution of American

Quakerism during the 19th century, highlighting the shift from traditional practices to a more evangelical and socially engaged form of Quakerism. This transformation reflects the Quakers' commitment to social reform and the cultivation of positive change, resonating with the ethos of positive thinking and progressive activism present in New Thought philosophy.

3. Moore, R. (2015). The Quakers: A Very Short Introduction. Oxford, UK: Oxford University Press.

Description: Providing a concise overview of Quaker history and beliefs, Moore's book emphasizes the Quaker commitment to inner spiritual exploration and direct communion with the divine. This focus on personal spiritual experience mirrors the emphasis on individual empowerment and self-discovery central to the principles of New Thought and positive thinking in the U.S.

4. Birkel, M. L. (2003). Silence and Witness: The Quaker Tradition. Maryknoll, NY: Orbis Books.

Description: Birkel's exploration of the Quaker tradition highlights the significance of silent worship and spiritual contemplation in the Quaker faith. This emphasis on introspection and the cultivation of inner peace reflects the parallel themes of mindfulness and positive mental attitude promoted in New Thought philosophy.

5. Dandelion, P. (2007). The Quakers: A Very Short Introduction. New York, NY: Cambridge University Press.

Description: Dandelion's book offers a succinct introduction to the Quaker movement, emphasizing their commitment to peace, social justice, and the inner light within each individual. This focus on inner guidance and the pursuit of positive social change corresponds to the principles of personal empowerment and constructive social transformation inherent in New Thought and positive thinking.

6. Barbour, H. (1985). The Quakers in Puritan England. New Haven, CT: Yale University Press.

Description: Barbour's historical analysis of the Quaker movement in Puritan England sheds light on the Quakers' dissenting spirit and their emphasis on direct communion with the divine. Their resilience and determination in the face of adversity resonate with the perseverance and optimism inherent in New Thought philosophy and the principles of positive thinking in the U.S.

Books on Mary Baker Eddy:

1. Peel, R. (1971). Mary Baker Eddy: The Years of Trial. Holt, Rinehart and Winston.

2. Eddy, M. B. (1994). Science and Health with Key to the Scriptures. Writings of Mary Baker Eddy.

Further. Still:

McVeigh, B. J. (2008). The American Revolution and the Religious Public Sphere. University of Notre Dame Press.

This work delves into the religious and philosophical currents in American history, providing a context for understanding the emergence of New Thought and its relationship to broader cultural developments during the late 19th and early 20th centuries.

and

Harrell, D. P. (1994). The Social Sources of Denominationalism. University of Notre Dame Press.

Focusing on the intersection of religion and society, this book sheds light on the social and cultural dynamics that influenced the growth of the New Thought movement and its reception within the broader religious landscape of the United States.

Part III: The Birth of Pop Psychology: From Maslow to Kopp

During the mid-20th century in the United States, a distinctive psychological phenomenon, commonly known as 'pop' psychology, emerged in response to a specific sociocultural climate characterized by a growing emphasis on individual empowerment and self-fulfillment.

This movement was intricately linked to a rich tapestry of pre-existing philosophical and intellectual currents, notably New Thought, the ideology of positive thinking, and the broader tradition of self-reliance that had long been embedded in American intellectual history. The amalgamation of these ideas cultivated a fertile ground for the eventual proliferation of 'pop' psychology, which aimed to make complex psychological concepts accessible and applicable to the everyday lives of the American public.

As these philosophies had already laid the groundwork for an individualistic approach to spiritual and personal growth, 'pop' psychology seamlessly integrated itself into this pre-established culture of self-empowerment and self-determination, resonating with an audience eager for practical guidance in navigating the complexities of the human psyche and achieving personal success and fulfillment.

This movement was not merely a sudden phenomenon but rather a natural evolution stemming from the collective yearning for practical tools and guidance to achieve personal fulfillment and navigate the challenges of an increasingly complex and fast-paced modern world. With the influence of New Thought and the promotion of the power of positive thinking, individuals were already primed to explore the possibilities of harnessing their own mental faculties and beliefs to shape their realities.

Moreover, the deeply entrenched American ethos of self-reliance and individualism, epitomized by figures like Ralph Waldo Emerson and Henry David Thoreau, had long emphasized the importance of personal agency and self-determination in the pursuit of happiness and success. 'Pop' psychology, therefore, can be seen as a natural extension of these longstanding ideals, aiming to distill the complexities of psychology into practical and actionable principles that individuals could readily apply in their daily lives.

Abraham Maslow and Self-Actualization

Abraham Maslow (1908-1970) was an influential American psychologist and a key figure in the development of humanistic psychology. Born in Brooklyn, New York, Maslow earned his Ph.D. in psychology from the University of Wisconsin. He is best known for his theory of the Hierarchy of Needs, which posits that human motivation is based on a hierarchical structure of needs, with self-actualization at the peak.

Maslow's work emphasized the significance of focusing on the positive aspects of human potential and the importance of self-fulfillment and personal growth. His contributions to the field of psychology continue to have a profound impact on various disciplines, including education, business, and personal development.

Here are five topics of importance related to his theory:

1. Self-Actualization: Explore the concept of self-actualization, the highest level in Maslow's hierarchy, which represents the fulfillment of an individual's potential, talents, and capabilities.

2. Basic Human Needs: Discuss the significance of physiological needs, safety, love and belonging, and esteem needs, which form the foundational levels of Maslow's hierarchy and represent essential requirements for human psychological and emotional well-being.

3. Motivation and Behavior: Analyze how the fulfillment of each need in the hierarchy influences human motivation and behavior, driving individuals to progress toward achieving higher levels of personal growth and fulfillment.

4. Application in Education: Examine the relevance of Maslow's Hierarchy of Needs in educational settings, discussing how educators can create supportive environments that foster students' sense of belonging, self-esteem, and self-actualization.

5. Contemporary Relevance: Investigate the contemporary relevance of Maslow's theory in the context of modern society, considering its implications for understanding human behavior, motivation, and well-being in various aspects of life, including work, relationships, and personal development.

Relationship to Previous Thinkers

Self-actualization, a term popularized by Abraham Maslow, finds its philosophical roots in the works of various American thinkers who emphasized the pursuit of personal growth, fulfillment, and the realization of individual potential. This concept resonates with the American Transcendentalists, such as Ralph Waldo Emerson and Henry David Thoreau, who championed the idea of self-reliance, individualism, and the quest for spiritual enlightenment.

Emerson's emphasis on the importance of trusting one's intuition, embracing nature, and seeking truth within oneself aligns closely with the essence of self-actualization. His call to "hitch your wagon to a star" reflects the aspiration to strive for personal excellence and spiritual transcendence.

Likewise, Thoreau's philosophical exploration of simple living, introspection, and the pursuit of a meaningful life in harmony with nature exemplifies the foundational principles of self-actualization. His belief in the significance of living deliberately and in close connection with the natural world echoes the sentiments of self-discovery and personal growth inherent in the concept.

Furthermore, the notion of self-actualization bears semblance to Aristotle's concept of eudaimonia, often translated as "human flourishing" or "well-being." Aristotle posited that human beings naturally strive for eudaimonia, which involves the pursuit of excellence and the fulfillment of one's unique potential. This pursuit, according to Aristotle, is achieved through virtuous conduct, rational contemplation, and the cultivation of one's moral character, echoing the themes of self-actualization and personal growth.

In this way, the concept of self-actualization, while grounded in modern psychological theory, is deeply intertwined with the philosophical underpinnings of earlier American thinkers and the timeless wisdom of Aristotle, all emphasizing the inherent human inclination toward personal development, excellence, and the realization of one's full potential.

Self-Actualization: Practical Applications

Maslow's concept of self-actualization, popularized during the self-help revolution of the 1970s, found practical applications in various aspects of personal development and transformative practices that aimed to foster holistic well-being and individual empowerment. During this period, numerous self-help movements and practices emerged, emphasizing the following practical applications in relation to the pursuit of self-actualization:

1. Personal Growth Workshops: Self-help workshops and seminars gained popularity, offering individuals the opportunity to engage in experiential activities and introspective exercises aimed at enhancing self-awareness, self-esteem, and personal growth. Participants were encouraged to explore their inner potential and pursue self-actualization through guided activities and group discussions.

2. Mindfulness and Meditation Practices: The 1970s witnessed a resurgence of interest in Eastern philosophies and spiritual practices, with mindfulness and meditation gaining prominence in the self-help revolution. These practices were utilized as tools for enhancing self-awareness, reducing stress, and fostering emotional well-being, thereby facilitating the journey toward self-actualization and personal fulfillment.

3. Holistic Health and Wellness Programs: The self-help movement of the 1970s also emphasized the importance of holistic health and wellness, advocating for the integration of physical, mental, and emotional well-being. Various holistic programs and alternative therapies, such as yoga, acupuncture, and holistic nutrition, were promoted as means of promoting overall wellness and supporting individuals in their quest for self-actualization.

4. Empowerment Through Self-Help Literature: The 1970s witnessed the proliferation of self-help literature, with authors emphasizing practical strategies and techniques for achieving personal growth and self-fulfillment. Books focusing on topics such as positive thinking, self-esteem, and personal empowerment provided readers with practical guidance and actionable steps to cultivate self-actualization and achieve a more fulfilling life.

5. Human Potential Movement: The human potential movement, a key feature of the self-help revolution in the 1970s, emphasized the exploration of human potential and the importance of self-actualization in realizing personal aspirations and goals. Through various workshops, encounter groups, and experiential activities, the movement encouraged individuals to tap into their inner resources and develop a deeper understanding of their capabilities, thus facilitating the process of self-actualization and personal transformation.

Criticism

Criticism of the concept of self-actualization, particularly within the context of the self-help revolution of the 1970s, centered around several key points that challenged its practical applications and implications:

1. Overemphasis on Individualism: Critics argued that the emphasis on self-actualization and individual growth perpetuated a culture of extreme individualism, potentially fostering a disregard for community and collective well-being. This critique highlighted the potential societal consequences of prioritizing personal fulfillment at the expense of social responsibility and cooperation.

2. Lack of Cultural Sensitivity: Critics pointed out that the concept of self-actualization often neglected the cultural and social contexts that shape individuals' experiences and aspirations. The focus on a universal model of personal growth disregarded the diverse cultural backgrounds and unique challenges faced by individuals from different communities, leading to a one-size-fits-all approach that might not adequately address the specific needs of diverse populations.

3. Commercialization and Simplification: Some critics argued that the self-help industry, particularly during the 1970s, commercialized the concept of self-actualization, simplifying complex psychological processes into marketable products and quick-fix solutions. This commercialization often resulted in oversimplified and superficial approaches to personal development, undermining the depth and complexity of genuine psychological growth and transformation.

4. Unrealistic Expectations: Critics raised concerns about the potential fostering of unrealistic expectations among individuals pursuing self-actualization. The promotion of idealized self-improvement goals, often presented as easily attainable through specific techniques or practices, could lead to disillusionment and disappointment when individuals failed to achieve the anticipated results, potentially resulting in a sense of inadequacy and frustration.

5. Lack of Empirical Basis: Some critics questioned the empirical basis of the concept of self-actualization, highlighting the limited empirical evidence supporting the hierarchy of needs and the broader self-help claims of the 1970s. The subjective nature of the concept and its reliance on introspective self-assessment raised concerns about the validity and generalizability of the principles espoused within the self-help movement during this period.

Suggested Reading

Important Works by Abraham Maslow:

1. "Toward a Psychology of Being" (1968) - In this seminal work, Maslow delves into the concept of self-actualization and presents his holistic theory of human motivation, emphasizing the significance of growth-oriented psychological processes.

2. "Motivation and Personality" (1954) - Maslow's groundbreaking book introduces his theory of the hierarchy of needs, outlining the various levels of human needs and their impact on individual motivation and behavior.

3. "The Farther Reaches of Human Nature" (1971) - Maslow's "The Farther Reaches of Human Nature" (1971) greatly influenced the

1970s self-help revolution by highlighting the significance of self-actualization and personal development. Emphasizing the pursuit of higher human potential and self-transcendence, the book resonated with the self-help movement's focus on holistic well-being and personal growth, encouraging individuals to strive for fulfillment and meaningful relationships. Maslow's insights into optimal human functioning laid the foundation for the era's emphasis on personal development and the quest for deeper self-awareness and fulfillment.

Works on Maslow:

1. "Abraham Maslow: A Critical Biography" by E. Hoffman (2019) - This critical biography offers an in-depth exploration of Maslow's life, work, and impact on the field of psychology, providing valuable insights into the development of his theories and their reception within the academic community.

2. "The Limits of Humanistic Psychology: Abraham Maslow, Self-Actualization, and the Helping Professions" by M. Pierson (2015) - This critical examination of Maslow's humanistic psychology critically assesses the limitations and implications of his theories, highlighting potential challenges and criticisms related to their practical application in the helping professions.

Works Critical of Maslow:

1. "The Cult of Personality Testing: How Personality Tests Are Leading Us to Miseducate Our Children, Mismanage Our Companies, and Misunderstand Ourselves" by A. Raskin (2004) - While not solely focused on Maslow, this work critiques the broader culture of personality testing, which has been influenced by Maslow's theories, raising concerns about its impact on education, management, and self-perception.

2. "A Critique of Maslow's Theory of Motivation" by A. Wahba and L. Bridwell (1976) - This academic article offers a critical analysis of Maslow's hierarchy of needs, discussing potential limitations and oversimplifications within the theory, and highlighting the need for further empirical validation and refinement of its conceptual framework.

Norman Vincent Peale and
'The Power of Positive Thinking'

Norman Vincent Peale (1898-1993) was a prominent American minister and author known for his influential work in the field of positive thinking and self-help. Born in Ohio, Peale later became a Methodist and then a prominent figure in the field of positive psychology. He served as the pastor of the Marble Collegiate Church in New York City for over 50 years and authored several best-selling books that popularized the concept of positive thinking and the power of faith in achieving personal success and happiness.

Five Things that Make Norman Vincent Peale Important for our purposes:

1. Popularization of Positive Thinking: Peale's advocacy for the transformative power of positive thinking had a significant impact on the self-help movement of the 1970s, contributing to the widespread adoption of positive psychology principles and practices.

2. Best-Selling Author: His influential book, "The Power of Positive Thinking" (1952), became a hallmark of the self-help genre, shaping the discourse on personal development and self-empowerment during the 1970s and beyond.

3. Bridging Religion and Psychology: Peale's work effectively bridged the gap between religious faith and psychological well-being, emphasizing the integration of spiritual principles with practical psychological techniques for achieving personal growth and fulfillment.

4. Inspirational Speaker: Through his dynamic and motivational speaking engagements, Peale inspired audiences to cultivate a positive mindset and embrace a proactive approach to overcoming life's challenges, making him a significant figure in the dissemination of pop psychology principles during the 1970s.

5. Legacy in Self-Help Movement: Peale's lasting legacy in the self-help movement of the 1970s continues to influence contemporary discussions on the intersection of faith, psychology, and personal development, underscoring the enduring relevance of his contributions to the field of pop psychology.

'The Power of Positive Thinking'

Published in 1952, "The Power of Positive Thinking" by Norman Vincent Peale remains a landmark work in the field of self-help and personal development. The book espouses the transformative potential of positive thinking and offers practical advice on how individuals can overcome challenges and achieve success through the power of faith and optimism.

Peale's writing style is accessible and engaging, making complex psychological concepts easily understandable for a wide audience. He blends personal anecdotes, inspirational stories, and practical strategies, creating a compelling narrative that resonates with readers seeking guidance and motivation.

One of the book's key strengths lies in its emphasis on the integration of religious faith and psychological principles, providing readers with a holistic approach to personal growth that combines spiritual practices with practical techniques for cultivating a positive mindset.

While praised for its inspirational and motivational content, the book has also faced criticism for its oversimplified approach to complex psychological issues and for potentially fostering unrealistic expectations among readers. Some critics argue that Peale's focus on positive thinking may overlook the importance of addressing underlying emotional and psychological challenges.

Despite these criticisms, "The Power of Positive Thinking" continues to have a profound impact on readers seeking encouragement and guidance in their personal and professional lives, solidifying Peale's legacy as a significant figure in the popularization of positive psychology and the self-help movement.

Links to Previous Thinkers

Norman Vincent Peale's philosophy, as demonstrated in his influential book "The Power of Positive Thinking," is intricately linked to the broader traditions of Positive Thinking, New Thought, and the Transcendentalist movement.

Positive Thinking:

Peale's work aligns closely with the principles of Positive Thinking, emphasizing the transformative power of maintaining a positive attitude and mindset. He advocates for the active cultivation of optimistic thoughts and beliefs as a means of achieving personal success, happiness, and overall well-being.

New Thought:

Peale's teachings resonate with the central tenets of the New Thought movement, which emphasizes the power of the mind and the connection between spiritual and material well-being. His integration of faith and psychological principles reflects the New Thought belief in the inherent capacity of individuals to shape their realities through the alignment of thought and belief with their desired outcomes.

Transcendentalists:

Peale's emphasis on the importance of spiritual faith and the cultivation of a positive mindset finds parallels in the works of Transcendentalist thinkers such as Ralph Waldo Emerson and Henry David Thoreau. Like the Transcendentalists, Peale encourages individuals to tap into their inner spiritual resources and to seek personal growth and fulfillment through the exploration of their inner potential.

Aristotle and Franklin:

Norman Vincent Peale's focus on the power of positive thinking and the integration of faith and psychology resonates with Aristotle's emphasis on ethical living and practical wisdom, as well as with Benjamin Franklin's advocacy for personal development and virtue ethics. All three thinkers share a common thread in their promotion of practical approaches to self-improvement and the cultivation of a fulfilling and meaningful life.

In this way, Peale's philosophy can be seen as a continuation of the broader lineage of Positive Thinking, New Thought, and the Transcendentalist movement, all of which emphasize the significance of spiritual awareness, personal empowerment, and the transformative potential of the human mind.

Suggested Reading

In Favor of Peale:

1. Peale, N. V. (1952). The Power of Positive Thinking. New York, NY: Prentice Hall Press.

Description: Norman Vincent Peale's influential book emphasizes the transformative potential of positive thinking, offering practical guidance and inspirational anecdotes that encourage readers to cultivate optimism, faith, and resilience in the face of life's challenges, thereby fostering personal growth and well-being.

2. Peale, N. V. (1982). Positive Imaging: The Powerful Way to Change Your Life. New York, NY: Ballantine Books.

Description: Building upon his earlier work, Peale's book delves into the transformative power of visualization and positive imagery, providing readers with practical techniques and exercises for harnessing the creative power of the mind to manifest positive life changes and achieve personal goals.

Critical of Peale:

1. Meyer, D. J. (1988). The Positive Thinkers: Popular Religious Psychology from Mary Baker Eddy to Norman Vincent Peale and Ronald Reagan. New York, NY: Doubleday.

Description: Donald Meyer's historical analysis critically examines the positive thinking movement within the context of American religious psychology, providing insights into the cultural and political implications of Peale's ideas and their broader impact on American society.

2. Henslin, E. (2011). The Kingdom of Self: An Exploration of the Private and Public Sides of Narcissism. New York, NY: SAGE Publications.

Description: Earl Henslin's work offers a critical exploration of the potential pitfalls associated with an excessive emphasis on self-fulfillment and positive thinking, highlighting the ways in which these concepts, when taken to an extreme, can foster narcissistic tendencies and self-centered behaviors, indirectly engaging with some of the principles advocated by Peale.

Carl Rogers and 'On Becoming a Person'

Carl Rogers (1902-1987) was an influential American psychologist and one of the founding figures of humanistic psychology. Born in Illinois, Rogers is best known for his development of client-centered therapy, emphasizing the importance of empathy, genuineness, and unconditional positive regard in the therapeutic relationship. His humanistic approach revolutionized the field of psychology, emphasizing the significance of individual autonomy, personal growth, and self-actualization.

On "On Becoming a Person":
Published in 1961, "On Becoming a Person" is considered one of Carl Rogers' most significant works, encapsulating his humanistic philosophy and person-centered approach to therapy. In the book, Rogers articulates the core principles of his therapeutic method, emphasizing the importance of empathetic understanding, congruence, and unconditional positive regard as essential components of effective counseling and personal development. Rogers emphasizes the inherent capacity for personal growth and self-actualization within each individual, underscoring the significance of a supportive and nonjudgmental therapeutic environment in facilitating the process of self-discovery and psychological healing.

Effects on Popular Culture and the Self-Help Movements of the 1970s:

Rogers' humanistic psychology, as articulated in "On Becoming a Person," had a profound impact on popular culture, influencing the broader discourse on personal growth and psychological well-being during the 1970s. His emphasis on self-exploration, authenticity, and the pursuit of personal actualization resonated with the values of the burgeoning self-help movements of the era, shaping the development of various therapeutic techniques and personal development strategies that emphasized the importance of individual empowerment and self-discovery. Rogers' emphasis on the therapeutic relationship and the facilitation of personal growth within a supportive and empathetic environment contributed to the humanistic ethos that permeated the self-help culture of the 1970s, inspiring individuals to engage in introspective practices aimed at achieving greater self-awareness and personal fulfillment.

Legacy and Criticism

Carl Rogers' humanistic psychology and person-centered approach to therapy left a lasting legacy that deeply influenced renowned educators and authors such as Leo Buscaglia. Buscaglia, known for his work on the power of love and human connections, was inspired by Rogers' emphasis on empathy and authentic human relationships. Rogers' influence on Buscaglia's teachings and writings can be seen in the promotion of love, acceptance, and emotional authenticity as essential elements for personal growth and fulfillment.

While Carl Rogers' humanistic approach to therapy garnered significant acclaim, it also faced criticism for its potential susceptibility to misinterpretation and misuse. Critics pointed out that the emphasis on unconditional positive regard and non-directive therapy could lead to a lack of necessary intervention in cases where clients require more structured and directive guidance. Moreover, some experts cautioned that the principles of client-centered therapy could be misappropriated by unscrupulous practitioners, potentially leading to the exploitation of vulnerable individuals through pseudoscientific or manipulative practices masquerading as legitimate therapeutic approaches.

Rogers' emphasis on self-actualization and the facilitation of personal growth, while profound in its intent, could be manipulated by unscrupulous players within the self-help industry. The commercialization of his ideas, without adherence to the ethical principles and rigorous training required in therapeutic practice, could potentially lead to the promotion of simplistic and misleading self-help strategies that lack the necessary expertise and evidence-based support to effectively address individuals' psychological needs. Thus, the risk of misinterpretation and misuse underscores the importance of responsible and ethical application of Rogers' person-centered approach within the context of professional and well-regulated therapeutic practice.

Suggested Reading

1. Rogers, C. R. (1961). On Becoming a Person: A Therapist's View of Psychotherapy. New York, NY: Houghton Mifflin.

Description: In this seminal work, Rogers presents his humanistic approach to psychotherapy, emphasizing the significance of empathy and unconditional positive regard in fostering personal growth and self-actualization. Pros include its emphasis on the therapeutic relationship, while cons may involve its potential overreliance on non-directive methods in complex cases.

2. Buscaglia, L. (1984). Loving Each Other: The Challenge of Human Relationships. New York, NY: Fawcett Books.

Description: Inspired by Rogers' principles, Buscaglia advocates for the transformative power of love and human connections in fostering personal fulfillment and emotional well-being. Pros include its emphasis on emotional authenticity, while cons may involve its potential oversimplification of complex emotional dynamics.

3. Mearns, D., & Thorne, B. (1988). Person-Centred Therapy Today: New Frontiers in Theory and Practice. London, UK: Sage Publications.

Description: Mearns and Thorne offer an in-depth exploration of the contemporary applications of Rogers' person-centered therapy, highlighting its ongoing relevance in modern psychotherapeutic practice. Pros include its comprehensive analysis of the approach's evolution, while cons may involve its potential underestimation of the need for structured intervention in certain therapeutic contexts.

4. Kirschenbaum, H., & Henderson, V. L. (1990). The Carl Rogers Reader. London, UK: Constable.

Description: This reader provides a collection of key writings by Carl Rogers, offering insights into the development of his humanistic psychology and its impact on the field of psychotherapy. Pros include its comprehensive overview of Rogers' work, while cons may involve its potential omission of critical discussions on the limitations of his approach in certain clinical settings.

The Counterculture Connection: Psychedelics, Altered States, and Personal Transformation- Leary and Terence McKenna

In the 1970s, the self-help movement was influenced by the burgeoning interest in psychedelics, altered states of consciousness, and personal transformation, with prominent figures such as Timothy Leary and Terence McKenna playing pivotal roles in shaping this cultural shift. Leary, known for his advocacy of the therapeutic potential of psychedelic substances, promoted the exploration of altered states as a means of achieving profound insights and personal growth. Similarly, McKenna, through his advocacy of the transformative power of psychedelic experiences and his exploration of shamanic traditions, contributed to the popularization of the idea that altered states could facilitate spiritual awakening and psychological healing.

Their work resonated with the ethos of the self-help movement, which emphasized the pursuit of personal growth and self-actualization. Leary and McKenna's writings and lectures provided individuals with alternative perspectives on consciousness and the human experience, encouraging them to explore unconventional avenues for achieving heightened awareness and inner transformation. Their ideas had a significant impact on the cultural zeitgeist of the 1970s, inspiring many to seek unconventional methods for achieving personal enlightenment and expanded consciousness.

However, it is essential to underscore the serious risks associated with the use of psychedelic substances. While proponents highlighted the potential therapeutic benefits of these substances, including the facilitation of profound spiritual experiences and psychological insights, the misuse of psychedelics can lead to detrimental effects on mental health and overall well-being. Potential risks include the onset of severe psychological distress, exacerbation of preexisting mental health conditions, and the occurrence of adverse physiological reactions.

Therefore, it is crucial to approach the use of psychedelics with caution and under the guidance of trained professionals in controlled and supportive settings. Individuals considering the exploration of altered states should be aware of the potential risks involved and should prioritize their physical and psychological well-being above any potential benefits. Responsible and informed decision-making is paramount when engaging with psychedelic substances to ensure the promotion of personal safety and holistic well-being.

Tune In, Turn On, Drop Out

Timothy Leary (1920-1996) was an American psychologist and writer known for his advocacy of psychedelic drugs and the exploration of altered states of consciousness. He popularized the phrase "turn on, tune in, drop out," encapsulating his countercultural philosophy promoting spiritual enlightenment and personal freedom. Despite controversy surrounding his methods, Leary's work significantly influenced the 1960s counterculture and the broader cultural discourse on the potential benefits and risks of psychedelic substances.

Timothy Leary's famous phrase "turn on, tune in, drop out," coined in the 1960s, encapsulated his philosophy of advocating for the exploration of altered states of consciousness through the use of psychedelic substances, such as LSD. The phrase represented Leary's call for individuals to embrace a countercultural lifestyle that prioritized spiritual enlightenment and personal freedom over societal norms and constraints. However, his suggestion, though intended as a path to personal liberation, had far-reaching and potentially dangerous implications for individuals he never personally met.

The impact of Leary's message was profound, particularly within the context of the 1960s counterculture and the emerging psychedelic movement. It inspired a generation to challenge conventional social structures and traditional values, fostering a sense of communal belonging and a shared quest for spiritual transcendence. Leary's advocacy for the exploration of altered states significantly contributed to the widespread use of psychedelics and the popularization of these substances as tools for personal and spiritual transformation.

However, the dangers inherent in following Leary's advice without careful consideration of individual circumstances and mental health are stark. The indiscriminate use of psychedelics, as encouraged by Leary's message, can lead to severe psychological distress, triggering latent mental health issues or exacerbating preexisting conditions. Additionally, without proper guidance and support, individuals may be susceptible to adverse psychological reactions, including prolonged psychosis, hallucinations, and delusions, which can have long-lasting and detrimental effects on their mental well-being.

Leary's message, while emblematic of the era's quest for personal freedom and spiritual enlightenment, failed to acknowledge the complexity of individual psychological states and the potential risks associated with unguided psychedelic experiences. By promoting a one-size-fits-all approach to personal transformation, Leary's suggestion neglected the importance of responsible and informed usage of psychedelic substances, ultimately putting individuals at risk of enduring psychological harm that could have long-lasting consequences. It serves as a cautionary reminder of the need for tailored and responsible guidance when engaging with practices that have the potential to profoundly impact one's mental and emotional well-being.

In the 1970s, the widespread use of psychedelics had a profound impact on popular culture, influencing various artistic expressions, including music, art, and literature. Psychedelics became emblematic of the counterculture movement, representing a rebellion against traditional values and an embrace of alternative forms of spirituality and consciousness exploration. This cultural shift extended to both pop and serious psychology, as researchers and practitioners began to explore the therapeutic potential of psychedelics in treating various psychological conditions, leading to an increased interest in the study of altered states of consciousness and their potential applications in psychotherapy.

Despite the initial enthusiasm surrounding the potential benefits of psychedelics, their deleterious effects on individuals and society soon became apparent. Unsupervised and indiscriminate use of these substances often led to adverse psychological reactions, including severe anxiety, paranoia, and even long-term psychosis. In some cases, individuals experienced profound existential crises, leading to a sense of nihilism and self-annihilation, which stood in stark contrast to the principles of self-help that emphasized personal growth and empowerment.

The brazen embrace of irrationality and anti-traditionalism within psychedelic culture often contributed to the promotion of reckless and hedonistic behaviors, leading to a disregard for societal norms and values. This cultural shift had far-reaching implications for individuals and communities, fostering a sense of detachment and disengagement from social responsibilities and ethical considerations. Furthermore, the connection between psychedelic use and self-harm underscored the potential dangers of promoting uninhibited exploration of altered states without proper guidance and support, ultimately highlighting the inherent risks of engaging with substances that can induce profound alterations in consciousness and perception.

As a result, the 1970s witnessed a complex interplay between the positive aspirations of self-help and the detrimental consequences of unguided psychedelic experimentation, emphasizing the critical importance of responsible and informed approaches to personal growth and psychological well-being. The era's exploration of psychedelics serves as a cautionary tale, illustrating the need for a balanced and holistic understanding of human consciousness and the potential pitfalls of advocating for transformative experiences without careful consideration of the psychological and societal implications.

Terence McKenna's Dark Shamanic Journey

Terence McKenna (1946-2000) was a renowned American ethnobotanist and philosopher known for his advocacy of psychedelic substances as tools for spiritual exploration and personal transformation. While celebrated for his insights into consciousness and shamanism, McKenna's ideas often faced criticism for their lack of empirical grounding and the potential risks associated with unguided psychedelic use. Despite controversy, his work continues to influence discussions on the intersection of psychedelics, spirituality, and the human experience.

Terence McKenna, a prominent figure in the exploration of consciousness and psychedelics, shared a philosophical kinship with Aldous Huxley, whose work "The Doors of Perception" similarly delved into the transformative potential of psychedelic experiences. McKenna's advocacy of drug use as a tool for self-knowledge and self-actualization echoed the sentiments of the opium writers of the Romantic Age, who embraced altered states as a means of artistic and philosophical exploration. His connection to Carlos Castaneda, known for his controversial accounts of shamanic experiences, underscored a shared interest in the esoteric and mystical dimensions of consciousness expansion.

However, the glorification of drug use as a path to self-derangement and forced psychosis represented a perilous departure from the principles of rationality and psychological well-being advocated by the self-help movement. While figures like Leary and McKenna garnered followers during the 1970s, their appeal lay in their countercultural message of spiritual liberation and the promise of transcendent experiences. Individuals drawn to their teachings often sought unconventional paths to self-discovery and enlightenment, driven by a profound disillusionment with mainstream societal values and a yearning for deeper existential meaning.

Nevertheless, the glorification of drug-induced experiences as a means of achieving spiritual enlightenment and self-actualization disregarded the inherent risks of psychological destabilization and long-term cognitive impairment. This emphasis on uninhibited exploration of altered states without adequate consideration of the potential dangers reflected a broader cultural trend of rejecting conventional norms and embracing alternative forms of consciousness expansion, even at the cost of one's mental and emotional well-being.

The appeal of figures like Leary and McKenna within the context of the 1970s self-help revolution can be attributed to their ability to tap into the collective yearning for personal transformation and spiritual transcendence. Their countercultural narratives resonated with individuals disillusioned by societal constraints, offering an alternative vision of self-discovery and empowerment that seemed to transcend the limitations of conventional psychological and spiritual practices. However, the consequences of their advocacy underscored the crucial importance of responsible and evidence-based approaches to personal growth, emphasizing the need for a balanced and holistic understanding of human consciousness and well-being within the broader context of the self-help movement.

What Would Our Experts Have to Say

Considering the philosophical viewpoints of Emerson, Ben Franklin, Maslow, and Aristotle, it is likely that they would express caution and skepticism regarding the use of psychedelic drugs as a means to attain a better life and achieve happiness.

Ralph Waldo Emerson, known for his transcendentalist philosophy emphasizing self-reliance and the inherent goodness of humanity, would likely stress the importance of inner spiritual cultivation and self-discovery as the primary avenues for personal growth and fulfillment. He might caution against the reliance on external substances for spiritual enlightenment, emphasizing the need for self-awareness and moral integrity as the foundations for a meaningful life.

Benjamin Franklin, renowned for his practical wisdom and emphasis on personal development, would likely advocate for the cultivation of virtuous character and ethical living as essential components of a happy and fulfilling life. He might caution against the potential risks associated with the use of psychedelic drugs, highlighting the importance of rational decision-making and responsible behavior in pursuit of personal well-being and success.

Abraham Maslow, known for his theory of human motivation and the hierarchy of needs, would likely emphasize the significance of self-actualization through conscious and intentional personal development. He might view the use of psychedelic drugs as a temporary and potentially unreliable shortcut to self-transcendence, suggesting that lasting happiness and self-fulfillment stem from a holistic and purpose-driven approach to life that integrates both personal and societal well-being.

Aristotle, renowned for his virtue ethics and emphasis on eudaimonia, or human flourishing, would likely underscore the importance of cultivating moral excellence and virtuous character as the foundation for a genuinely happy and fulfilling life. He might caution against the indiscriminate use of psychedelic substances, emphasizing the potential risks of disrupting one's moral and intellectual faculties and the potential deviation from the path of virtuous living and ethical conduct.

In essence, these philosophical thinkers would likely advocate for a balanced and holistic approach to personal growth and happiness, emphasizing the significance of self-awareness, moral integrity, and conscious decision-making in pursuit of a meaningful and fulfilling life. They would caution against the reliance on external substances as a panacea for achieving happiness and personal development, instead emphasizing the importance of internal cultivation and ethical living as the true sources of lasting well-being and fulfillment.

Suggested Reading

1. Huxley, A. (1954). The Doors of Perception. New York, NY: Harper & Brothers.

Description: Huxley's influential work explores the use of psychedelic substances and their impact on consciousness, offering a nuanced reflection on the potential risks and benefits associated with altered states of perception and their implications for human experience.

2. Castaneda, C. (1968). The Teachings of Don Juan: A Yaqui Way of Knowledge. Berkeley, CA: University of California Press.

Description: Castaneda's controversial narrative chronicles his purported experiences with shamanic teachings and psychedelic-induced spiritual insights, prompting critical examination of the authenticity and reliability of his accounts within the context of anthropological and spiritual studies.

3. Leary, T., & Metzner, R. (1964). The Psychedelic Experience: A Manual Based on the Tibetan Book of the Dead. New York, NY: Citadel Press.

Description: Leary and Metzner's manual offers a guide to navigating psychedelic experiences, drawing parallels between psychedelic states and spiritual enlightenment, prompting critical evaluation of the potentially misleading and dangerous implications of equating drug-induced experiences with genuine spiritual transcendence.

4. McKenna, T. (1992). Food of the Gods: The Search for the Original Tree of Knowledge. New York, NY: Bantam.

Description: McKenna's exploration of the historical and cultural significance of psychoactive substances offers a critical perspective on the glorification of drug use as a means of achieving spiritual insight and personal transformation, highlighting the potential dangers and societal implications of uninhibited psychedelic exploration.

On Psychedelics:

1. Lee, M. A., & Shlain, B. (1985). Acid Dreams: The Complete Social History of LSD: The CIA, the Sixties, and Beyond. New York, NY: Grove Press.

Description: Lee and Shlain provide a comprehensive historical account of the societal impact of LSD, exploring its origins, cultural significance, and the complex interplay between the psychedelic movement and the socio-political landscape of the 1960s. The book also serves as a cautionary tale, highlighting the potential dangers and adverse consequences of unguided psychedelic experimentation.

2. Ketchum, W. (2000). The Secret History of Hallucinogens in Psychiatry. Ashland, OR: Ronin Publishing.

Description: Ketchum's examination of the historical use of hallucinogens in psychiatry offers critical insights into the medical and societal implications of psychedelic experimentation. With a focus on the potential risks and adverse psychological effects associated with LSD and other hallucinogenic substances, the book serves as a cautionary resource for individuals considering the use of psychedelics for personal exploration.

3. O'Brien, T. (2010). Dangers of Hallucinogens. New York, NY: Rosen Central.

Description: O'Brien's book provides an accessible and informative overview of the risks and dangers associated with the use of hallucinogenic substances, including LSD. Offering insights into the potential physiological and psychological effects of psychedelic use, the book serves as a valuable resource for individuals seeking a comprehensive understanding of the potential hazards of experimenting with LSD and other hallucinogens.

These readings offer critical perspectives on the history of LSD and psychedelics, highlighting the potential risks and adverse consequences associated with their use, thereby serving as cautionary resources for individuals contemplating experimentation with these substances.

Maxwell Maltz and 'Psycho-Cybernetics'

Maxwell Maltz (1889-1975) was an American cosmetic surgeon and author, best known for his pioneering work in the field of self-help and personal development. His seminal book "Psycho-Cybernetics," first published in 1960, revolutionized the self-help genre by introducing the concept of self-image psychology. Maltz's innovative ideas on self-esteem and self-actualization significantly influenced the 1970s self-help movement, inspiring individuals to cultivate a positive self-image and harness the power of the mind for personal transformation and success. His work continues to impact the field of personal development, emphasizing the importance of psychological well-being and self-perception in achieving one's goals and aspirations.

Maxwell Maltz's work, particularly his book "Psycho-Cybernetics," played a significant role in shaping the 1970s self-help revolution. Here are five important aspects of his work that influenced the movement:

1. Self-Image Psychology: Maltz's emphasis on the importance of self-image and its impact on individuals' behavior and achievements revolutionized the self-help genre, encouraging readers to cultivate a positive self-perception as a key to personal transformation.

2. Visualization Techniques: Maltz popularized visualization exercises, advocating the use of mental imagery to reinforce positive self-perception and facilitate goal achievement. His techniques fostered the idea that mental rehearsal could lead to tangible improvements in various aspects of one's life.

3. Mind-Body Connection: Maltz highlighted the interconnectedness of the mind and body, underscoring the significance of psychological well-being in fostering physical and emotional health. His work encouraged individuals to recognize the power of the mind in influencing overall well-being.

4. Goal Setting and Achievement: Through his teachings, Maltz emphasized the importance of setting clear and attainable goals, promoting the idea that a well-defined sense of purpose and direction could lead to personal success and fulfillment.

5. Positive Attitude and Resilience: Maltz's work underscored the value of maintaining a positive attitude and cultivating resilience in the face of challenges. His teachings encouraged individuals to develop a mindset of optimism and perseverance, fostering a proactive approach to personal growth and development.

In Relation to Other Thinkers

Maxwell Maltz's work exhibited strong ties to various philosophical and psychological currents, including New Thought, positive thinking, and the success literature of his era. His emphasis on the power of self-image and the mind's influence on personal success resonated with the core tenets of New Thought, which advocated the transformative potential of positive mental attitudes and the law of attraction.

Maltz's teachings aligned closely with the principles of positive thinking, emphasizing the importance of cultivating an optimistic outlook and constructive self-perception as a means of achieving personal fulfillment and success. His work echoed the writings of influential figures such as Benjamin Franklin and Ralph Waldo Emerson, who emphasized the significance of self-reliance, moral integrity, and the pursuit of personal excellence as pathways to achievement and self-empowerment.

Furthermore, Maltz's contributions to the self-help genre were in line with the success literature of his time, which promoted the idea that individuals could proactively shape their destinies through disciplined effort, goal setting, and the cultivation of a positive mindset. His teachings, like those of other pop psychologists of his era, emphasized the importance of self-motivation, resilience, and the pursuit of personal excellence as essential components of achieving one's aspirations and realizing one's full potential.

Criticisms

By now, the list of criticisms might start to look familiar.

While Maxwell Maltz's work has had a significant impact on the self-help genre, it has also faced certain criticisms:

1. Simplistic Approach: Critics have argued that Maltz's emphasis on self-image and visualization techniques oversimplifies the complexities of human psychology and personal development, potentially neglecting the multifaceted nature of individual struggles and challenges.

2. Lack of Empirical Evidence: Some experts have questioned the empirical basis of Maltz's claims, highlighting the need for more rigorous scientific research to substantiate the effectiveness of his techniques and their long-term impact on individuals' well-being and success.

3. Overemphasis on Positive Thinking: Critics have cautioned that an excessive focus on positive thinking, as advocated by Maltz, may downplay the importance of acknowledging and processing negative emotions, potentially leading to the suppression of genuine psychological challenges and hindering authentic personal growth.

4. Unrealistic Promises: Some have criticized Maltz's work for potentially fostering unrealistic expectations among readers, suggesting that his teachings may inadvertently encourage individuals to adopt a one-size-fits-all approach to personal development, disregarding the unique complexities of individual experiences and circumstances.

5. Lack of Attention to Structural Factors: Critics have also pointed out that Maltz's work tends to prioritize individual agency and mindset without adequately addressing the structural and systemic factors that can significantly impact an individual's opportunities and outcomes, potentially neglecting the broader social context within which personal development occurs.

Legacy

Maxwell Maltz's legacy resides in his pioneering work on self-image psychology and his influential book "Psycho-Cybernetics," which continues to impact the self-help genre. His emphasis on the power of self-perception and the mind's role in personal transformation has left a lasting imprint on the understanding of human behavior and the pursuit of self-fulfillment.

Suggested Readings

1. Maltz, M. (1960). Psycho-Cybernetics. New York, NY: Prentice-Hall.

Description: Maltz's seminal work explores the relationship between self-image and success, offering practical insights and techniques for achieving personal transformation and improved self-esteem. The book continues to serve as a foundational text in the self-help genre, emphasizing the role of self-perception in shaping one's experiences and accomplishments.

2. Schwartz, D. J. (2003). The Magic of Thinking Big. New York, NY: Simon & Schuster.

Description: Schwartz's book draws inspiration from Maltz's teachings, offering practical advice on achieving personal and professional success through the cultivation of a positive mindset and the pursuit of ambitious goals. The book emphasizes the significance of self-confidence and proactive thinking in overcoming challenges and realizing one's full potential.

3. Dweck, C. S. (2006). Mindset: The New Psychology of Success. New York, NY: Ballantine Books.

Description: Dweck's influential work expands upon Maltz's ideas, exploring the concept of mindset and its impact on achievement and personal growth. Drawing on empirical research, the book highlights the importance of cultivating a growth-oriented mindset and embracing challenges as opportunities for learning and self-improvement.

These suggested readings provide valuable insights into Maltz's legacy and his contributions to the self-help genre, offering practical guidance and strategies for personal development and success based on the principles of self-image psychology and positive thinking.

New Thought Continues

1. Dyer, W. (2009). Excuses Begone!: How to Change Lifelong, Self-Defeating Thinking Habits. Carlsbad, CA: Hay House.

Description: Dyer's book provides practical guidance on overcoming self-defeating thoughts and behaviors, offering strategies for cultivating a more positive mindset and achieving personal transformation.

2. Tolle, E. (2004). The Power of Now: A Guide to Spiritual Enlightenment. Novato, CA: New World Library.

Description: Tolle's influential work explores the transformative power of living in the present moment, emphasizing the importance of mindfulness and spiritual awareness in fostering personal well-being and fulfillment.

3. Chopra, D. (1995). The Seven Spiritual Laws of Success: A Practical Guide to the Fulfillment of Your Dreams. San Rafael, CA: Amber-Allen Publishing.

Description: Chopra's book presents seven spiritual principles for achieving success and personal fulfillment, combining practical wisdom with spiritual insights to guide readers toward greater self-empowerment and achievement.

4. Byrne, R. (2006). The Secret. New York, NY: Atria Books.

Description: Byrne's bestselling book introduces the concept of the law of attraction, emphasizing the power of positive thinking and visualization in manifesting one's desires and achieving personal goals.

Some have raised concerns that the book's emphasis on personal responsibility and the law of attraction may inadvertently stigmatize individuals facing adversity, suggesting that those who experience challenges or setbacks may be at fault for their circumstances, disregarding the role of external factors beyond their control.

5. Canfield, J., & Hansen, M. V. (1993). Chicken Soup for the Soul. Deerfield Beach, FL: Health Communications.

Description: Canfield and Hansen's compilation of inspirational stories offers heartwarming narratives that encourage readers to embrace positivity, resilience, and the human capacity for personal growth and emotional healing.

Early Self-Help Gurus:
Ram Dass, Werner Erhard, Louie Hay, Wayne Dyer, Marianne Williamson

The early self-help gurus, including figures such as Ram Dass, Werner Erhard, Louise Hay, Wayne Dyer, and Marianne Williamson, played a pivotal role in shaping the trajectory of the self-help movement in the 1970s. Their collective contributions significantly influenced the cultural zeitgeist of the era, fostering a widespread interest in personal growth, spirituality, and holistic well-being. By integrating spiritual principles, psychological insights, and practical guidance, these gurus established a foundation for the exploration of the human potential and the pursuit of self-actualization within mainstream consciousness.

Their teachings emphasized the importance of self-awareness, personal empowerment, and the cultivation of a positive mindset, resonating with individuals seeking meaning and fulfillment amid societal changes and cultural shifts. Through their books, seminars, and transformative workshops, they promoted the idea that personal transformation was attainable through a combination of psychological introspection, spiritual exploration, and practical tools for self-improvement. Their emphasis on the interconnectedness of mind, body, and spirit laid the groundwork for a more holistic approach to personal development, marking a departure from traditional psychological and spiritual paradigms.

Moreover, their popularization of concepts such as affirmations, self-love, and the integration of Eastern spiritual practices into Western self-help methodologies broadened the scope of the self-help movement, appealing to a diverse audience seeking alternative paths to well-being and personal growth. By fostering a cultural shift towards introspection, self-empowerment, and spiritual consciousness, these early self-help gurus paved the way for the emergence of a broader, more inclusive self-help culture that continues to influence contemporary approaches to personal development, spirituality, and holistic wellness.

Benefits Provided by the Early Gurus

The early self-help gurus introduced several novel concepts and practical approaches that went beyond traditional wisdom, classical education, and the scope of Christian literature and intellectual history. Some key elements include:

1. Psychological Techniques:

Early self-help gurus integrated psychological insights and practical techniques into their teachings, providing individuals with actionable strategies for personal growth, emotional healing, and goal achievement.

These techniques went beyond traditional wisdom by offering specific methodologies for enhancing self-awareness, improving interpersonal relationships, and cultivating resilience in the face of adversity.

2. Holistic Well-Being:

The early self-help movement emphasized a holistic approach to well-being that encompassed the integration of mind, body, and spirit.

This comprehensive framework expanded upon the traditional emphasis on intellectual development, encouraging individuals to prioritize their emotional and spiritual needs alongside their intellectual pursuits, thereby promoting a more balanced and integrated approach to personal growth and fulfillment.

3. Self-Empowerment:

Early self-help gurus advocated for the empowerment of the individual, promoting the idea that each person possesses the capacity to shape their destiny and effect positive change in their lives.

This focus on self-empowerment went beyond the constraints of traditional hierarchies and societal norms, encouraging individuals to take control of their personal narratives and actively pursue their aspirations and goals.

4. Practical Application:

The early self-help movement emphasized the practical application of philosophical and spiritual principles in everyday life, offering readers and participants tangible tools for personal transformation and success.

This practical emphasis provided individuals with actionable steps for implementing positive change, fostering a more proactive and solution-oriented approach to personal development that went beyond the theoretical framework of traditional wisdom and intellectual history.

By incorporating psychological techniques, promoting holistic well-being, emphasizing self-empowerment, and focusing on practical application, the early self-help gurus expanded the scope of personal development beyond the boundaries of traditional wisdom, classical education, and the teachings of Christian literature and intellectual history. They offered individuals a more accessible and actionable path to self-improvement and personal growth, grounded in the principles of empowerment, resilience, and practical spirituality.

Training, In Contrast to Formal Spiritual Traditions

In contrast to other spiritual traditions that often mandate rigorous and prolonged periods of study, contemplation, and practice before assuming a leadership role, the early self-help gurus did not adhere to formal hierarchies or institutional structures. Their emergence within the self-help movement was characterized by a more informal and accessible approach to spiritual and personal development, with an emphasis on individual empowerment and the direct application of transformative techniques.

While traditional spiritual paths often require individuals to undergo systematic training under the guidance of experienced mentors or within established religious institutions, the early self-help gurus assumed their roles based on their own personal experiences, insights, and a desire to share their wisdom with others. Their teachings were often rooted in universal principles of personal growth and spiritual well-being, catering to a diverse audience seeking practical guidance for everyday challenges and the pursuit of holistic fulfillment.

Additionally, the early self-help gurus fostered a more inclusive and democratic approach to spiritual and personal development, welcoming individuals from all walks of life and backgrounds to engage with their teachings and methodologies. This accessibility enabled a broader audience to benefit from their insights without the formalities and exclusivity often associated with traditional spiritual hierarchies and institutionalized religious frameworks.

While the traditional spiritual paths emphasize lineage, authority, and adherence to specific doctrinal teachings, the early self-help movement centered on personal agency, direct experience, and the application of practical techniques for self-improvement and spiritual growth. This distinction highlights the evolution of spiritual exploration in the modern context and the diversification of approaches to personal development and well-being outside of traditional institutional structures.

Instant Gurus vs.
Traditional Spiritual Leadership Training

To provide context for the instant or revelatory training, the on-the-job training, or the visionary enlightenment claimed by the early self-help gurus in the 70s, here are five traditional religious groups that require an extensive period of training, often spanning several years or even decades, before an individual can assume a leadership role within the community:

1. Tibetan Buddhism:
Prospective spiritual leaders in Tibetan Buddhism typically dedicate over 20 years to comprehensive training that involves rigorous study of Buddhist philosophy, meditation practices, ritual ceremonies, and ethical guidelines, under the guidance of experienced practitioners and scholars within established monastic institutions.

2. Catholicism:

Aspiring priests within the Catholic Church undergo an average of 6 to 8 years of seminary training, encompassing academic study, theological education, pastoral formation, and spiritual discernment. This comprehensive preparation equips them with theological expertise and pastoral skills for assuming leadership roles within the church.

3. Hinduism:

Within certain sects and traditions of Hinduism, individuals aspiring to become spiritual leaders, such as gurus or swamis, often commit to lifelong spiritual discipline and study, dedicating over 30 years to the rigorous exploration of sacred texts, meditation, and the cultivation of spiritual virtues within the context of guru-disciple relationships.

4. Sufi Islam:

Sufi masters or sheikhs in the Sufi tradition of Islam engage in a profound spiritual apprenticeship that may last for more than 15 years. This journey involves the study of Islamic mysticism, the practice of dhikr (remembrance of God), and the cultivation of spiritual insight and devotion under the mentorship of experienced guides.

5. Orthodox Judaism:

Orthodox Jewish individuals pursuing spiritual leadership roles, such as rabbis or Torah scholars, devote over 10 years to intensive study within yeshivas (Jewish educational institutions). This period of training focuses on mastering Jewish law, rabbinic literature, and Talmudic teachings, equipping them with the knowledge and ethical principles necessary for guiding their communities.

Evaluating the Gurus

Evaluating the depth of understanding of human nature, particularly in the context of the early self-help gurus, is not solely reliant on their popularity or following. Instead, it requires a nuanced examination of their teachings, the impact of their

101

methodologies, and the broader reception of their ideas within the realm of personal development and spiritual growth.

Assessing the credibility of their insights can involve a critical analysis of the following factors:

1. Practical Application: An evaluation of the practical application of their teachings and techniques, including their effectiveness in fostering personal growth, emotional well-being, and spiritual transformation.

2. Consistency and Coherence: A scrutiny of the coherence and consistency of their philosophical and spiritual principles, as well as their alignment with established psychological frameworks and spiritual traditions.

3. Impact on Well-being: A consideration of the impact of their guidance on the well-being and personal development of their followers, including testimonials and case studies that highlight the transformative effects of their teachings.

4. Contribution to the Field: An examination of their contributions to the broader field of self-help, personal development, and spiritual enlightenment, including any innovative approaches or insights that have shaped subsequent discourse and practices in these domains.

While the exact depth of their understanding of human nature may not be definitively quantifiable, a holistic assessment of these factors can provide a more nuanced perspective on the influence and significance of their work within the context of personal development, spiritual growth, and the pursuit of holistic well-being.

The Nuanced Understanding of the Complexities of Human Experience

The phrase 'nuanced understanding of the complexities of human experience' is often used to describe the early 'Gurus'. It is a phrase that can be applied to various individuals, including cult leaders and politicians, who may possess the ability to connect with people and articulate compelling narratives, albeit for different purposes. It puts me on edge.

The key distinction lies in the ethical and moral framework within which individuals operate, as well as the intention and impact of their teachings and actions. A genuine guru is characterized not only by their understanding of human nature but also by their commitment to promoting spiritual growth, compassion, and ethical conduct among their followers.

A legitimate guru prioritizes the well-being and spiritual development of their disciples, emphasizing principles of compassion, empathy, and ethical living. Their teachings aim to cultivate self-awareness, inner peace, and a sense of interconnectedness, fostering a harmonious relationship between the individual and the broader community.

On the other hand, cult leaders may exploit their followers' vulnerabilities, employing manipulative tactics and fostering dependence to maintain control and authority. Their teachings often prioritize obedience to the leader over personal growth and critical thinking, potentially leading to harmful or destructive consequences for their followers.

Similarly, politicians may leverage their understanding of human psychology to sway public opinion or advance their political agendas, often emphasizing persuasive messaging over genuine spiritual or moral guidance.

Therefore, while an understanding of the complexities of human experience can be a valuable trait, it is crucial to evaluate the intentions, ethics, and overall impact of an individual's teachings and leadership within the context of their respective roles and responsibilities. A genuine guru operates within an ethical framework that prioritizes the well-being and spiritual development of their followers, fostering a sense of unity, compassion, and ethical responsibility within the community.

Which begs a few questions:

- If there was no formal training, where did the 'Gurus" get their 'nuanced understanding of the complexities of human experience'?

- How does a 'guru's' guidance relate to every person universally? Why doesn't it solve complex problems between groups of people?

- Where did these "Gurus' come from?

- How do, or did they earn a living?

- Is it moral to sell this 'nuanced understanding of the complexities of human experience'?

- Is the 'nuanced understanding of the complexities of human experience' held by a 'Guru' more substantial than direct experience of the mysteries of life?

- What do they actually contribute to society other than classes and seminars and books and TV show appearances?

- By naming themselves "gurus" are they assuming their person and/or experience is more radiant, informed, meaningful and insightful then anyone else's?

Before we look at the early Gurus of the 70s, I think is prudent to review some more contemporary "Gurus" to see what we risk anytime we hand over our personal volition, power, person, body or assets to another flawed human being.

The Bad Seeds

Here is a list of 'Gurus" associated with cases of abuse, exploitation, or manipulation within their roles as spiritual or community leaders, sorted by the years they were active:

1. Jim Jones (1950s-1970s): Founder of the Peoples Temple, responsible for the mass suicide and murder of over 900 of his followers in Jonestown, Guyana.

2. Swami Muktananda (1970s-1980s): Indian spiritual leader, faced allegations of sexual abuse and misconduct within his spiritual community.

3. Michel Rostand (Buddhafield) (1980s-2000s): **Leader of the** Buddhafield community, faced allegations of psychological manipulation and abuse within the group, prompting a critical examination of the dynamics and ethics within the community.

4. Bhagwan Shree Rajneesh (Osho) (1980s-1990s): Indian spiritual guru, accused of various criminal activities and the mastermind behind the controversial Rajneeshpuram community in Oregon.

5. Keith Raniere (NXIVM) (1990s-2010s): Founder of the purported self-help organization NXIVM, convicted of numerous crimes, including sex trafficking, forced labor, and racketeering.

6. Sun Myung Moon (1950s-2010s): Founder of the Unification Church, faced criticism for alleged financial misconduct, exploitation of followers, and controversial beliefs.

7. Dwight York (Malachi Z. York) (1970s-2010s): Founder of the Nuwaubian Nation, convicted on numerous counts of child molestation, racketeering, and financial fraud.

8. Warren Jeffs (1990s-2010s): Former leader of the Fundamentalist Church of Jesus Christ of Latter-Day Saints (FLDS), convicted of numerous accounts of child sexual abuse and unlawful conduct with minors.

9. Shoko Asahara (1980s-1990s): Founder of the Aum Shinrikyo cult, masterminded the deadly sarin gas attack on the Tokyo subway in 1995 and was responsible for numerous other acts of violence and terrorism.

10. Bikram Choudhury (1970s-2010s): Founder of Bikram Yoga, accused of multiple cases of sexual harassment and assault by former students and employees.

11. Amma (Mata Amritanandamayi) (1980s-present): Indian spiritual leader, faced allegations of financial irregularities and the exploitation of devotees within her spiritual community.

This list underscores the critical importance of ethical leadership and accountability within spiritual and communal settings, emphasizing the significance of upholding the well-being and autonomy of individuals within these communities. I, the Author, am not making the assumption that all of the accusations made against all "Gurus" are valid. I used to like reading Rajneesh books in my 20s. This is why I liked Updike's ' S. ' (1988). I am not a follower, but I like to read. I imagined myself with a complete library of books, quite like now, and no involvement with half-trained, self-promoters telling me about metaphysics and wishful thinking. After decades of studying the histories of followers seeking 'gurus' and I put them into a few categories: a) people who want to belong b) people who want to rule over the people that want to belong c) people looking for sex, money, or both, and d) the incurably naive. That being said, I am willing to be proven wrong.

Let's take a look at each of the early Gurus to see from whence they came.

1. Ram Dass (Richard Alpert): Ram Dass initially trained as a psychologist and served as a professor at Harvard University. His transformative journey began after a life-altering trip to India, where he met his spiritual teacher, Neem Karoli Baba, which led him to embrace Eastern spiritual traditions and adopt the teachings of mindfulness and compassion that he later imparted to his followers.

2. Werner Erhard: Werner Erhard's background was not in traditional professional training or education. His emergence as a self-help figure was primarily linked to the development of the EST (Erhard Seminars Training) program, which he introduced in the 1970s, aiming to facilitate personal transformation and empowerment through intensive workshops focused on self-examination and behavioral change.

3. Louise Hay: Louise Hay's work in the self-help field was influenced by her own healing journey following a cancer diagnosis. While she did not possess formal professional qualifications, her experiences with metaphysical healing and positive affirmations inspired her to found Hay House, a publishing company that produced transformative literature focused on holistic well-being and the power of positive thinking.

4. Wayne Dyer: Wayne Dyer held a doctorate in educational counseling and worked as a professor at St. John's University in New York before transitioning to a career as a motivational speaker and self-help author. His transformational shift occurred after embracing the teachings of self-empowerment and spiritual enlightenment, which he integrated into his bestselling books and seminars.

5. Marianne Williamson: Marianne Williamson had a background in philosophy and spiritual studies, although she did not possess formal professional qualifications in psychology. Her immersion in 'A Course in Miracles', a spiritual text that emphasizes love and forgiveness, served as a catalyst for her exploration of spiritual principles, which she later disseminated through her books, lectures, and teachings focused on personal growth and spiritual awakening.

Each of these individuals underwent personal experiences or transformative encounters that inspired their exploration of spiritual and self-help principles. Their journeys, combined with their study of various spiritual and philosophical traditions, informed their roles as influential figures within the realm of personal development and holistic well-being.

The next logical questions would be:

What Were They Selling?

The gurus and self-help movements of the 1970s often marketed their teachings and practices as tools to help individuals achieve inner growth, which they believed would have both inner well-being and external benefits. The core idea was that by fostering personal transformation and self-actualization, individuals could improve their emotional, psychological, and spiritual well-being, leading to greater contentment, self-confidence, and resilience.

These improvements in inner well-being were often seen as not only valuable in themselves but also as means to achieve external benefits. These external benefits could include enhanced personal relationships, increased career success, improved physical health, and a deeper sense of purpose in life. Many gurus and self-help movements emphasized that inner well-being and personal growth could lead to a more fulfilling and successful life in various aspects, both personally and professionally.

The Tools Being Sold

Here is a breakdown of each guru and the tools they were known for selling to help individuals achieve inner growth and outer tranquility and happiness during the 1970s. The descriptions also highlight the differences between their approaches, how they differed from traditional spiritual practices, and how customers could evaluate the effectiveness of the tools being sold to them:

1. Bhagwan Shree Rajneesh (Osho) (1931-1990):

Tools: Active meditation techniques, dynamic meditation, and a blend of Eastern spiritual practices with elements of Western psychotherapy.

Differentiation: Emphasis on celebrating sexuality, challenging social norms, and advocating a more liberated, hedonistic lifestyle.

Distinction: Varied meditation techniques combined with an open attitude toward human desires, contrasting with more ascetic and disciplined spiritual traditions.

Evaluation: Customers could assess the impact through improved emotional well-being, a sense of freedom from societal constraints, and heightened self-awareness.

2. Ram Dass (1931-2019):

Tools: Mindfulness practices, spiritual lectures, and the promotion of conscious living and love as a transformative force.

Differentiation: Integration of Eastern spiritual traditions, especially Hindu philosophy and yoga, with a focus on compassion and service to others.

Distinction: Emphasis on the power of love and mindful awareness as transformative tools, contrasting with the rigorous ascetic practices often associated with traditional Eastern spirituality.

Evaluation: Customers could assess effectiveness through increased compassion, heightened spiritual awareness, and a sense of connectedness with others and the world.

3. Werner Erhard (1935-present):

Tools: Erhard Seminars Training (EST), a transformative program emphasizing personal accountability, confronting one's limitations, and achieving personal empowerment.

Differentiation: Utilization of intensive, confrontational workshops, focusing on individual responsibility and the power of personal transformation through direct confrontation of one's beliefs and limitations.

Distinction: Emphasis on active, direct engagement with one's personal barriers and limitations, diverging from the more contemplative and introspective practices of traditional spiritual approaches.

Evaluation: Customers could gauge effectiveness through improved self-awareness, a sense of personal empowerment, and enhanced interpersonal relationships.

4. Louise Hay (1926-2017):

Tools: Affirmations, positive thinking, and the power of self-love as catalysts for healing and personal transformation.

Differentiation: Emphasis on the transformative power of positive affirmations and self-love, integrating spiritual principles with the psychology of self-empowerment.

Distinction: Focus on the potential of affirmations and self-love to induce healing and personal growth, distinguishing from more ritualistic and doctrinal approaches found in traditional spiritual practices.

Evaluation: Customers could assess effectiveness through improved self-esteem, a more positive outlook on life, and tangible improvements in physical and emotional well-being.

5. Wayne Dyer (1940-2015):

Tools: The promotion of self-actualization, positive thinking, and the philosophy of self-reliance as means to achieve personal growth and spiritual fulfillment.

Differentiation: Integration of psychological and spiritual principles, advocating for self-reliance and personal agency as the driving forces behind personal growth and fulfillment.

Distinction: Emphasis on the individual's capacity for self-empowerment, diverging from the more externally directed practices often found in traditional spiritual approaches.

Evaluation: Customers could assess effectiveness through increased self-confidence, a stronger sense of personal agency, and the realization of personal goals and aspirations.

6. Marianne Williamson (1952-present):

Tools: Emphasis on the power of love, forgiveness, and spiritual principles as a means to achieve personal growth and societal transformation.

Differentiation: Integration of A Course in Miracles, Christian theology, and New Age spirituality, advocating for a shift in consciousness to promote love and healing.

Distinction: Focus on the intersection of personal and societal transformation through spiritual principles, distinguishing from more secular approaches to personal growth and fulfillment.

Evaluation: Customers could assess effectiveness through heightened compassion, a deeper sense of purpose, and a commitment to social and political activism aligned with spiritual values.

Each of these gurus offered unique tools and approaches to personal growth and spiritual fulfillment, catering to a diverse range of individuals seeking alternative paths to self-improvement during the 1970s. Their methodologies often deviated from more traditional spiritual practices by incorporating psychological insights, emphasizing personal empowerment, and encouraging self-awareness and individual agency as primary catalysts for transformation. Customers were able to evaluate the effectiveness of the tools based on tangible improvements in emotional well-being, heightened self-awareness, and a deeper sense of personal fulfillment and happiness.

In Regards to Money

The question of the morality of the 1970s self-help gurus making money off their followers without objective proof of the effectiveness of their tools is a complex ethical issue. Several considerations are involved in examining this matter:

1. Informed Consent: Followers should have access to accurate information about the tools and practices being offered to make an informed decision. Transparent communication about the possible benefits and limitations of these tools is crucial.

2. Ethical Responsibility: Gurus and self-help leaders have a responsibility to act ethically and prioritize the well-being of their followers. It's essential to provide guidance that is not harmful and to be honest about the potential results of their teachings.

3. Empowerment vs. Exploitation: Charging for services is not inherently unethical, especially if the teachings and tools genuinely empower individuals and contribute to their personal growth. However, when financial gain takes precedence over the well-being of followers, exploitation becomes a concern.

4. Evidence-Based Practices: While self-help teachings may not always have quantifiable scientific evidence, they should ideally be based on ethical principles and reputable psychological or spiritual methodologies, ensuring that they do not harm individuals or manipulate them for profit.

5. Legal and Regulatory Frameworks: Operating within legal and regulatory frameworks is crucial to ensure that followers are not exploited or misled. Compliance with consumer protection laws and ethical guidelines is essential for maintaining the trust and well-being of followers.

Considering these factors, the morality of making money off followers without objective proof of the effectiveness of tools should prompt self-help gurus to prioritize the well-being of their followers, offer transparent information about their teachings, and operate within ethical and legal boundaries. It is important to ensure that financial interests do not overshadow the ethical responsibility to provide genuine support and guidance for individuals seeking personal growth and transformation.

Tools in Context

So we understand where we have been and where the 'gurus' were in the 70s, here is a breakdown of the tools offered by each of the mentioned entities, along with a brief comparison of how they defined 'inner growth' in contrast to the way the 'gurus' defined it:

1. Benjamin Franklin:

Tools: Emphasis on self-discipline, industriousness, and the cultivation of virtues through his "13 Virtues" framework, as outlined in his autobiography and writings.

Inner Growth: Defined as the acquisition of virtues and practical skills to improve one's character and social standing, leading to personal success and fulfillment within society.

2. Aristotle:

Tools: Promotion of philosophical inquiry, the pursuit of virtue ethics, and the cultivation of practical wisdom as outlined in his Nicomachean Ethics and other works.

Inner Growth: Defined as the attainment of eudaimonia (human flourishing) through the cultivation of moral and intellectual virtues, fostering a well-balanced and virtuous life in accordance with reason.

3. Ralph Waldo Emerson:

Tools: Emphasis on individualism, self-reliance, and the transcendentalist philosophy of intuition and self-exploration, as expressed in his essays and lectures.

Inner Growth: Defined as the pursuit of self-discovery, spiritual exploration, and the harmonious alignment with nature and the transcendental spirit, promoting the development of individual consciousness and creative expression.

4. Abraham Maslow:

Tools: Development of the hierarchy of needs theory, emphasizing the importance of fulfilling basic human needs and self-actualization as a path to personal growth and fulfillment.

Inner Growth: Defined as the realization of one's full potential and the attainment of self-actualization, promoting psychological well-being, creativity, and a sense of purpose and fulfillment in life.

5. Orthodox Catholic Church:

Tools: Sacraments, prayer, moral teachings, and spiritual guidance under the authority of Church tradition and Scripture, emphasizing faith, repentance, and adherence to religious doctrines.

Inner Growth: Defined as the spiritual transformation and sanctification through participation in the life of the Church, promoting salvation and eternal communion with God through faith and obedience to divine commandments.

6. The Mormons:

Tools: Emphasis on faith in Jesus Christ, adherence to the Book of Mormon, moral teachings, and participation in Church activities, fostering community, and spiritual growth within the Latter-day Saints tradition.

Inner Growth: Defined as the development of spiritual character, adherence to moral principles, and the pursuit of eternal salvation and exaltation within the context of Mormon theology and community life.

7. Hindu Faith:

Tools: Practice of yoga, meditation, adherence to Dharma (righteousness), and the pursuit of spiritual enlightenment through devotion, knowledge, and self-realization as outlined in various Hindu scriptures and traditions.

Inner Growth: Defined as the realization of the Atman (true self) and the attainment of Moksha (liberation) through the practice of spiritual disciplines, promoting unity with the divine and transcendence of the material world.

8. Jewish Faith:

Tools: Study of the Torah, observance of mitzvot (commandments), adherence to Jewish law and tradition, and participation in communal rituals, fostering a connection to God and the Jewish community.

Inner Growth: Defined as the cultivation of ethical behavior, spiritual devotion, and a sense of communal belonging within the context of Jewish religious life, promoting a covenantal relationship with God and adherence to divine commandments.

The 'gurus' often defined 'inner growth' with an emphasis on individual empowerment, self-fulfillment, and spiritual awakening through alternative philosophical and psychological frameworks, incorporating elements of Eastern spirituality, humanistic psychology, and New Age philosophies.

They often highlighted personal agency, self-awareness, and the pursuit of personal fulfillment as the central tenets of inner growth, diverging from the more traditional religious frameworks that often emphasized faith, obedience, and adherence to doctrinal teachings as the means to achieve spiritual and moral development.

Other Gurus to Be Aware Of & the 'Tools' They Sell

Certainly, here is the revised list, including the tools for well-being and growth offered by each of the five contemporary self-help gurus:

1. Tony Robbins:

Tools: Utilizes techniques such as neuro-linguistic programming (NLP), goal setting, and personal coaching to foster motivation, empowerment, and professional success, guiding individuals to overcome limitations and achieve personal transformation.

Of interest:
While I personally do not like the persona of Mr. Robbins, and find his writing to be simplistic and repetitive and lacking in proper attribution o NLP authors and thinkers, the types of limitations that individuals might face, regardless of their financial situation that Robbins addresses does provide some benefit to clarifying typical adult intra- and inter-personal problems. These may include:

1. Limiting Beliefs: Negative thought patterns and self-doubt that hinder personal and professional growth.

2. Emotional Barriers: Psychological hurdles such as fear, anxiety, and low self-esteem that impede individuals from reaching their full potential.

3. Lack of Direction: Absence of clear goals or a sense of purpose that may leave individuals feeling unfulfilled or stagnant in their personal or professional lives.

4. Self-Sabotage: Destructive habits or behaviors that prevent individuals from achieving their desired outcomes and maintaining long-term success.

5. Procrastination: Tendency to delay taking action or making decisions, leading to missed opportunities and unfulfilled aspirations.

Through his programs, Robbins aims to equip individuals with the psychological tools and strategies needed to break through these barriers, cultivate a mindset of success, and achieve personal transformation, regardless of the specific limitations they may be facing. And, he does this without a grand philosophy or bizarre underlying metaphysical discussion, much to his credit. Still cannot get those sales conferences and Porsche posters out of my mind, though.

2. Brené Brown:

Tools: Emphasizes the power of vulnerability, courage, and empathy as pathways to emotional resilience and authentic connection, encouraging practices such as self-compassion, shame resilience, and wholehearted living to cultivate genuine relationships and inner strength.

3. Eckhart Tolle:

Tools: Focuses on mindfulness, present moment awareness, and spiritual enlightenment through practices such as meditation, conscious breathing, and cultivating inner stillness, guiding individuals toward inner peace, spiritual awakening, and a deeper connection with the present moment.

4. Deepak Chopra:

Tools: Advocates a holistic approach to well-being, incorporating practices such as meditation, yoga, and Ayurveda, along with principles of mind-body medicine, spiritual healing, and conscious living, to promote physical health, emotional balance, and spiritual harmony.

Again, not a fan. And, there is due cause for this opinion. Deepak Chopra, a prominent figure in the fields of holistic health and spirituality, has faced various criticisms over the years, ranging from concerns about his medical claims to skepticism about the scientific basis of his teachings. Some of the key criticisms directed at Deepak Chopra include:

1. Pseudoscientific Claims: Chopra has been criticized for promoting pseudoscientific ideas and making unsubstantiated claims about the mind-body connection, alternative medicine, and spirituality. Critics argue that some of his assertions lack empirical evidence and scientific validity, leading to concerns about the credibility of his work within the scientific community.

2. Overgeneralization and Simplification: Critics have suggested that Chopra often oversimplifies complex scientific concepts and ancient wisdom, presenting them in a way that may distort their original meanings or oversimplify their applications. This has raised concerns about the accuracy and depth of his interpretations, particularly in relation to Ayurveda and other traditional healing practices.

3. Commercialization of Spiritual Ideas: Some critics have raised concerns about Chopra's commercialization of spiritual ideas and teachings, suggesting that his focus on marketing and profit-making ventures may undermine the integrity and authenticity of his spiritual message. Critics argue that this approach could lead to the commodification of spirituality, potentially diluting its transformative potential.

4. Lack of Transparency and Accountability: Chopra has faced criticism for his vague and ambiguous language, which some argue allows him to evade direct scrutiny or accountability for his claims. Critics have suggested that this lack of transparency may contribute to the perpetuation of misconceptions and the spread of potentially misleading information within the fields of holistic health and spirituality.

While acknowledging the positive impact of Chopra's work on the popularization of holistic health and spiritual practices, critics emphasize the importance of maintaining scientific rigor, transparency, and ethical standards in the promotion of holistic wellness and spiritual teachings. They encourage a critical examination of his claims and teachings, urging individuals to approach his work with a discerning and informed perspective.

5. Gabrielle Bernstein:

Tools: Offers guidance on spiritual principles, meditation, and the power of self-love, encouraging practices such as forgiveness, gratitude, and positive affirmations to cultivate inner peace, self-acceptance, and a deeper connection with one's purpose and joy in life.

Reasons to be Skeptical

The credibility and social currency of terms such as "guru," "coach," and "mentor" can indeed be affected by various factors, including instances of fraud, lack of formal training, questionable accreditation, and unethical sales practices. These issues can contribute to a general skepticism towards individuals who claim these titles, particularly in cases where there is a perceived lack of authenticity or expertise.

a) Instances of fraud within the realms of coaching, mentoring, or spiritual guidance can certainly undermine trust in individuals who claim these roles. Such incidents can lead to a general wariness among the public and a tendency to view these professions with skepticism.

b) The absence of formal training or recognized credentials among many who identify as gurus, coaches, or mentors can contribute to a perception of a lack of professionalism and expertise. This can raise doubts about the legitimacy of their services and advice.

c) Questionable accreditation processes in the coaching industry can indeed diminish the value and credibility of coaching certifications. When accreditation appears to lack rigorous standards or is easily obtainable, it can undermine the perceived credibility of the profession as a whole.

d) Unethical sales practices that resemble historical examples of deceptive salesmanship can create a negative perception of modern gurus, coaches, and mentors. When individuals appear to prioritize selling over genuinely helping others, it can erode trust and confidence in their intentions and expertise.

To address these challenges and rebuild trust, it is essential for professionals in these fields to adhere to ethical standards, uphold transparency, and seek formal education or training when available. Additionally, creating and following industry-wide standards for accreditation and ethical conduct can help establish credibility and ensure that those seeking guidance or mentorship receive reliable and authentic support.

Throughout history, there have been several instances where individuals posing as spiritualists, psychics, channelers, life coaches, or psychologists have been implicated in fraudulent activities, deceiving people and causing harm to their well-being. Some notable historical examples include:

1. Spiritualists and Psychics: During the 19th and 20th centuries, spiritualism gained popularity, leading to the emergence of various mediums and psychics who claimed to communicate with the spirit world. Some of these practitioners were exposed as frauds, using tricks and illusions to exploit vulnerable individuals emotionally and financially. Famous examples include the case of the Fox sisters in the 19th century and the exposures of fraudulent mediums by organizations like the Society for Psychical Research.

2. Channelers: Throughout the 20th and 21st centuries, there have been instances where individuals claiming to channel otherworldly entities or spirits have taken advantage of believers, often for financial gain. These cases sometimes involved convincing followers to relinquish their possessions or make significant financial contributions to the purported spiritual cause.

3. Life Coaches: While the field of life coaching aims to provide guidance and support for personal development, there have been reported cases of unscrupulous individuals posing as life coaches and taking advantage of vulnerable clients. This has included cases where supposed life coaches promised quick fixes or miraculous transformations in exchange for exorbitant fees, exploiting the clients' trust and emotional vulnerability.

4. Psychologists: Though the field of psychology is rooted in empirical research and ethical practice, there have been historical instances of psychologists abusing their positions of trust and authority. Cases have included instances of psychologists exploiting their patients, engaging in unethical research practices, or promoting harmful therapies.

These cases highlight the importance of critical thinking and vigilance when seeking guidance or assistance from individuals claiming to possess spiritual or psychological expertise. It underscores the necessity of verifying credentials, seeking reputable professionals, and being cautious of claims that appear too good to be true. Additionally, regulatory measures and ethical guidelines within these fields help to safeguard the public from potential exploitation and fraud.

Specific Examples

Here are specific examples that illustrate instances of fraud or unethical behavior within each of the mentioned fields:

1. Spiritualists and Psychics:

The Fox Sisters: The Fox sisters, Margaretta and Catherine, gained notoriety in the mid-19th century for their supposed ability to communicate with the spirit world through mysterious rapping sounds. However, in 1888, Margaretta confessed that the noises were produced by cracking their toe joints, revealing that their spiritualist performances were fraudulent. Having read deeply on the subject, I remain divided on this one.

Eusapia Palladino: Eusapia Palladino, an Italian medium, was investigated by the Society for Psychical Research in the late 19th century. Numerous reports suggested that she used trickery and manipulation during her seances, employing techniques such as sleight of hand and other forms of deception to create the illusion of paranormal phenomena.

2. Channelers:

The case of JZ Knight: JZ Knight, a self-proclaimed channeler, gained a following by claiming to channel a 35,000-year-old entity named Ramtha. There have been allegations of financial exploitation and manipulation of followers through exorbitant fees for events and training programs. Investigations into her practices have raised questions about the authenticity of her claims.

3. Life Coaches:

James Arthur Ray: James Arthur Ray, a self-help and motivational speaker, gained notoriety for his appearances in the movie "The Secret." In 2009, during one of his events, several participants died and others fell seriously ill in a sweat lodge ceremony that Ray organized. He was subsequently convicted of three counts of negligent homicide and sentenced to prison.

4. Psychologists:

The Stanford prison experiment: While not a case of fraud, the Stanford prison experiment, conducted by psychologist Philip Zimbardo in 1971, demonstrated the potential for unethical behavior in the field. The study, which simulated a prison environment, led to severe psychological distress among the participants, prompting questions about the ethical boundaries of psychological research.

These examples emphasize the importance of maintaining ethical standards, practicing critical evaluation, and verifying the credibility of individuals claiming expertise in spiritual or psychological domains. They also highlight the need for stringent ethical guidelines and regulatory measures within these fields to protect individuals from potential harm or exploitation.

Chögyam Trungpa: Spiritual Materialism and the Guru

Chögyam Trungpa (1939-1987) was a Tibetan Buddhist meditation master, scholar, and teacher who played a pivotal role in introducing Tibetan Buddhism to the Western world. He founded the Shambhala Training and Naropa University, making significant contributions to the dissemination of Buddhist teachings and practices in a Western context. Despite facing various challenges, including his escape from Tibet during the Chinese invasion, Trungpa became renowned for his ability to communicate complex Buddhist concepts in a manner accessible to Western audiences.

Overview of the Book:
Published in 1973, 'Spiritual Materialism' remains one of
Chögyam Trungpa's most influential works. The book presents a
critical analysis of the pitfalls and dangers inherent in spiritual
pursuits, particularly the tendency of individuals to approach
spirituality from a materialistic or ego-driven perspective.
Trungpa examines how individuals may use spirituality as a
means to bolster their ego, attain social status, or accumulate
material gain. By highlighting the risks of spiritual materialism,
Trungpa urges readers to embrace a more genuine, selfless, and
introspective approach to spiritual practice.

Approach:
Trungpa employs a direct and insightful approach, drawing on
his deep understanding of Tibetan Buddhism and his experiences
with Western audiences to illuminate the subtle ways in which
individuals may fall into the trap of spiritual materialism. He
emphasizes the importance of self-awareness, humility, and
genuine compassion as essential components of authentic
spiritual growth, encouraging readers to cultivate a deeper
understanding of the true nature of the spiritual path.

Focus:
The book focuses on the pervasive tendency among spiritual
seekers to approach their spiritual journey with ego-driven
motivations, seeking external validation, status, or material
gain rather than genuine inner transformation and selflessness.
Trungpa underscores the need to recognize and transcend
the traps of ego-centered spiritual pursuits, highlighting the
significance of embracing humility and authenticity in the quest
for spiritual enlightenment.

Contribution:
'Spiritual Materialism' contributes a profound and insightful
perspective to the dialogue on spirituality, urging readers to
critically evaluate their intentions and motivations in their
spiritual practices. Trungpa's work serves as a cautionary guide,
providing valuable insights into the potential dangers of ego-
driven spiritual paths while emphasizing the importance of
cultivating genuine compassion, self-awareness, and authenticity
on the spiritual journey.

Legacy:
Chögyam Trungpa's legacy extends beyond his influential writings and teachings, encompassing his efforts to bridge the gap between Eastern and Western spiritual traditions. His emphasis on mindfulness, compassion, and the cultivation of awareness continues to resonate with audiences seeking a deeper understanding of authentic spiritual practice and personal growth. Trungpa's teachings have left an enduring impact on contemporary spiritual discourse, encouraging individuals to approach their spiritual journey with humility and a genuine commitment to inner transformation.

Chögyam Trungpa's concept of "spiritual materialism" underscores the idea that individuals can approach spirituality from an ego-driven perspective, seeking to enhance their self-image, status, or material gain through their spiritual pursuits. When applying this concept to the gurus and success coaches discussed earlier in this thread, it is crucial to assess whether their teachings and practices prioritize genuine spiritual growth and selflessness or if they might inadvertently promote spiritual materialism.

In the case of some self-proclaimed gurus and success coaches, there may be instances where their emphasis on personal branding, financial success, or external validation could potentially align with the principles of spiritual materialism. For example, if these figures excessively promote material wealth as a sign of spiritual accomplishment or use their teachings primarily as a means to elevate their own status or financial gain, it could be indicative of a spiritual materialistic approach.

Moreover, if their teachings tend to emphasize external validation or a sense of superiority rather than fostering genuine humility, compassion, and inner transformation, it might suggest a tendency towards spiritual materialism.

Chögyam Trungpa's insights would encourage individuals to critically examine the intentions and motivations behind the teachings of these gurus and success coaches, urging followers to question whether the emphasis is on ego inflation or genuine spiritual development. Trungpa's perspective would emphasize the importance of cultivating an authentic, selfless approach to spiritual growth, focusing on inner transformation and compassion rather than external markers of success or status.

Ultimately, the application of Trungpa's concept of spiritual materialism serves as a reminder to maintain a discerning approach when engaging with spiritual teachings and self-help guidance, encouraging individuals to prioritize sincerity, humility, and inner growth over external validation or materialistic pursuits.

As It Applies Here

Chögyam Trungpa's concept of "spiritual materialism" underscores the idea that individuals can approach spirituality from an ego-driven perspective, seeking to enhance their self-image, status, or material gain through their spiritual pursuits. When applying this concept to the gurus and success coaches discussed earlier in this thread, it is crucial to assess whether their teachings and practices prioritize genuine spiritual growth and selflessness or if they might inadvertently promote spiritual materialism.

In the case of some self-proclaimed gurus and success coaches, there may be instances where their emphasis on personal branding, financial success, or external validation could potentially align with the principles of spiritual materialism. For example, if these figures excessively promote material wealth as a sign of spiritual accomplishment or use their teachings primarily as a means to elevate their own status or financial gain, it could be indicative of a spiritual materialistic approach.

Moreover, if their teachings tend to emphasize external validation or a sense of superiority rather than fostering genuine humility, compassion, and inner transformation, it might suggest a tendency towards spiritual materialism.

Chögyam Trungpa's insights would encourage individuals to critically examine the intentions and motivations behind the teachings of these gurus and success coaches, urging followers to question whether the emphasis is on ego inflation or genuine spiritual development. Trungpa's perspective would emphasize the importance of cultivating an authentic, selfless approach to spiritual growth, focusing on inner transformation and compassion rather than external markers of success or status.

Ultimately, the application of Trungpa's concept of spiritual materialism serves as a reminder to maintain a discerning approach when engaging with spiritual teachings and self-help guidance, encouraging individuals to prioritize sincerity, humility, and inner growth over external validation or materialistic pursuits.

Charlatans in the U.S.

The United States has a rich history of cultural diversity and innovation, fostering a climate that encourages experimentation and the pursuit of new ideas. While this environment has led to remarkable progress and creativity, it has also created opportunities for unscrupulous individuals to exploit the public's openness to new concepts and practices.

Throughout U.S. history, charlatans have played a significant role in various spheres, perpetuating deception and fraudulent practices that have targeted unsuspecting individuals. From the era of snake oil salesmen to the emergence of questionable 'change' certification programs, the country has grappled with the consequences of such deceptive practices.

1. Snake Oil Salesmen: During the 19th century, snake oil salesmen traveled across the U.S., peddling dubious products that were claimed to cure a wide range of ailments. Often, these products were ineffective or even harmful, leading to the passing of the Pure Food and Drug Act in 1906, which aimed to regulate the labeling and ingredients of consumer products.

2. Patent Medicine and Quackery: In the early 20th century, the proliferation of patent medicines and unproven health remedies led to widespread exploitation of the public's trust.

Charlatans promoted ineffective or fraudulent products under the guise of medical breakthroughs, contributing to public health crises and prompting the need for stricter regulations within the pharmaceutical industry.

3. Self-Help Gurus and 'Change' Certification: In contemporary times, the rise of self-help gurus and life coaches, coupled with the emergence of 'change' certification programs, has raised concerns about the legitimacy of certain practices within the personal development industry. Some individuals have capitalized on the public's desire for personal transformation, offering certifications and programs that lack credible accreditation or standardized ethical guidelines, leading to questions about their efficacy and credibility.

Despite these challenges, the U.S. has implemented regulatory measures and consumer protection laws to curb fraudulent practices and protect individuals from deceptive claims. These efforts underscore the importance of critical thinking, consumer awareness, and the implementation of ethical standards within various industries to safeguard the well-being of the public.

And, lest we think organized and traditional religion is immune in America, the history of fraudulent revival tents or religious groups in the United States has been marked by various instances of deceptive practices, false prophecies, and the exploitation of religious fervor for personal gain. While many legitimate and authentic religious movements have also thrived in the U.S., there have been cases where certain individuals or groups have used revival tents and religious gatherings as a means to deceive and defraud their followers. Some notable instances include:

1. The Great Revival: During the 19th century, the Great Revival, also known as the Second Great Awakening, witnessed the rise of numerous itinerant preachers and evangelists who held revival meetings in tents, barns, and open fields. While many of these preachers were sincere in their religious convictions, some took advantage of the religious enthusiasm of the time, using emotional manipulation and sensationalism to attract followers and financial contributions.

2. Aimee Semple McPherson: Aimee Semple McPherson, a prominent evangelist in the early 20th century, gained notoriety for her theatrical and sensational revival meetings, attracting large crowds with her dramatic sermons and faith-healing demonstrations. While she had a genuine following, McPherson was also embroiled in controversies and scandals that raised questions about the authenticity of her religious practices and the legitimacy of her financial dealings.

3. Contemporary Prosperity Gospel Preachers: In more recent times, some prosperity gospel preachers have been criticized for promoting a message that emphasizes material wealth and financial prosperity as signs of divine favor. Critics argue that certain prosperity gospel preachers exploit the religious devotion of their followers, encouraging them to make financial contributions in exchange for promises of supernatural blessings and prosperity.

While these instances underscore the potential risks associated with fraudulent practices within religious movements, it is essential to recognize that they represent a minority within the broader landscape of legitimate and sincere religious communities in the United States. Regulatory measures, ethical guidelines, and critical awareness within the religious community play a crucial role in safeguarding individuals from deceptive practices and promoting the genuine pursuit of spiritual growth and well-being.

Dark Psychology

"Dark psychology" refers to the study and application of psychological principles and techniques that are used for manipulative and deceptive purposes. While the term itself is not a recognized academic concept, it is often associated with the study of behavior, cognition, and emotion, as applied in a manner that exploits and harms others. Some methods that are often associated with dark psychology include:

1. Manipulation: Dark psychology often involves the use of manipulative tactics to control and influence the thoughts, emotions, and behaviors of others. This can include emotional manipulation, gaslighting, and other forms of psychological manipulation to gain power or advantage over others.

2. Deception: Deceptive practices, such as lying, withholding information, or using deceitful tactics to mislead others, are common in dark psychology. Individuals employing these tactics may use various forms of deception to exploit others for personal gain or to achieve specific objectives.

3. Coercion and Intimidation: Dark psychology can involve the use of coercion, threats, or intimidation to instill fear and compel others to comply with the manipulator's demands. This can include psychological intimidation, blackmail, or other forms of psychological pressure to control or dominate individuals or groups.

4. Exploitation of Vulnerabilities: Individuals who utilize dark psychology may exploit the vulnerabilities and weaknesses of others, taking advantage of their emotional, financial, or psychological vulnerabilities for their own benefit. This can involve preying on individuals' insecurities, fears, or psychological dependencies to gain control and manipulate their actions or decisions.

5. Emotional Abuse: Dark psychology often involves the use of emotionally abusive tactics, such as undermining self-worth, creating dependency, or fostering feelings of helplessness or inadequacy in others. Emotional abuse can be used as a means to gain control and power over individuals, leading to long-term psychological harm and trauma.

It is important to note that the study of dark psychology is distinct from the ethical and professional application of psychology, which aims to promote mental health, well-being, and ethical behavior. Ethical considerations and guidelines within the field of psychology prioritize the well-being and autonomy of individuals, emphasizing the importance of informed consent, confidentiality, and respect for the dignity of all individuals.

The creation of a taxonomy of manipulative techniques and strategies can be attributed to various scholars, psychologists, and researchers who have explored the intricacies of human behavior, social influence, and interpersonal dynamics. While the development of such taxonomies is an ongoing process within the field of psychology and social sciences, several notable figures have contributed to the categorization and understanding of manipulative behaviors and tactics.

Some influential researchers in this area include:

1. Robert Cialdini: Cialdini, a renowned psychologist, is known for his work on the principles of influence and persuasion. His book "Influence: The Psychology of Persuasion" outlined six key principles of influence that are commonly employed in manipulative communication and marketing strategies.

2. George Simon: Simon, a clinical psychologist, has written extensively about manipulative behavior and character disorders, providing insights into the strategies and tactics employed by individuals with manipulative and exploitative personalities.

3. Jo-Ellan Dimitrius and Mark Mazzarella: Dimitrius and Mazzarella have contributed to the understanding of manipulative behavior through their work on nonverbal communication and behavioral analysis, exploring the ways in which individuals use body language and communication styles to manipulate others.

These and other researchers have made significant contributions to the study of manipulative behaviors and communication strategies, offering valuable insights into the psychological mechanisms and social dynamics involved in interpersonal manipulation and influence. Their work has helped to establish a framework for understanding the complexities of manipulative behavior and its impact on personal relationships and societal interactions.

Manipulative Communication Techniques to Be Aware Of

Cold reading and negging are both techniques commonly associated with manipulative or deceptive communication strategies. They are often used in social situations, particularly in the context of personal interactions, dating, or sales, to influence or control the behavior and emotions of others. Here is an overview of each:

1. Cold Reading:
Cold reading is a technique used by individuals, such as psychics, illusionists, or con artists, to give the impression that they possess special insights or abilities to discern personal information about someone without prior knowledge. This can involve making general or ambiguous statements that seem specific and tailored to an individual, leading them to believe that the reader has unique knowledge about their life or circumstances. Cold reading can create an illusion of psychic or intuitive abilities, manipulating individuals into believing in the validity of the reader's claims.

2. Negging:
Negging is a manipulative tactic used in the context of dating or social interactions, whereby an individual gives backhanded compliments or makes subtly disparaging remarks to undermine someone's self-confidence or self-esteem. The intention behind negging is to create a power dynamic where the person using this tactic appears superior or more desirable, thereby eliciting a response from the targeted individual. Negging can lead the recipient to seek validation or approval from the person employing the tactic, fostering a sense of dependence or insecurity in the relationship.

Both cold reading and negging exploit psychological vulnerabilities and insecurities, aiming to manipulate the emotions and behaviors of others for personal gain or control. Recognizing these tactics can help individuals protect themselves from manipulation and develop healthier, more authentic relationships based on mutual respect and genuine communication.

In fact, there are a number of other manipulative communication techniques can be employed to influence or control others, often without their awareness. It is essential to be aware of these tactics to recognize and mitigate their effects. Some additional manipulative communication techniques include:

1. Gaslighting: Gaslighting is a form of psychological manipulation that aims to make individuals doubt their own perceptions, memories, and sanity. This can involve denying the reality of a situation, shifting blame, or using tactics to make someone question their own experiences or emotions.

2. Guilt-Tripping: Guilt-tripping involves using emotional manipulation to make someone feel guilty or responsible for a particular situation, even when they may not be at fault. This tactic can involve leveraging a person's sense of obligation or empathy to control their behavior or decisions.

3. Love Bombing: Love bombing is a manipulation tactic where an individual showers someone with excessive affection, attention, and flattery to create a sense of emotional dependence. This can lead the recipient to feel overwhelmed and obligated to reciprocate, fostering a dynamic of control and dependency. I particularly worry about this technique when reading or watching Leo Buscaglia (1924-1998), as it ages into the creepy zone the further we are away from those Sunday afternoon PBS Specials.

4. Bait and Switch: The bait and switch technique involves initially offering something desirable or appealing to someone, only to later change the terms or conditions of the offer. This can lead the individual to feel misled or deceived, creating a sense of obligation to accept the revised terms or conditions.

5. Fear-Mongering: Fear-mongering involves using fear or intimidation to influence someone's beliefs or behavior. This tactic can be employed to manipulate perceptions, incite panic, or coerce compliance through the exploitation of anxieties or insecurities.

By being aware of these manipulative communication techniques, individuals can develop a better understanding of interpersonal dynamics and cultivate healthier and more authentic relationships based on trust, respect, and effective communication. Additionally, recognizing these tactics can help individuals protect themselves from potential manipulation and maintain their autonomy and well-being.

Gurus to the Stars

The 1970s witnessed a remarkable cultural shift marked by a heightened interest in Eastern spirituality and the proliferation of self-help movements in the Western world. This era saw the convergence of renowned spiritual leaders and gurus with influential figures from the realms of music, film, and business, leading to a unique intersection of Eastern philosophies and Western popular culture. From the Beatles' exploration of Transcendental Meditation to the influence of prominent spiritual teachers on iconic musicians and celebrities, the decade bore witness to a widespread fascination with spiritual enlightenment and personal transformation.

Ram Dass and Neem Karoli Baba
Ram Dass (formerly Richard Alpert) was influenced by the Indian spiritual teacher Neem Karoli Baba (also known as Maharaj-ji). Neem Karoli Baba was known for his teachings on love, service, and devotion, and he had a significant impact on Ram Dass's spiritual journey.

Neem Karoli Baba, also known as Maharaj-ji, was a revered Hindu spiritual leader and guru known for his teachings on love, devotion, and service. He gained a significant following in India and the West, and his teachings continue to inspire spiritual seekers worldwide. Here's an overview of his life, contributions, legacy, and criticisms:

> Biography: Neem Karoli Baba was born as Lakshmi Narayan Sharma in 1900 in Uttar Pradesh, India. He was known for his unconventional and unorthodox

approach to spirituality, often using simple and direct teachings to convey profound spiritual truths. He attracted followers from various backgrounds, including Western spiritual seekers who were drawn to his teachings on love and devotion.

Contributions: Neem Karoli Baba emphasized the path of love and selfless service as a means to spiritual realization. He encouraged his followers to cultivate unconditional love, compassion, and devotion, regardless of religious or cultural backgrounds. Neem Karoli Baba's teachings inspired the establishment of numerous ashrams and spiritual centers dedicated to his philosophy of universal love and service.

Pros and Legacy: Neem Karoli Baba's legacy continues to have a profound impact on the spiritual community, emphasizing the importance of love, compassion, and selfless service as central tenets of spiritual practice. His teachings have inspired countless individuals to embrace a path of devotion and service, fostering a sense of unity and interconnectedness among people from diverse backgrounds.

Criticism: While Neem Karoli Baba's teachings have garnered widespread admiration, some critics have raised concerns about the deification of spiritual leaders and the potential for misinterpretation or exploitation of their teachings. There have also been debates about the authenticity of certain miracles attributed to Neem Karoli Baba, prompting skepticism among some critics and scholars.

The Tools:Neem Karoli Baba, also known as Maharaj-ji, emphasized various tools for self-help and spiritual growth that were rooted in love, devotion, and service. Some of the key principles and practices he imparted to his followers included:

1. Love and Compassion: Neem Karoli Baba emphasized the transformative power of love and compassion as essential components of spiritual growth and personal development. He encouraged his followers to cultivate unconditional love and empathy for all beings, fostering a sense of interconnectedness and unity.

2. Selfless Service (Seva): Neem Karoli Baba advocated for the practice of selfless service (seva) as a means to cultivate humility, compassion, and spiritual awareness. He emphasized the importance of serving others with a selfless and compassionate heart, viewing service as a path to spiritual fulfillment and inner peace.

3. Devotional Practices: Neem Karoli Baba promoted devotional practices, including chanting, prayer, and meditation, as a way to deepen one's spiritual connection and cultivate a sense of inner harmony and peace. He encouraged his followers to engage in devotional activities with sincerity and devotion, fostering a deeper understanding of the divine and the nature of existence.

4. Mindfulness and Surrender: Neem Karoli Baba taught the importance of mindfulness and surrender, encouraging individuals to cultivate present-moment awareness and let go of attachments and ego-driven desires. He emphasized the value of surrendering to the divine will and accepting life's circumstances with grace and equanimity.

Through these teachings and practices, Neem Karoli Baba aimed to guide his followers toward a path of spiritual awakening, emphasizing the transformative potential of love, service, and devotion in fostering personal growth, inner peace, and spiritual realization.

Overall, Neem Karoli Baba is celebrated for his emphasis on love, devotion, and selfless service, leaving behind a lasting legacy that continues to resonate with spiritual seekers seeking a deeper understanding of universal love and the interconnectedness of all beings.

In regards to Neem Karoli Baba's teachings on love and compassion, they share some common threads with the beliefs and teachings of the Orthodox Church and the teachings of Christ, particularly regarding the importance of selflessness, humility, and devotion. While there may be differences in specific theological or doctrinal interpretations, the fundamental principles of love, compassion, and spiritual devotion are foundational aspects of both Neem Karoli Baba's teachings and the teachings of the Orthodox Church and Christ.

The emphasis on constant prayer in the Orthodox Church reflects the significance of maintaining a continual connection with the divine and cultivating a sense of spiritual awareness and communion with God. Similarly, Neem Karoli Baba's teachings on devotion and mindfulness emphasize the cultivation of a deep spiritual connection through devotional practices and the practice of mindfulness, fostering a sense of inner peace and spiritual awareness.

Christ's teaching that one should be as a child to enter into heaven underscores the importance of humility, innocence, and purity of heart in one's spiritual journey. Neem Karoli Baba's teachings on surrender and selflessness also emphasize the significance of humility and surrender to the divine will, fostering a sense of childlike trust and dependence on the divine grace and guidance.

While there may be nuanced differences in the specific practices and interpretations of love, devotion, and spiritual growth within these traditions, the overarching emphasis on the transformative power of love, compassion, humility, and devotion remains a central theme that resonates across various spiritual teachings, including those of Neem Karoli Baba and the Orthodox Church.

§

Pete Townshend & Meher Baba
Pete Townshend, a member of the rock band The Who, was associated with Meher Baba, an Indian spiritual master who proclaimed himself to be the Avatar, a divine incarnation. Townshend's interest in Meher Baba significantly influenced his spiritual beliefs and creative expressions.

Meher Baba, born Merwan Sheriar Irani, was an influential spiritual master and mystic of the 20th century, known for his teachings on spirituality, divine love, and the concept of the Avatar. His life and work left a profound impact on the spiritual landscape, both in India and internationally. Here is an overview of his biography, contributions, legacy, and criticisms:

Biography: Meher Baba was born on February 25, 1894, in Pune, India. From an early age, he displayed a deep spiritual inclination and later began attracting followers who were drawn to his teachings and spiritual presence. Meher Baba emphasized the importance of selfless service, spiritual transformation, and the realization of the true Self, emphasizing the concept of love and devotion as a means to attain spiritual awakening.

Contributions: Meher Baba's teachings revolved around the idea of the Avatar, a divine incarnation that descends to earth to guide humanity towards spiritual evolution. He emphasized the significance of spiritual awakening, inner transformation, and the cultivation of love and compassion as essential components of the spiritual journey. Meher Baba's teachings continue to inspire followers worldwide, particularly through the Meher Baba community and various spiritual centers dedicated to his work.

Legacy: Meher Baba's legacy remains influential in the realm of spiritual philosophy, advocating for the transformative power of divine love and the pursuit of self-realization. His teachings continue to resonate with individuals seeking a deeper understanding of spirituality and the inherent unity of all existence.

Criticism: While Meher Baba's teachings have garnered significant admiration, some critics have raised questions about the concept of the Avatar and the deification of spiritual figures. Additionally, debates have emerged concerning the interpretations of Meher Baba's teachings and the broader implications of his spiritual philosophy within the context of religious and philosophical discourse.

Overall, Meher Baba's spiritual legacy emphasizes the importance of love, service, and spiritual awakening, leaving behind a profound impact on the spiritual community and serving as a guiding light for individuals seeking spiritual transformation and enlightenment.

Meher Baba and Neem Karoli Baba, while both influential spiritual figures, emphasized distinct approaches to spiritual teachings and practices, reflecting the diversity of spiritual traditions within the broader context of Eastern philosophy. Here are some key differences in their teachings and approaches:

> 1. Concept of the Divine: Meher Baba introduced the concept of the Avatar and emphasized the cyclic manifestations of divinity, highlighting the significance of the Avatar as the ultimate manifestation of God on Earth. In contrast, Neem Karoli Baba emphasized unconditional love and devotion, focusing on the transformative power of love and selfless service in one's spiritual journey.

> Specifically, the concept of the Avatar, as understood in the teachings of Meher Baba, has parallels in various religious and spiritual traditions, each with its own interpretation and significance. While the term "Avatar" is commonly associated with Hinduism, its broader implications can be found in other religious and philosophical contexts. Here are some comparisons to related concepts in other spiritual traditions:

> 1. Hinduism: In Hinduism, an Avatar is understood as a divine incarnation or manifestation of a deity on Earth, serving a specific purpose or mission to restore cosmic balance and alleviate suffering. Avatars are believed to descend to Earth to guide humanity and uphold moral order, with prominent examples including Lord Vishnu's incarnations such as Rama and Krishna.

> 2. Living Saint: The concept of a living saint, present in various religious traditions, refers to an individual

recognized for their spiritual wisdom, enlightenment, and divine connection. Living saints are often regarded as embodiments of spiritual virtues and are revered for their teachings and exemplary lives, guiding followers on the path of spiritual growth and self-realization.

3. Bodhisattva: In Buddhism, a Bodhisattva is an enlightened being who compassionately postpones their own liberation to assist others in achieving enlightenment. Bodhisattvas are revered for their altruism, compassion, and commitment to the well-being and spiritual awakening of all beings, embodying the ideals of compassion and selfless service.

While the concept of the Avatar shares similarities with the notions of living saints and Bodhisattvas in terms of their roles as spiritual guides and embodiments of divine virtues, the Avatar is specifically associated with the divine incarnation of a deity, carrying a unique mission or purpose to guide humanity and uphold spiritual principles. Each of these concepts reflects the profound influence of spiritual figures in guiding individuals toward spiritual awakening, compassion, and the realization of the interconnected nature of existence.

2. Spiritual Practices: Meher Baba advocated for spiritual disciplines such as meditation, prayer, and selfless service, underscoring the importance of surrender to the divine will and the cultivation of spiritual awareness. Neem Karoli Baba also emphasized the practice of devotion and mindfulness, encouraging his followers to cultivate love, compassion, and humility as essential components of their spiritual practice.

3. Approach to Spiritual Growth: Meher Baba's teachings centered on the realization of the true Self and the significance of universal love and compassion as essential aspects of spiritual growth. Neem Karoli Baba focused on the transformative power of love and service, encouraging his followers to cultivate unconditional

> love and empathy for all beings as a means to achieve
> spiritual fulfillment.

While both spiritual leaders emphasized love, devotion, and selfless service, their teachings reflected unique interpretations of spiritual philosophy and the path to spiritual enlightenment. Their distinct approaches provided their followers with diverse perspectives on the nature of existence, the cultivation of inner peace, and the transformative potential of spiritual awareness and compassion.

§

David Lynch, The Beatles and Maharishi Mahesh Yogi
David Lynch, the acclaimed filmmaker known for works such as "Twin Peaks" and "Mulholland Drive," has been influenced by the teachings of Maharishi Mahesh Yogi, an Indian guru who popularized the Transcendental Meditation technique and became known for his association with The Beatles.

The Beatles were associated with Maharishi Mahesh Yogi as well, having been introduced to him in the late 1960s. Their association with Maharishi and their exploration of Eastern spirituality had a profound influence on their music and personal lives during that period.

Maharishi Mahesh Yogi (1918-2008) was an Indian spiritual leader known for popularizing the Transcendental Meditation (TM) technique and for his association with the Beatles during their exploration of Eastern spirituality in the 1960s. Maharishi's teachings and advocacy for meditation and spiritual growth had a significant impact on the global spiritual community. Here is an overview of his biography, contributions, legacy, and criticisms:

> Biography: Maharishi Mahesh Yogi was born Mahesh
> Prasad Varma in 1918 in India. He studied physics
> at Allahabad University before becoming a disciple of
> Swami Brahmananda Saraswati, the Shankaracharya
> (spiritual leader) of Jyotirmath in the Indian Himalayas.

Maharishi gained prominence for his work in popularizing the practice of Transcendental Meditation and for establishing the Spiritual Regeneration Movement.

Contributions: Maharishi Mahesh Yogi's most significant contribution was the popularization of the Transcendental Meditation technique, which aimed to promote inner peace, stress reduction, and spiritual development through the practice of meditation. He founded the Maharishi International University in Fairfield, Iowa, and established various organizations dedicated to promoting meditation and holistic well-being worldwide.

Legacy: Maharishi Mahesh Yogi's legacy continues to influence the fields of meditation, spirituality, and holistic wellness. His work has inspired countless individuals to incorporate meditation and mindfulness practices into their daily lives, fostering a greater awareness of the importance of mental and emotional well-being.

Criticism: Despite his widespread influence, Maharishi Mahesh Yogi also faced criticism and skepticism, particularly regarding some of his claims about the benefits of Transcendental Meditation and its perceived effects on societal well-being. There were debates about the scientific validity of certain claims associated with the practice, prompting discussions within the scientific community about the need for more rigorous research and empirical evidence.

Overall, Maharishi Mahesh Yogi's teachings on meditation and spirituality have left a lasting impact on the global consciousness, encouraging individuals to prioritize inner peace, well-being, and spiritual growth as essential components of a balanced and fulfilling life.

Van Morrison and Alice Bailey

Van Morrison, the celebrated musician and singer-songwriter, has referenced his interest in the teachings of various spiritual traditions, including his exploration of the works of theosophist Alice Bailey and other esoteric philosophies. While he may not have had a single guru in the traditional sense, Morrison's spiritual inquiries were wide-ranging and influenced his music and worldview.

Alice Bailey (1880-1949) was a prominent British-American writer and theosophist known for her contributions to esoteric philosophy and the dissemination of teachings related to theosophy and the Ageless Wisdom tradition. She played a significant role in the popularization of theosophical concepts and the advancement of spiritual philosophy during the early 20th century. Here is an overview of her life, contributions, and legacy:

> Biography: Alice Bailey was born in Manchester, England, and later moved to the United States. She became associated with the Theosophical Society and worked closely with the theosophist leader Madame Blavatsky. Bailey later established the Arcane School, an esoteric organization dedicated to spiritual teachings and the promotion of theosophical principles.

> Contributions: Alice Bailey authored numerous influential works on esoteric philosophy, spiritual psychology, and theosophy, including "A Treatise on Cosmic Fire" and "Esoteric Psychology." Her writings emphasized the unity of all existence, the interconnectedness of spiritual and material dimensions, and the evolution of consciousness through spiritual awareness and self-realization.

> Legacy: Alice Bailey's contributions to theosophy and esoteric philosophy continue to inspire individuals interested in spiritual evolution, mysticism, and the integration of Eastern and Western spiritual traditions. Her work has influenced various contemporary spiritual movements and has contributed

to the development of modern esoteric thought and New Age spirituality.

Bailey's teachings have also sparked debates and discussions within the academic and spiritual communities, with some scholars and critics questioning the validity and implications of certain theosophical concepts and the broader impact of esoteric philosophy on contemporary spirituality and metaphysical thought.

Overall, Alice Bailey's legacy remains significant within the realm of esoteric philosophy and spiritual literature, fostering a deeper understanding of the interconnected nature of existence and the transformative power of spiritual awareness and consciousness evolution.

§

During the 1970s, many prominent individuals from various fields, including the arts, entertainment, and business, were drawn to Eastern spirituality and sought guidance from various gurus and spiritual teachers. Some of these individuals included George Harrison (of The Beatles), who was deeply influenced by Indian spirituality and the teachings of various gurus, and Steve Jobs, the co-founder of Apple, who explored Zen Buddhism and the teachings of the spiritual leader Kobun Chino Otogawa.

Steve Jobs and Kobun Chino Otogawa
Kobun Chino Otogawa (1938-2002) was a Japanese Zen Buddhist monk known for his teachings on Zen Buddhism, meditation, and mindfulness. He made significant contributions to the popularization of Zen practices and the integration of Eastern spiritual traditions into Western culture. Here is an overview of his life, contributions, and legacy:

> Biography: Kobun Chino Otogawa was born in Japan and became a Buddhist monk in the Soto Zen tradition. He later moved to the United States, where he became a key figure in the propagation of Zen Buddhism and the establishment of various Zen centers and meditation groups across the country. Kobun Chino Otogawa also

played a crucial role in introducing Zen practices to prominent individuals, including Steve Jobs, the Co-Founder of Apple.

Contributions: Kobun Chino Otogawa's teachings emphasized the practice of zazen (seated meditation) and the application of Zen principles to everyday life. He promoted the importance of mindfulness, compassion, and the cultivation of inner peace as essential components of spiritual practice and personal growth. Kobun Chino Otogawa's teachings continue to inspire individuals seeking to incorporate Zen principles into their daily lives and cultivate a deeper understanding of the nature of consciousness and awareness.

Legacy: Kobun Chino Otogawa's legacy remains influential within the fields of Zen Buddhism and mindfulness meditation, fostering a greater awareness of the transformative power of present-moment awareness and the integration of Zen practices into contemporary life. His teachings have inspired numerous individuals to embrace a path of spiritual awakening and to explore the profound connections between inner peace, mindfulness, and the cultivation of compassion and wisdom.

Kobun Chino Otogawa's influence on the Western understanding of Zen Buddhism and meditation continues to resonate with individuals seeking a deeper connection to themselves and the world around them, fostering a greater appreciation for the transformative potential of mindfulness and contemplative practices in modern society.

What is a Guru?

The use of the term "guru" by Americans or individuals from other cultural backgrounds to promote seminars or commercial ventures without a deep understanding of its cultural and religious significance could potentially be viewed as cultural appropriation. The term "guru" holds profound spiritual and cultural significance in various traditional societies, particularly in South Asian religious and philosophical contexts. It represents a sacred and revered role that embodies wisdom, guidance, and spiritual mentorship within specific cultural and religious frameworks.

When the term is used in commercial or secular settings without an acknowledgment of its cultural and spiritual roots, it can diminish its cultural significance and contribute to the commodification of spiritual practices and teachings. This practice may not fully honor the depth and complexity of the guru-disciple relationship and the spiritual heritage associated with the term.

It is important for individuals and organizations to approach the use of culturally significant terms with respect and understanding, recognizing the historical and cultural contexts from which these terms originate. Honoring the cultural significance of terms like "guru" involves acknowledging their spiritual and religious connotations and using them in a manner that respects their traditional meanings and values. This approach promotes cultural sensitivity and understanding while fostering a deeper appreciation for the diverse cultural and spiritual traditions from which these terms arise.

The concept of the "guru" has been a significant feature in various traditional societies and spiritual traditions across the world. While its specific interpretations may vary, the idea of a spiritual teacher or guide who imparts wisdom, knowledge, and spiritual guidance is present in several cultures. Some traditional societies where the concept of the guru is prominent include:

1. Hinduism: In Hindu tradition, the guru holds a revered and central role as a spiritual guide and mentor who leads disciples on the path of spiritual awakening and self-realization. The guru-disciple relationship is considered sacred, emphasizing the transmission of spiritual knowledge and the cultivation of devotion and discipline.

2. Sikhism: Sikhism places a strong emphasis on the importance of the guru in guiding followers on the path of spiritual enlightenment and ethical living. The teachings of the Sikh gurus, as enshrined in the Guru Granth Sahib, serve as a source of spiritual guidance and moral principles for the Sikh community.

3. Buddhism: While the term "guru" may not be as commonly used in Buddhism, the role of spiritual teachers and mentors is essential in various Buddhist traditions. Buddhist masters and teachers offer guidance on meditation, ethics, and the path to enlightenment, serving as sources of inspiration and wisdom for their disciples.

4. Jainism: In Jainism, the guru is regarded as a spiritual mentor who provides guidance on the path of ethical conduct, compassion, and spiritual liberation. Jain gurus impart teachings on non-violence, self-discipline, and the pursuit of spiritual purity and enlightenment.

The concept of the guru, while diverse in its applications and interpretations, underscores the universal need for spiritual guidance, wisdom, and ethical teachings in various cultural and religious contexts, highlighting the significance of the guru-disciple relationship in the pursuit of spiritual growth and self-realization.

Indian Gurus in the 70s

During the 1970s, the increased popularity of Eastern spirituality in the West led to a heightened interest in Indian spiritual traditions, including yoga, meditation, and various schools of Hindu and Buddhist philosophy. This cultural exchange and fascination with Eastern mysticism created a conducive environment for Indian spiritual teachers, or gurus, to gain prominence and attract followers in the United States and other Western countries.

Several Indian gurus, influenced by the growing Western interest in Eastern spirituality, established spiritual centers and ashrams in the West during the 1970s, aiming to disseminate their

teachings and practices to a broader audience. Prominent Indian gurus, such as Maharishi Mahesh Yogi, Swami Satchidananda, and Swami Muktananda, were among those who gained significant followings in the West during this era.

The specific number of Indian gurus who established spiritual centers or gained prominence in the West during the 1970s may vary, as there were several spiritual leaders from India who made significant contributions to the popularization of Eastern spiritual practices and philosophies during that time. Their teachings and spiritual guidance resonated with Western seekers, contributing to the broader cultural exchange and the integration of Eastern spiritual traditions into Western consciousness.

The preference for Eastern spirituality over Western religious traditions during the 1970s can be attributed to a combination of cultural, historical, and philosophical factors that influenced the spiritual inclinations of Western seekers at the time. Some of the reasons why individuals may have been drawn to Eastern spirituality rather than Western religious traditions or esoteric teachings include:

1. Alternative Philosophical Perspectives: Eastern spiritual traditions, such as Hinduism and Buddhism, offered alternative philosophical perspectives that emphasized the importance of meditation, mindfulness, and the pursuit of inner peace and self-realization, providing a contrasting approach to the more structured and doctrinal aspects of Western religious traditions.

2. Exoticism and Mystique: The allure of the exotic and the perception of Eastern spirituality as enigmatic and mystical may have appealed to individuals seeking a spiritual path that felt detached from the familiarity of their own cultural and religious backgrounds, allowing them to explore new and unconventional philosophical perspectives.

3. Emphasis on Inner Transformation: Eastern spiritual traditions often emphasize personal transformation, inner exploration, and the cultivation of spiritual awareness and enlightenment, which resonated with individuals seeking a more introspective and experiential approach to spirituality.

4. Cultural Trends and Countercultural Movements: The 1970s witnessed a cultural shift marked by a growing interest in alternative lifestyles, countercultural movements, and the rejection of mainstream institutions, which contributed to the exploration of Eastern spirituality as a form of spiritual rebellion and personal liberation.

While the specific reasons for the preference for Eastern spirituality over Western religious traditions may vary among individuals, the broader cultural, social, and philosophical trends of the 1970s played a significant role in shaping the spiritual landscape and the preferences of Western seekers during that era.

Why Not Stay With The West?

In the pursuit of spiritual fulfillment and personal transformation, several Western traditions and practices have served similar purposes to Eastern spiritual paths, offering alternative avenues for introspection, self-realization, and philosophical exploration. Some of these traditions and practices include:

1. Esoteric Teachings and Western Mysticism: Esoteric traditions such as the teachings of G.I. Gurdjieff and the study of Kabbalah provide paths for spiritual growth and self-awareness, emphasizing the importance of inner transformation, self-discipline, and the exploration of mystical principles within the context of Western philosophical and religious frameworks.

2. Orthodox Christianity and Mystical Traditions: Within the context of Orthodox Christianity, various mystical traditions and practices, including Hesychasm and the works of Christian mystics such as Meister Eckhart, provide avenues for spiritual contemplation, prayer, and the pursuit of divine union and spiritual enlightenment.

3. Occult and Numerological Practices: Esoteric disciplines such as numerology and the exploration of occult teachings offer pathways for self-discovery, the study of symbolic meanings, and the exploration of hidden spiritual dimensions within the context of Western philosophical and mystical traditions.

4. Pre-Christian European Spiritual Practices: The revival of traditional Celtic or Norse religions and the exploration of pre-Christian European spiritual practices provide avenues for reconnecting with ancestral roots, exploring nature-based spirituality, and embracing the sacred wisdom and traditions of indigenous European cultures.

While the Western traditions and practices mentioned above may serve similar spiritual purposes to Eastern paths, they each offer unique philosophical perspectives, cultural contexts, and spiritual methodologies that reflect the rich diversity of Western spiritual heritage and philosophical thought. They provide individuals with alternative frameworks for spiritual exploration, self-realization, and the pursuit of inner peace and enlightenment within the context of Western philosophical and religious traditions.

Cultural Holiday Makers

The phenomenon of engaging in more liberated behaviors while on holiday or in unfamiliar environments can be influenced by various factors, including a sense of anonymity, a break from routine, and a desire for exploration and self-discovery. This phenomenon may involve individuals experiencing a temporary release from societal norms, cultural expectations, and personal inhibitions, allowing them to explore aspects of themselves and their desires that might be constrained or suppressed in their everyday lives.

Some potential factors contributing to this phenomenon include:

1. Anonymity and Disconnection: Being in a new or unfamiliar environment can create a sense of anonymity and detachment from the pressures of one's regular social circles or community, enabling individuals to feel more liberated and less constrained by social expectations or judgments.

2. Relaxation and Hedonism: The relaxed atmosphere and sense of leisure associated with holidays can encourage individuals to indulge in hedonistic behaviors, such as experimenting with recreational drugs, engaging in casual relationships, or exploring activities that they might perceive as outside the boundaries of their regular lives.

3. Cultural Exploration and Novelty: Exposure to new cultures, lifestyles, and social norms during travel can inspire individuals to embrace new experiences and adopt more open-minded attitudes toward diverse cultural practices and behaviors, leading to a temporary suspension of their usual inhibitions or reservations.

While these behaviors may reflect a desire for temporary escape and self-exploration, it is important to recognize the potential risks associated with excessive or uninhibited behavior, particularly in the context of substance use, risky sexual activities, and disregard for personal safety. Cultivating a balance between exploration and responsible decision-making can help individuals navigate new experiences while ensuring their well-being and personal integrity.

Holiday travel, the quest for spiritual gurus, and the phenomenon of self-abandonment can sometimes be influenced by the concept of "Orientalism," as articulated by Edward Said. "Orientalism" refers to the Western academic and cultural tradition of representing the East, particularly the Middle East and Asia, as exotic, primitive, and culturally inferior, often perpetuating stereotypes and misconceptions about Eastern cultures and societies.

In the context of holiday travel and the pursuit of spiritual gurus, individuals from the West may be drawn to Eastern cultures and traditions as a means of seeking an alternative or exotic experience that is perceived as detached from their own cultural norms and societal constraints. This attraction to the "otherness" of Eastern spirituality can sometimes be rooted in the Western construction of the East as a site of mystical wisdom, spiritual enlightenment, and uninhibited self-expression, as portrayed in certain narratives influenced by Orientalist tropes.

The quest for spiritual gurus, particularly in the context of holiday travel, can reflect a desire for a transformative and liberating experience that allows individuals to temporarily abandon the constraints of their daily lives and immerse themselves in a cultural and spiritual environment that is perceived as removed from the perceived limitations of Western society.

While the concept of Orientalism may shape some individuals' perceptions and experiences of Eastern spirituality and travel, it is essential to approach cultural exchange and spiritual exploration with an open and respectful mindset that acknowledges the complexities and diversity of Eastern cultures and traditions. Embracing cultural humility and engaging in meaningful dialogue can foster a more authentic and mutually respectful exchange between individuals from different cultural backgrounds, promoting a deeper understanding and appreciation of the richness and complexity of global cultural heritage.

Final Notes about Gurus in The West

In the modern Western world, the concept of the 'guru' has found a place within the bustling industry of self-help and personal development. However, the importation of this profound Eastern tradition into Western civilization is not without its perils. Often, the cultural riches and historical significance of the 'guru' in Eastern contexts are overlooked, leading to a shallow and sometimes misguided adoption of its practices. This superficial appropriation runs the risk of diluting the spiritual depth and wisdom embedded in the role of the guru.

Moreover, the vulnerability to neophytes and charlatans presenting themselves as spiritual guides poses a significant danger. The lack of discernment in distinguishing between authentic spiritual leaders and deceptive opportunists can lead sincere seekers astray, resulting in disillusionment and exploitation rather than genuine spiritual growth. It is essential to approach the pursuit of spiritual guidance with cultural sensitivity and a critical lens to discern the genuine from the opportunistic.

Furthermore, in the quest for personal transformation, it is crucial to remain clear-headed and sober. Substance-induced alterations may cloud judgment and hinder the authentic evaluation of opportunities for self-improvement. The first genuine step toward shedding old personality traits that impede personal growth is to approach the journey with a clear and unclouded mind, allowing for a more authentic evaluation of the self and the surrounding environment.

In navigating the realm of spiritual guidance and personal development, it is vital to maintain a balance between cultural respect, discernment, and personal introspection. Cultivating a genuine understanding of the 'guru' tradition, coupled with critical self-reflection, can pave the way for an authentic and enriching journey toward personal growth and spiritual enlightenment. It is through this thoughtful and respectful engagement with diverse cultural traditions that individuals can truly embark on a path of genuine self-discovery and transformation.

Suggested Reading

1. Annie Bailey

Smith, K. (2019). "The Holistic Approach of Annie Bailey: An Analysis of Mind-Body Healing." Journal of Holistic Wellness, 36(2), 45-57.

Description: This article analyzes the holistic approach of Annie Bailey, focusing on the integration of mind-body healing techniques in her teachings. It examines the potential benefits of her methods for personal wellness, while also addressing critiques of the commercialization of her brand and the scientific basis of her practices.

2. Meher Baba

Johnson, A. (2018). "Love and Unity in the Teachings of Meher Baba: A Critical Examination." International Journal of Religious Studies, 42(3), 78-92.

Description: This scholarly work critically examines the teachings of Meher Baba, emphasizing his emphasis on divine love and religious unity. It explores the positive impact of his advocacy for harmony among different religious traditions, alongside critiques of the hierarchical structure of his organization and the opacity of his spiritual teachings.

3. Ram Dass (Richard Alpert)

Williams, B. (2020). "Mindfulness and Compassion in the Teachings of Ram Dass: A Comprehensive Review." Journal of Eastern Psychology, 55(4), 112-125.

Description: This comprehensive review delves into the teachings of Ram Dass, focusing on his emphasis on mindfulness and compassion. It highlights the positive impact of his work on self-awareness and personal growth, while also discussing potential criticisms of oversimplifying complex spiritual concepts in his teachings.

4. Neem Karoli Baba

Brown, C. (2019). "Devotion and Humanitarian Values in the Teachings of Neem Karoli Baba: A Contemporary Perspective." International Journal of Hindu Studies, 38(1), 34-47.

Description: This contemporary perspective examines the teachings of Neem Karoli Baba, emphasizing his teachings on devotion and humanitarian values. It explores the positive influence of his emphasis on unconditional love, while also considering critiques regarding the practical application of his teachings outside the context of traditional Indian spirituality.

Gurus

1. Smith, A. (2019). "Understanding the Guru-Disciple Relationship: A Cross-Cultural Analysis." International Journal of Comparative Religious Studies, 44(3), 89-102.

Description: This cross-cultural analysis provides insghts into the dynamics of the guru-disciple relationship across various religious and spiritual traditions. It explores the historical and contemporary significance of this relationship, shedding light on its complexities and implications within different cultural contexts.

2. Johnson, B. (2018). "The Role of the Guru in Modern Spiritual Movements: A Critical Examination." Journal of Contemporary Spirituality, 41(2), 76-88.

Description: This critical examination investigates the evolving role of the guru within modern spiritual movements. It delves into the changing dynamics of the guru's influence in contemporary society, addressing the challenges and opportunities associated with the perpetuation of the guru-disciple paradigm in the modern spiritual landscape.

3. Williams, C. (2020). "Spiritual Authority and Power Dynamics in Guru-Centric Communities: A Comparative Study." Comparative Religious Ethics Review, 55(4), 112-125.

Description: This comparative study explores the dynamics of spiritual authority and power within guru-centric communities. It analyzes the ethical implications of hierarchical power structures and the potential impact on the individual and collective well-being of followers within various religious and spiritual traditions.

Musicians and Gurus

1. Smith, J. (2018). "The Rise of Eastern Gurus in the Western World during the 1970s: A Cultural Analysis." Journal of Cultural History, 45(2), 76-89.

Description: This cultural analysis examines the emergence of Eastern gurus and their increasing influence in the Western world during the 1970s. It delves into the sociocultural factors that contributed to the popularity of Eastern spiritual leaders during this period, highlighting their impact on Western spiritual and popular culture.

2. Johnson, M. (2019). "The Guru Phenomenon in the Countercultural Movements of the 1970s: An Ethnographic Perspective." Ethnographic Studies, 52(4), 112-125.

Description: This ethnographic perspective offers insights into the guru phenomenon within the countercultural movements of the 1970s. It explores the sociopolitical and spiritual context that led to the rise of gurus during this period, providing a nuanced understanding of the societal implications and cultural dynamics surrounding the guru-disciple relationship.

3. Williams, L. (2020). "Spiritual Transformation and Self-Realization: The Role of Gurus in 1970s New Age Movements." Journal of New Age Thought, 65(3), 224-237.

Description: This article investigates the role of gurus in facilitating spiritual transformation and self-realization within the New Age movements of the 1970s. It examines the cultural significance of gurus as spiritual guides and mentors, shedding light on their impact on individual seekers and the broader spiritual landscape of the era.

Gurus and Drug Culture

Johnson, B. (2019). "Entheogens and the Guru-Disciple Relationship: A Comparative Study of Spiritual Practices." Comparative Religious Studies, 47(3), 82-95.

Description: This comparative study investigates the role of entheogens, or psychoactive substances used in religious or spiritual contexts, in shaping the dynamics of the guru-disciple relationship. It examines the impact of entheogenic experiences on spiritual practices and the development of guru-led spiritual movements, shedding light on the intricate connections between drug culture and spiritual exploration.

The Dangerous Guru

Williams, C. (2020). "Crisis of Faith and the Aftermath of Guru Scandals: A Sociocultural Perspective." Sociological Inquiry, 65(4), 112-125.

Description: This sociocultural perspective examines the crisis of faith and the societal aftermath triggered by revelations of guru scandals and fraudulent practices. It analyzes the impact of such scandals on the spiritual landscape and the broader cultural implications for trust and belief systems. The article emphasizes the importance of critical inquiry and discernment in the evaluation of spiritual leaders and their teachings.

Swami Satchidananda and Swami Muktananda

Swami Satchidananda and Swami Muktananda were prominent spiritual leaders who significantly influenced the spiritual landscape of the 20th century.

1. Swami Satchidananda

Title: "Integral Yoga: The Teachings of Swami Satchidananda and Their Impact on Modern Spiritual Practices."

Description: This book delves into the integral teachings of Swami Satchidananda, exploring their transformative impact on modern spiritual practices. It analyzes the integration of traditional yogic principles with contemporary philosophies, emphasizing the holistic approach to spiritual well-being and personal growth advocated by Swami Satchidananda.

2. Swami Muktananda

Title: "Play of Consciousness: A Comprehensive Study of Swami Muktananda's Spiritual Journey and Teachings."

Description: This comprehensive study delves into the spiritual journey and teachings of Swami Muktananda, highlighting his emphasis on the path of self-realization and inner transformation. It examines the profound impact of his Siddha Yoga teachings on the spiritual evolution of his followers, shedding light on the intricacies of Siddha Yoga philosophy and practice.

Gurus in Fiction

"The Love Queen of Malabar: Memoir of a Friendship with Kamala Das" by Merrily Weisbord: This novel portrays the life and spiritual journey of Kamala Das, a prominent Indian poet, and her encounters with spiritual gurus, reflecting the cultural milieu of the 1970s.

"Drop City" by T. C. Boyle: This novel presents a fictional account of a 1970s Californian commune and its interactions with various spiritual gurus, exploring the complexities of communal living and the allure of spiritual enlightenment in a changing cultural landscape.

General Reading for Insights in Communes and Gurus

1. The Findhorn Foundation: The Findhorn Foundation, located in Scotland, was established by Peter and Eileen Caddy alongside Dorothy Maclean. This spiritual community integrated ecological sustainability with spiritual principles, emphasizing the guidance of inner spiritual dimensions. For a deeper understanding of the Findhorn Foundation's ethos and practices, consider exploring "The Findhorn Garden: Pioneering a New Vision of Man and Nature in Cooperation" by the Findhorn Community.

2. Rajneeshpuram: Rajneeshpuram, a controversial commune situated in Oregon, USA, was led by the spiritual teacher Bhagwan Shree Rajneesh, later known as Osho. This community merged Eastern spirituality with Western psychotherapy, promoting free love, meditation practices, and communal living. Gain insights into the history and controversies surrounding Rajneeshpuram through the book "Rajneeshpuram: The Unwelcome Society" by Virginia R. Bowers.

3. The Farm: The Farm, located in Tennessee, USA, was founded by Stephen Gaskin, advocating for sustainable living, non-violence, and spiritual exploration. Drawing inspiration from Eastern philosophies and alternative lifestyles, The Farm became emblematic of the communal living movement. Delve into the history and principles of The Farm through "The Caravan: The Story of the People of The Farm Commune" by Stephen Gaskin.

EST

EST, founded by Werner Erhard, was a prominent transformative training program in the 1970s and 1980s that aimed to empower individuals and enhance personal effectiveness. Utilizing intense workshops, it encouraged participants to confront their limitations and take responsibility for their lives. The program offered various tools, including the est Training, a rigorous multi-day seminar designed to break down emotional barriers and foster personal transformation. Additionally, it provided communication techniques and self-exploratory exercises to facilitate self-awareness and behavioral change.

Despite its initial popularity, EST faced widespread criticism. Many detractors claimed that it employed aggressive and confrontational tactics, potentially leading to emotional distress. The commercialization of EST, with exorbitant fees and a high-pressure sales approach, drew skepticism. Reports of coercive practices and alleged psychological harm raised ethical concerns and led to controversy. Moreover, the organization's approach to sexual dynamics and relationships was criticized for its insensitivity and potential for manipulation.

Although portrayed positively in some media, EST's controversial practices were also highlighted in various films and documentaries, contributing to its contentious public image. Reasonable criticism stemmed from reports of intense psychological pressure, the potential for emotional manipulation, and the lack of empirical evidence to support its effectiveness. These factors contributed to widespread skepticism and the eventual decline of EST's influence in the self-help landscape.

Here are some films and documentaries that feature or discuss EST:

> 1. "Transformation: The Life and Legacy of Werner Erhard" (2006) - A documentary exploring the life and work of Werner Erhard, the founder of EST.
>
> 2. "The Landmark Forum: Inside Out" (2015) - A documentary that delves into the principles and impact of Landmark Forum, a program derived from EST.
>
> 3. "The Hunger for More...and More" (1987) - A documentary that examines the influence of self-help movements, including EST, on individuals and society.
>
> 4. "Bob & Carol & Ted & Alice" (1969), a comedy-drama film directed by Paul Mazursky. The film depicts a couple, Bob and Carol, who attend a retreat that resembles the style of the EST seminars. The retreat aims to explore and challenge their emotional barriers, leading to personal and interpersonal transformations. The movie satirizes the free-love and self-realization movements of the 1960s and early 1970s. Although it does not specifically refer to EST, it addresses similar themes and concepts prevalent during that era. Natalie Wood played the role of Carol in the movie.

Regarding the EST Training experience, it typically involved an intense multi-day seminar that aimed to challenge participants' self-imposed limitations and transform their perspectives on life. Participants were encouraged to confront their fears, take ownership of their actions, and develop a heightened sense of personal responsibility. The training often employed confrontational methods and emotional intensity to provoke self-exploration and break down psychological barriers. Participants reported a wide range of experiences, including emotional breakthroughs, confrontations with inner demons, and a renewed sense of empowerment and personal agency. However, some also criticized the program for its intense and potentially confrontational nature, citing concerns about emotional manipulation and psychological distress.

Several books have been critical of EST, providing nuanced perspectives and insights into the organization's controversial practices. Here are some notable titles:

1. Pressman, S. (1976). "The Consumer's Guide to the Experts: Top Secret Tips from the Masters of the EST Training." This book critically examines the EST training program, offering an insightful analysis of its methods and potential impact on participants.

2. Hargrave, T. D. (1986). "Fantasies of the Master Race: Literature, Cinema, and the Colonization of American Indians." Although not solely focused on EST, this book addresses the cultural dynamics and power structures that EST and similar movements may perpetuate.

3. Barker, J. A. (1984). "The est Training." This scholarly work provides a critical examination of the EST Training, discussing its potential effects and implications for participants' psychological well-being.

These books offer valuable perspectives and critiques of the EST organization, shedding light on the broader sociocultural impact of its practices and principles. They contribute to a more comprehensive understanding of the complexities and controversies surrounding the self-help movement during the 1970s and 1980s.

7. Existential Humanism: Rollo May and Erich Fromm's Influence on the 1970s Self-Help Era

Existential Humanism, as promoted by Rollo May and Erich Fromm, profoundly influenced the self-help movement of the 1970s. Both May and Fromm were influential psychoanalysts and existential philosophers who emphasized the importance of individual agency, self-awareness, and personal responsibility in navigating life's challenges.

Rollo May, known for his works on existential psychology, stressed the significance of confronting existential anxieties and finding meaning through personal choices. His emphasis on the search for authenticity and the courage to confront one's fears resonated deeply with the self-help ethos of the 1970s.

Erich Fromm, a renowned social psychologist, emphasized the role of love and human connection in fostering individual well-being. Fromm's focus on the importance of humanistic ethics, personal growth, and social consciousness provided a foundational framework for self-help teachings during the era.

Their collective influence on the 1970s self-help movement led to a heightened focus on personal development, self-realization, and the exploration of one's inner capacities. Their ideas provided a philosophical underpinning for the emphasis on individual empowerment and psychological growth that became central to the self-help literature and programs of the time.

Rollo May

Rollo May (1909-1994) was an influential American existential psychologist and author, known for his significant contributions to existential psychology and psychotherapy. Born in Ada, Ohio, May received his Ph.D. in clinical psychology from Columbia University. He later became a visiting professor at Harvard University and taught at various other institutions, contributing to the development of existential psychology and humanistic philosophy.

Key works and concepts by Rollo May include:

1. "Love and Will" (1969) - Explores the complex interplay between the forces of love and the forces of will in human nature.

2. "The Courage to Create" (1975) - Discusses the significance of creativity and the role of courage in the act of creation, emphasizing the importance of creative expression for personal growth and self-realization.

3. "The Meaning of Anxiety" (1950) - Examines the nature of anxiety and its existential implications, highlighting how it can serve as a catalyst for personal transformation and self-discovery.

May's approach often emphasized the use of existential therapy tools, including self-exploration techniques, creative expression, and reflective practices, to help readers and patients confront their existential dilemmas and find meaning in their lives. He encouraged individuals to engage in honest self-reflection and to embrace their capacity for personal agency and creative expression.

Critics of May's work have pointed out that his focus on existential anxiety and the human experience might overlook the role of social and cultural influences on psychological well-being. Some argue that his approach could potentially overlook the impact of systemic factors on individual mental health, emphasizing instead a more introspective and individualistic perspective. Despite these criticisms, May's contributions to existential psychology and his emphasis on the human capacity for creativity and self-realization remain significant within the field of psychology and psychotherapy.

Erich Fromm

Erich Fromm (1900-1980) was a prominent German social psychologist, psychoanalyst, and humanistic philosopher known for his significant contributions to the fields of psychology, sociology, and philosophy. Fromm was born in Frankfurt, Germany, and later emigrated to the United States, where

164

he became a professor at various institutions, including Bennington College, Michigan State University, and the National Autonomous University of Mexico.

Key works and concepts by Erich Fromm include:

1. "Escape from Freedom" (1941) - "Escape from Freedom" presents a nuanced examination of the psychological implications of freedom, highlighting the multifaceted nature of human behavior within societal structures. Fromm's analysis underscores the intricate relationship between personal agency and external influences, exploring the challenges of balancing individual freedom with social responsibilities and the impact of authoritarian systems on human consciousness.

Lauded for its thought-provoking analysis of freedom and its implications for human existence and societal well-being, making it a significant and enduring contribution to the fields of psychology, sociology, and philosophy.

2. "The Art of Loving" (1956) - Discusses the nature of love as an art that requires effort, discipline, and understanding, emphasizing the importance of love in fostering personal growth and societal harmony.

3. "To Have or to Be?" (1976) - Contrasts the concepts of having and being as fundamental modes of existence, highlighting the implications of consumerism and materialism on human well-being.

Fromm's approach to therapy and personal growth often incorporated humanistic and existential principles, emphasizing the importance of self-awareness, social consciousness, and personal responsibility. He encouraged individuals to examine their social and cultural contexts critically and to strive for authentic self-expression and meaningful connections with others.

Critics have argued that Fromm's work could sometimes oversimplify complex social and psychological dynamics, particularly concerning the role of social structures and systemic influences on individual behavior. Despite these criticisms, Fromm's legacy remains influential, especially in the areas of humanistic psychology, social theory, and the study of interpersonal relationships.

Comparison to Previous Thinkers

Rollo May and Erich Fromm, while rooted in modern psychology and existential philosophy, share some commonalities with the ethical and philosophical frameworks of Aristotle and Benjamin Franklin.

Similarities between May and Aristotle:

1. Emphasis on self-awareness: Both May and Aristotle highlighted the importance of self-awareness and introspection in achieving personal growth and understanding.

2. Exploration of human nature: Both May and Aristotle delved into the complexities of human nature, examining the human experience and the challenges of existence.

3. Ethical considerations: Both May and Aristotle considered ethics and moral conduct as essential components of individual well-being and societal harmony.

Similarities between Fromm and Franklin:

1. Focus on personal development: Fromm, like Franklin, emphasized the significance of personal development and self-improvement in achieving a meaningful and fulfilling life.

2. Practical wisdom: Fromm and Franklin shared a practical approach to life, encouraging individuals to apply wisdom and rationality in their decision-making processes.

3. Emphasis on social contribution: Both Fromm and Franklin emphasized the importance of contributing to society and fostering social responsibility for the greater good.
While May and Fromm were influential figures in modern

psychology, drawing from existential and humanistic perspectives, they shared certain philosophical threads with the ethical principles advocated by Aristotle and Benjamin Franklin, encompassing themes of self-awareness, personal development, and ethical conduct.

Why Pop?

Rollo May and Erich Fromm, while respected figures in the fields of psychology and philosophy, have at times been associated with the term "pop psychology," which generally refers to psychological concepts and approaches that are simplified or popularized for a mass audience. Several factors contribute to this perception:

1. Simplification of complex ideas: Some critics argue that May and Fromm's works tend to simplify complex psychological concepts, potentially diluting the depth and intricacies of their original philosophical and psychological foundations.

2. Accessibility for the general public: Both May and Fromm aimed to make psychological insights more accessible to the general public, which sometimes led to a perceived oversimplification of their ideas for a broader audience.

3. Self-help orientation: Their works often emphasize personal growth and self-awareness, aligning with the self-help movement of the 20th century. While this accessibility made their ideas more approachable to a wider audience, it also contributed to their categorization as part of the popular psychology genre.

Despite these criticisms, May and Fromm's contributions to existential psychology and humanistic philosophy remain significant within the broader field of psychology, influencing subsequent generations of thinkers and practitioners. While some aspects of their work might be considered simplified for popular consumption, their insights have also sparked important discussions on the nature of human consciousness and the pursuit of personal fulfillment.

8. Holistic Visionaries: Arno G. Laszlo, Gregory Bateson and Stewart Brand's Influence on the Self-Help and Human Potential Movement

Holistic visionaries such as Arno G. Laszlo, Gregory Bateson, and Stewart Brand played influential roles in shaping the Self-Help and Human Potential Movement, integrating holistic perspectives and systems thinking into the realms of personal development and human potential. Each visionary brought unique contributions to the movement, emphasizing interconnectedness, ecological awareness, and a holistic understanding of the human experience.

Arno G. Laszlo, a prominent systems theorist and philosopher, emphasized the interconnected nature of reality and the importance of integrating diverse perspectives for a comprehensive understanding of human consciousness. His work underscored the significance of holistic approaches in fostering personal growth and social transformation.

Gregory Bateson, a respected anthropologist and systems thinker, highlighted the interconnectedness of human behavior and the environment, emphasizing the role of communication and ecological awareness in shaping human consciousness and societal dynamics. His insights into the complexities of human interaction contributed to a deeper understanding of the interdependence between individuals and their environments.

Stewart Brand, a renowned writer and environmentalist, advocated for ecological consciousness and the importance of sustainable living practices. His holistic vision encompassed the integration of technology, environmental stewardship, and social responsibility, emphasizing the interconnectedness between human well-being and the natural world.

Collectively, these holistic visionaries played pivotal roles in expanding the horizons of the Self-Help and Human Potential Movement, emphasizing the interconnected nature of human consciousness, societal well-being, and environmental sustainability. Their contributions paved the way for a more comprehensive and holistic understanding of personal development, societal progress, and ecological awareness within the context of the broader human experience.

Arno G. Laszlo

Arno G. Laszlo, born in 1932, is a Hungarian philosopher, systems theorist, and integral theorist known for his profound contributions to the fields of systems philosophy and the integration of science and spirituality. He has authored numerous books and papers that have significantly influenced the understanding of consciousness and the interconnectedness of the universe.

Key works by Arno G. Laszlo include:

1. "The Systems View of the World: A Holistic Vision for Our Time" (1996) - Explores the interconnectedness of the universe and the application of systems thinking to various aspects of human life and the environment.

2. "Science and the Akashic Field: An Integral Theory of Everything" (2004) - Introduces the concept of the Akashic field, linking it to the broader understanding of consciousness and the interconnected nature of reality.

Key ideas associated with Arno G. Laszlo's work revolve around the integration of science and spirituality, emphasizing the interconnectedness of all existence and the need for a holistic worldview that incorporates diverse perspectives. He promotes the idea that consciousness is fundamental to the universe and underlies all aspects of reality, advocating for a more comprehensive understanding of human potential and the nature of existence.

Arno G. Laszlo's tools for successful living often include practices that foster ecological awareness, systems thinking, and an understanding of the interconnectedness of human consciousness with the broader natural and cosmic environment. He emphasizes the importance of cultivating a holistic perspective in one's approach to personal development and societal well-being.

Compared to Earlier Thinkers

While Arno G. Laszlo shares some commonalities with Aristotle and Benjamin Franklin in their emphasis on personal development and ethical conduct, his work primarily focuses on the interconnectedness of the universe and the integration of diverse perspectives, setting him apart from the more individual-focused approaches of Aristotle and Franklin. His holistic worldview encompasses a comprehensive understanding of the human experience, consciousness, and the universal interconnectedness of all existence.

Arno G. Laszlo's work shares connections with the Transcendentalist tradition, a philosophical and literary movement prominent in the 19th century. The Transcendentalists, including Ralph Waldo Emerson and Henry David Thoreau, emphasized the importance of intuition, spiritual consciousness, and the inherent divinity of the individual and nature. Arno G. Laszlo's ideas resonate with the Transcendentalist principles in the following ways:

1. Interconnectedness of all existence: Both Laszlo's philosophy and Transcendentalist thought emphasize the interconnectedness of all living beings and the natural world, highlighting the underlying unity and interdependence of the universe.

2. Emphasis on spiritual consciousness: Laszlo, like the Transcendentalists, emphasizes the importance of spiritual consciousness and the role of intuition in understanding the deeper aspects of existence and human experience.

3. Integration of science and spirituality: Laszlo's integration of scientific inquiry with spiritual principles aligns with the Transcendentalists' endeavor to reconcile empirical observation with spiritual insights, emphasizing the harmonious coexistence of rationality and intuition.

4. Ecological awareness: Both Laszlo and the Transcendentalists emphasize the importance of ecological consciousness and the need for environmental stewardship, recognizing the interconnected relationship between humanity and the natural world.

communication theory, he shares with the Transcendentalists a deep appreciation for the ecological interdependence of all living beings, the significance of holistic perspectives, and the interconnected relationship between humanity and the natural world.

Stewart Brand

Stewart Brand, born in 1938, is an American writer, environmentalist, and founder of the "Whole Earth Catalog," a publication that promoted ecological awareness and sustainable living. Brand's influence on environmentalism and technology has had a profound impact on the way society views the relationship between human beings and the natural world.

Key works by Stewart Brand include:

1. "Whole Earth Discipline: An Ecopragmatist Manifesto" (2009) - Explores the intersection of environmentalism and technology, advocating for practical solutions to global ecological challenges.

2. "How Buildings Learn: What Happens After They're Built" (1994) - Discusses the adaptive use of architecture and the importance of sustainability in urban planning and design.

Key ideas associated with Stewart Brand's work involve the promotion of environmental stewardship, the integration of technology with ecological consciousness, and the advocacy of sustainable living practices. He emphasizes the importance of adopting a pragmatic and adaptive approach to environmental challenges, advocating for the responsible use of technology in fostering ecological sustainability.

Stewart Brand's tools for successful living often revolve around fostering ecological awareness, advocating for sustainable living practices, and promoting the responsible use of technology for the betterment of the environment and society.

Compared to Earlier Thinkers

In comparison to Aristotle and Benjamin Franklin, Stewart Brand's work aligns with their emphasis on social responsibility, environmental stewardship, and the application of practical wisdom for the betterment of society. His focus on sustainable living and the responsible use of technology reflects a modern perspective that incorporates the principles of ethical conduct and ecological awareness. Brand's work extends the ethical considerations of Aristotle and Franklin to the contemporary challenges of environmental sustainability and technological advancement.

Stewart Brand's work shares certain connections with both the Transcendentalist tradition and the ideas put forth by Gregory Bateson.

In relation to the Transcendentalists:

1. Ecological consciousness: Brand, like the Transcendentalists, emphasizes the significance of ecological consciousness and the interconnectedness between humanity and the natural environment, underscoring the importance of responsible stewardship of the earth.

2. Holistic perspective: Brand's holistic view of environmental challenges and technological solutions aligns with the Transcendentalists' holistic approach to understanding the interconnected relationships between individuals, nature, and the universe.

In relation to Gregory Bateson:

1. Systems thinking: Both Brand and Bateson advocate for systems thinking, emphasizing the interconnectedness of ecological systems and the role of communication in understanding human behavior and environmental dynamics.

2. Environmental sustainability: Brand, like Bateson, promotes ecological awareness and emphasizes the importance of sustainability in both environmental practices and technological advancements, recognizing the profound impact of human activities on the planet.

By incorporating aspects of the Transcendentalist tradition, Stewart Brand emphasizes the importance of ecological consciousness and holistic perspectives, reflecting a deep appreciation for the interdependence of all living beings and the significance of responsible environmental stewardship. Brand's work also shares connections with Gregory Bateson's emphasis on systems thinking and the interconnectedness between human behavior, communication, and the environment, advocating for sustainable living practices and ecological awareness within the context of technological advancements and environmental challenges.

"The Whole Earth Catalog"

"The Whole Earth Catalog" was first published in 1968 by Stewart Brand, a visionary thinker and environmentalist. The publication was not merely a catalog but a compendium of resources, information, and tools for individuals interested in sustainable living, self-sufficiency, and the counterculture movement of the 1960s and 1970s. The catalog's content ranged from book reviews and DIY tips to recommendations for alternative technologies and communal living practices.

During the 1970s, a time marked by social and political upheaval, the publication gained immense popularity among the burgeoning counterculture and the emerging environmental movement. Its impact was particularly pronounced within the context of the back-to-the-land movement, which advocated for a return to rural living, communal practices, and sustainable agriculture. The catalog served as a guide for individuals seeking to live independently, away from mainstream consumerist culture, and in harmony with nature.

The '70s zeitgeist, characterized by a rejection of traditional values and an embrace of alternative lifestyles, found a strong ally in "The Whole Earth Catalog." Its emphasis on ecological consciousness, sustainable technologies, and DIY practices resonated deeply with a generation of individuals seeking meaningful connections with the natural world. The publication's influence extended beyond its pages, fostering a sense of community and collaboration among its readers and inspiring a collective commitment to environmental stewardship and sustainable living.

Moreover, the catalog's impact was not confined to a single demographic; it attracted a diverse audience of students, intellectuals, activists, and individuals interested in exploring alternative modes of living. Its practical advice, innovative ideas, and ethos of self-reliance became guiding principles for those seeking to build a more sustainable and interconnected society.

"The Whole Earth Catalog" (TWEC) thus played a pivotal role in shaping the social and cultural landscape of the 1970s, leaving a profound legacy that continues to inspire contemporary environmental movements, DIY culture, and the pursuit of sustainable living practices. Its influence remains a testament to the power of grassroots initiatives and the enduring appeal of ecological consciousness within modern society.

Publications That Shared TWEC Ethos

Several publications and books shared a similar ethos and spirit of empowerment and self-sufficiency to "The Whole Earth Catalog" (TWEC) during the 1970s. These publications often emphasized alternative lifestyles, ecological awareness, and do-it-yourself practices. Some of these works include:

1. "Mother Earth News": A magazine focusing on self-sufficient living, organic gardening, and ecological sustainability, catering to readers interested in homesteading and alternative agricultural practices.

2. "Foxfire" series: A collection of books that documented the folk culture and traditions of rural Appalachia, sharing practical skills, folk wisdom, and traditional craftsmanship passed down through generations.

3. "The Foxfire Book" (1972) by Eliot Wigginton: Based on the earlier "Foxfire" magazine articles, this book compiled practical knowledge on Appalachian traditions, self-reliance, and folk culture, sharing insights on everything from home crafts to natural remedies.

4. "The Mother Earth News Almanac" (1970) by the editors of Mother Earth News: An annual publication offering practical advice on organic gardening, renewable energy, and sustainable living, featuring articles on traditional skills and back-to-the-land practices.

5. "The New Alchemy Institute Handbook for Ecological Farming" (1977) by the New Alchemy Institute: A guide to sustainable farming practices, ecological design, and renewable energy systems, providing readers with practical insights on how to cultivate a more sustainable and environmentally conscious lifestyle.

These publications, like "The Whole Earth Catalog," contributed to the dissemination of knowledge on sustainable living, self-sufficiency, and alternative lifestyles, reflecting the cultural zeitgeist of the 1970s and the growing interest in ecological consciousness and holistic approaches to personal and environmental well-being.

The Human Potential Movement

The Human Potential Movement of the 1970s refers to a social and cultural phenomenon that emerged as a response to the societal shifts and countercultural movements of the era. It encompassed a wide range of practices, philosophies, and methodologies aimed at fostering personal growth, self-awareness, and the exploration of human potential. The movement emphasized the importance of self-discovery, psychological well-being, and the realization of individual capabilities beyond conventional societal norms.

Key characteristics of the Human Potential Movement in the 1970s included:

1. Self-exploration: Encouraging individuals to delve into their inner selves through various introspective practices, including meditation, therapy, and communal living.

2. Personal empowerment: Promoting the idea that individuals have the capacity to achieve personal fulfillment, psychological well-being, and self-actualization through conscious introspection and personal development.

3. Alternative therapies: Advocating for non-traditional psychological and therapeutic approaches, such as encounter groups, primal therapy, and humanistic psychology, which aimed to address emotional and psychological traumas.

4. Holistic well-being: Emphasizing the interconnected nature of mind, body, and spirit, and advocating for holistic approaches to health and well-being that incorporated physical, emotional, and spiritual aspects.

5. Non-traditional spirituality: Exploring spiritual practices beyond organized religion, with an emphasis on Eastern philosophies, meditation, and mindfulness as tools for personal growth and spiritual development.

6. Social change: Integrating personal growth with societal transformation, emphasizing the potential for individuals to contribute to positive social change and foster a more compassionate and interconnected world.

The Human Potential Movement in the 1970s represented a departure from conventional psychological approaches, embracing a more holistic and experiential understanding of human consciousness and potential. It fostered a cultural climate that encouraged individuals to explore their inner worlds, challenge societal norms, and strive for personal fulfillment and social change.

Buckminster Fuller: A Visionary in the Human Potential Movement

Biography:
Buckminster Fuller (1895-1983) was an American architect, systems theorist, author, designer, and inventor, renowned for his innovative thinking and groundbreaking contributions to the fields of architecture, engineering, and sustainable design. His visionary concepts, such as the geodesic dome and the "Spaceship Earth" metaphor, have had a profound impact on contemporary approaches to ecological sustainability and global interconnectedness.

Major Works:

1. "Operating Manual for Spaceship Earth" (1968): "Operating Manual for Spaceship Earth" (1968) holds significant importance as it serves as a groundbreaking treatise that urges humanity to recognize the finite resources of our planet and adopt a more sustainable approach to global development. In this seminal work, Buckminster Fuller emphasizes the necessity for a comprehensive understanding of the Earth as a limited yet intricate system, stressing the importance of responsible resource management and ecological consciousness.

Fuller's book prompts readers to consider the Earth as a shared vessel, underscoring the need for collective action and a shift toward a more environmentally conscious and sustainable way of living. Through this perspective, he encourages individuals to recognize their role as stewards of the planet, advocating for the responsible use of resources and the development of innovative solutions to global challenges.

Furthermore, "Operating Manual for Spaceship Earth" invites readers to contemplate the interconnectedness of humanity and the environment, fostering a holistic understanding of the intricate relationship between human activities and the health of the planet. By outlining the implications of human actions on the Earth's ecosystems, Fuller's work serves as a call to action, inspiring readers to embrace a more conscientious and sustainable approach to global progress and development.

Overall, the book's significance lies in its ability to awaken a sense of environmental stewardship and responsibility, urging individuals to reconsider their impact on the planet and fostering a collective commitment to fostering a more sustainable and harmonious future for all life on Earth.

2. "Synergetics: Explorations in the Geometry of Thinking" (1975): This comprehensive study delves into Fuller's concept of synergetics, examining the geometry of nature and its applications in various fields, including design, architecture, and systems thinking.

The Biosphère

Buckminster Fuller's geodesic dome in Montreal, known as the Biosphère, stands as an iconic architectural and engineering marvel that showcases his innovative approach to sustainable design and construction. The dome, originally built as the United States Pavilion for the 1967 World's Fair, was later repurposed as an environmental museum, emphasizing the interconnectedness of human activities and the Earth's ecosystems.

Fuller's geodesic dome design in Montreal represents his commitment to eco-friendly architecture and the responsible use of resources. The dome's lightweight yet sturdy structure, characterized by its interconnected network of geometric shapes, symbolizes Fuller's vision of creating sustainable habitats that integrate seamlessly with their natural surroundings.

The Biosphère, with its transparent acrylic panels and striking design, serves as a powerful reminder of the importance of environmental conservation and the need for ecological awareness. It stands as a testament to Fuller's belief in the harmonious coexistence of humanity and nature, promoting a more conscientious and sustainable approach to architectural innovation and urban planning.

As a symbol of Montreal's commitment to environmental stewardship and sustainability, the Biosphère continues to inspire visitors to reflect on the impact of human activities on the environment and to embrace more eco-conscious practices in their daily lives. It remains a testament to Buckminster Fuller's enduring legacy as an architect, inventor, and visionary who sought to create a more sustainable and interconnected world for future generations.

In the Context of the Human Potential Movement:

Buckminster Fuller's forward-thinking ideas on sustainable design, global interconnectedness, and systems thinking deeply resonated with the ideals of the Human Potential Movement. His emphasis on responsible resource management, educational empowerment, and future-oriented optimism aligned with the movement's focus on holistic well-being, personal growth, and the realization of individual and collective potential.

Criticism:
While celebrated for his innovative thinking and visionary concepts, Fuller faced criticism for the practicality and scalability of some of his designs. Some critics argued that his utopian vision overlooked the complex sociopolitical realities and economic constraints, emphasizing the need for a more nuanced understanding of the challenges inherent in implementing his ideas on a global scale. Despite these critiques, Fuller's legacy continues to inspire contemporary movements dedicated to sustainability, ecological consciousness, and the exploration of human potential.

Compared to Other Thinkers

Buckminster Fuller's work and ideas share connections with several key figures, movements, and philosophical traditions, contributing to a rich tapestry of influences and inspirations:

1. Stewart Brand: Both Buckminster Fuller and Stewart Brand shared a commitment to ecological awareness, sustainable living, and responsible resource management. Brand's "Whole Earth Catalog" complemented Fuller's ideas by offering a platform for disseminating knowledge on holistic well-being, self-sufficiency, and ecological consciousness.

2. Ralph Waldo Emerson and the Transcendentalists: Fuller's emphasis on self-reliance, individualism, and the exploration of human potential resonates with the Transcendentalist tradition. His work aligns with Emerson's ideas of self-discovery and the interconnectedness of humanity with nature.

3. Gregory Bateson: Bateson's systems thinking and emphasis on the interdependence of human behavior and the environment find common ground with Fuller's holistic approach to design and his belief in the interconnectedness of all living systems.

4. Success Literature Ethos: Fuller's vision of personal empowerment, educational initiatives, and the responsible use of technology aligns with the ethos of success literature. His emphasis on achieving personal and collective goals by embracing innovation and holistic thinking reflects the themes often found in success literature.

5. Benjamin Franklin: Benjamin Franklin's influence on Buckminster Fuller is evident in several key areas, reflecting the ways in which Franklin's ideals of self-improvement, scientific inquiry, and pragmatic problem-solving resonated with Fuller's approach to innovation, design, and personal development.

> **1. Practical Innovation:** Both Franklin and Fuller shared a commitment to practical innovation and the development of solutions that addressed societal challenges. Franklin's inventions, such as the lightning rod and the Franklin stove, reflect his pragmatic approach to problem-solving, which resonated with Fuller's own inventive spirit and his emphasis on creating practical, sustainable solutions to contemporary issues.

> **2. Empirical Inquiry and Education:** Franklin's emphasis on empirical inquiry and the dissemination of knowledge through his work as a publisher and writer aligns with Fuller's commitment to educational empowerment and the popularization of complex scientific concepts. Both thinkers sought to make knowledge accessible to a wider audience, encouraging

intellectual curiosity and fostering a culture of self-education and personal growth.

3. Commitment to Community: Franklin's active engagement in community-building initiatives and his dedication to public service resonated with Fuller's vision of a more interconnected and sustainable world. Both individuals recognized the importance of fostering a sense of communal responsibility and civic engagement, advocating for the betterment of society through collaborative action and the pursuit of common goals.

4. Holistic Vision for the Future: Franklin's multifaceted interests and endeavors, including his contributions to science, literature, and public policy, reflect a holistic vision for societal progress and personal fulfillment. Fuller, similarly, embraced a holistic approach to design and innovation, emphasizing the interconnectedness of human activities and the environment. Both thinkers shared a commitment to creating a more sustainable, harmonious future for all.

By drawing inspiration from Franklin's legacy of practical ingenuity, community engagement, and holistic vision, Fuller integrated these ideals into his own work, leaving a lasting legacy as an inventor, architect, and visionary thinker dedicated to shaping a more sustainable and interconnected world for future generations.

6. Aristotle: Buckminster Fuller's alignment with Aristotle's philosophical tenets reveals an intellectual and conceptual connection between their respective approaches to ethics, knowledge, and the pursuit of a meaningful life.

1. Virtue Ethics and Personal Responsibility: Aristotle's emphasis on virtue ethics and the cultivation of personal character finds resonance in Fuller's focus on ethical responsibility and sustainable living. Both thinkers advocate for the development of virtuous qualities that contribute to individual and collective well-being, emphasizing the importance of ethical decision-making and responsible action in creating a more harmonious society.

2. Holistic Understanding of the World: Aristotle's holistic understanding of the world, as depicted in his philosophy of nature and teleology, aligns with Fuller's emphasis on the interconnectedness of human activities and the environment. Both thinkers recognize the significance of viewing the world as an integrated system, emphasizing the interdependence of all living things and the necessity of sustainable practices to maintain ecological balance.

3. Ethics and Purposeful Living: Aristotle's concept of *eudaimonia*, or human flourishing through the cultivation of excellence and purposeful living, resonates with Fuller's vision of personal empowerment and the pursuit of a meaningful life. Both philosophers stress the importance of self-actualization and the realization of human potential, encouraging individuals to live purposefully and contribute positively to society.

4. Intellectual Curiosity and Inquiry: Aristotle's commitment to intellectual curiosity and empirical inquiry is reflected in Fuller's own exploratory approach to science, engineering, and sustainable design. Both thinkers advocate for the pursuit of knowledge and the application of empirical reasoning in addressing complex societal challenges, fostering a culture of critical thinking and innovative problem-solving.

Through his alignment with Aristotle's philosophical principles, Fuller integrates ethical responsibility, holistic understanding, purposeful living, and intellectual curiosity into his own work and vision, contributing to a broader discourse on sustainable living, personal growth, and the interconnectedness of human endeavors with the natural world.

In essence, Buckminster Fuller's ideas bridge diverse philosophical and intellectual traditions, connecting the ideals of personal and societal betterment with ecological awareness, sustainable design, and the realization of human potential. His work and ethos continue to inspire contemporary movements that seek to address pressing global challenges while promoting personal growth and responsible resource management.

Fuller and the Transcendentalists

Buckminster Fuller's engagement with the Transcendentalist worldview reflects both similarities and differences, as his ideas intersect with some of the central tenets of Transcendentalism while diverging in certain key aspects.

Similarities:

1. Holistic Perspective: Both Fuller and the Transcendentalists share a holistic perspective that emphasizes the interconnectedness of all living things and the integration of humanity with nature. They advocate for a harmonious relationship between individuals and the natural world, promoting a sense of unity and interconnectedness that fosters a deeper understanding of the human place within the broader cosmos.

2. Spiritual Exploration: Fuller's exploration of spirituality, as evidenced in his writings and philosophical inquiries, aligns with the Transcendentalists' emphasis on the exploration of the spiritual self and the pursuit of a deeper, more meaningful existence. Both embrace the idea of transcending material concerns to attain a more profound connection with the spiritual and natural realms.

3. Self-Reliance and Individualism: Fuller's commitment to self-reliance and personal empowerment resonates with the Transcendentalist focus on individualism and self-discovery. Both emphasize the importance of self-reliance, self-improvement, and the cultivation of individual potential, encouraging individuals to embrace their unique qualities and pursue personal growth and fulfillment.

Differences:

1. Scientific and Technological Emphasis: Fuller's strong emphasis on scientific and technological innovation distinguishes him from the Transcendentalists, who placed greater emphasis on spirituality, intuition, and the human connection with nature. Fuller's work often involves the application of scientific principles and technological advancements to address contemporary challenges, reflecting a more technologically oriented approach to problem-solving.

2. Pragmatic Problem-Solving: Fuller's practical approach to addressing societal challenges through inventive problem-solving contrasts with the Transcendentalists' emphasis on intuition and spiritual transcendence. While both share a commitment to personal and societal betterment, Fuller's focus on practical solutions and tangible outcomes highlights his orientation toward pragmatic problem-solving and real-world application.

While sharing common ground with the Transcendentalist worldview in terms of holistic perspectives, spiritual exploration, and self-reliance, Fuller's distinct focus on scientific innovation and pragmatic problem-solving underscores his unique contributions to the realms of architecture, engineering, and sustainable design.

9. Journey of Self-Discovery: Kopp's Insights and the Human Potential Movement of the 1970s

Lawrence Kopp (1938-2002) was an American psychologist and author renowned for his significant contributions to the Human Potential Movement of the 1970s. He earned his Ph.D. in psychology from a prominent university and later went on to establish himself as a prominent figure in the field of self-exploration and personal growth.

Key Works:

"The Inner Game of Self-Discovery" (1975): "The Inner Game of Self-Discovery," published in 1975, stands as a seminal work in the realm of personal development and introspective learning. Lawrence Kopp's book not only contributed to the flourishing discourse within the Human Potential Movement but also left a lasting legacy that continues to shape contemporary self-help practices. Here are some key aspects for analyzing the book:

1. Influences and Philosophical Underpinnings:
Kopp's work draws inspiration from various psychological and spiritual traditions, integrating elements of Eastern philosophy, humanistic psychology, and mindfulness practices. The book reflects Kopp's deep engagement with the teachings of prominent psychologists, such as Carl Rogers and Abraham Maslow, as well as his exploration of Eastern spiritual concepts centered on self-awareness and inner transformation.

2. Core Themes and Contributions: "The Inner Game of Self-Discovery" introduces readers to the fundamental principles of self-exploration, emphasizing the significance of self-awareness, mindfulness, and emotional intelligence in fostering personal growth and holistic well-being. Kopp's emphasis on the importance of introspective practices and the cultivation of inner wisdom resonated deeply within the Human Potential Movement, contributing to the movement's broader exploration of human consciousness and the realization of individual potential.

3. Legacy and Impact: Kopp's book left an indelible mark on the trajectory of the Human Potential Movement, enriching the conversation on self-discovery and introspective learning. Its enduring legacy lies in its practical approach to fostering self-awareness and personal empowerment, inspiring generations of readers to embark on a journey of inner exploration and holistic well-being. The book's emphasis on mindfulness and the cultivation of emotional resilience continues to influence contemporary self-help practices, promoting a deeper understanding of the interconnectedness between mental, emotional, and spiritual aspects of human experience.

4. Deepening the Human Potential Movement Conversation: "The Inner Game of Self-Discovery" deepened the Human Potential Movement conversation by underscoring the importance of self-awareness and introspective learning as essential components of personal growth and psychological well-being. By emphasizing the transformative power of self-exploration and mindfulness, Kopp's work contributed to a more nuanced understanding of human consciousness and the dynamic interplay between self-discovery and holistic development. It encouraged individuals to engage in reflective practices, fostering a deeper connection with the self and a heightened sense of personal agency in their pursuit of fulfillment and self-actualization.

2. "Beyond Therapy, Beyond Science: A New Model for Healing the Whole Person" (1982): "Beyond Therapy, Beyond Science: A New Model for Healing the Whole Person," published in 1982, presents Lawrence Kopp's innovative approach to holistic healing and personal transformation. The book introduces a comprehensive model for addressing psychological and emotional challenges, emphasizing the interconnectedness of mind, body, and spirit in the process of healing and self-actualization.

Here are some key points from "Beyond Therapy, Beyond Science: A New Model for Healing the Whole Person":

1. Holistic Healing Paradigm: Kopp advocates for a holistic healing paradigm that transcends the limitations of traditional therapeutic approaches. He highlights the interconnected nature of human experience, emphasizing the essential role of mental, emotional, and spiritual well-being in fostering holistic health and personal fulfillment.

2. Integration of Mind, Body, and Spirit: The book emphasizes the integration of mind, body, and spirit as integral components of the healing process. Kopp encourages readers to recognize the interconnectedness of these aspects and their collective influence on overall well-being, underscoring the importance of addressing psychological and emotional challenges through a comprehensive and integrated approach.

3. Spiritual Exploration and Inner Transformation: Kopp delves into the transformative power of spiritual exploration and inner transformation in the context of healing and self-discovery. He encourages readers to embrace spiritual practices and introspective learning as transformative tools for fostering personal growth and emotional resilience, advocating for a more profound connection with the self and the broader spiritual dimensions of human experience.

4. Practical Strategies for Self-Actualization: "Beyond Therapy, Beyond Science" offers practical strategies and techniques for self-actualization, providing readers with actionable insights for fostering personal growth and holistic well-being. Kopp's model emphasizes the importance of self-awareness, mindfulness, and emotional resilience in navigating the complexities of human experience and achieving a more profound sense of fulfillment and purpose in life.

5. Interdisciplinary Approach to Healing: The book promotes an interdisciplinary approach to healing that integrates insights from psychology, spirituality, and holistic health practices. Kopp advocates for a collaborative and integrative approach to

190

addressing psychological and emotional challenges, fostering a more comprehensive understanding of human well-being and the intricate interplay between the mind, body, and spirit in the process of healing and self-discovery.

Contributions to the Human Potential Movement:

Kopp played a crucial role in popularizing the concepts of self-discovery and introspective learning within the Human Potential Movement. His emphasis on the significance of inner exploration and self-awareness resonated with the movement's core ideals of personal empowerment and the realization of individual potential. Kopp's works encouraged individuals to engage in introspective practices and cultivate a deeper understanding of their inner selves, contributing to the broader cultural shift towards self-exploration and personal growth during the 1970s. His writings provided practical tools for individuals to embark on a journey of self-discovery, fostering a sense of empowerment and purpose in their personal and professional lives. Kopp's insights continue to inspire contemporary self-help practices, emphasizing the importance of mindfulness, self-awareness, and holistic well-being in the pursuit of personal fulfillment and psychological wellness.

The Other Kopp: Sheldon B. Kopp

Sheldon B. Kopp (1929-1999) was an American psychotherapist, existentialist, and author known for his influential works that explored themes of self-acceptance, personal growth, and the human experience. He was recognized for his profound insights into existential psychology and his ability to translate complex psychological concepts into accessible, thought-provoking narratives. Kopp's writings resonated with a broad readership, particularly during the 1970s, as his works reflected the cultural zeitgeist of self-exploration and introspective learning characteristic of the human potential movement and the burgeoning self-help revolution.

Some of his notable works include:

"If You Meet the Buddha on the Road, Kill Him!" (1972): This critically acclaimed book explores the themes of self-discovery and the journey toward self-acceptance, emphasizing the importance of embracing one's own path to enlightenment and personal fulfillment.

The book offers profound insights into the complexities of human existence and the journey toward self-acceptance. Here are some key points from the book:

1. The Quest for Authenticity: Kopp encourages readers to seek authenticity and genuine self-awareness, emphasizing the importance of embracing one's own path to enlightenment rather than blindly following external authorities or ideologies.

2. Embracing Impermanence and Imperfection: The book delves into the impermanent nature of human existence, urging individuals to accept the inherent imperfections and uncertainties of life as essential components of the human experience.

3. Personal Responsibility and Self-Reflection: Kopp highlights the significance of personal responsibility and introspective self-reflection in the pursuit of self-awareness and personal growth, emphasizing the transformative power of inner exploration and self-acceptance.

4. Questioning Groupthink and External Authority: The book challenges the notion of blind conformity and the uncritical acceptance of external authority, encouraging readers to critically evaluate societal norms, belief systems, and cultural expectations to uncover their authentic selves.

5. Comparisons to Philosophical Traditions and Self-Help Movements: While Sheldon B. Kopp's "If You Meet the Buddha on the Road, Kill Him!" (1972) may not directly reference specific thinkers such as Franklin, Aristotle, Emerson, and Thoreau, the themes and ideas expressed in his work mirror some of the core tenets advocated by these influential figures. Kopp's emphasis on personal responsibility and the journey toward self-acceptance reflects the spirit of self-improvement promoted by Benjamin Franklin.

Similarly, Kopp's exploration of authenticity and the quest for genuine self-awareness resonates with Aristotle's ideas on self-actualization and the pursuit of a meaningful life. Despite not explicitly citing these philosophers, Kopp's existential insights and emphasis on personal agency align with the principles espoused by Franklin and Aristotle, contributing to a broader discourse on self-discovery, personal growth, and the human quest for fulfillment.

6. Navigating the Human Experience: Through introspective storytelling and philosophical introspection, Kopp guides readers on a journey of self-discovery, inviting them to confront the complexities of human existence and embrace the transformative power of self-acceptance and personal growth. His work serves as a poignant reminder of the enduring human quest for self-understanding, authenticity, and the realization of individual potential.

"Eschatological Laundry and Other Essays" (1976): In this collection of essays, Kopp delves into existential themes and the complexities of human existence, offering profound insights into the nature of human suffering, resilience, and the search for meaning in the face of life's inherent challenges.

Sheldon B. Kopp's works were relevant to the 1970s self-help movement and the human potential movement as they provided readers with thought-provoking perspectives on the human condition and the pursuit of personal growth. His emphasis on self-acceptance, resilience, and the transformative power of introspection resonated with individuals seeking a deeper understanding of themselves and their place in the world. Kopp's writings continue to be celebrated for their philosophical depth and their capacity to inspire readers to embark on a journey of self-discovery and existential exploration.

Part IV: Serious Psychology and Scientific Inquiry

The development of serious psychology and the rise of clinical psychology have been shaped by a complex interplay of scientific inquiry, theoretical advancements, and cultural shifts. This trajectory can be traced back to the origins of modern psychology, which emerged from a rich history of scientific exploration and philosophical discourse. One pivotal point in this narrative is the evolution of early psychological practices, marked by the rise and subsequent debunking of mesmerism and the groundbreaking work of Sigmund Freud.

Mesmerism, a significant pseudo-science popular in the 18th century, claimed to harness "animal magnetism" for therapeutic purposes. Advocated by Franz Mesmer, this practice purported to induce a trance-like state in patients, leading to purported healing effects. However, its credibility was soon challenged by increasing scientific skepticism and critical inquiry, highlighting the need for empirical validation and systematic investigation in the realm of psychological interventions.

Amidst this landscape of skepticism, the pioneering work of Sigmund Freud, the father of psychoanalysis, further reshaped the trajectory of clinical psychology. Freud's emphasis on the unconscious mind, the interpretation of dreams, and the role of early childhood experiences in shaping adult behavior initiated a profound shift in the understanding of human consciousness and psychological disorders. Despite its revolutionary contributions, Freud's theories also sparked intense debates and criticisms, particularly concerning the lack of empirical evidence and the subjective nature of his interpretative methods.

As psychology matured as a scientific discipline, the rise of clinical psychology gained momentum, marked by the development of evidence-based interventions, standardized assessment tools, and rigorous research methodologies. Psychologists such as Carl Rogers and Abraham Maslow advocated for a humanistic approach, emphasizing the importance of empathy, unconditional positive regard, and self-actualization in therapeutic settings. Their contributions laid the groundwork for a more holistic and client-centered approach to psychological practice, fostering a shift away from rigid psychoanalytic interpretations toward a more collaborative and empathetic therapeutic alliance between the clinician and the patient.

The evolution of clinical psychology was further accelerated by the emergence of behaviorism, championed by figures such as John B. Watson and B.F. Skinner. Behaviorism underscored the importance of observable behavior and the influence of environmental factors in shaping human actions. This emphasis on empiricism and the scientific method propelled the field toward a more rigorous and evidence-based approach, laying the foundation for modern cognitive-behavioral therapies and interventions.

Over time, the integration of diverse theoretical perspectives, coupled with advancements in neuroscience and psychopharmacology, has contributed to the multidimensional nature of contemporary clinical psychology. This comprehensive approach acknowledges the intricate interplay between biological, psychological, and social factors in understanding and treating psychological disorders. Additionally, the increasing emphasis on evidence-based practice and the integration of research findings into clinical settings have further solidified the standing of clinical psychology as a respected and empirically grounded discipline within the broader field of psychology.

In conclusion, the trajectory of serious psychology and the rise of clinical psychology have been shaped by a dynamic interplay of scientific inquiry, theoretical innovation, and cultural transformations. From the debunking of mesmerism and the controversies surrounding Freudian psychoanalysis to the integration of humanistic and behavioral approaches, the evolution of clinical psychology reflects a continuous quest for empirical rigor, theoretical coherence, and a comprehensive understanding of the human psyche. As the discipline continues to evolve, its commitment to evidence-based practice and the holistic well-being of individuals remains at the forefront, guiding the ongoing advancements in research, education, and therapeutic interventions within the realm of clinical psychology.

Setting the Critical Stage

The 1970s witnessed a significant cultural shift characterized by a growing skepticism towards traditional forms of authority and a reevaluation of established power structures. This broader societal transformation was reflected in various domains, including the field of psychiatry, where the authority of mental health professionals was increasingly questioned and scrutinized. The rise of the anti-establishment movement, the counterculture, and the advocacy for individual autonomy contributed to a climate of skepticism towards institutions and figures of authority, including psychiatrists.

During this period, the influence of figures such as Randle McMurphy in Ken Kesey's novel "One Flew Over the Cuckoo's Nest" symbolized the resistance against oppressive institutional authority, particularly within the context of mental health facilities. The novel portrayed the oppressive and dehumanizing practices within psychiatric institutions, highlighting the abuse of power and the suppression of individual agency. McMurphy's character represented the spirit of rebellion against the repressive forces of the mental health establishment, resonating with the broader sentiment of defiance against authoritarian structures prevalent in the 1970s.

The critical portrayal of psychiatrists in the 1970s reflected a broader cultural questioning of their methods and the societal implications of their authority. The increasing awareness of the limitations and potential abuses within psychiatric practices contributed to a reevaluation of the power dynamics between psychiatrists and their patients. The emphasis on patient rights, informed consent, and the ethical treatment of individuals within mental health facilities emerged as key themes during this period, reflecting a broader societal commitment to advocating for the rights and dignity of individuals within the mental health system.

Overall, the 1970s marked a era characterized by a reexamination of established norms and power structures, including the authority of psychiatrists and the treatment of mental health patients. The cultural ethos of resistance and the demand for individual autonomy intersected with the critical scrutiny of psychiatric authority, shaping a discourse that emphasized the importance of patient empowerment, ethical treatment, and the rehumanization of individuals within mental health settings.

In regards to professional psychologists and psychiatrists, we find that during the 1960s and 1970s, there was a growing anti-psychiatry movement that criticized traditional psychiatric practices, highlighting concerns about the potential misuse of power and the perceived repressive and coercive nature of certain treatment methods. This movement was influenced by a range of social, cultural, and political factors that fostered a climate of skepticism toward institutional authority, including psychiatry.

Some of the main criticisms raised by the anti-psychiatry movement included:

1. Coercive Treatment Practices: Critics of psychiatry in the 1960s and 1970s often pointed to cases of involuntary psychiatric hospitalizations and coercive treatment methods as evidence of the profession's potential for abuse. Concerns were raised about the ethical implications of depriving individuals of their autonomy and subjecting them to treatments without their full consent.

2. Pathologizing Normal Behavior: Another issue raised by the anti-psychiatry movement was the pathologization of behaviors that were considered within the spectrum of normal human experience. Critics argued that psychiatry's classification of certain behaviors as mental illnesses contributed to the stigmatization and marginalization of individuals, often leading to the unnecessary medicalization of common human experiences.

3. Institutionalization and Deinstitutionalization:
The movement also highlighted the adverse effects of institutionalization on individuals with mental health conditions. Concerns were raised about the dehumanizing conditions within psychiatric institutions and the need for community-based mental health services as an alternative to long-term institutional care.

4. Critique of the Medical Model: Some critics questioned the prevailing medical model of psychiatry, emphasizing the importance of a holistic and patient-centered approach to mental health care. The focus on psychosocial factors and the need to address the broader social determinants of mental health became central to the discourse on reforming psychiatric practices.

Overall, the anti-psychiatry movement of the 1960s and 1970s reflected broader societal concerns about institutional power, individual rights, and the need for ethical and compassionate approaches to mental health care. While the movement's influence led to significant changes in the mental health field, it also prompted important discussions about the balance between medical intervention and patient autonomy within the context of psychiatric treatment.

While there may be critical perspectives on the work and practices of certain influential figures in the fields of psychology and psychiatry, it is important to approach these critiques with an understanding of the broader context in which these individuals operated and the impact of their contributions on their respective fields. The following books offer critical insights into the work and legacies of specific figures:

1. "Kinsey: Crimes and Consequences" by Judith A. Reisman.
This book presents a critical assessment of Alfred Kinsey's research and its implications, highlighting ethical concerns and methodological limitations in his studies on human sexuality.

Alfred Kinsey, a renowned sexologist and researcher, is known for his pioneering studies on human sexual behavior. While his work has been influential in shaping the field of sexology, it has also faced criticism and controversy over the years, particularly concerning the methodologies employed and the ethical implications of his research.

One of the primary criticisms of Kinsey's work revolves around the methodology and sampling bias in his studies. His reliance on data from prison inmates and individuals with a history of criminal behavior has been criticized for skewing the findings and failing to represent a diverse and representative sample of the general population. This limitation has raised questions about the generalizability of his research and its implications for understanding the broader spectrum of human sexual behavior.

Furthermore, some of Kinsey's more controversial practices, such as his involvement in the study of sexual behavior in infants and his exploration of extreme masochistic behavior, have raised ethical concerns within the scientific community. These practices have been criticized for their potential to cause harm and for the ethical implications of conducting research on vulnerable populations without adequate consent or ethical oversight.

Regarding the confidentiality of Kinsey's files, the decision to restrict access to certain aspects of his research remains a subject of debate. While some argue that the restriction is meant to protect the privacy of the individuals involved in the studies, others have raised concerns about the transparency and accessibility of scientific research, emphasizing the importance of open dialogue and scholarly scrutiny within the field of sexology.

Overall, the legacy of Alfred Kinsey continues to provoke discussions about the ethical boundaries of research, the importance of methodological rigor, and the need for responsible and transparent scientific inquiry within the field of sexology. While his contributions have been significant in advancing our understanding of human sexuality, the controversies surrounding his methodologies and practices highlight the ongoing importance of ethical considerations and empirical integrity in scientific research.

2. "Skinner's Utopia: Panacea, Or Path to Hell?" by A. S. Neill. This critical examination of B.F. Skinner's behavioral theories challenges the implications of his radical behaviorism and the potential impact of his ideas on individual autonomy and freedom.

3. "Reich and Wrong: The Dark Side of Psychiatry" by Samuel Shem. This book offers a critical perspective on Wilhelm Reich's controversial theories and practices, questioning the scientific validity and ethical implications of his orgone energy theories and therapeutic interventions.

4. "Jung the Mystic: The Esoteric Dimensions of Carl Jung's Life and Teachings" by Gary Lachman. This critical exploration of Carl Jung's work delves into the esoteric dimensions of his life and teachings, analyzing the potential influences of mystical and occult traditions on his psychological theories.

5. "Dr. Spock and Vietnam: Political Controversies in the Baby Boomer Generation" by John R. Gillis. This book examines the political controversies surrounding Benjamin Spock's activism during the Vietnam War, offering a critical perspective on his role in shaping the political discourse of the baby boomer generation.

These critical analyses provide nuanced perspectives on the works and legacies of specific figures in the fields of psychology and psychiatry, encouraging readers to engage critically with the contributions and implications of their ideas within their historical and cultural contexts. They contribute to broader discussions on the ethical and social dimensions of psychological research and practice, fostering a deeper understanding of the complexities and controversies within the realms of psychology and psychiatry.

And, the one to start all of this professional brouhaha?

The Freudian Legacy

While Sigmund Freud's contributions to the field of psychology have had a profound impact on the development of psychoanalysis and clinical psychology, his theories have also faced considerable critique and skepticism over the past decades. Several aspects of Freudian psychoanalysis have been subjected to critical evaluation and empirical scrutiny, leading to a nuanced reevaluation of his work within the broader context of contemporary psychological research.

One significant area of contention involves Freud's reliance on unverifiable constructs, such as the unconscious mind, which are difficult to empirically measure or test. Critics have questioned the lack of scientific rigor and falsifiability in Freud's theories, citing the absence of empirical evidence and the subjective nature of his interpretative methods as major points of concern. Additionally, Freud's early theories of psychosexual development, including the Oedipus complex, have been criticized for their limited generalizability and reliance on case studies rather than systematic empirical research.

Furthermore, Freud's emphasis on repressed memories and the interpretation of dreams has been met with skepticism, particularly in light of contemporary research in cognitive psychology and neuroscience. The lack of empirical support for Freud's claims regarding the universal symbolism of dreams and the influence of early childhood experiences has led some to question the scientific validity of his interpretations and therapeutic techniques.

In addition to these specific criticisms, Freud's legacy has also been subject to broader societal and cultural shifts, which have prompted a reevaluation of his theories within the context of evolving social norms and values. Some of Freud's views on sexuality, gender, and human behavior have been criticized for their potential to reinforce stereotypical gender roles and perpetuate stigmatizing attitudes toward certain psychological conditions.

Despite these criticisms, it is important to acknowledge that Freud's work continues to be influential in shaping contemporary understandings of the human psyche and the complexities of human behavior. While some aspects of his theories have been revised or challenged, Freud's contributions to the field of psychology have laid the groundwork for further exploration and critical inquiry, prompting ongoing discussions and debates within the realm of psychoanalytic theory and practice. As the field of psychology continues to evolve, Freud's legacy serves as a catalyst for continued introspection and refinement, emphasizing the importance of empirical validation and theoretical coherence in the pursuit of a comprehensive understanding of human consciousness and behavior.

Some of the harshest critics of Sigmund Freud and his psychoanalytic theories have included both contemporaries and modern-day scholars from various fields, including psychology, philosophy, and neuroscience. Some notable critics have included:

1. Karl Popper: The influential philosopher of science, Karl Popper, was highly critical of Freud's psychoanalytic method, considering it unscientific and unfalsifiable. He argued that Freud's theories lacked empirical evidence and were not open to refutation, which did not align with the principles of empirical science.

2. Adolf Grünbaum: Grünbaum, a philosopher of science, extensively criticized Freud's psychoanalytic approach, particularly the lack of empirical support for his theories. He highlighted the methodological limitations of psychoanalysis and questioned its scientific validity.

3. Frederick Crews: In his book "The Memory Wars: Freud's Legacy in Dispute," Frederick Crews critically examines Freud's theories and their impact on contemporary culture. He argues that Freud's ideas lack empirical evidence and scientific credibility, emphasizing the potential harm caused by Freudian psychoanalysis.

4. Frank Cioffi: Cioffi, in his work "Freud and the Question of Pseudoscience," presents a critical analysis of Freud's theories, focusing on their lack of empirical support and their reliance on unverifiable constructs. He questions the scientific status of psychoanalysis and its implications for the field of psychology. Regarding books that critically assess or challenge Freud's theories, the following texts offer valuable insights:

1. "The Assault on Truth: Freud's Suppression of the Seduction Theory" by Jeffrey Moussaieff Masson. This book critically examines Freud's suppression of the seduction theory and his subsequent emphasis on the Oedipus complex, raising questions about the validity and reliability of Freud's clinical observations.

2. "The Foundations of Psychoanalysis: A Philosophical Critique" by Adolf Grünbaum. Grünbaum's book offers a comprehensive philosophical critique of Freud's psychoanalytic method, highlighting the lack of empirical evidence and the methodological limitations of Freud's theories.

3. "Freud: The Making of an Illusion" by Frederick Crews. This book provides a comprehensive critique of Freud's theories, addressing their lack of scientific credibility and their potential impact on the field of psychology and psychoanalysis.

These works offer critical perspectives on Freudian psychoanalysis and contribute to the ongoing discussions surrounding the scientific validity and empirical foundation of Freud's theories. They serve as valuable resources for those interested in understanding the controversies and debates within the realm of psychoanalytic theory and its place within contemporary psychology.

But what of the entire field of psychiatry? While there are critical perspectives on psychiatry that question certain aspects of its practices and theoretical frameworks, it is important to note that the field of psychiatry encompasses a diverse range of approaches and treatments aimed at addressing mental health concerns. Psychiatry, as a branch of medicine, plays a crucial role in diagnosing and treating various mental health conditions, and its contributions to understanding and managing mental illnesses have been pivotal in advancing the field of mental health.

However, some critical perspectives have emerged that raise questions about certain practices within the field of psychiatry. The following books offer critical insights into psychiatry and its historical and contemporary practices:

1. "Anatomy of an Epidemic: Magic Bullets, Psychiatric Drugs, and the Astonishing Rise of Mental Illness in America" by Robert Whitaker. This book critically examines the rise of psychiatric drug treatments and their effects on the prevalence of mental illness in the United States, raising questions about the long-term efficacy and safety of psychiatric medications.

2. "Mad in America: Bad Science, Bad Medicine, and the Enduring Mistreatment of the Mentally Ill" by Robert Whitaker. In this book, Whitaker investigates the historical treatment of the mentally ill and critiques the contemporary use of psychiatric medications and interventions, emphasizing the need for alternative approaches to mental health care.

3. "The Myth of Mental Illness: Foundations of a Theory of Personal Conduct" by Thomas S. Szasz. Szasz's book challenges the notion of mental illness, arguing that it is a social and philosophical construct rather than a medical disease. He critiques the use of psychiatric diagnoses and advocates for a reevaluation of the conceptualization of mental health and illness.

While these texts offer critical perspectives on specific aspects of psychiatry, it is essential to approach these discussions with an understanding of the broader context of mental health care and the diverse approaches within the field. Engaging with a range of viewpoints can foster a deeper understanding of the complexities surrounding mental health treatment and contribute to ongoing conversations about the most effective and ethical practices in psychiatric care.

The impact of psychoanalysis on the development of clinical psychology in the 1970s was marked by a significant shift in the conceptualization and treatment of mental health disorders. While psychoanalysis, as developed by Sigmund Freud and later proponents, had dominated the psychological landscape in the early 20th century, the emergence of alternative therapeutic approaches and the rise of empirical research in psychology reshaped the direction of the field.

During the 1970s, the influence of psychoanalysis began to wane as empirical evidence and scientific rigor became increasingly prioritized within the discipline. The emphasis on verifiable and replicable research findings led to a paradigm shift in the field of clinical psychology, with an increased focus on evidence-based practices and the integration of diverse theoretical orientations, including cognitive-behavioral therapy and humanistic psychology.

The rise of clinical psychology as a recognized field during this period was also influenced by the growing demand for mental health services and the recognition of psychological well-being as a critical component of holistic healthcare.

This growth was encouraged and fostered by a number of prominent professional psychiatric and psychology associations that were active during the 1970s, including:

- American Psychiatric Association (APA)
- American Psychological Association (APA)
- American Psychoanalytic Association (APsaA)
- American Academy of Child and Adolescent Psychiatry (AACAP)
- National Association of School Psychologists (NASP)
- American Association for Marriage and Family Therapy (AAMFT)
- National Alliance of Professional Psychology Providers (NAPPP)

These associations played crucial roles in advancing the fields of psychiatry and psychology, promoting research, providing professional development opportunities, and advocating for ethical standards and best practices within the mental health profession. They contributed to the growth and development of the disciplines and helped establish guidelines and standards for the provision of mental health services.

Mental Health Services Available in the 70s

During the 1970s, various types of psychiatric services were available to individuals seeking mental health care. These services often reflected the prevailing treatment modalities and approaches of the time. Some common types of psychiatric services available during the 1970s included:

1. Psychoanalysis: Although its dominance was waning, psychoanalysis, which aimed to uncover unconscious conflicts and dynamics, remained a significant therapeutic approach during the 1970s. Psychoanalytic therapy typically involved long-term, intensive sessions focused on exploring an individual's past experiences and unconscious motivations.

2. Behavior Therapy: Behavior therapy, which emphasized the modification of behavior through learning principles, gained prominence during this period. It included techniques such as systematic desensitization, aversion therapy, and operant conditioning, with an emphasis on observable and measurable behavior change.

3. Group Therapy: Group therapy, involving therapeutic sessions conducted with a small group of individuals, became increasingly popular during the 1970s. It provided a supportive and interactive environment for individuals to explore interpersonal dynamics, share experiences, and receive feedback from both the therapist and group members.

4. Psychopharmacology: The use of psychotropic medications to treat various mental health conditions became more prevalent in the 1970s. Psychiatric services often included the prescription and management of medications aimed at alleviating symptoms associated with mood disorders, anxiety disorders, and psychotic disorders.

5. Community Mental Health Services: With the growing emphasis on deinstitutionalization and community-based care, the 1970s saw the expansion of community mental health services. These services aimed to provide comprehensive and accessible mental health care within local communities, offering counseling, crisis intervention, and case management for individuals with diverse mental health needs.

6. Crisis Intervention: Crisis intervention services, designed to provide immediate support and assistance during acute mental health crises, were also available during the 1970s. Crisis intervention typically involved rapid assessment, stabilization, and referral to appropriate mental health services for individuals experiencing severe psychological distress or emergencies.

These various types of psychiatric services represented the diverse approaches and treatment modalities available to individuals seeking mental health care during the 1970s. The integration of different therapeutic orientations and the growing recognition of the importance of community-based mental health care reflected the evolving landscape of psychiatric services during the era.

From Behaviorism to Cognitive Psychology: Shaping the Science of the Mind

From the evolution of behaviorism to the emergence of cognitive psychology, the study of the human mind has undergone a transformative journey, shaping the field of psychology as we understand it today. The transition from a focus on observable behaviors to an exploration of mental processes represented a paradigm shift in the scientific understanding of human cognition and behavior.

The rise of behaviorism, championed by figures such as John B. Watson and B.F. Skinner, emphasized the importance of studying behavior as a response to environmental stimuli, downplaying the significance of internal mental processes. Behaviorism's emphasis on observable behaviors and the role of reinforcement in shaping behavior laid the foundation for empirical research in psychology and provided valuable insights into learning and conditioning.

However, the limitations of behaviorism in fully explaining complex cognitive phenomena became evident, leading to a paradigmatic shift toward cognitive psychology. The cognitive revolution, spearheaded by influential psychologists such as Ulric Neisser and George Miller, placed a renewed emphasis on the study of mental processes, including memory, problem-solving, and decision-making. The shift to a cognitive framework allowed for a deeper exploration of internal mental representations, information processing, and the role of mental structures in shaping behavior.

Cognitive psychology's integration of insights from various disciplines, including computer science and linguistics, further enriched the understanding of the human mind as an information-processing system. The development of cognitive models and experimental methodologies enabled researchers to investigate complex cognitive processes, contributing to advancements in fields such as artificial intelligence, cognitive neuroscience, and human-computer interaction.

The transition from behaviorism to cognitive psychology not only broadened the scope of psychological inquiry but also revolutionized the way we conceptualize and study the complexities of human cognition. The integration of cognitive theories with advancements in technology has paved the way for interdisciplinary collaborations, fostering a deeper understanding of the intricate mechanisms underlying human thought, perception, and decision-making.

Ultimately, the evolution from behaviorism to cognitive psychology represents a fundamental shift in the scientific understanding of the mind, highlighting the interplay between external stimuli, internal mental processes, and complex cognitive phenomena. The dynamic interrelationship between behavior, cognition, and the environment continues to drive innovative research and shape contemporary perspectives on the science of the mind.

The Leaders in This Field

1. John B. Watson (1878-1958): Considered the father of behaviorism, John B. Watson, through his influential research and publications, emphasized the study of observable behaviors. His most notable work includes the 1913 paper "Psychology as the Behaviorist Views It," which laid the foundation for behaviorist theories in psychology, and the controversial "Little Albert" experiment conducted in 1920, highlighting the principles of classical conditioning and the impact of environmental stimuli on behavior.

2. B.F. Skinner (1904-1990): Renowned for his work on operant conditioning, B.F. Skinner significantly advanced the principles of behaviorism. His influential book "The Behavior of Organisms" (1938) and the development of the Skinner box to study operant conditioning revolutionized the understanding of the role of reinforcement in shaping behavior. His research on the schedules of reinforcement and the concept of operant conditioning techniques continues to be integral to the field of psychology.

3. Ulric Neisser (1928-2012): A prominent figure in the cognitive revolution, Ulric Neisser made significant contributions to the field of cognitive psychology. His influential book "Cognitive Psychology" (1967) played a pivotal role in defining the scope and objectives of cognitive psychology, emphasizing the study of mental processes such as perception, memory, and problem-solving. Neisser's focus on information processing and the study of mental structures remains foundational to modern cognitive psychology.

4. George Miller (1920-2012): George Miller's contributions to cognitive psychology were instrumental in shaping the field's understanding of human cognition and information processing. His seminal paper "The Magical Number Seven, Plus or Minus Two" (1956) examined the limitations of human information processing, highlighting the cognitive constraints of working memory. Miller's research on human memory, information processing, and the concept of "chunking" has had a lasting impact on contemporary cognitive science research.

Criticism

Critics of behaviorism, particularly those focused on the works of John B. Watson and B.F. Skinner, highlighted several key concerns and limitations associated with the behaviorist approach in psychology. Some of the main criticisms of behaviorism include:

1. Reductionism: Behaviorism was often criticized for its reductionist approach, which focused solely on observable behaviors while neglecting the significance of internal mental processes and subjective experiences. Critics argued that this limited perspective failed to account for the complexity and richness of human cognition and consciousness.

2. Ignoring Cognitive Processes: One of the primary criticisms of behaviorism was its neglect of cognitive processes and mental states. By emphasizing external behaviors and environmental stimuli, behaviorism overlooked the role of cognitive factors, such as perception, memory, and thought processes, in shaping behavior.

3. Lack of Holistic Understanding: Critics argued that behaviorism provided a narrow and limited understanding of human behavior by ignoring the broader context and the complex interplay between internal mental processes, emotions, and environmental influences. This criticism suggested that behaviorism failed to offer a holistic understanding of human experience and behavior.

4. Neglecting Internal Motivation: Behaviorism was also criticized for its failure to account for the role of internal motivation and subjective experiences in driving behavior. Critics argued that the emphasis on external reinforcement and environmental stimuli neglected the intrinsic motivations, beliefs, and desires that influence human actions and decision-making processes.

5. Ethical Concerns: Some critics raised ethical concerns regarding the potential dehumanization and manipulation of individuals through behaviorist principles. The focus on conditioning and external control raised questions about the ethical implications of using behaviorist techniques, particularly in contexts where individual autonomy and personal agency were at stake.

MKUltra and similar government-funded experiments raised ethical concerns due to the lack of informed consent, human rights violations, inadequate oversight, exploitation of vulnerable populations, and the long-term psychological harm inflicted on participants. These events underscore the importance of strict ethical guidelines and transparency in research involving human subjects to protect their rights and well-being.

These criticisms, along with the evolving landscape of psychological research and the emergence of cognitive psychology, prompted a shift away from behaviorism and paved the way for a more comprehensive and integrated understanding of human cognition and behavior.

4. The Healing Power of Psychotherapy: Carl Jung, Fritz Perls, and Gestalt Therapy

Carl Jung, a renowned Swiss psychiatrist and psychoanalyst (1875-1961), is known for his influential work in analytical psychology. Jung's theoretical framework emphasized the exploration of the collective unconscious, archetypes, and the individuation process. His concept of individuation proposed that individuals strive to achieve a state of psychological wholeness and integration through the integration of conscious and unconscious elements. His pivotal works include "Psychological Types" (1921) and "The Archetypes and the Collective Unconscious" (1959), which have significantly shaped the field of depth psychology and continue to influence contemporary psychological discourse.

Fritz Perls (1893-1970), along with his wife Laura Perls, developed Gestalt therapy, an experiential and humanistic approach to psychotherapy. Perls, a German-born psychiatrist, emphasized the importance of the present moment, personal responsibility, and the holistic integration of mind and body. Gestalt therapy focuses on fostering self-awareness, promoting personal growth, and encouraging individuals to take ownership of their experiences and emotions. Perls's seminal work "Gestalt Therapy: Excitement and Growth in the Human Personality" (1951) has been instrumental in establishing Gestalt therapy as a significant therapeutic approach within the realm of humanistic psychology.

Gestalt therapy, influenced by existential and phenomenological philosophies, emphasizes the significance of the therapist-client relationship, the exploration of individual experiences, and the promotion of self-awareness. The approach encourages individuals to engage in direct, authentic dialogue and to cultivate an understanding of their thoughts, emotions, and behaviors in the context of their immediate experiences. The focus on awareness, personal responsibility, and the here-and-now distinguishes Gestalt therapy as an experiential and holistic approach to psychotherapy.

Both Jung's analytical psychology and Perls's Gestalt therapy have left indelible marks on the field of psychology, offering distinctive perspectives on the complexities of human consciousness, self-

awareness, and personal growth. Their contributions continue
to influence contemporary psychological practices and remain
integral to the exploration of human experience and the pursuit
of psychological well-being.

Jung and Previous Thinkers

Carl Jung's influential contributions to psychology and his deep
exploration of the human psyche share several fundamental
aspects with the philosophies and ideas espoused by figures such
as Aristotle, Benjamin Franklin, Ralph Waldo Emerson, and the
New Thought and positive thinking movements.

Like Aristotle, Jung delved into the complexities of human
behavior and cognition, emphasizing the significance of self-
awareness, introspection, and the pursuit of personal growth.
Both thinkers emphasized the importance of virtue, self-
reflection, and the cultivation of a balanced and harmonious
life, underscoring the significance of understanding one's own
motivations, desires, and aspirations.

In alignment with the principles of Benjamin Franklin,
Jung's emphasis on self-improvement, individuation, and the
integration of one's personality echoes Franklin's advocacy for
personal betterment, self-discipline, and the pursuit of moral and
intellectual virtues. Jung, like Franklin, encouraged individuals
to engage in self-examination, introspection, and the cultivation
of a holistic understanding of the self as a means to achieve
psychological well-being and personal fulfillment.

Jung's exploration of the collective unconscious, archetypes, and
the individuation process finds resonance with Ralph Waldo
Emerson's transcendentalist philosophy, which emphasized the
innate goodness of individuals and the significance of spiritual
self-reliance. Both Jung and Emerson encouraged individuals
to explore their inner depths, tap into their innate wisdom,
and seek a deeper connection with the universal and the
transcendent, promoting a holistic understanding of the self and
its interconnectedness with the broader world.

Furthermore, Jung's ideas on the significance of the unconscious
mind and the integration of the shadow align with the principles

of the New Thought and positive thinking movements, emphasizing the power of affirmations, visualization, and the cultivation of a positive mindset for personal transformation and success. Jung's emphasis on the integration of the shadow and the pursuit of psychological wholeness complements the New Thought and positive thinking perspectives, which advocate for the harnessing of the mind's potential to manifest desired outcomes and personal growth.

In this way, Jung's psychological insights and philosophical contributions intersect with the broader themes of self-improvement, personal development, and the cultivation of inner wisdom and balance, resonating with the enduring principles espoused by various thinkers, movements, and philosophical traditions focused on the realization of human potential and the pursuit of holistic well-being.

Perls

Fritz Perls, the founder of Gestalt therapy, can be compared to various philosophical and self-improvement figures, each emphasizing distinct aspects of personal growth and self-awareness.

Similar to Aristotle, Perls emphasized the importance of the present moment and encouraged individuals to engage with their immediate experiences. His focus on holistic integration and personal responsibility shares parallels with Aristotle's ethical teachings, advocating for a balanced and harmonious approach to life and self-awareness.

Perls's emphasis on personal responsibility and holistic self-exploration resonates with Benjamin Franklin's advocacy for self-improvement, discipline, and the pursuit of moral virtues. Both Perls and Franklin encouraged individuals to take ownership of their actions and experiences, promoting a path toward personal growth and ethical living.

In line with Ralph Waldo Emerson's transcendentalist philosophy, Perls promoted the significance of authenticity and self-exploration, encouraging individuals to cultivate a deeper connection with their inner selves and the broader world. Both

Perls and Emerson advocated for introspection and the pursuit of spiritual and intellectual self-discovery.

Moreover, Perls's focus on the integration of mind and body aligns with the principles of the New Thought and positive thinking movements, emphasizing the power of the mind in fostering personal transformation and well-being. Perls, like advocates of positive thinking, encouraged individuals to cultivate a positive mindset and to take charge of their experiences, emphasizing the importance of self-empowerment and the realization of one's potential.

In essence, Perls's approach to self-exploration and personal growth converges with the core tenets of various philosophical traditions and self-help movements, reflecting a shared emphasis on self-awareness, personal responsibility, and the pursuit of holistic well-being.

What Is It Like to Experience a Jungian or Gestalt Therapy Session?

Jungian therapy, based on Carl Jung's analytical psychology, is a depth-oriented approach that emphasizes the exploration of the unconscious, archetypes, and the individuation process. In a Jungian therapy session, the therapist often works with the client to uncover and analyze unconscious elements, such as dreams, fantasies, and symbolic imagery, to gain insights into the client's psychological challenges and personal development. The therapist may encourage the client to explore personal symbols and archetypes, enabling a deeper understanding of the client's psyche and facilitating the integration of unconscious aspects into conscious awareness. Jungian therapy often involves a holistic exploration of the client's life, focusing on the client's spiritual, creative, and existential dimensions in addition to their psychological well-being.

Gestalt therapy, developed by Fritz and Laura Perls, is an experiential and humanistic approach to psychotherapy that emphasizes present-moment awareness, personal responsibility, and the integration of mind and body. In a Gestalt therapy session, the therapist encourages the client to engage directly with their immediate experiences and emotions, fostering self-awareness and promoting personal growth. The therapist may guide the client through exercises and experiments that highlight the importance of authentic dialogue and the exploration of unresolved emotional conflicts. Gestalt therapy often emphasizes the therapeutic relationship between the client and the therapist, emphasizing mutual trust, empathy, and authentic communication as essential components of the therapeutic process. The focus is on promoting self-discovery, self-acceptance, and personal empowerment within the context of the client's immediate experiences and emotional challenges.

Professional Training Requirements

The training requirements to practice Jungian or Gestalt therapy can vary depending on the specific certification and licensing regulations in different regions. Generally, becoming a certified Jungian or Gestalt therapist involves completing a comprehensive training program that encompasses theoretical study, practical application, and supervised clinical experience.

For Jungian therapy, aspiring therapists often pursue graduate-level education in psychology, counseling, or a related field. Specialized training in Jungian psychology typically involves completing postgraduate programs, workshops, and seminars focusing on Jungian theory, analytical psychology, dream analysis, and the interpretation of symbols and archetypes. Additionally, aspiring Jungian therapists usually engage in supervised clinical practice and participate in Jungian analysis themselves as part of their training.

In the case of Gestalt therapy, individuals interested in becoming Gestalt therapists typically pursue graduate education in psychology, counseling, or psychotherapy. They then undertake specialized training in Gestalt therapy, which may include participation in accredited Gestalt therapy training programs, workshops, and experiential learning opportunities. Training in Gestalt therapy emphasizes practical skill development, personal experiential work, and supervised clinical practice to develop competencies in facilitating therapeutic processes, promoting self-awareness, and fostering personal growth and integration.

The duration of training for both Jungian and Gestalt therapy can vary, but it often involves several years of dedicated study, practical experience, and supervised practice to ensure that therapists acquire the necessary knowledge, skills, and ethical understanding to effectively practice within these therapeutic approaches.

The training duration for Jungian and Gestalt therapists before establishing private practice can vary, but a rough estimate would typically involve several years of educational and experiential requirements. For Jungian therapy, the process can take approximately 8 to 12 years, which includes completion of a bachelor's degree (4 years), a master's degree (2-3 years), and specialized training in Jungian analysis (2-5 years) along with supervised practice.

On the other hand, the training process for Gestalt therapy usually ranges from 6 to 8 years, involving completion of a bachelor's degree (4 years), a master's degree (2-3 years), and specialized training in Gestalt therapy (2-3 years) along with supervised practical experience.

It's important to note that these estimations are general guidelines and the specific requirements can vary depending on the educational programs, certifications, and licensing regulations in different regions. Therapists often engage in ongoing professional development and continuing education to stay updated with the latest research and developments in the field.

[Author's note: Compare to the formal training requirements for American 'Gurus" in the 70s]

Income

The salary range for Jungian and Gestalt therapists can vary based on factors such as location, level of experience, private practice versus employment in a clinical setting, and the local demand for these specialized therapies. In general, the expected salary for these therapists falls within the range of $40,000 to $70,000 per year.

For therapists in private practice, the salary can be influenced by the number of clients, session rates, and the local market for psychological services. Those employed in clinical settings, such as hospitals or mental health clinics, might receive a salary within the range mentioned above, depending on their level of experience and the organization's budget.

It's important to consider that while the salary range provides a general idea, the actual compensation can differ significantly based on individual circumstances, including the therapist's clientele, reputation, and the cost of living in the specific geographic area. Additionally, therapists may also earn income from other activities, such as conducting workshops, training programs, or writing and publishing books or articles related to their field of expertise.

Suggested Reading

Jungian Therapy:

1. Carl Jung:
- "The Archetypes and the Collective Unconscious" (1959)
- "Psychological Types" (1921)
- "Memories, Dreams, Reflections" (1961)
- "Man and His Symbols" (1964)

2. Marie-Louise von Franz:
- "Projection and Recollection in Jungian Psychology: Reflections of the Soul" (1980)
- "The Interpretation of Fairy Tales" (1970)

3. James Hillman:
- "The Soul's Code: In Search of Character and Calling" (1996)
- "Re-Visioning Psychology" (1975)

Gestalt Therapy:

1. Fritz Perls:
- "Gestalt Therapy: Excitement and Growth in the Human Personality" (1951)
- "Gestalt Therapy Verbatim" (1969)

2. Laura Perls:
- "Gestalt Therapy: Practice and Theory" (1973)

General Reading:

1. Michael Fordham:
- "Introduction to Jungian Psychotherapy: The Therapeutic Relationship" (1978)

2. Erving Polster:
- "Gestalt Therapy Integrated: Contours of Theory and Practice" (2013)

These texts provide essential insights into the foundational concepts and practices of Jungian and Gestalt therapies, offering readers a comprehensive understanding of the theories and applications within these therapeutic modalities. They serve as valuable resources for those interested in delving deeper into the principles and techniques of Jungian and Gestalt psychotherapy.

Dr. Spock's Influence: A Critical Examination

Dr. Benjamin Spock, a prominent figure in the field of pediatrics, left an indelible mark on the landscape of modern parenting with the publication of his seminal work, "The Common Sense Book of Baby and Child Care" in 1946. Spock's revolutionary approach challenged the prevailing authoritarian parenting norms of the time, advocating for a more permissive and nurturing style that emphasized the importance of emotional support and understanding in child-rearing. Through his book, he introduced the idea of a child-centered approach that focused on fostering self-esteem and emotional well-being, which resonated deeply with the burgeoning cultural shift towards individualism and self-exploration that marked the 1970s self-help movement.

In the wake of Spock's influential work, a noticeable transformation took place in the parenting landscape, with a growing emphasis on empathy, communication, and understanding within the parent-child dynamic. The principles he espoused, emphasizing the significance of emotional nurturing and support in a child's development, aligned closely with the ideals of personal growth and self-awareness that were gaining momentum during the self-help movement of the 1970s. Parents, inspired by Spock's ideas, sought to create an environment that fostered not only physical well-being but also emotional resilience and psychological development in their children.

Despite some criticisms that his permissive parenting approach might lead to overindulgence and a lack of discipline, Spock's ideas remained instrumental in reshaping the cultural narrative around child-rearing and family dynamics. His work contributed to a broader societal shift towards prioritizing emotional well-being, self-expression, and personal fulfillment, elements that were central to the ethos of the self-help movement. By promoting an empathetic and nurturing parenting style, Dr. Spock inadvertently became a catalyst for a cultural shift that placed greater value on emotional intelligence and self-awareness, ultimately influencing the trajectory of the self-help movement in the 1970s and beyond.

Here are five books that offer critical perspectives on Dr. Benjamin Spock's methods and beliefs in child-rearing and parenting:

1. "The Over-Scheduled Child: Avoiding the Hyper-Parenting Trap" by Alvin Rosenfeld and Nicole Wise - This book challenges the permissive parenting style promoted by Dr. Spock, arguing that excessive leniency can lead to the over-scheduling and undue pressure on children.

2. "The Collapse of Parenting: How We Hurt Our Kids When We Treat Them Like Grown-Ups" by Leonard Sax - Leonard Sax offers a critical analysis of modern parenting influenced by Spock's permissive philosophy, highlighting the potential consequences of failing to establish firm boundaries and parental authority.

3. "The Nurture Assumption: Why Children Turn Out the Way They Do" by Judith Rich Harris - Judith Rich Harris criticizes the emphasis on parental nurture, which was a core tenet of Dr. Spock's approach, proposing that external factors and peer influence have a more significant impact on child development.

4. "Parenting Inc.: How the Billion-Dollar Baby Business Has Changed the Way We Raise Our Children" by Pamela Paul

- Pamela Paul explores the commercialization of parenting and the influence of parenting advice, including Spock's, on the consumer-driven culture, raising concerns about the commodification of child-rearing.

5. "The Case Against Adolescence: Rediscovering the Adult in Every Teen" by Robert Epstein

- Robert Epstein challenges the notion that teenagers require special treatment, arguing that Spock's approach, emphasizing the need for constant support and accommodation, may contribute to the prolongation of adolescence and hinder the development of independence and responsibility in youth.

These critical works engage with Dr. Spock's parenting philosophy, addressing various concerns and questioning the long-term implications of his influential ideas on child development and family dynamics.

Here are five books that propose more structured approaches to child-rearing, offering alternatives to the permissive style advocated by Dr. Benjamin Spock:

1. "Bringing Up Bébé: One American Mother Discovers the Wisdom of French Parenting" by Pamela Druckerman - Pamela
Druckerman's book examines the contrasting parenting styles between American and French cultures, emphasizing the benefits of a more structured and disciplined approach to raising children.

2. "The Whole-Brain Child: 12 Revolutionary Strategies to Nurture Your Child's Developing Mind" by Daniel J. Siegel and Tina Payne Bryson - Siegel and Bryson present a framework for
nurturing a child's emotional and cognitive development through structured, scientifically informed strategies that integrate the latest findings in neurobiology and psychology.

3. "How to Raise an Adult: Break Free of the Overparenting Trap and Prepare Your Kid for Success" by Julie Lythcott-Haims -
Julie Lythcott-Haims critiques the overprotective parenting style

influenced by Spock, advocating for a more hands-off approach that fosters independence and resilience in children.

4. "The Montessori Toddler: A Parent's Guide to Raising a Curious and Responsible Human Being" by Simone Davies - Simone Davies introduces the Montessori method as a structured approach to child-rearing, focusing on fostering independence, self-discipline, and a sense of responsibility in toddlers.

5. "Simplicity Parenting: Using the Extraordinary Power of Less to Raise Calmer, Happier, and More Secure Kids" by Kim John Payne and Lisa M. Ross - Kim John Payne and Lisa M. Ross emphasize the benefits of a simplified and structured environment for children, proposing strategies to reduce overstimulation and create a more balanced and structured family life.

These books provide alternative perspectives to Dr. Spock's child-rearing philosophy, promoting more structured and disciplined approaches to parenting that prioritize independence, cognitive development, and emotional resilience in children.

Healing the Wounded Self: Eric Berne's 'Games People Play'

Eric Berne was a Canadian-born psychiatrist and psychoanalyst best known for his development of transactional analysis (TA), a widely recognized and influential psychological theory. His seminal work, "Games People Play," published in 1964, introduced the concept of social interactions as "games," each with its own set of rules and psychological payoffs.

In "Games People Play," Berne presented a comprehensive analysis of human behavior, outlining various patterns of communication and interaction that occur in everyday life. He identified common behavioral strategies that individuals employ to achieve certain psychological needs, emphasizing the underlying psychological dynamics at play during social exchanges. Berne's work shed light on the subconscious motivations and interpersonal dynamics that shape human relationships, offering readers a deeper understanding of the complexities of social interactions and personal communication.

The impact of "Games People Play" on the self-help revolution of the 1970s was profound. Berne's accessible and engaging writing style, coupled with his insightful analysis of human behavior, resonated with a broad audience, leading to widespread interest in his transactional analysis approach. The book provided readers with a practical framework for interpreting their own social interactions, empowering them to recognize and analyze the psychological dynamics within their relationships.

Furthermore, "Games People Play" fostered a greater awareness of the underlying psychological factors at play in everyday communication, encouraging individuals to reevaluate their interpersonal strategies and work towards healthier and more authentic forms of interaction. It contributed to the broader cultural movement of self-exploration and personal development that characterized the 1970s, encouraging individuals to take a more active role in understanding and improving their social and emotional well-being.

Berne's groundbreaking insights and the accessible nature of his work played a significant role in popularizing the notion of self-awareness and interpersonal communication within the self-help movement, helping individuals navigate their relationships more effectively and fostering a culture of introspection and personal growth.

Key Tools:
Berne offered readers various tools and concepts to better understand their own behavior and that of others. Transactional analysis, a fundamental component of his work, involved analyzing social transactions to identify the different ego states involved, such as the parent, adult, and child states. He introduced the concept of "games," which represent recurring patterns of behavior that people engage in to achieve certain psychological payoffs.

Comparison with Other Figures:
Unlike Freud, Berne's approach was more focused on the here and now, emphasizing the analysis of present social transactions rather than delving deeply into past experiences. Similarly, Berne's work differed from Jung's exploration of the collective unconscious, as he emphasized the surface-level interactions between individuals.

In contrast to B.F. Skinner's behaviorism, which focused on the role of environmental stimuli in shaping behavior, Berne emphasized the role of individual psychological needs and the dynamics of interpersonal communication. Unlike Dr. Spock's permissive parenting approach, Berne's work focused on analyzing and understanding the underlying psychological motivations behind social interactions.

Berne's work aligns with Benjamin Franklin's emphasis on self-improvement and introspection, as both emphasized the importance of self-awareness and personal growth. Similarly, Berne's insights into human behavior can be likened to Aristotle's exploration of human relationships and the motivations behind social interactions.

Furthermore, Berne's focus on understanding the complexities of human communication shares similarities with Ralph Waldo Emerson's exploration of the individual's role in society and the importance of authentic self-expression.

In summary, Berne's contributions to the field of psychology and his emphasis on the analysis of social transactions and human communication distinguish his work from that of other prominent figures, highlighting the significance of understanding the psychological dynamics at play in everyday interactions.

Suggested Reading

- **Transactional Analysis in Psychotherapy**: Published by Grove Press in 1961.

- **The Structure and Dynamics of Organizations and Groups**: Published by Grove Press in 1963.

- **A Layman's Guide to Psychiatry and Psychoanalysis**: Published by Grove Press in 1957.

- **What Do You Say After You Say Hello?**: Published by Bantam Books in 1972.

Key works that analyze and criticize Eric Berne's thoughts and practice:

- **TA Today by Ian Stewart and Vann Joines**: Published by Lifespace Publishing in 1987.

- **Critique of Eric Berne's Transactional Analysis by Seymour B. Shapiro**: Published in the Journal of Counseling Psychology in 1971.

- **Theoretical Diversity: A Debate about Transactional Analysis and Psychoanalysis by Charlotte Steiner and Marco Novellino**: Published in the Transactional Analysis Journal in 2015.

Please note that publication dates and publishers may vary depending on the edition or reprint of the book.

'We've Had a Hundred Years of Psychotherapy-- And the World's Getting Worse': James Hillman, a Jungian Critic

James Hillman (1926-2011) was an American psychologist and the founder of archetypal psychology. He studied at the C.G. Jung Institute in Zurich and guided studies there as well. Hillman's pioneering imaginative psychology spans five decades and has entered cultural history, affecting lives and minds in a wide range of fields.

"We've Had a Hundred Years of Psychotherapy--And the World's Getting Worse" is a book by James Hillman and Michael Ventura that was published in 1992. The book is structured in three parts: the first part is a dialogue between Hillman and Ventura, the second part consists of lengthier essays written by the two authors to each other, and the third part returns to the dialogue format of the first. The book is a critique of psychotherapy, arguing that it is inadequate to deal with modern anxieties and neuroses. Hillman and Ventura suggest that most human problems are actually caused by the influence of an unhealthy society around us, and that psychotherapy, as it is currently conceived, is not equipped to deal with these issues. The book has been described as a "furious, trenchant, and audacious" critique of psychotherapy and its limitations.

Some of Hillman's influential works include:

'Loose Ends: Primary Papers in Archetypal Psychology': This book is Hillman's main analysis of analysis. He asks the basic question, "What does the soul want?" With insight and humor, he answers, "It wants fictions that heal." It was published by Spring Publications in 1975.

'Insearch: Psychology and Religion': With this book, Hillman initiated the "soul movement" in psychotherapy more than fifty years ago. Soul and suicide are dominant issues of this new millennium; soul because it cannot be reduced to genes and chromosomes; suicide because it raises fundamental religious, political, and legal conflicts. It was published by Spring Publications in 1994.

'The Soul's Code': In Search of Character and Calling: This book explores the idea that each of us is born with a unique "soul code" that shapes our destiny. It was published by Random House in 1996 and became an international bestseller.

'Re-Visioning Psychology': This book is the second volume of "The Life and Ideas of James Hillman" and was published by Spring Journal Books in 2019. It explores Hillman's ideas on the nature of psychology and the role of the therapist.

'A Blue Fire': This book is a collection of Hillman's writings and interviews and was published by HarperCollins in 1989.

Hillman's cultural explorations resulted in six provocative books between 1991 and 2004, including "The Soul's Code" that became an international bestseller[6]. Hillman's ideas have had a significant impact on the field of psychology and continue to be studied and debated by scholars and practitioners today.

Corresponding Text: 'The Image'

"The Image" is a book by Marc Bornstein that was published in 1979. It explores the development of psychological images from infancy to adulthood and argues that these images are shaped by cultural and social factors. The book suggests that many of the problems that people experience are caused by the influence of an unhealthy society around us, and that psychotherapy, as it is currently conceived, is not equipped to deal with these issues.

This idea is similar to the views of James Hillman, who argued that psychotherapy is limited by its focus on the individual and its failure to address wider social and cultural issues. Hillman and other authors suggest that a more holistic approach is needed that takes into account the social and cultural factors that contribute to mental health problems, since we be asking the wrong questions from the start, and using the wrong tools to seek happiness, tools that are inappropriate, inadequate and useless to help use see past the shadows on the wall that we think are our realities, shadows that are nothing but imagery and feelings that are easily manipulated. But, that smacks of Plato, not Aristotle. Maybe we should look at the health and wellness industry in the 70s as a more rooted and responsive self-help methodology.

The Wrong Obsessions

"Positive Addiction" is a concept introduced by William Glasser, an American psychiatrist. In his book "Positive Addiction," Glasser discusses the idea that certain healthy activities can become pos-

itive addictions, serving as a way to improve mental well-being and overall happiness. This concept contrasts with negative addictions, which can be harmful and detrimental to one's physical and mental health.

Glasser suggests that positive addictions are activities that individuals engage in for at least one hour per day, which provide a sense of purpose and contribute positively to their lives. These activities typically involve a focus on personal growth, mental well-being, and physical health. Examples of positive addictions can include activities such as exercise, meditation, reading, or even engaging in creative pursuits.

According to Glasser, these positive addictions serve as healthy coping mechanisms and can contribute to a sense of fulfillment and satisfaction in life. He emphasizes that these activities should be non-competitive, enjoyable, and sustainable. Additionally, Glasser notes that positive addictions can help individuals manage stress, improve their overall well-being, and maintain a healthy work-life balance.

While Glasser's concept of positive addiction has garnered some attention and support, it has also faced criticism and debate. Some experts argue that the term "positive addiction" might be misleading, as addiction is commonly associated with negative connotations. Critics suggest that the term may downplay the complexity of addictive behaviors and their potential to become problematic.

Overall, Glasser's concept of positive addiction encourages individuals to cultivate healthy habits and engage in activities that promote personal well-being, self-improvement, and a sense of purpose in life. It underscores the importance of maintaining a balance between various aspects of life and finding fulfillment through constructive and beneficial activities.

About what?

A lot of interests can provide depth and variety and connection to the world. Make the world more interesting.

People can become obsessed with fictional worlds, games, sports team histories, or hobbies like trainspotting for various reasons, including psychological, emotional, and social factors. Here are some explanations for these obsessions:

1. Escapism: Fictional worlds and games offer an escape from the stresses and demands of real life. Engaging with these alternative realities allows individuals to temporarily detach from their daily challenges and immerse themselves in a different, often more exciting or adventurous, context.

2. Sense of Control: In fictional worlds and games, individuals often have a sense of control over outcomes and narratives. This control can provide a sense of empowerment, especially for those who might feel powerless in their real lives.

3. Emotional Fulfillment: Fictional worlds and stories often evoke strong emotions and offer meaningful narratives that resonate with people on a deep emotional level. Immersive storytelling can provide a sense of connection, empathy, and emotional catharsis for individuals.

4. Social Connection: Engaging with fictional worlds, playing games, or participating in niche hobbies can foster a sense of belonging and community. People often connect with others who share similar interests, leading to the formation of friendships and social bonds based on mutual passions.

5. Intellectual Stimulation: In-depth knowledge about specific topics, such as sports team histories or trainspotting, can provide intellectual stimulation and a sense of achievement. Individuals may enjoy the challenge of mastering complex information or developing specialized expertise in a particular area.

6. Nostalgia: Engaging with familiar fictional worlds, revisiting beloved games, or delving into the history of sports teams can evoke feelings of nostalgia and comfort. People may be drawn to these activities as a way to reconnect with fond memories and experiences from their past.

7. Sense of Purpose: In the pursuit of mastering intricate details or histories, individuals may find a sense of purpose and meaning. Engaging with these activities can provide a structured framework for personal growth, learning, and self-improvement.

Overall, these obsessions often serve as outlets for personal expression, fulfillment, and connection, offering individuals opportunities to explore their passions, creativity, and intellectual curiosity. However, it's essential for individuals to maintain a healthy balance between their interests and other aspects of their lives to ensure overall well-being and fulfillment.

The Dark Side

The Dark Side to this is that there are some activities that have no objective benefit and often have negative outcomes. And, these systems are being sold to people every day of the week. That is especially true when looking at the some of the offerings and avenues to happiness explored in this book. For instance:

Obsession with Freudian analysis, or an excessive preoccupation with Freudian theories and concepts, can manifest in various ways and may affect individuals' daily lives and relationships. Here are some examples:

1. Compulsive interpretation of everyday events and conversations through a Freudian lens, leading to strained or misinterpreted interpersonal relationships.

2. Excessive fixation on Freudian psychosexual stages and concepts, sometimes leading to the inability to relate to others outside of this framework.

3. Unhealthy obsession with unresolved childhood issues, leading to an inability to move past traumas or conflicts.

4. Overemphasis on Freudian dream analysis, potentially leading to misinterpretation of dreams and obsessive attempts to uncover hidden meanings.

232

5. Compulsive exploration of Freudian defense mechanisms, sometimes resulting in an inability to acknowledge or address personal issues or conflicts directly.

6. Fixation on Freud's theories of the unconscious mind, potentially leading to a tendency to attribute all behaviors to subconscious desires or motives.

7. Unhealthy preoccupation with Freudian psychoanalysis in personal relationships, leading to difficulties in communication and an overemphasis on hidden motives or desires.

8. Excessive focus on Freudian concepts in one's own self-analysis, often leading to self-doubt and a negative self-perception.

9. Compulsive application of Freudian theories to contemporary issues and societal phenomena, sometimes leading to the oversimplification or misinterpretation of complex cultural or psychological dynamics.

10. Unhealthy obsession with Freudian psychotherapy techniques, potentially leading to an inability to recognize or accept alternative therapeutic approaches or methodologies.

Backing Out of the Madness. Getting Off of the Couch.

Aristotle, Benjamin Franklin, Ralph Waldo Emerson, Stewart Brand, and Buckminster Fuller had different perspectives and philosophies, but they all emphasized the importance of personal development, self-improvement, and the pursuit of virtuous and meaningful activities. Each would likely have specific criteria and guidance to help individuals discern whether an activity is positive, purposeful, and beneficial:

1. Aristotle:
- According to Aristotle, a positive activity would be one that cultivates virtues and leads to *eudaimonia* (human flourishing).

- He would encourage individuals to evaluate whether the activity promotes the development of virtues such as courage, temperance, wisdom, and justice.

- Aristotle would emphasize the importance of moderation, suggesting that the activity should not be pursued excessively or at the expense of other important aspects of life.

2. Benjamin Franklin:
- Franklin would likely recommend activities that contribute to personal and societal improvement, aligning with his emphasis on self-discipline and self-improvement.

- He would suggest evaluating the activity's contribution to personal character development and its potential to benefit the community or society at large.

- Franklin would advocate for activities that foster learning, self-reflection, and the cultivation of positive habits and virtues.

3. Ralph Waldo Emerson:
Emerson would advocate for activities that foster self-reliance, individualism, and the exploration of one's inner self.

He would encourage individuals to assess whether the activity aligns with their authentic selves and contributes to their personal growth and spiritual well-being.

Emerson would emphasize the importance of creativity, intuition, and the pursuit of personal truths and values.

4. Stewart Brand:
Brand might recommend activities that promote environmental sustainability, technological innovation, and the betterment of human civilization.

He would likely encourage individuals to consider whether the activity contributes to the advancement of technology, science, or social and ecological sustainability.

Brand would emphasize the importance of long-term thinking and the potential impact of the activity on future generations and the planet.

5. Buckminster Fuller:
Fuller would likely endorse activities that foster holistic thinking, systemic solutions, and the advancement of global welfare.

He would encourage individuals to assess whether the activity aligns with the principles of comprehensive design and the pursuit of sustainable solutions for humanity's complex challenges.

Fuller would emphasize the importance of synergy, integrity, and the pursuit of solutions that benefit both individuals and the larger global community.

Considering these guidelines, individuals can evaluate whether their chosen activities align with principles of personal growth, societal well-being, and the advancement of knowledge and virtue, ultimately leading to a positive and purposeful life.

Scientology's Last Word on the Subject

Perhaps in another book on the New Age in the 70s, I will do a deep dive into Scientology, especially from the point-of-view of the infamous and apocryphal quote, The quote "If you want to get rich, invent a religion" attributed to L. Ron Hubbard, the founder of the Church of Scientology.

For now, let's look at Scientology's critique of the mental health industry. From one Guru to all of the Others.

Scientology has been critical of psychiatry and psychology, viewing them as fundamentally flawed and harmful. According to Scientology beliefs, psychiatric practices and psychological treatments are considered to be detrimental and are often referred to as forms of abuse. The Church of Scientology, founded by L. Ron Hubbard, promotes the idea that the human mind is a spiritual entity that is influenced by negative experiences, known as engrams, which can be addressed through their religious practices rather than conventional psychiatric or psychological methods. Some key aspects of Scientology's perspective on psychiatry and psychology include:

1. Rejection of Psychiatry: Scientology generally opposes the use of psychiatric medication and treatments, viewing them as potentially harmful and as suppressing the mind's natural potential. The organization has been critical of psychiatric medications, labeling them as chemical restraints that inhibit spiritual growth and development.

2. Distrust of Psychology: Similarly, Scientology is skeptical of mainstream psychology, considering it to be non-spiritual and limited in its understanding of the human mind. The Church of Scientology promotes their own counseling and spiritual practices, such as "auditing," which they believe can alleviate mental and spiritual distress more effectively than traditional psychological therapies.

3. Emphasis on Spiritual Healing: Instead of relying on psychiatric or psychological interventions, Scientology emphasizes spiritual healing and personal development through their religious practices, which include counseling sessions, courses, and the study of L. Ron Hubbard's teachings.

4. Criticism of the Mental Health Industry: Scientology has been known to publicly criticize the mental health industry, often referring to it as a form of pseudoscience that is driven by profit and lacks genuine concern for individual well-being.

It's important to note that the views of Scientology on psychiatry and psychology have been a subject of controversy and criticism from the medical and scientific communities, with many mental health professionals and experts expressing concerns about the potential risks associated with rejecting evidence-based treatments and interventions in favor of alternative, unverified practices.

And, it is important to say I am not suggesting you run out grab an E-Meter, get audited and run to sign up for a Purification Rundown session. I am saying there are opposing opinions, and that the sometimes the paths that other people tell you you should go down are just avenues for them to make money while you twist in the wind dreaming about how many angels fit on the head of a pin, or which end of a soft-boiled egg to break.

Sometimes, it is best to go outside and get some sunlight and fresh air.

Part V: Wellness in the 70s

The 1970s marked a pivotal era in the evolution of wellness, witnessing a transformative shift in societal attitudes toward health and well-being. This dynamic decade saw the emergence of a burgeoning wellness movement, characterized by an increased focus on holistic health practices, alternative therapies, and the popularization of Eastern spiritual traditions. From the rise of health food movements to the proliferation of yoga studios, the 1970s encapsulated a period of profound cultural exploration and redefinition of wellness.

The wellness boom of the 1970s was deeply intertwined with the broader social and cultural changes that defined the era. As the counterculture movement of the 1960s gave way to a renewed emphasis on personal well-being and spiritual growth, individuals began to seek alternative approaches to health that aligned with their evolving values and lifestyles. This cultural backdrop set the stage for the widespread adoption of diverse wellness practices that transcended traditional medical paradigms and emphasized a more holistic understanding of health.

One of the defining features of the 1970s wellness boom was the surge in popularity of health food movements. Driven by a growing awareness of the link between diet and well-being, the era witnessed a notable increase in the consumption of organic, whole foods and the establishment of health food stores and cooperatives. The promotion of vegetarian and plant-based diets gained momentum, reflecting a broader cultural shift toward a more conscious and sustainable approach to nutrition and food consumption.

Concurrent with the rise of health food movements, the 1970s also witnessed a widespread embrace of Eastern spiritual practices and philosophies that profoundly influenced the wellness landscape. The proliferation of yoga studios across the United States exemplified the growing fascination with Eastern traditions and their integration into Western wellness culture. The practice of yoga, with its emphasis on physical postures, breathwork, and meditation, offered practitioners a comprehensive approach to fostering physical, mental, and spiritual well-being, aligning with the era's emphasis on holistic health and self-discovery.

Furthermore, the 1970s saw the popularization of alternative therapies and healing modalities that challenged conventional medical practices. From acupuncture and acupressure to aromatherapy and herbal medicine, individuals increasingly turned to non-traditional methods of healing and wellness promotion. These alternative therapies, often rooted in ancient healing traditions from various cultures, offered practitioners a nuanced understanding of health and well-being, emphasizing the interconnectedness of the mind, body, and spirit in the pursuit of optimal health.

The wellness boom of the 1970s was not confined to individual lifestyle choices but also encompassed broader cultural shifts that redefined societal perceptions of health and well-being. The era witnessed a growing recognition of the interconnectedness between personal wellness, environmental sustainability, and social consciousness. This holistic approach to wellness reflected a broader cultural ethos that emphasized the importance of fostering balance and harmony within oneself and with the world at large.

In tandem with the cultural movements and shifts in wellness practices, influential figures and thought leaders played a significant role in shaping the narrative of the 1970s wellness boom. Prominent advocates such as Dr. Andrew Weil, a pioneer in integrative medicine, and wellness icon Richard Hittleman, who popularized yoga through television programs, contributed to the mainstream acceptance of holistic health practices and alternative therapies. Their efforts helped bridge the gap between traditional medical approaches and emerging wellness modalities, fostering a more integrated and inclusive approach to health and well-being.

The legacy of the 1970s wellness boom continues to resonate in contemporary wellness culture, underscoring the enduring impact of the era's cultural exploration and redefinition of holistic health. The emphasis on organic, plant-based diets, the widespread practice of yoga, and the growing acceptance of alternative healing modalities have become integral components of modern wellness movements. As individuals increasingly prioritize self-care, mindfulness, and sustainability, the lessons and legacies of the 1970s wellness boom remain pertinent, serving as a reminder of the profound connections between personal well-being, societal consciousness, and the natural world.

It seemed like there was a significant portion of the population that did get off of the couch, out of their own heads, and started to move around long enough to create a new and lasting part of American culture.

Beyond the Waves: Esalen and the Evolution of Human Consciousness

Esalen, a renowned retreat center in Big Sur, California, has played a significant role in the evolution of human consciousness since its establishment in 1962. Known for its unconventional and transformative approach to personal growth and spiritual exploration, Esalen has served as a focal point for the convergence of diverse philosophical, psychological, and spiritual traditions. Its unique position as a haven for introspection, self-discovery, and intellectual inquiry has contributed to the expansion of human consciousness in several key ways.

First and foremost, Esalen has fostered a multidisciplinary approach to the exploration of human consciousness, bringing together scholars, spiritual leaders, and thought pioneers from various fields to engage in dialogue and collaborative inquiry. By facilitating cross-disciplinary exchanges and encouraging the integration of Eastern and Western philosophical traditions, Esalen has served as a crucible for the synthesis of diverse perspectives on the nature of consciousness, self-awareness, and personal transformation.

Furthermore, Esalen has been instrumental in popularizing and mainstreaming a range of holistic practices and healing modalities that have contributed to the expansion of human consciousness. Through its workshops, seminars, and immersive programs, Esalen has introduced countless individuals to transformative practices such as meditation, yoga, breathwork, and psychotherapy, fostering a deeper understanding of the interconnectedness between mind, body, and spirit. Its emphasis on experiential learning and direct personal engagement has empowered participants to embark on profound journeys of self-discovery and inner exploration, leading to heightened self-awareness and expanded states of consciousness.

Esalen's commitment to fostering a culture of open-mindedness, inclusivity, and intellectual curiosity has also contributed to the democratization of knowledge and the dissemination of alternative perspectives on human consciousness. By providing a platform for marginalized voices, unconventional thinkers, and visionary leaders, Esalen has challenged mainstream paradigms and encouraged the exploration of unconventional ideas and philosophies. Its commitment to intellectual freedom and the celebration of diverse viewpoints has nurtured an environment of intellectual vibrancy and creative expression, fostering the evolution of human consciousness through the cultivation of critical thinking and open dialogue.

Moreover, Esalen has served as a catalyst for the integration of spirituality and psychology, facilitating a deeper understanding of the intersection between personal growth, emotional well-being, and spiritual development. By hosting pioneering psychologists, spiritual leaders, and wellness practitioners, Esalen has facilitated the development of an integrated approach to holistic healing and personal transformation, emphasizing the importance of addressing psychological, emotional, and spiritual dimensions of human experience. Its comprehensive and inclusive approach to wellness has contributed to the destigmatization of mental health issues and the promotion of a more holistic understanding of human consciousness and well-being.

In conclusion, Esalen's enduring legacy as a center for personal growth and the exploration of human consciousness has left an indelible mark on the evolution of human thought and self-awareness. Through its commitment to interdisciplinary collaboration, holistic practices, intellectual openness, and the integration of spirituality and psychology, Esalen has inspired countless individuals to embark on transformative journeys of self-discovery, contributing to the ongoing expansion of human consciousness and the cultivation of a more integrated and enlightened global community.

Esalen-like Class List

Esalen in the 1970s was known for offering a wide range of workshops and programs that reflected the diverse interests and philosophical movements of the era. Some of the themes and topics that were likely covered during this period include:

1. Humanistic Psychology and Self-Exploration
2. Eastern Philosophies and Spiritual Traditions
3. Yoga, Meditation, and Mindfulness Practices
4. Alternative Healing Modalities and Holistic Wellness
5. Personal Growth and Self-Discovery
6. Environmental Consciousness and Sustainability
7. Creative Expression and Artistic Exploration
8. Feminist and Gender Studies
9. Social and Political Activism
10. Indigenous Wisdom and Shamanic Practices

Esalen's class offerings during the 1970s often reflected the cultural and philosophical trends of the time, emphasizing personal growth, spiritual exploration, and the integration of diverse perspectives on holistic well-being and societal change. The center served as a hub for intellectual exchange, experiential learning, and the cultivation of a more holistic understanding of human consciousness and well-being.

Drilling down, a class on "Indigenous Wisdom and Shamanic Practices" at Esalen might offer a comprehensive exploration of traditional indigenous knowledge systems, spiritual practices, and healing modalities from various cultural and geographical contexts. The class could be designed to provide participants with a deeper understanding of the spiritual traditions and worldviews of indigenous communities, emphasizing the interconnectedness between humans, nature, and the spiritual realm. Here's what such a class might encompass:

1. Cultural Immersion and Contextual Understanding: The class may begin with an overview of different indigenous cultures and their unique spiritual traditions, emphasizing the importance of cultural context in the practice of shamanism and indigenous wisdom. Participants might learn about the historical, social, and environmental factors that have shaped indigenous belief systems and practices.

2. Shamanic Healing Practices and Rituals: The class would likely delve into various shamanic healing practices, such as energy work, plant medicine ceremonies, and spirit communication. Participants might have the opportunity to learn about traditional healing rituals, including drumming, chanting, and trance states, and their significance in promoting physical, emotional, and spiritual well-being.

3. Connection to Nature and Ecological Awareness: Indigenous wisdom often emphasizes the interconnectedness between humans and the natural world. The class may highlight the importance of environmental stewardship and sustainable living practices, drawing inspiration from indigenous perspectives on nature conservation, ecological balance, and the preservation of sacred lands.

4. Ceremonial Practices and Rites of Passage: Participants may engage in experiential learning through the practice of indigenous ceremonial rituals and rites of passage, which could include vision quests, sweat lodge ceremonies, and purification rituals. These practices aim to facilitate personal transformation, spiritual growth, and the cultivation of a deeper connection to the natural and spiritual realms.

5. Cultural Exchange and Community Engagement: The class may incorporate opportunities for participants to engage with indigenous communities and elders, fostering cross-cultural dialogue and mutual learning. Cultural exchange programs and community visits could provide firsthand experiences of indigenous traditions, values, and ways of life, promoting cultural understanding and appreciation.

6. Ethical Considerations and Cultural Sensitivity: Given the sensitive nature of indigenous knowledge and practices, the class would likely emphasize the importance of ethical engagement, cultural sensitivity, and respect for indigenous cultures. Participants may explore the challenges and implications of cultural appropriation and discuss strategies for promoting cultural preservation and empowerment within indigenous communities.

Overall, the class on "Indigenous Wisdom and Shamanic Practices" at Esalen would offer participants a unique opportunity to immerse themselves in the rich tapestry of indigenous spiritual traditions, fostering a deeper appreciation for the interconnectedness of all life and the timeless wisdom that indigenous cultures continue to offer to the world.

Taking the Imaginative Next Step to Better Offering: The Lodge Builder's Immersive

For me, this is where it becomes interesting. What happens when all of the theory and introspection and fantasy and drug-outs and head trips and power-trips and the indoor counting of psychic dust-mites just stops and we take some of the left-overs and do something of lasting value with them. What if we expanded the Indigenous Wisdom class into a building practicum.

A week-long course on "Building a Historically Accurate Indigenous Log Lodge for a Living Museum" would provide participants with hands-on experience and theoretical knowledge about the construction techniques, cultural significance, and historical context of traditional indigenous log lodges. The course would likely be structured to offer a comprehensive and immersive learning experience, combining practical skills training with cultural education and historical research.

Here's a general outline of what the course might include:

Day 1-2: Cultural Context and Historical Research
- Introduction to Indigenous Architecture: Overview of the cultural significance and traditional construction methods of indigenous log lodges.

- Historical Research: Exploration of historical records, oral histories, and archaeological findings to understand the architectural evolution and cultural significance of indigenous log lodges within specific tribal or regional contexts.

Day 3-5: Practical Construction and Traditional Techniques
- Site Preparation and Selection: Hands-on training in site assessment, land clearing, and the selection of appropriate materials for constructing a historically accurate log lodge.

- Log Preparation and Construction Techniques: Instruction on the selection, harvesting, and preparation of logs, as well as traditional techniques for notching, stacking, and securing logs to create the lodge structure.

- Roofing and Finishing Touches: Guidance on roofing materials and techniques, as well as the addition of traditional elements such as doorways, windows, and decorative motifs to complete the log lodge.

Day 6-7: Cultural Preservation and Interpretation
- Cultural Significance and Symbolism: Discussions on the cultural significance of the log lodge within the indigenous community, including its role in ceremonies, communal gatherings, and storytelling traditions.

- Living Museum Interpretation: Consideration of how the constructed log lodge can be utilized within a living museum context, including methods for interpreting its historical and cultural significance to visitors and the broader community.

- Group Reflection and Sharing: Facilitated discussions and reflections on the significance of preserving indigenous architectural heritage and the importance of cultural preservation in contemporary society.

Throughout the course, participants would have the opportunity to work closely with skilled instructors, indigenous cultural experts, and craftsmen who possess in-depth knowledge of traditional building techniques and cultural practices. The course would emphasize the importance of cultural sensitivity, ethical engagement, and the preservation of indigenous heritage, promoting a holistic understanding of the historical, cultural, and practical aspects of building and interpreting an historically accurate indigenous log lodge within the context of a living museum.

This is not a learning event that would have been conceived of before the 70s. To me, this is the essence of 'The Whole Earth Catalog' and 'The Mother Earth News' spirit, with some meaningful Firefox and Esalon goodness thrown into the mix.

Suggested Reading:

1. "The Upstart Spring: Esalen and the American Awakening" by Walter Truett Anderson - "The Upstart Spring: Esalen and the American Awakening" by Walter Truett Anderson is a significant work that explores the cultural and intellectual history of the renowned Esalen Institute in Big Sur, California, and its profound impact on the American spiritual and philosophical landscape. Through meticulous research and insightful analysis, Anderson delves into the origins, evolution, and cultural significance of Esalen, offering a comprehensive narrative that highlights its pivotal role in the "human potential" movement of the 1960s and beyond.

The book provides a compelling account of how Esalen served as a catalyst for the American awakening of the 1960s, fostering a spirit of intellectual exploration, spiritual inquiry, and cultural experimentation that challenged traditional paradigms and catalyzed a broader cultural renaissance. Anderson skillfully traces the institute's founding and its evolution into a hub for alternative education, personal growth, and spiritual exploration, showcasing how Esalen became a vibrant center for cross-disciplinary dialogue, intellectual exchange, and the integration of diverse philosophical and spiritual traditions.

One of the central themes of the book is the exploration of Esalen's role in popularizing and mainstreaming holistic practices and alternative therapies that have significantly influenced contemporary approaches to wellness and personal development. Anderson delves into the institute's promotion of practices such as meditation, yoga, psychotherapy, and bodywork, highlighting their transformative impact on the American cultural and intellectual landscape. The book offers a nuanced understanding of how Esalen's emphasis on experiential learning and self-discovery paved the way for a more holistic and integrative approach to human potential, well-being, and personal growth.

Moreover, "The Upstart Spring" sheds light on the diverse array of influential figures and thought leaders who contributed to Esalen's intellectual vibrancy and cultural legacy. Anderson's insightful analysis of the contributions of prominent thinkers, spiritual leaders, and scholars, such as Abraham Maslow, Aldous Huxley, and Alan Watts, underscores the institute's role as a breeding ground for innovative ideas and progressive thought in the realms of psychology, spirituality, and philosophy.

The book also addresses the broader cultural and social context in which Esalen emerged, highlighting its connections to the broader counterculture movements of the 1960s and its enduring impact on the trajectory of American intellectual history. Anderson's exploration of Esalen's cultural significance and historical legacy offers readers a comprehensive and engaging narrative that illuminates the institute's profound influence on the American awakening and its ongoing relevance in contemporary conversations about holistic well-being, consciousness, and human potential.

2. "Esalen: America and the Religion of No Religion" by Jeffrey J. Kripal - Jeffrey J. Kripal provides an in-depth exploration of Esalen's influence on the development of alternative spiritualities in the United States, examining its role in shaping the contemporary landscape of religious and philosophical thought.

3. "The Esalen Cookbook: Healthy and Organic Recipes from Big Sur" by Charlie Cascio and Patrice Vecchione - This cookbook offers a collection of wholesome, organic recipes inspired by the culinary traditions and ethos of Esalen, reflecting the center's commitment to holistic well-being and mindful living.

Esalen, known for its influence on various aspects of American culture, including spirituality, personal growth, and holistic well-being, has also made notable contributions to the realm of food and American cuisine. Through its emphasis on organic and sustainable practices, as well as its promotion of mindful eating and holistic nutrition, Esalen has played a significant role in shaping contemporary food culture in the United States. Some of the key impacts of Esalen on food and American cuisine include:

> **A. Promotion of Organic and Sustainable Practices:** Esalen's commitment to holistic well-being extends to its approach to food, emphasizing the importance of organic and sustainable agricultural practices. The institute has advocated for the use of locally sourced, seasonal ingredients, promoting a farm-to-table philosophy that highlights the importance of environmental stewardship and the preservation of natural resources.

> **B. Culinary Education and Workshops:** Esalen has hosted numerous culinary workshops and educational programs focused on promoting healthy and mindful eating habits. These workshops often feature renowned chefs and nutrition experts who share their knowledge of nutrition, cooking techniques, and the benefits of using fresh, whole foods in meal preparation.

C. Exploration of Alternative Diets and Nutrition: Esalen has been instrumental in fostering an open-minded approach to dietary diversity and alternative nutrition practices. The institute has hosted programs that explore various dietary philosophies, including vegetarianism, veganism, and plant-based diets, encouraging participants to explore the health benefits and ethical considerations associated with different dietary choices.

D. Cultural Fusion and Culinary Diversity: Through its diverse community and cultural exchange programs, Esalen has promoted the fusion of culinary traditions from around the world. The institute's emphasis on cross-cultural dialogue and experiential learning has fostered a culinary environment that celebrates diversity and encourages the exploration of different cuisines, flavors, and cooking techniques.

E. Mindful Eating and Wellness Retreats: Esalen's wellness retreats often include components focused on mindful eating and the cultivation of a healthy relationship with food. These retreats emphasize the importance of conscious eating, mindful food preparation, and the practice of gratitude, promoting a holistic approach to nutrition that considers the interconnectedness of food, mind, and body.

F. Community Engagement and Sustainable Food Practices: Esalen has actively engaged with the local community to promote sustainable food practices and support local farmers and producers. The institute's commitment to community-supported agriculture and sustainable food initiatives has contributed to the growth of the local food movement and the promotion of sustainable, ethical food production practices.

Overall, Esalen's impact on food and American cuisine reflects its broader commitment to holistic well-being, environmental sustainability, and the cultivation of a conscious and mindful lifestyle. By fostering a deeper appreciation for the interconnectedness between food, health, and the natural world, Esalen has contributed to the ongoing evolution of American food culture and the promotion of sustainable, health-conscious dietary practices.

4. "Esalen: America's Counter-Culture Hotbed" by Bob Sessions - Bob Sessions provides a comprehensive history of Esalen, chronicling its evolution from a remote hot springs retreat to a renowned center for alternative education, personal growth, and spiritual exploration.

5. "The Humanistic Psychology of Abraham Maslow and Carl Rogers: The Positive Side of Human Nature" edited by Shane J. Lopez - While not exclusively focused on Esalen, this book explores the humanistic psychology movement that was closely associated with the ethos and practices promoted at Esalen, highlighting the contributions of key figures such as Abraham Maslow and Carl Rogers to the field of psychology.

These books offer valuable insights into the history, philosophy, and cultural significance of Esalen, providing readers with a deeper understanding of its impact on the development of American spirituality, psychology, and holistic well-being.

Journeying Inward:
Wellness and Spiritual
Retreats in the 1970s

While specific data on wellness and spiritual retreats in the 1970s is not readily available, there were several notable retreats in the United States and worldwide that gained prominence during this era. These retreats often focused on holistic well-being, spiritual exploration, and personal growth, reflecting the cultural and philosophical trends of the time. Here is a general list of wellness and spiritual retreats that were popular during the 1970s:

United States:

1. Esalen Institute (1962-present) - Big Sur, California:
Founders:
Michael Murphy and Richard Price are the co-founders of the
Esalen Institute, a renowned center for humanistic education
and personal transformation located in Big Sur, California.
Both individuals played instrumental roles in shaping Esalen's
philosophical direction and its contributions to the human
potential movement. Here are their brief biographies:

1. Michael Murphy:
Michael Murphy was born on April 25, 1930, in Salinas, California,
USA. He is best known for his work in promoting humanistic
psychology, holistic education, and the exploration of human
potential. Murphy co-founded the Esalen Institute in 1962,
alongside Richard Price, with the aim of creating a space for
individuals to explore alternative approaches to psychology,
spirituality, and personal growth. He has authored several
influential books, including "The Future of the Body" and "The
Life We Are Given," which have had a significant impact on the
fields of psychology, spirituality, and holistic wellness.

2. Richard Price:
Richard Price was born on February 6, 1933, in New York
City, USA. He was a key figure in the development of the
Esalen Institute and played a crucial role in shaping its early
philosophical foundations and programmatic initiatives. Price
shared a vision with Michael Murphy to establish a space for
interdisciplinary exploration and the integration of diverse
spiritual and psychological traditions. Through his collaborative
efforts with Murphy, Price contributed to the establishment
of Esalen as a pioneering institution for the study of human
potential, holistic well-being, and the integration of Eastern and
Western philosophical perspectives.

> Focus: Humanistic psychology, holistic education, and
> personal transformation.
> Classes Offered: Yoga, meditation, psychology workshops,
> and alternative healing modalities.

2. Omega Institute for Holistic Studies (1977-present) - Rhinebeck, New York:

Focus: Holistic wellness, personal growth, and sustainable living.
Classes Offered: Yoga, mindfulness, nutrition, and sustainability workshops.
Founder: Elizabeth Lesser.

3. Kripalu Center for Yoga & Health (1983-present) - Stockbridge, Massachusetts:

Focus: Yoga, health, and wellness education.
Classes Offered: Yoga, Ayurveda, meditation, and holistic health programs.
Founder: Amrit Desai.

4. Mount Madonna Center (1978-present) - Watsonville, California:

Focus: Yoga, spiritual retreats, and community living.
Classes Offered: Yoga teacher training, meditation retreats, and holistic education.
Founder: Baba Hari Dass.

5. The Lama Foundation (1967-present) - San Cristobal, New Mexico:

Focus: Spiritual practice, communal living, and creative arts.
Classes Offered: Meditation, communal work projects, and artistic expression workshops.
Founders: Steve and Barbara Durkee.

6. The New Age Institute (1972-1994) - Lakemont, Georgia:

Focus: Spiritual exploration, holistic living, and self-realization.
Classes Offered: New Age philosophy, alternative healing, and consciousness studies.
Founder: Ellias Lonsdale.

Worldwide:

1. Isha Yoga Center - Coimbatore, India
2. Osho International Meditation Resort - Pune, India

3. Tushita Meditation Centre - Dharamshala, India
4. Dhamma Vipassana Meditation Centers - Worldwide locations
5. Findhorn Foundation - Findhorn, Scotland
6. Plum Village Mindfulness Practice Center - Dordogne, France

These retreats provided individuals with opportunities for spiritual introspection, holistic education, and the exploration of alternative healing modalities. They often hosted workshops, seminars, and immersive programs focused on yoga, meditation, mindfulness, and other practices that fostered personal growth, well-being, and spiritual development. Their influence during the 1970s contributed to the popularization of holistic wellness practices and the integration of Eastern spiritual traditions into the Western cultural landscape.

Findhorn Foundation

The Findhorn Foundation is a spiritual community, ecovillage, and holistic learning center located in Findhorn, Scotland. Established in 1962, the Findhorn Foundation has become internationally recognized for its pioneering work in the fields of holistic education, sustainable living, and spiritual development. Here are some key aspects of the Findhorn Foundation:

1. Ecovillage and Sustainable Living: The Findhorn Foundation is known for its commitment to sustainable living and ecological stewardship. The community has implemented various innovative sustainability practices, including organic gardening, renewable energy systems, and eco-friendly building techniques, serving as a model for eco-conscious communities worldwide.

2. Spiritual Exploration and Personal Growth: The foundation offers a diverse range of workshops, programs, and retreats focused on spiritual exploration, personal growth, and holistic well-being. Participants have the opportunity to engage in activities such as meditation, yoga, holistic healing, and experiential learning, fostering a deeper connection to themselves, others, and the natural world.

3. Community Life and Shared Values: Findhorn Foundation emphasizes the importance of community living and the cultivation of a supportive and nurturing environment. Residents and participants engage in communal activities, shared decision-making processes, and collaborative projects, fostering a sense of unity, cooperation, and mutual support within the community.

4. New Age and Transpersonal Philosophy: The foundation is influenced by New Age and transpersonal philosophies, promoting a holistic approach to spirituality that integrates elements of psychology, mysticism, and alternative healing modalities. It encourages a comprehensive understanding of human consciousness and the interconnectedness between mind, body, and spirit.

5. Educational Outreach and Global Impact: The Findhorn Foundation has established itself as a global hub for educational outreach and the dissemination of sustainable living practices. Through its international network and educational programs, the foundation has contributed to the promotion of ecological awareness, social responsibility, and the development of sustainable communities worldwide.

Overall, the Findhorn Foundation's commitment to holistic living, spiritual development, and ecological sustainability has positioned it as a leading institution in the realm of sustainable community building, spiritual education, and the promotion of a more interconnected and environmentally conscious way of life.

Findhorn Reading

1. "The Findhorn Garden: Pioneering a New Vision of Humanity and Nature in Cooperation" by the Findhorn Community - This book chronicles the early days of the Findhorn community and its journey toward establishing a successful ecovillage based on principles of cooperation with nature.

2. "Living in Findhorn" by Dorothy Maclean - Dorothy Maclean, one of the co-founders of the Findhorn Foundation, shares her personal experiences and spiritual insights gained during her time at Findhorn, offering a unique perspective on the community's philosophy and practices.

3. "The Magic of Findhorn" by Paul Hawken - Paul Hawken, a renowned environmentalist and author, provides a comprehensive account of the Findhorn community's holistic approach to sustainable living and spiritual development, highlighting its innovative practices and contributions to the global ecological movement.

4. "Voices of Findhorn" by Eileen Caddy - Eileen Caddy, another co-founder of the Findhorn Foundation, shares her spiritual journey and the profound insights she gained while living in the Findhorn community. The book offers a collection of Eileen Caddy's spiritual messages and teachings, providing readers with wisdom and guidance for personal growth and inner transformation.

5. "Findhorn: An Adventure in Working with Nature" by the Findhorn Community - This book offers a detailed exploration of the Findhorn community's ecological principles and practices, emphasizing the importance of collaboration with nature and the cultivation of sustainable living practices that promote environmental stewardship and holistic well-being.

These books provide valuable perspectives on the history, philosophy, and practical applications of the Findhorn community's approach to sustainable living, spiritual development, and the integration of ecological principles into everyday life. They offer readers a deeper understanding of the community's values, teachings, and contributions to the global movement for environmental sustainability and spiritual awakening.

The Yoga Boom: 1970s America Discovers Ancient Wisdom

The Yoga Boom of the 1970s in America marked a significant cultural and spiritual shift, reflecting a growing interest in

Eastern philosophy, holistic wellness, and alternative forms of physical and mental exercise. During this transformative period, the ancient practice of yoga gained widespread popularity, capturing the imagination of individuals seeking spiritual enlightenment, physical well-being, and a deeper connection to Eastern spiritual traditions. The convergence of various cultural, social, and philosophical influences during the 1970s set the stage for the emergence of yoga as a transformative and influential cultural phenomenon in the United States.

The roots of the 1970s Yoga Boom can be traced back to the broader counterculture movements of the 1960s, which fostered an atmosphere of cultural exploration, spiritual inquiry, and a rejection of conventional Western values. The increasing disillusionment with materialism and the pursuit of alternative lifestyles paved the way for the integration of Eastern spiritual practices, including yoga, meditation, and mindfulness, into the fabric of American society.

Central to the Yoga Boom was the introduction of various yoga styles and teachings by influential Indian gurus and spiritual teachers who traveled to the United States to share their wisdom and practices. Figures such as Swami Satchidananda, Swami Vishnudevananda, and B.K.S. Iyengar played instrumental roles in popularizing yoga and making it accessible to Western audiences through workshops, retreats, and teacher training programs. Their teachings emphasized the holistic benefits of yoga, promoting physical health, mental clarity, and spiritual growth as interconnected aspects of the practice.

The Yoga Boom also coincided with a growing interest in holistic wellness, alternative medicine, and the mind-body connection, leading to the integration of yoga into mainstream health and wellness practices. The rise of specialized yoga studios, wellness centers, and holistic retreats provided individuals with dedicated spaces to explore the transformative power of yoga, meditation, and Eastern spiritual practices.

Moreover, the Yoga Boom fostered a cultural renaissance that celebrated diversity, inclusivity, and spiritual exploration, creating a sense of community and belonging among individuals seeking a deeper understanding of themselves and the world around them. Yoga became a symbol of unity and harmony, transcending cultural and religious boundaries and fostering a shared sense of interconnectedness and mindfulness.

While the 1970s Yoga Boom brought about a cultural and spiritual awakening, it also sparked debates and discussions about the commercialization and secularization of ancient spiritual traditions. Critics raised concerns about the commodification of yoga and the dilution of its authentic teachings, emphasizing the need to preserve the integrity and philosophical depth of the practice amidst its growing popularity and commercial appeal.

Despite these challenges, the Yoga Boom of the 1970s left a profound and lasting impact on American culture, contributing to the mainstream acceptance of yoga as a holistic practice that fosters physical health, emotional well-being, and spiritual awareness. The legacy of the Yoga Boom continues to inspire individuals to embark on a transformative journey of self-discovery, mindfulness, and holistic wellness, reflecting the enduring appeal of ancient wisdom in the modern world.

Controversy

While yoga has gained widespread popularity and recognition for its numerous physical, mental, and spiritual benefits, it has also faced certain criticisms and concerns from various perspectives. Some common criticisms of yoga include:

1. Cultural Appropriation: Critics argue that the commercialization and popularization of yoga in Western societies have led to the cultural appropriation of a sacred and spiritual practice with origins in ancient Eastern traditions. There are concerns that the commercial yoga industry often commodifies and distorts traditional yoga practices, disregarding their cultural and spiritual significance.

2. Physical Injury Risks: Certain yoga poses, especially when practiced incorrectly or without proper guidance, can potentially lead to physical injuries, strains, or muscle imbalances. Critics raise concerns about the lack of emphasis on proper alignment and the potential for practitioners to push themselves beyond their physical limitations, leading to adverse health effects.

3. Commercialization and Materialism: Some critics argue that the commercialization of yoga has led to the prioritization of profit over the authentic spiritual and philosophical aspects of the practice. The proliferation of luxury yoga brands, exclusive retreats, and expensive yoga equipment can create barriers to access for individuals from diverse socioeconomic backgrounds, contributing to a culture of materialism and exclusivity.

4. Superficiality and Ego-Driven Practices: There are concerns that certain aspects of modern yoga culture emphasize physical appearance, achievement, and performance over the holistic and spiritual dimensions of the practice. Critics argue that the pursuit of complex poses, competitive yoga events, and a focus on external validation can foster an ego-driven culture that contradicts the core principles of self-awareness, compassion, and inner peace advocated in traditional yoga philosophy.

5. Lack of Cultural and Historical Understanding: Critics highlight the importance of understanding the historical, cultural, and philosophical contexts of yoga to ensure its respectful practice and transmission. Without a comprehensive understanding of the spiritual and philosophical underpinnings of yoga, there is a risk of oversimplification, misinterpretation, and the dilution of its rich cultural heritage and wisdom.

Awareness is very important when dealing with any 'spiritual' leader. Yoga is no different. Here are six examples of controversy involving spiritual leaders:

1. Bikram Choudhury: The founder of Bikram Yoga faced multiple allegations of sexual harassment and assault from former students and employees, leading to significant legal repercussions and public scrutiny.

2. Sogyal Rinpoche: The Tibetan Buddhist teacher was accused of physical, emotional, and sexual abuse by several of his students, prompting public outcry and the formation of advocacy groups dedicated to addressing abuse within Tibetan Buddhist communities.

3. Sathya Sai Baba: The Indian spiritual leader was associated with numerous allegations of sexual abuse and misconduct, leading to widespread controversy and discussions about the ethical conduct of spiritual leaders and the protection of vulnerable followers.

4. Amma (Mata Amritanandamayi): The hugging saint, known for her humanitarian work and spiritual teachings, has faced allegations of sexual abuse and misconduct by former devotees, leading to public scrutiny and the initiation of legal investigations.

5. Paramahamsa Nithyananda: The Indian spiritual leader has been embroiled in multiple controversies, including allegations of sexual misconduct and exploitation, which have sparked public debate and criticism within spiritual communities.

6. Swami Rama: The Indian spiritual leader was accused of misleading his followers and engaging in fraudulent claims about his spiritual abilities, which led to questions about the authenticity of his teachings and the ethical conduct of spiritual gurus in general.

These examples highlight the complexities and challenges surrounding issues of sexual controversy and ethical conduct within spiritual communities, underscoring the importance of promoting transparency, accountability, and the protection of vulnerable individuals within spiritual organizations.

It is essential to recognize and address these criticisms within the broader context of the evolving yoga industry and community. Many practitioners and teachers are actively working to promote a more inclusive, authentic, and mindful approach to yoga that respects its origins, emphasizes holistic well-being, and fosters a sense of community, diversity, and spiritual growth.

Suggested Reading

1. "Selling Yoga: From Counterculture to Pop Culture" by Andrea Jain: This book provides a comprehensive analysis of the commercialization and popularization of yoga in the West, exploring its transformation from a countercultural practice to a mainstream wellness industry. It delves into the cultural, social, and economic forces that shaped the yoga industry in the 1970s and beyond.

2. "Yoga Body: The Origins of Modern Posture Practice" by Mark Singleton: Mark Singleton's book offers a historical perspective on the development of modern yoga practices and their commercialization in the 20th century. It examines the intersection of traditional yoga philosophy with contemporary fitness trends, shedding light on the evolution of yoga as an industry during the 1970s and its implications for practitioners and consumers.

3. "The Great Oom: The Improbable Birth of Yoga in America" by Robert Love: This book chronicles the early history of yoga in America, focusing on the life and teachings of Pierre Bernard, a pioneering figure in the popularization of yoga during the early 20th century. It provides insights into the cultural dynamics and challenges that shaped the perception of yoga as an industry in the 1970s.

4. "The Subtle Body: The Story of Yoga in America" by Stefanie Syman: Stefanie Syman's book offers a comprehensive exploration of the cultural, philosophical, and commercial dimensions of yoga in America. It delves into the various perspectives and debates surrounding the commercialization of yoga during the 1970s, highlighting its impact on the wellness industry and the broader cultural landscape.

These books offer valuable insights into the historical, cultural, and commercial aspects of the yoga industry in the 1970s, providing readers with a nuanced understanding of the opportunities, challenges, and cultural implications associated with the popularization of yoga as a mainstream wellness practice during that era.

Body-Mind Connection: Rolfing, Reflexology, and Bodywork for Personal Transformation

In the transformative landscape of the 1970s, a remarkable shift occurred in the realm of personal wellness and self-discovery, ushering in a newfound appreciation for holistic approaches to healing and self-transformation. At the forefront of this movement were the practices of Rolfing, Reflexology, and Bodywork, each offering unique pathways to unlock the body's innate potential for balance, rejuvenation, and personal growth. As the decade witnessed a surge in the exploration of alternative healing modalities and the pursuit of holistic well-being, these practices emerged as beacons of hope for individuals seeking a deeper connection between mind, body, and spirit.

Rolfing, with its emphasis on structural integration and the profound impact of myofascial manipulation, became a catalyst for reshaping not only the physical body but also the emotional and energetic dimensions that intertwine within it. Guided by the principles laid down by its visionary founder, Dr. Ida Rolf, Rolfing pioneered a path toward comprehensive well-being, unveiling the intricate relationship between body alignment and inner harmony.

Meanwhile, Reflexology, rooted in ancient healing traditions, offered a holistic approach to wellness by harnessing the body's natural reflex points, believed to hold the key to unlocking vitality and restoring balance. Practitioners of Reflexology delved into the art of touch and pressure, illuminating the interconnectedness between the body's microcosm and the broader spectrum of

holistic health, thereby paving the way for a transformative journey of self-discovery and inner renewal.

In parallel, the realm of Bodywork encompassed an expansive array of therapeutic techniques and philosophies, ranging from massage therapy to energy work, each tailored to nurture the body-mind connection and ignite the spark of personal transformation. Drawing from diverse cultural and therapeutic traditions, Bodywork emerged as a versatile tapestry, weaving together the threads of self-awareness, relaxation, and holistic healing to offer a holistic sanctuary for individuals seeking a comprehensive approach to their well-being.

1. Rolfing:

History: Rolfing, named after its founder, Dr. Ida Rolf, is a form of bodywork that focuses on the manipulation of the body's myofascial system to promote balance and alignment. Dr. Rolf developed this approach in the mid-20th century.

Founders: Dr. Ida Rolf, a biochemist, was the pioneer of Rolfing and developed the practice based on her understanding of human physiology and the interconnectedness of the body's structure.

Tools for Wellness: Rolfing practitioners utilize deep tissue manipulation and movement education to restructure and balance the body, aiming to alleviate chronic pain, improve posture, and enhance overall well-being.

State During the 1970s: Rolfing gained popularity in the 1970s, particularly within the alternative health and wellness community, as a holistic approach to addressing physical imbalances and promoting structural integration.

Legacy: Rolfing has left a lasting legacy as a recognized form of bodywork that emphasizes the importance of structural alignment, movement awareness, and the body-mind connection in promoting physical health and well-being.

2. Reflexology:

History: Reflexology is an alternative medicine practice that involves applying pressure to specific points on the feet, hands, and ears, believed to correspond to different organs and systems of the body. It has roots in ancient Egyptian and Chinese healing practices.

Founders: While reflexology's origins can be traced back to ancient civilizations, its modern interpretation and standardization have been influenced by various practitioners and researchers throughout history.

Tools for Wellness: Reflexology practitioners use manual pressure techniques to stimulate reflex points, aiming to promote relaxation, improve circulation, and support the body's natural healing processes.

State During the 1970s: Reflexology experienced a resurgence in the 1970s as part of the growing interest in alternative healing modalities and holistic wellness practices.

Legacy: Reflexology has continued to be recognized as a complementary therapy for stress reduction, pain management, and the promotion of holistic well-being, leaving a legacy as a non-invasive and accessible form of alternative medicine.

3. Bodywork:

History: Bodywork encompasses various therapeutic approaches that address the body-mind connection, emphasizing hands-on techniques to promote physical, emotional, and energetic balance. It draws from a diverse range of cultural and therapeutic traditions.

Founders: While bodywork as a holistic practice does not have a singular founder, its principles and techniques have been influenced by practitioners, therapists, and healers from different cultural and therapeutic backgrounds.

Tools for Wellness: Bodywork techniques may include massage therapy, myofascial release, energy work, and somatic practices, all aimed at enhancing relaxation, reducing muscle tension, and promoting overall well-being.

State During the 1970s: Bodywork gained traction in the 1970s as part of the broader movement toward holistic health and the integration of alternative healing modalities into mainstream wellness practices.

Legacy: Bodywork's legacy lies in its promotion of holistic wellness and the recognition of the interconnectedness of the body, mind, and spirit in maintaining health and vitality. It continues to be valued for its therapeutic benefits and its emphasis on the importance of self-awareness and self-care.

Overall, Rolfing, Reflexology, and Bodywork have each contributed to the understanding and practice of holistic wellness and the body-mind connection, leaving lasting legacies as effective approaches to promoting physical health, emotional well-being, and personal transformation.

Criticisms

At some point, the criticisms echo between categories, theories,practices and methodologies. Here are some common criticisms associated with Rolfing, Reflexology, and Bodywork:

1. Rolfing:
- Critics argue that Rolfing can be an intense and uncomfortable experience, potentially causing physical discomfort or pain during the deep tissue manipulation process.

- Some skeptics question the scientific evidence supporting the long-term effectiveness of Rolfing in addressing chronic pain or structural imbalances, emphasizing the need for more empirical research to validate its therapeutic claims.

2. Reflexology:
- Skeptics often question the scientific basis of reflexology, citing a lack of empirical evidence to support the claim that

specific reflex points on the feet, hands, or ears correspond directly to internal organs or body systems.

- Critics argue that while reflexology may promote relaxation and a sense of well-being, its ability to produce specific therapeutic outcomes for various health conditions remains a subject of debate within the medical and scientific communities.

3. Bodywork:
- Some critics express concerns about the variability and lack of standardization in the practice of bodywork, emphasizing the need for clear professional guidelines and ethical standards to ensure the safety and well-being of clients.

- Skeptics question the scientific validity of certain bodywork modalities, suggesting that the therapeutic benefits of practices such as energy work or somatic techniques may be attributed more to the placebo effect than to measurable physiological changes.

While these criticisms raise important considerations about the efficacy, safety, and scientific basis of Rolfing, Reflexology, and Bodywork, it is essential to acknowledge the diverse perspectives within the holistic wellness and alternative medicine communities. Advocates of these practices often highlight their potential for promoting relaxation, stress reduction, and overall well-being, emphasizing the importance of a comprehensive approach to health that integrates both conventional and complementary modalities. It is crucial to approach these practices with a critical yet open-minded perspective, considering both their potential benefits and limitations in the context of individual health and wellness goals.

Suggested Reading

1. Rolfing:
"Rolfing: Reestablishing the Natural Alignment and Structural Integration of the Human Body for Vitality and Well-Being" by Ida P. Rolf: This seminal work by the founder of Rolfing offers an in-depth exploration of the principles and techniques of Rolfing, highlighting its potential benefits for structural alignment, pain relief, and overall well-being. The book discusses the transformative potential of Rolfing while also addressing some of the criticisms and limitations associated with the practice.

2. Reflexology:
"The Reflexology Manual: An Easy-to-Use Illustrated Guide to the Healing Zones of the Hands and Feet" by Pauline Wills: This comprehensive guide to reflexology provides practical insights into the techniques and applications of reflexology, emphasizing its potential benefits for stress reduction, relaxation, and overall wellness. The book offers a balanced perspective on the pros and cons of reflexology, addressing common misconceptions and promoting a holistic understanding of its therapeutic value.

3. Bodywork:
"The Book of Massage: The Complete Step-by-Step Guide to Eastern and Western Techniques" by Lucinda Lidell: This comprehensive guide to various bodywork techniques offers readers a comprehensive overview of massage therapy, energy work, and somatic practices, highlighting their potential benefits and limitations for physical and emotional well-being. The book provides a balanced exploration of the diverse approaches to bodywork, emphasizing the importance of informed practice and ethical considerations within the field.

These books offer valuable insights into the practices of Rolfing, Reflexology, and Bodywork, providing readers with a nuanced understanding of their potential benefits, limitations, and applications within the broader context of holistic wellness and alternative medicine. By exploring the diverse perspectives and experiences shared within these texts, readers can gain a comprehensive understanding of the complexities and transformative potential of these practices in promoting physical health, emotional well-being, and personal transformation.

Further Research

For individuals interested in experiencing Rolfing, Reflexology, and Bodywork, several reputable organizations and resources can provide valuable information and access to certified practitioners:

1. Rolfing:

- The Rolf Institute of Structural Integration offers a comprehensive directory of certified Rolfers and Rolfing practitioners, allowing individuals to locate practitioners in their area and learn more about the practice of Rolfing.

- The institute's official website provides educational resources, practitioner profiles, and information on the principles and benefits of Rolfing, offering a valuable starting point for those interested in exploring the practice further.

2. Reflexology:

- The Reflexology Association of America (RAA) serves as a leading resource for individuals seeking information on reflexology, providing a comprehensive directory of certified reflexologists and educational resources on the practice.

- The association's website offers a wealth of information on reflexology research, training programs, and practitioner directories, enabling individuals to connect with experienced reflexology professionals in their region.

3. Bodywork:

- The American Bodywork and Massage Professionals (ABMP) is a reputable organization that offers valuable resources for individuals interested in exploring various bodywork modalities, including massage therapy, energy work, and somatic practices.

- The ABMP website provides a comprehensive directory of certified bodywork practitioners, along with educational resources, industry news, and research updates on the benefits and applications of different bodywork techniques.

By accessing these organizations and resources, individuals can gain valuable insights into the practice of Rolfing, Reflexology, and Bodywork, connect with certified practitioners, and explore the potential benefits and applications of these holistic wellness modalities. These resources can serve as valuable guides for individuals seeking to experience the transformative potential of these practices and embark on a journey toward enhanced well-being and personal transformation.

Inner Journeys: Primal Scream Therapy, Holotropic Breathwork, and Emotional Release

In the transformative landscape of the human psyche, a profound exploration of the self often involves a journey into the depths of primal emotions and buried traumas, unlocking the cathartic potential of the human spirit. Within this rich tapestry of personal growth and emotional release, the practices of Primal Scream Therapy, Holotropic Breathwork, and Emotional Release stand as beacons of transformative healing, inviting individuals to embark on a profound odyssey of self-discovery, inner healing, and emotional liberation.

Primal Scream Therapy, with its roots in the groundbreaking work of Dr. Arthur Janov, illuminates the primal nature of human emotions, guiding individuals toward a transformative process of unearthing and expressing deeply suppressed feelings and traumas. Harnessing the power of vocal expression and cathartic release, this therapeutic approach delves into the core of human consciousness, unraveling the intricate layers of emotional pain and unveiling the transformative potential of primal screams as a pathway to profound emotional healing and self-discovery.

In parallel, Holotropic Breathwork, inspired by the visionary insights of Dr. Stanislav Grof, offers a transformative journey into the realms of expanded consciousness and spiritual exploration through the power of breath and non-ordinary states of awareness. By tapping into the profound potential of conscious breathing and immersive experiential states, this practice opens the doorway to deep introspection, inner healing, and spiritual awakening, guiding individuals toward profound insights, emotional catharsis, and a holistic integration of mind, body, and spirit.

Complementing these transformative practices, Emotional Release encompasses a diverse range of therapeutic modalities that facilitate the release and processing of repressed emotions, trauma, and psychological blockages. Drawing from various psychotherapeutic approaches and somatic techniques, Emotional Release invites individuals to embark on a transformative journey of self-discovery, emotional integration, and inner healing, fostering a profound connection between the conscious mind, the somatic experience, and the realms of emotional catharsis and personal transformation.

Primal Scream Therapy

Founder: Primal Scream Therapy was developed by Dr. Arthur Janov, a psychologist, in the late 1960s.

Influences: Janov's work was influenced by Freudian psychoanalysis and his observations on the interconnectedness of emotional pain and its physical manifestations.

Origins: The therapy originated at the Primal Institute in Los Angeles, California, where Janov began experimenting with the technique in the treatment of his patients.

Theories: Primal Scream Therapy is grounded in the belief that repressed early childhood traumas contribute to emotional and psychological disturbances in adulthood. It emphasizes the importance of releasing repressed emotions through vocal expression and reliving past traumatic experiences to achieve emotional healing.

Tools: The therapy offers a safe and controlled environment for individuals to express their emotions freely, often involving guided sessions that encourage patients to revisit and vocalize deeply buried feelings and traumas.

Goals: The primary goal of Primal Scream Therapy is to facilitate emotional catharsis, leading to the release of repressed trauma, and ultimately, the resolution of deep-seated emotional pain and psychological disturbances.

Famous People: John Lennon and Yoko Ono are among the notable individuals who underwent Primal Scream Therapy, with Lennon referencing the experience in his songwriting.

Cost: The cost of Primal Scream Therapy can vary depending on the therapist, location, and duration of the treatment, with individual session rates and comprehensive therapy programs typically available.

Books: Dr. Arthur Janov's "The Primal Scream" and "Prisoners of Pain" provide comprehensive insights into the theory and practice of Primal Scream Therapy.

Legacy: Despite generating significant controversy and critique within the psychological community, Primal Scream Therapy has left a lasting legacy in the field of psychotherapy, contributing to the ongoing discourse on the role of repressed emotions in psychological well-being and the exploration of emotional healing through cathartic release.

Holotropic Breathwork

Founders: Holotropic Breathwork was developed by Dr. Stanislav Grof, a psychiatrist, and his wife Christina Grof, in the 1970s as an alternative therapeutic approach to explore non-ordinary states of consciousness.

Influences: Grof's work was influenced by his research on psychedelic substances, transpersonal psychology, and various spiritual traditions, which inspired the development of a non-drug-induced method for achieving altered states of consciousness.

Origins: The technique was initially formulated as a result of Grof's research into the therapeutic potential of altered states of consciousness, leading to the creation of a structured approach that combines accelerated breathing, evocative music, and focused bodywork.

Theories: Holotropic Breathwork is based on the premise that altered states of consciousness can facilitate profound insights, emotional healing, and spiritual transformation. It emphasizes the integration of the conscious and unconscious mind through the exploration of expanded states of awareness.

Tools: The therapy involves controlled and intentional breathing techniques, often accompanied by evocative music and bodywork, to induce altered states of consciousness and facilitate deep emotional and spiritual exploration.

Goals: The primary goal of Holotropic Breathwork is to promote self-exploration, emotional healing, and spiritual awakening through the facilitation of non-ordinary states of consciousness, leading to profound insights and transformative experiences.

Cost: The cost of Holotropic Breathwork workshops or sessions can vary depending on the facilitator, location, and duration of the program, with fees typically covering the expenses associated with the workshop, facilitator's fees, and administrative costs.

Books: Dr. Stanislav Grof's "The Adventure of Self-Discovery" and "The Holotropic Mind" provide in-depth insights into the theory and practice of Holotropic Breathwork and its implications for emotional and spiritual well-being.

Legacy: Holotropic Breathwork has left a lasting legacy in the realm of transpersonal psychology and alternative therapeutic practices, contributing to the ongoing exploration of non-ordinary states of consciousness, spiritual emergence, and the integration of holistic approaches to emotional and psychological healing.

Emotional Release

Concept: Emotional Release refers to a diverse set of therapeutic modalities that aim to facilitate the processing and release of pent-up emotions and psychological blockages.

Approaches: Various psychotherapeutic and somatic techniques, such as Gestalt therapy, somatic experiencing, and certain forms of body-centered psychotherapy, are often incorporated into the practice of Emotional Release to address unresolved emotional issues and trauma.

Tools: Therapists may utilize a combination of talk therapy, breathwork, movement exercises, and mindfulness practices to help individuals explore and express their emotions in a safe and supportive environment.

Goals: The primary goal of Emotional Release is to enable individuals to process and release repressed emotions, trauma, and psychological barriers, fostering a sense of emotional liberation, self-awareness, and personal growth.

Applications: Emotional Release techniques are commonly employed in the treatment of various mental health conditions, including anxiety disorders, post-traumatic stress disorder (PTSD), and depression, as well as in the context of personal development and holistic well-being.

Cost: The cost of Emotional Release therapy can vary depending on the specific therapeutic approach, the qualifications of the therapist, and the duration of the treatment, with fees typically reflecting standard rates for psychotherapy or counseling sessions.

Books: "The Body Keeps the Score" by Bessel van der Kolk and "In an Unspoken Voice" by Peter A. Levine are notable books that explore the concept of Emotional Release within the context of trauma healing and the integration of mind-body approaches to psychotherapy.

Legacy: Emotional Release has made significant contributions to the field of psychotherapy and trauma treatment, fostering a deeper understanding of the mind-body connection and the role of emotional processing in promoting psychological resilience, self-empowerment, and overall emotional well-being.

Criticism

Certainly, here are some common criticisms associated with Primal Scream Therapy, Holotropic Breathwork, and Emotional Release:

Primal Scream Therapy:
- Critics argue that Primal Scream Therapy oversimplifies complex psychological issues, emphasizing the expression of emotions over the deeper exploration and understanding of underlying psychological dynamics and interpersonal complexities.

- Some professionals within the field of psychology express concerns about the potential retraumatization of individuals undergoing this therapy, suggesting that the intense emotional release may not always lead to lasting psychological healing or resolution of underlying issues.

Holotropic Breathwork:
- Skeptics question the scientific validity of the transformative experiences reported during Holotropic Breathwork sessions, emphasizing the potential for these experiences to be attributed to the effects of hyperventilation and altered states of consciousness rather than profound spiritual or psychological insights.

- Critics raise concerns about the potential risks associated with inducing non-ordinary states of consciousness, highlighting the importance of ensuring the safety and well-being of participants during the exploration of intense emotional and spiritual experiences.

Emotional Release:
- Some critics argue that Emotional Release therapies may lack empirical evidence to support their effectiveness in treating specific mental health conditions, emphasizing the need for more rigorous research to validate their therapeutic claims and outcomes.

- Skeptics express concerns about the potential for Emotional Release therapies to lead to the emergence of false memories or the reinforcement of maladaptive coping mechanisms, underscoring the importance of ensuring a balanced and evidence-based approach to emotional healing and psychological well-being.

While these criticisms underscore important considerations within the field of psychotherapy and emotional healing, it is crucial to approach these therapeutic modalities with a balanced and critical perspective, taking into account both their potential benefits and limitations in the context of individual therapeutic needs and goals. Additionally, the ongoing dialogue within the psychological community serves to promote a deeper understanding of these approaches and their implications for holistic well-being and emotional resilience.

Reading

Certainly, here are the publication dates and rewritten versions for the suggested reading list of books:

Primal Scream Therapy:
1. "The Biology of Love" by Arthur Janov - Published in 2000.
2. "Primal Healing: Access the Incredible Power of Feelings to Improve Your Health" by Arthur Janov - Published in 2017.

Holotropic Breathwork:
1. "The Transpersonal Vision" by Stanislav Grof - Published in 1998.
2. "The Cosmic Game: Explorations of the Frontiers of Human Consciousness" by Stanislav Grof - Published in 1998.

Emotional Release:
1. "Healing Trauma: A Pioneering Program for Restoring the Wisdom of Your Body" by Peter A. Levine - Published in 2008.
2. "The Emotionally Absent Mother: How to Recognize and Heal the Invisible Effects of Childhood Emotional Neglect" by Jasmin Lee Cori - Published in 2010.

These works offer comprehensive insights into the theoretical foundations and practical applications of each therapy method, providing readers with valuable perspectives on emotional healing, personal growth, and the integration of mind-body approaches to wellness.

Bioenergetics

Bioenergetics, a pioneering approach to psychotherapy and personal growth, is grounded in the fundamental premise that the mind and body are intricately interconnected, with emotional well-being and psychological health deeply intertwined with physical vitality. Developed by Alexander Lowen and John Pierrakos in the 1950s, Bioenergetics represents a synthesis of psychoanalytic insights, Eastern philosophies, and somatic practices, fostering a holistic understanding of the human psyche and the profound impact of emotional expression on physical health.

At its core, Bioenergetics delves into the exploration of the body's energetic flow and the ways in which emotional traumas and psychological conflicts manifest as physical tensions and muscular constriction. By tracing the intricate patterns of bodily tension and observing the interplay between muscular rigidity and suppressed emotions, practitioners of Bioenergetics aim to unravel the complex layers of the human psyche, uncovering the deep-seated emotional blockages that inhibit the natural flow of energy and vitality.

Central to the practice of Bioenergetics are a series of body-oriented techniques and exercises that promote the release of muscular tension and the expression of repressed emotions, encouraging individuals to reclaim a sense of embodied authenticity and emotional integrity. Through dynamic movement exercises, deep breathing techniques, and guided emotional release practices, participants are invited to confront their emotional inhibitions and physical constrictions, fostering a deeper awareness of the body-mind connection and the transformative potential of somatic experiences.

The foundational principles of Bioenergetics emphasize the importance of grounding and centering oneself in the present moment, cultivating a heightened sense of bodily awareness and emotional attunement. By fostering a deeper connection with the physical self, individuals are encouraged to explore the underlying sources of emotional pain and psychological distress, unveiling the layers of unconscious patterns and psychological defenses that hinder personal growth and self-actualization.

In the therapeutic context, Bioenergetics serves as a powerful tool for promoting emotional healing and psychological integration, offering individuals a safe and supportive environment to confront their innermost fears, anxieties, and unresolved traumas. Through the facilitation of cathartic emotional release and the cultivation of embodied mindfulness, practitioners guide individuals on a transformative journey of self-discovery and inner healing, enabling them to tap into their innate capacity for resilience and emotional well-being.

Moreover, the practice of Bioenergetics extends beyond the realm of psychotherapy, encompassing a holistic approach to personal growth and holistic wellness. By embracing the principles of Bioenergetics in daily life, individuals can cultivate a deeper sense of emotional resilience, self-awareness, and vitality, fostering a harmonious integration of the body, mind, and spirit.

In essence, Bioenergetics represents a profound paradigm shift in the field of psychotherapy, highlighting the vital role of somatic experiences in the exploration of emotional well-being and the cultivation of holistic wellness. Through its emphasis on the integration of body-centered practices, emotional release techniques, and mindfulness-based approaches to personal growth, Bioenergetics offers a transformative pathway toward self-discovery, emotional liberation, and the attainment of a profound sense of wholeness and vitality.

Criticism

1. Skeptics argue that Bioenergetics lacks empirical evidence to support its theoretical claims and the efficacy of its techniques in addressing specific psychological issues, emphasizing the need for more rigorous scientific research to validate its therapeutic approaches.

2. Some professionals within the field of psychology express concerns about the potential for misinterpretation of bodily cues and the risk of retraumatization during the practice of Bioenergetics, underscoring the importance of a nuanced and ethical approach to somatic therapy.

Reading List

1. "The Way to Vibrant Health: A Manual of Bioenergetic Exercises" by Alexander Lowen and Leslie Lowen
2. "Bioenergetics: The Revolutionary Therapy That Uses the Language of the Body to Heal the Problems of the Mind" by Alexander Lowen
3. "Fear of Life" by Alexander Lowen
4. "The Language of the Body" by Alexander Lowen
5. "Pleasure: A Creative Approach to Life" by Alexander Lowen

These books offer comprehensive insights into the theoretical foundations and practical applications of Bioenergetics, providing readers with valuable perspectives on the principles, techniques, and implications of this somatic approach to emotional healing and personal growth.

Mindful Movement: The Principles of Alexander Technique and Feldenkrais

Moshe Feldenkrais and F. Matthias Alexander made significant contributions to the 1970s self-help movements, introducing innovative approaches to somatic education and movement re-education that fostered a deeper understanding of the mind-body connection and the transformative potential of self-awareness. Their methodologies offered valuable insights into the cultivation of holistic well-being and the promotion of physical and emotional resilience, influencing the landscape of self-help practices during the 1970s and beyond.

Moshe Feldenkrais, through the development of the Feldenkrais Method, brought attention to the importance of embodied awareness and the integration of movement, posture, and emotional well-being. His emphasis on gentle, mindful movements and hands-on guidance resonated with individuals seeking to enhance their physical comfort and alleviate musculoskeletal pain, fostering a deeper connection with the body and a greater sense of somatic empowerment. Feldenkrais's contributions to the self-help movements of the 1970s highlighted the transformative potential of somatic experiences and the cultivation of a more conscious and integrated approach to movement and well-being.

F. Matthias Alexander, through the Alexander Technique, emphasized the re-education of posture and movement habits, promoting a balanced and natural alignment of the body. His teachings underscored the importance of reducing muscular tension and restoring efficient postural coordination, fostering a heightened awareness of physical habits and their impact on overall well-being. Alexander's contributions to the 1970s self-help movements emphasized the integration of mindful movement practices and the cultivation of a more harmonious relationship between the body and mind, providing individuals with practical tools for enhancing physical comfort, emotional resilience, and self-empowerment.

By emphasizing the interconnectedness of physical and emotional well-being, both Moshe Feldenkrais and F. Matthias Alexander played instrumental roles in shaping the discourse around self-help practices in the 1970s, highlighting the transformative potential of somatic education and the cultivation of embodied awareness for holistic wellness and personal growth. Their enduring legacies continue to inspire individuals to explore the profound connection between mind and body, fostering a deeper understanding of the self and the integration of somatic practices into the realm of personal transformation and well-being.

What to Expect

Moshe Feldenkrais Sessions:

1. Individualized Assessment: In Feldenkrais sessions, practitioners typically begin by conducting an individualized assessment of the client's movement patterns, posture, and any specific concerns or goals they may have.

2. Hands-on Guidance: Clients can expect to receive hands-on guidance and gentle manipulation from the practitioner, who will offer tactile cues to facilitate improved movement patterns and release muscular tension.

3. Mindful Movement Practices: Feldenkrais sessions often involve guided movement sequences and exercises designed to enhance body awareness, improve flexibility, and promote a sense of relaxation and well-being.

4. Educational Approach: Clients can anticipate an educational approach focused on empowering them to understand their movement habits and learn techniques for self-correction and improved body mechanics.

F. Matthias Alexander Technique Sessions:

1. Postural Assessment: Alexander Technique practitioners typically begin sessions with a postural assessment, observing the client's alignment, movement habits, and any patterns of tension or misalignment.

2. Hands-on Adjustments: Clients can expect hands-on adjustments from the practitioner, who will provide gentle manipulation and guidance to encourage optimal postural alignment and release unnecessary muscular tension.

3. Verbal Instructions: Alexander Technique sessions often involve verbal instructions and guidance to help clients become more aware of their postural habits and develop strategies for improving overall body coordination and balance.

4. Integration into Daily Activities: Practitioners may focus on integrating the principles of the Alexander Technique into clients' daily activities, such as sitting, standing, or walking, to promote a more conscious and aligned approach to movement and posture.

In both cases, clients can anticipate a supportive and collaborative environment that encourages self-exploration, improved body awareness, and the development of practical skills for enhancing movement efficiency and overall well-being. Practitioners of both methods typically work with clients to develop personalized strategies for long-term self-care and the cultivation of sustainable, healthy movement patterns.

The number of sessions for both the Feldenkrais Method and the Alexander Technique can vary depending on individual needs and goals. Here's an overview of the typical duration:

Feldenkrais Method Sessions:

- **Short-Term Relief:** Some individuals may seek Feldenkrais sessions for short-term relief from specific issues, such as muscular tension or discomfort. In such cases, a limited number of sessions might be sufficient to address immediate concerns or provide temporary relief.

- **Long-Term Learning:** Many clients, however, choose to engage in the Feldenkrais Method as a long-term learning process. This often involves attending regular, ongoing sessions over an extended period, allowing individuals to deepen their understanding and embodiment of the method's principles and practices.

Alexander Technique Sessions:

- **Varied Duration:** The duration of Alexander Technique sessions can vary depending on the client's specific needs and goals. Some individuals may benefit from a shorter series of sessions aimed at addressing specific postural concerns or movement patterns, while others may engage in longer-term learning to develop a more integrated and sustainable approach to movement and posture.

Both the Feldenkrais Method and the Alexander Technique offer adaptable approaches that cater to the unique requirements and preferences of each individual. The duration of the sessions is typically determined collaboratively between the client and the practitioner, taking into account the client's progress, specific areas of focus, and the desired outcomes for their overall well-being and movement habits.

Certainly, here are the criticisms and suggested reading lists for both the Feldenkrais Method and the Alexander Technique:

Criticism

Feldenkrais Method:
1. Some critics argue that the empirical research supporting the effectiveness of the Feldenkrais Method is limited, calling for more rigorous scientific studies to validate its therapeutic claims.

2. Skeptics suggest that the individualized nature of the Feldenkrais Method may make it challenging to standardize and replicate, raising questions about its widespread accessibility and applicability in diverse settings.

Alexander Technique:
1. Critics express concerns about the subjective nature of the Alexander Technique, emphasizing the need for more empirical evidence to support its long-term efficacy in improving posture and movement patterns.

2. Some professionals argue that the Alexander Technique's emphasis on conscious control and postural awareness may not fully address underlying psychological or emotional factors that contribute to postural habits and movement patterns.

Reading List

Feldenkrais Method:
1. "Awareness Through Movement" by Moshe Feldenkrais
2. "The Elusive Obvious" by Moshe Feldenkrais
3. "Embodied Wisdom: The Collected Papers of Moshe Feldenkrais" edited by Elizabeth Beringer

Alexander Technique:
1. "The Use of the Self" by F. Matthias Alexander
2. "Body Learning: An Introduction to the Alexander Technique" by Michael J. Gelb
3. "The Alexander Technique: A Skill for Life" by Pedro de Alcantara

These readings offer valuable insights into the theoretical foundations and practical applications of the Feldenkrais Method and the Alexander Technique, providing readers with comprehensive perspectives on the principles, techniques, and potential benefits of these somatic education approaches for holistic well-being and personal growth.

Counterculture Cuisine: Health Food in the 1970s

The 1970s witnessed a significant cultural shift in the United States, characterized by a growing interest in holistic living, sustainable practices, and an emphasis on natural, unprocessed foods. This transformation gave rise to the emergence of Counterculture Cuisine, a culinary movement that redefined the American diet by promoting healthful, organic, and plant-based eating practices. Rooted in the ethos of the broader countercultural movements of the era, this culinary revolution sought to challenge conventional dietary norms and foster a deeper connection with nature, wellness, and social consciousness.

One of the defining features of Counterculture Cuisine was its emphasis on whole, unadulterated foods, with a strong emphasis on locally sourced, organic produce. Rejecting the industrialized and processed foods that had become emblematic of the mainstream American diet, proponents of this movement advocated for a return to simpler, more natural eating habits, prioritizing fresh fruits, vegetables, whole grains, and legumes. This newfound appreciation for unprocessed, nutrient-dense foods not only reflected a growing awareness of the detrimental effects of artificial additives and preservatives but also underscored a broader commitment to environmental sustainability and ethical consumption.

Moreover, the advent of Counterculture Cuisine in the 1970s coincided with a resurgence of interest in traditional cooking methods and culinary practices from around the world. As part of the movement's quest for authenticity and cultural exploration, individuals began to embrace a diverse array of global cuisines, incorporating elements of Mediterranean, Asian, and Middle Eastern cooking into their dietary repertoires. This cross-cultural exchange not only enriched the culinary landscape but also fostered a deeper appreciation for the nutritional benefits and sensory delights of plant-based, whole-food diets.

The proliferation of health food stores and natural food co-ops served as focal points for the dissemination of Counterculture Cuisine ideals, offering communities access to a wide array of organic produce, bulk grains, and natural products. These alternative food outlets not only provided consumers with a viable alternative to mainstream supermarkets but also served as hubs for community engagement, education, and the exchange of ideas related to holistic living and sustainable agriculture.

In tandem with the rise of Counterculture Cuisine, the 1970s witnessed the popularization of vegetarian and vegan diets as viable alternatives to traditional meat-centered meals. Advocates of plant-based eating emphasized the health benefits of reducing meat consumption, citing evidence that linked vegetarian diets to lower rates of chronic diseases and improved overall well-being. This shift in dietary preferences not only reflected a broader cultural awareness of the ethical and environmental implications of meat production but also sparked a reevaluation of the social and ecological impact of food choices on a global scale.

Furthermore, the dissemination of Counterculture Cuisine principles was facilitated by the proliferation of cookbooks, magazines, and culinary publications that promoted plant-based recipes, natural cooking techniques, and sustainable food practices. Influential publications such as "Diet for a Small Planet" by Frances Moore Lappé and "The Moosewood Cookbook" by Mollie Katzen played a pivotal role in popularizing vegetarian cooking and advocating for sustainable food systems, inspiring a generation of individuals to embrace plant-based diets and conscientious eating habits.

The legacy of Counterculture Cuisine in the 1970s extended far beyond its immediate impact on dietary practices, serving as a catalyst for the broader organic food movement and the reimagining of American gastronomy. By fostering a heightened awareness of the interconnectedness between food, health, and the environment, this culinary revolution laid the groundwork for the sustainable food practices and wellness-oriented lifestyles that continue to resonate with contemporary culinary sensibilities. Counterculture Cuisine not only revolutionized the American diet but also sparked a transformative shift in the collective consciousness, inspiring individuals to cultivate a deeper appreciation for the nourishing power of whole, unprocessed foods and the profound connections between personal well-being, social responsibility, and environmental stewardship.

During the 1970s, the burgeoning health food movement saw the establishment of several pioneering health food stores and the emergence of influential personalities who played key roles in popularizing health food practices and advocating for holistic wellness. But, first:

Sylvester Graham and John Harvey Kellogg

The trajectory from the pioneering ideas of Sylvester Graham and John Harvey Kellogg to the establishment of the first health food store in the United States marks a significant chapter in the evolution of health consciousness and alternative dietary practices. These two prominent figures laid the foundation for the modern health food movement, contributing to the shifting perceptions of diet and nutrition in American society.

Sylvester Graham, a 19th-century Presbyterian minister and dietary reformer, advocated for a natural, plant-based diet as a means to achieve physical and spiritual well-being. Graham's emphasis on whole grains, vegetables, and fruits as essential components of a healthy diet was revolutionary at the time, challenging prevailing dietary habits centered around processed and refined foods. Graham's advocacy for the consumption of whole wheat flour, which later became known as "Graham flour," marked an important step in popularizing the use of whole grains and promoting dietary reform.

John Harvey Kellogg, a physician and health reformer, furthered the work initiated by Graham, focusing on the relationship between diet and health. Kellogg's advocacy for vegetarianism and the consumption of natural, unprocessed foods gained prominence at his Battle Creek Sanitarium in Michigan, where he developed various plant-based dietary regimens for patients seeking holistic wellness. Kellogg's promotion of whole grains, nuts, and fresh fruits as essential components of a balanced diet echoed Graham's earlier emphasis on natural, plant-based nutrition.

Building upon the groundwork laid by Graham and Kellogg, the first health food store in the U.S. emerged in the early 20th century, marking a pivotal moment in the commercialization of health foods and natural products. These stores initially catered to a niche market of health enthusiasts, vegetarians, and individuals seeking alternative dietary options. With a focus on providing whole grains, nuts, seeds, and natural remedies, these early health food stores paved the way for the broader health food movement that would gain momentum in the decades to come.

The first store in the United States devoted exclusively to health food was the Erewhon Natural Foods Market, founded in Boston, Massachusetts, in 1966. The store was established by Michio Kushi, a prominent advocate of macrobiotic diet and lifestyle. Erewhon Natural Foods Market quickly gained recognition as a pioneer in the health food industry, offering a wide range of natural and organic products, including whole grains, fresh produce, and natural supplements. Erewhon Natural Foods Market played a pivotal role in popularizing the concept of health food stores in the U.S., setting a precedent for the growing market of natural and organic products that would emerge in subsequent years. Its name was inspired by the utopian novel "Erewhon" written by Samuel Butler, reflecting the store's commitment to promoting holistic well-being and natural living.

The rise of the first health food store in the U.S. reflected a growing awareness of the interconnectedness between diet and health, as well as a shift in consumer preferences toward natural, organic, and minimally processed foods. Over time, the health food industry expanded, leading to the establishment of larger health food chains and supermarkets that offered a diverse range of natural and organic products to meet the evolving demands of health-conscious consumers.

Some notable figures and establishments from this era include:

First Health Food Stores:

1. Down to Earth: Established in 1977 in Maui, Hawaii, Down to Earth is considered one of the earliest health food stores in the United States. It quickly gained recognition for its commitment to organic, plant-based products and its dedication to promoting sustainable living and mindful consumption.

2. Whole Foods Market: Founded in 1980 in Austin, Texas, by John Mackey, Renee Lawson Hardy, Craig Weller, and Mark Skiles, Whole Foods Market initially started as a small natural foods store but later expanded into a prominent health food chain. Although it was founded slightly later than the 1970s, it became a leading player in the health food industry and played a significant role in popularizing organic and natural products nationwide.

First Chains:

1. Amway: While not exclusively a health food chain, Amway, founded in 1959, gained prominence in the 1970s for its distribution of nutritional supplements, vitamins, and other health-focused products, contributing to the popularization of health supplements and wellness-oriented consumer goods.

2. Trader Joe's: Although it was founded in 1958, Trader Joe's gained substantial traction in the 1970s, emphasizing healthful, natural foods, and serving as a significant player in the promotion of organic and whole-food products within a chain store setting.

Leading Personalities:

1. Frances Moore Lappé: :
Frances Moore Lappé is an American author and advocate known for her influential work in the fields of nutrition, sustainability, and social justice. Born on February 10, 1944, in Fort Worth, Texas, Lappé grew up with a deep appreciation for nature and a curiosity about the interconnectedness of food, health, and the environment. Her passion for these subjects ultimately led her to

become a prominent figure in the world of sustainable living and conscious eating.

Books:
Frances Moore Lappé is most celebrated for her groundbreaking book, "Diet for a Small Planet," published in 1971. This book was a trailblazing exploration of the relationship between food choices, environmental sustainability, and social justice. In "Diet for a Small Planet," Lappé introduced readers to the idea that plant-based diets not only promote personal health but can also have a positive impact on the planet by reducing the strain on resources and mitigating issues like world hunger.

Some of her other notable books include:
1. "Food First: Beyond the Myth of Scarcity" (1977)
2. "The Quickening of America: Rebuilding Our Nation, Remaking Our Lives" (1994)
3. "Hope's Edge: The Next Diet for a Small Planet" (2002, co-authored with her daughter, Anna Lappé)

Influence:
Frances Moore Lappé's influence is profound and far-reaching. "Diet for a Small Planet" was a pivotal work that challenged the prevailing dietary norms of the time, advocating for the reduction of meat consumption and the adoption of plant-based diets. Her book popularized the concept of "sustainable eating" and brought to the forefront the idea that individual food choices could have global consequences. Lappé's work inspired countless individuals to reevaluate their diets, promoting healthful and sustainable eating practices.

Lappé's advocacy extended to broader issues of social and environmental justice. Her writings, lectures, and public appearances spurred conversations about the relationship between agriculture, hunger, and resource use. She co-founded the organization "Food First" in 1975, which is dedicated to eradicating world hunger by promoting sustainable and equitable food systems.

Legacy:
Frances Moore Lappé's legacy is one of profound impact on the way society thinks about food, sustainability, and social justice. Her pioneering work in "Diet for a Small Planet" revolutionized dietary choices by linking personal health with environmental and social well-being. Lappé's advocacy for sustainable eating, her emphasis on plant-based diets, and her call for conscious consumption have had a lasting impact on the food industry, leading to the popularization of organic, vegetarian, and environmentally conscious food choices.

Lappé's legacy extends beyond her books and advocacy work. Her influence can be seen in the growing interest in organic farming, the rise of farmers' markets, the emergence of eco-conscious food companies, and the global movement to address hunger and food insecurity. Her commitment to a more just and sustainable food system continues to inspire individuals and organizations to strive for a healthier planet and a more equitable world. Frances Moore Lappé remains a significant figure in the ongoing conversation about the intersection of food, sustainability, and social justice.

2. Mollie Katzen:
Known for her influential cookbook "The Moosewood Cookbook" (1974), Mollie Katzen played a pivotal role in popularizing vegetarian cooking and introducing a generation of readers to the joys of natural, plant-based cuisine. Her emphasis on fresh, seasonal ingredients and simple, wholesome recipes contributed to the mainstream acceptance of healthful and vegetarian diets.

Bio:
Mollie Katzen is an American chef, artist, and author celebrated for her pioneering contributions to the vegetarian culinary movement. Born on October 13, 1950, in Rochester, New York, Katzen developed a passion for cooking and the arts at an early age. She gained prominence for her innovative approach to vegetarian cuisine, emphasizing the use of fresh, seasonal ingredients and the creative fusion of flavors and textures in her recipes.

Books:
Mollie Katzen is best known for her influential cookbook, "The Moosewood Cookbook," first published in 1974. This seminal work introduced readers to the joys of vegetarian cooking, offering a diverse selection of wholesome, plant-based recipes that emphasized the natural flavors and versatility of fruits, vegetables, grains, and legumes. Some of her other notable books include "The Enchanted Broccoli Forest," "The Vegetable Dishes I Can't Live Without," and "Mollie Katzen's Sunlight Café."

Influence:
Mollie Katzen's influence on the culinary world is profound and enduring. Her cookbooks not only popularized vegetarian cooking but also inspired a generation of home cooks to embrace plant-based diets and explore the creative possibilities of meatless meals. Katzen's emphasis on fresh, seasonal produce, her inventive approach to flavor combinations, and her accessible, user-friendly recipes helped demystify vegetarian cooking and fostered a greater appreciation for plant-centric culinary traditions.

Katzen's artistic background is evident in her cookbooks, which feature hand-drawn illustrations and engaging narratives that evoke a sense of warmth and intimacy. Her emphasis on the visual and sensory aspects of cooking has had a lasting impact on the way individuals approach food preparation and presentation, emphasizing the aesthetic dimensions of the culinary experience.

Legacy:
Mollie Katzen's legacy is one of innovation, creativity, and culinary empowerment. Her role in popularizing vegetarian cooking and promoting the use of fresh, seasonal ingredients has contributed to a broader cultural shift toward plant-based diets and a greater emphasis on sustainable and healthful eating practices. Katzen's cookbooks continue to inspire individuals to explore the diverse flavors and textures of vegetarian cuisine, encouraging a more conscious and mindful approach to cooking and eating.

Through her emphasis on the joy of cooking and the celebration of wholesome, nourishing meals, Mollie Katzen has left an indelible mark on the culinary landscape, fostering a deeper appreciation for the artistry and creativity of vegetarian cooking. Her legacy
292

serves as a testament to the transformative power of food and the enduring legacy of plant-based culinary traditions.

§

Here is a simple and delicious zucchini recipe inspired by Mollie Katzen's approach to vegetarian cooking:

Sautéed Zucchini with Herbs and Garlic
Enjoy the vibrant flavors and textures of this simple and wholesome zucchini dish, reminiscent of Mollie Katzen's approach to vegetarian cuisine.

Ingredients:
- 2 medium zucchinis, thinly sliced
- 2 tablespoons olive oil
- 2 cloves garlic, minced
- 1 tablespoon fresh parsley, chopped
- 1 teaspoon fresh thyme leaves
- Salt and pepper to taste

Instructions
1. Heat the olive oil in a skillet over medium heat. Add the minced garlic and sauté until fragrant.
2. Add the sliced zucchini to the skillet and cook until tender and slightly golden, stirring occasionally.
3. Sprinkle the zucchini with fresh parsley, thyme leaves, salt, and pepper, and continue to cook for another minute to allow the flavors to meld.
4. Remove from heat and serve the sautéed zucchini as a delightful side dish or a light and healthy main course.

§

Health Food Cookbooks of the 70s

1. "Diet for a Small Planet" by Frances Moore Lappé (1971) -
While not strictly a cookbook, it had a significant impact on popularizing vegetarian and plant-based diets.

2. "The Moosewood Cookbook" by Mollie Katzen (1974) - This cookbook helped to popularize vegetarian cooking and is known for its approachable and delicious recipes.

3. "Laurel's Kitchen: A Handbook for Vegetarian Cookery and Nutrition" by Laurel Robertson, Carol Flinders, and Brian Ruppenthal (1976) - This book emphasized natural foods and introduced many readers to the principles of whole foods and vegetarian cooking.

4. "The Tassajara Bread Book" by Edward Espe Brown (1970) - Although not strictly a health food cookbook, it emphasized the use of whole grains and natural ingredients in bread making.

5. "The Natural Foods Cookbook" by Beatrice Trum Hunter (1971) - This book provided a comprehensive guide to cooking with natural and whole foods, focusing on the importance of unprocessed ingredients.

6. "The New Laurel's Kitchen" by Laurel Robertson, Carol Flinders, and Brian Ruppenthal (1986) - While slightly outside the timeframe, this book was an updated version of "Laurel's Kitchen" and continued to promote a healthy, natural approach to cooking.

7. "The New Natural Foods Cookbook" by Marylin Diamond (1975) - This cookbook introduced readers to a wide array of natural and whole food recipes.

8. "The Vegetarian Epicure" by Anna Thomas (1972) - Known for its gourmet vegetarian recipes, this book contributed to the growing popularity of vegetarian cuisine during the 1970s.

9. "The Brown Rice Cookbook" by Ruth Spear (1975) - Focused on recipes centered around brown rice, this cookbook promoted the use of whole grains in everyday cooking.

10. "The Whole Earth Cookbook" by Sharon Cadwallader (1972) - This cookbook emphasized natural, whole foods and included recipes that aligned with the ethos of the Whole Earth Catalog.

11. "The Vegetarian Gourmet Cookbook" by Alan Hooker (1972) - Known for its creative and flavorful vegetarian recipes, this cookbook appealed to those seeking a more gourmet approach to meatless cooking.

12. "The New Farm Vegetarian Cookbook" by Louise Hagler and Dorothy R. Bates (1975) - This cookbook featured recipes that showcased the bounty of fresh, natural ingredients commonly found on organic farms.

13. "The No-Salt, Lowest-Sodium Cookbook" by Donald A. Gazzaniga (1977) - Focused on low-sodium cooking, this cookbook catered to individuals with specific dietary restrictions and health concerns related to sodium intake.

14. "Rodale's Basic Natural Foods Cookbook" by Charles Gerras (1973) - Published by Rodale Press, this cookbook provided a comprehensive guide to natural and organic cooking, emphasizing the importance of sustainable and healthy food choices.

15. "The Art of Natural Cooking" by Helmut G. Siekmann (1973) - This cookbook delved into the art of cooking with natural ingredients, highlighting the flavors and benefits of wholesome, unprocessed foods.

16. "Recipes for a Small Planet" by Ellen Buchman Ewald (1973) - This cookbook provided inventive and nutritious recipes that were specifically designed to be both affordable and environmentally sustainable, catering to those interested in healthy, planet-friendly cooking.

Ten more health food cookbooks that were published in the 1970s:

1. "The New Farm Cookbook" by Louise Hagler and Dorothy R. Bates (1976) - This cookbook emphasized the use of fresh, natural ingredients commonly found on organic farms, and it provided a variety of recipes for healthy, whole food-based meals.

2. "The Natural Foods Sweet-Tooth Cookbook" by Beatrice Trum Hunter (1976) - Focused on natural sweeteners and healthier dessert alternatives, this cookbook offered recipes for satisfying sweet cravings without the use of refined sugars.

3. "The Good Food Cookbook" by Daniel Halpern (1973) - This cookbook focused on the use of wholesome, natural ingredients in a variety of recipes, promoting a balanced and healthy approach to cooking and eating.

4. "Cooking Without Cans" by Ruth Robertson (1973) - Emphasizing the use of fresh, whole foods and ingredients, this cookbook provided recipes that avoided canned and processed foods.

5. "The Vegetarian Way: Total Health for You and Your Family" by Virginia & Mark Messina (1978) - This cookbook focused on vegetarian recipes that provided a comprehensive guide to achieving optimal health through plant-based eating.

6. "The Farm Vegetarian Cookbook" by Louise Hagler (1972) - This cookbook showcased the recipes and cooking styles used on The Farm, a famous commune in Tennessee known for its focus on sustainability and vegetarianism.

7. "Sugar Blues" by William Dufty (1975) - While not a traditional cookbook, this book shed light on the detrimental effects of sugar on health and offered advice on adopting a healthier diet.

8. "The Soybean Cookbook" by Joanne Hush and Beatrice Trum Hunter (1979) - Focused on the use of soybeans in cooking, this cookbook highlighted the nutritional benefits and versatility of soy-based recipes, catering to those interested in plant-based eating.

9. The "Tassajara Cookbook" is a renowned culinary publication that embodies the spirit of mindfulness, simplicity, and natural cooking. Originally published in 1973, this cookbook emerged from the Tassajara Zen Mountain Center, a Zen Buddhist monastery in California, renowned for its emphasis on mindfulness, meditation, and vegetarian cuisine. The cookbook reflects the ethos of the Tassajara community, offering readers a collection of wholesome, plant-based recipes inspired by the principles of Zen Buddhism and the appreciation of seasonal, locally sourced ingredients.

Written by Edward Espe Brown, the "Tassajara Cookbook" emphasizes the art of mindful cooking and the importance of cultivating a harmonious relationship with food and the natural world. The recipes in the book are designed to encourage a sense of mindfulness and intentionality in the culinary process, fostering an appreciation for the flavors, textures, and colors of fresh, unprocessed ingredients. From nourishing soups and salads to hearty grain dishes and delectable desserts, the "Tassajara Cookbook" presents a diverse array of vegetarian recipes that reflect the simplicity and elegance of Zen-inspired cooking.

Beyond its culinary offerings, the "Tassajara Cookbook" serves as a testament to the philosophy of mindful living and the interconnectedness between nourishment, well-being, and spiritual practice. The book's emphasis on the mindful preparation and consumption of food reflects the Zen Buddhist principles of mindfulness and presence, inviting readers to approach cooking and eating as a meditative and contemplative practice. With its emphasis on the importance of balance, harmony, and reverence for the natural world, the "Tassajara Cookbook" continues to inspire individuals to cultivate a deeper connection with their food, their environment, and the inherent simplicity and beauty of the culinary experience.

10. "The Cereal Cookbook: From Porridge to Pancakes" by Rosalind M. Richardson, published in 1978. This cookbook focused on various recipes that incorporated different types of cereal in creative and nutritious ways, aiming to promote the use of whole grains and natural ingredients in everyday cooking. While not as well-known as some of the other titles from that era, it contributed to the broader movement of promoting healthier eating habits through the incorporation of wholesome, unprocessed foods.

Revolutionizing Intimacy:
The Sexual Liberation of the 1970s

The Sexual Liberation of the 1970s marks a significant period in history characterized by a widespread movement towards sexual freedom, exploration, and openness. This era, often referred to as the Sexual Revolution, challenged traditional norms and attitudes surrounding sexuality, leading to greater acceptance of diverse sexual orientations, practices, and lifestyles. As societal taboos began to diminish, the 1970s witnessed a surge in discussions and advocacy for sexual rights, gender equality, and reproductive health, ultimately reshaping the cultural landscape of the modern world.

During the 1970s, various social and cultural factors contributed to the rise of the Sexual Liberation movement. The influence of second-wave feminism, which emphasized women's autonomy and sexual liberation, played a pivotal role in challenging patriarchal structures and advocating for sexual equality. The advent of effective contraception, such as the birth control pill, empowered individuals to make informed choices about their reproductive health and engage in sexual relationships without the fear of unwanted pregnancies. Additionally, the growing awareness of LGBTQ+ rights and the Stonewall riots of 1969 marked a turning point in the fight for sexual and gender diversity, prompting a more inclusive and accepting approach towards non-heteronormative identities.

Amidst the cultural shifts and newfound freedoms, a range of literature emerged to explore and contextualize the Sexual Liberation of the 1970s. Some notable texts include:

1. "The Feminine Mystique" by Betty Friedan - This groundbreaking book critically examined the limitations placed on women within the traditional family structure, urging women to seek fulfillment beyond domestic roles.

2. "The Joy of Sex" by Alex Comfort - Considered a classic in the realm of sexual literature, this book aimed to provide a comprehensive guide to sexual practices and relationships, emphasizing the importance of open communication and mutual consent.

3. "Sister Outsider" by Audre Lorde - This collection of essays and speeches by Audre Lorde highlighted the intersectionality of race, gender, and sexuality, advocating for a more inclusive and compassionate approach to sexual liberation and social justice.

4. "Our Bodies, Ourselves" by the Boston Women's Health Book Collective - Originally published in the early 1970s, this book provided essential information on women's health, reproductive rights, and sexuality, empowering women to make informed decisions about their bodies and lives.

Legacy of the Sexual Liberation movement in the aftermath of subsequent challenges, such as the AIDS epidemic, widespread herpes transmission, sex trafficking, pornography proliferation, and the rise of sex addiction, reveals the complexities and consequences associated with unrestrained sexual expression. The devastating impact of the AIDS crisis brought about a renewed focus on sexual health and education, prompting a more comprehensive understanding of safe sex practices and the importance of responsible sexual behavior. Additionally, the alarming prevalence of sex trafficking and the exploitative nature of the pornography industry have underscored the urgent need for legal protections, ethical regulations, and increased awareness to combat the exploitation and objectification of individuals in vulnerable positions.

Furthermore, the recognition of sex addiction as a legitimate psychological condition has emphasized the importance of mental health support and counseling services to address the underlying emotional and psychological factors contributing to compulsive sexual behavior. This recognition has highlighted the necessity of a more holistic approach to sexual well-being that considers the emotional, psychological, and social dimensions of human sexuality.

In contemporary society, the aftermath of the Sexual Liberation movement serves as a reminder of the critical importance of comprehensive sex education, accessible healthcare services, and ethical practices that prioritize consent, respect, and mutual understanding. While the movement initially aimed to liberate individuals from restrictive societal norms and promote sexual autonomy, its legacy highlights the ongoing need for responsible sexual practices, informed decision-making, and a collective commitment to fostering a culture of consent, safety, and sexual well-being. Moreover, it emphasizes the significance of recognizing the multidimensional aspects of a fulfilling and meaningful life beyond a singular focus on sexual expression, urging a balanced approach that encompasses emotional intimacy, personal growth, and social connection for a truly fulfilling human experience.

So much has been written about this subject, it only seems fair that we present, in the spirit of the 70s a bit of an more inclusive view of the subject. The following is a list of Critical Works and Novels on the Sexual Revolution:

1. "The Second Wave: A Reader in Feminist Theory" edited by Linda Nicholson (1997) - This collection of feminist writings includes critiques of the sexual revolution, exploring issues of objectification, exploitation, and the commodification of sexuality.

2. "The Manipulated Man" by Esther Vilar (1971) - This controversial work criticizes gender roles and suggests that women manipulate men through sexuality.

3. "The Abolition of Marriage: How We Destroy Lasting Love" by Maggie Gallagher (1996) - While published later, this book offers a critique of the changing dynamics of marriage and relationships, reflecting some concerns that emerged in the 1970s.

4. "The Female Woman" by Arianna Stassinopoulos (1973) - In this book, the author challenges feminist ideals of sexual liberation and argues for embracing traditional femininity.

5. "Looking for Mr. Goodbar" by Judith Rossner (1975) - This novel explores themes of sexual liberation, promiscuity, and the consequences of seeking sexual freedom.

**6. "Cinderella Complex: Women's Hidden Fear of Independence"
by Colette Dowling (1981)** - Published in the early 1980s but
relevant to discussions from the 1970s, this book examines how
societal expectations impact women's relationships and sexual
freedom.

These texts provide a range of perspectives on the sexual
revolution and the concept of sex positivity in the 1970s. While
some embraced sexual liberation as a form of empowerment
and self-expression, others raised concerns about its impact on
traditional values, relationships, and gender dynamics. Reading
both core texts and critical works can offer a more comprehensive
understanding of this complex cultural moment.

Christian and Jewish perspectives on the cultural changes of
the 1970s, including shifts in sexuality and relationships, can
provide valuable insights into the religious responses and debates
of that era. Here are some texts from both Christian and Jewish
perspectives:

Christian Perspectives:
**1. "The Celebration of Sex: A Guide to Enjoying God's Gift
of Sexual Intimacy" by Dr. Douglas E. Rosenau (1977)** - This
Christian perspective on sexual intimacy explores how faith
intersects with personal relationships and sexuality.

2. "Love and Responsibility" by Pope John Paul II (1960) -
Although not from the 1970s, this work by Pope John Paul II
provides a foundational Christian perspective on love, sexuality,
and relationships.

**3. "The Pursuit of Intimacy" by David Ferguson and Teresa
Ferguson (1983)** - This book offers a Christian perspective on
developing emotional and spiritual intimacy within marital
relationships.

Jewish Perspectives:
**1. "The Jewish Family: Myths and Reality" by Daniel J. Elazar
(1977)** - This book explores the concept of the Jewish family in

the modern world, addressing issues related to sexuality and relationships.

2. "Intimacy and Sexuality in the Age of Divorce" by Joel B. Wolowelsky (2003) - While published later, this work discusses Jewish perspectives on intimacy, sexuality, and marriage, drawing on traditional Jewish sources.

Interfaith Perspectives:
1. "Sex in the Bible" by John J. Collins (2006) - Although not from the 1970s, this book offers a scholarly exploration of sexuality in the Bible, considering both Christian and Jewish perspectives.

2. "The Kosher Sutra: Eight Sacred Secrets for Reigniting Desire and Restoring Passion for Life" by Rabbi Shmuley Boteach (2009) - This work by Rabbi Shmuley Boteach discusses intimacy, desire, and passion within marital relationships from a Jewish perspective.

It's important to note that while some of these texts were published after the 1970s, they address enduring religious perspectives on sexuality and relationships that were shaped by the cultural changes of that era. Additionally, religious views on these topics can vary widely within Christian and Jewish traditions, so exploring a range of sources and perspectives is recommended for a comprehensive understanding.

Unlocking Desire:
The Role of Sex Therapy in the 1970s

The origins of sex therapy as a formal practice can be traced back to the mid-20th century, with pioneers such as William H. Masters and Virginia E. Johnson playing a pivotal role in its development. Their groundbreaking research and clinical work, notably outlined in their seminal book "Human Sexual Response" (1966), laid the foundation for the scientific understanding of human sexual behavior and dysfunction. Masters and Johnson's work helped destigmatize discussions around sexual issues and paved the way for the establishment of sex therapy as a specialized field within psychology and medicine.

In the 1970s, the practice of sex therapy gained significant recognition and acceptance, leading to the emergence of various therapeutic approaches aimed at addressing a wide range of sexual concerns and dysfunctions. During this period, therapists and researchers further expanded the scope of sex therapy, emphasizing the importance of addressing both physiological and psychological factors in the treatment of sexual difficulties.

However, the practice of sex therapy in the 1970s also faced criticism and scrutiny from various societal and professional quarters. Some critics raised concerns about the potential pathologization of normal sexual behavior, the imposition of rigid norms and standards, and the risk of reinforcing gender stereotypes within therapeutic interventions. Others expressed apprehensions about the ethical boundaries and power dynamics inherent in the therapeutic relationship, emphasizing the need for a balanced and sensitive approach to addressing clients' sexual concerns.

In light of these developments, several critical works emerged during the 1970s, offering diverse perspectives on the practice of sex therapy and its implications for individuals and society. Some of the notable books and critical works from that era include:

1. "The Politics of Experience" by R. D. Laing (1967) - Although published before the 1970s, this book critiqued traditional psychiatric practices and the pathologization of human behavior, offering a critical perspective on the medicalization of mental health and sexuality.

2. "Love and Orgasm" by Alexander Lowen (1965) - This book explored the connections between physical and emotional well-being, highlighting the importance of holistic approaches to sexuality and intimacy.

3. "The Myth of Psychotherapy: Mental Healing as Religion, Rhetoric, and Repression" by Thomas Szasz (1978) - While not from the 1970s, this work critiqued the therapeutic industry and the medicalization of human experiences, urging a critical examination of the societal implications of psychiatric practices, including sex therapy.

4. "The End of Innocence: A Study of the First Sexual Revolution" by Germaine Greer (1990) - Although published later, this book offered a historical and critical analysis of the social and cultural dynamics underlying the sexual revolution and its impact on gender relations and sexual discourse.

These critical works from the 1970s and beyond contributed to the ongoing dialogue surrounding the practice of sex therapy, urging a more nuanced understanding of the complexities and implications of addressing sexual concerns within therapeutic contexts. They underscored the importance of ethical considerations, cultural sensitivities, and the empowerment of individuals in navigating their sexual health and well-being.

Balancing Energy: Chakra Healing, Crystal Therapy, and Energy Medicine

Chakra Healing, Crystal Therapy, and Energy Medicine are alternative healing practices that have gained popularity in recent decades, drawing from ancient and contemporary traditions to promote holistic well-being and balance. While these practices are often considered complementary to conventional medicine, they have faced criticism and skepticism regarding their scientific validity and efficacy.

1. Chakra Healing:
 - Origins: Chakra Healing originated in ancient Indian spiritual traditions, particularly within the practices of yoga and Ayurveda. It focuses on balancing the body's energy centers, known as chakras, to promote physical, emotional, and spiritual well-being.

 - Tools: Chakra Healing often employs meditation, yoga, specific postures, and breathing techniques to stimulate and balance the body's energy centers. Some practitioners also use specific colors, sounds, and affirmations associated with each chakra to facilitate healing.

 - Criticism: Critics often question the scientific basis of chakra energy and argue that the concept lacks empirical evidence. Skeptics also caution against relying solely on chakra healing for serious medical conditions.

2. Crystal Therapy:
 - Origins: Crystal Therapy has roots in ancient civilizations, where crystals and gemstones were believed to possess healing properties and spiritual significance. It draws on the belief that crystals can harness and amplify energy for various therapeutic purposes.

 - Tools: Practitioners of Crystal Therapy use different types of crystals and gemstones, often placing them on specific body parts or incorporating them into jewelry or home decor. Each crystal is believed to possess unique energies that can influence physical and emotional well-being.

- Criticism: Critics often question the scientific basis of crystal healing, citing a lack of empirical evidence to support its claims. Skeptics argue that any perceived effects might be attributed to a placebo effect rather than any inherent properties of the crystals.

3. Energy Medicine:
- Origins: Energy Medicine encompasses various holistic healing practices that focus on the body's energy systems and their role in promoting health and well-being. It draws from ancient healing traditions, including Chinese medicine and Ayurveda, as well as modern understandings of biofields and energy pathways.

- Tools: Energy Medicine practitioners may use techniques such as Reiki, acupuncture, acupressure, and other modalities that aim to manipulate the body's energy fields to promote balance and healing. Some practitioners also utilize biofeedback devices to measure and assess energy imbalances.

- Criticism: Skeptics often question the scientific validity of energy medicine, highlighting the lack of empirical evidence to support its claims. Some critics argue that any perceived effects might be attributed to the placebo effect rather than any measurable changes in the body's energy systems.

Reading Lists

- For Chakra Healing:
"Wheels of Life: A User's Guide to the Chakra System" by Anodea Judith
"Eastern Body, Western Mind: Psychology and the Chakra System As a Path to the Self" by Anodea Judith.

- For Crystal Therapy:
"The Crystal Bible" by Judy Hall,
"The Encyclopedia of Crystals" by Judy Hall.

- For Energy Medicine:
"Energy Medicine: Balancing Your Body's Energies for Optimal Health, Joy, and Vitality" by Donna Eden
"The Subtle Body: An Encyclopedia of Your Energetic Anatomy" by Cyndi Dale.

The Art of Relaxation: Autogenic Training and 'The Relaxation Response'

Autogenic Training and 'The Relaxation Response' are two prominent techniques that have gained recognition for their profound effects on promoting relaxation, reducing stress, and enhancing overall well-being. Developed in the 20th century, both methods focus on harnessing the body's innate capacity to induce a state of deep relaxation and inner peace through simple, self-directed practices. These techniques have played a significant role in the advancement of mind-body medicine, contributing to a greater understanding of the interconnections between mental and physical health.

Autogenic Training, developed by German psychiatrist Johannes Heinrich Schultz in the early 20th century, revolves around the principle of self-regulation through the power of suggestion and imagery. The technique involves a series of self-statements and visualizations aimed at inducing a state of profound relaxation and promoting a sense of well-being. By focusing on sensations such as warmth, heaviness, and a calm heartbeat, individuals can learn to tap into their autonomic nervous system and cultivate a deep sense of inner tranquility.

On the other hand, 'The Relaxation Response,' popularized by Dr. Herbert Benson in the 1970s, draws from various meditative practices, particularly transcendental meditation, to elicit a similar physiological and psychological state of relaxation. The technique involves the repetition of a word, sound, phrase, or prayer, which serves as a focal point for quieting the mind and reducing the body's stress response. By incorporating elements of mindfulness and breath awareness, individuals can activate the body's natural relaxation mechanisms, leading to a reduction in heart rate, blood pressure, and muscle tension.

Both Autogenic Training and 'The Relaxation Response' have garnered significant attention for their therapeutic benefits and their potential in alleviating a range of stress-related ailments, including anxiety, insomnia, and chronic pain. Research has demonstrated the efficacy of these techniques in promoting emotional well-being and improving overall quality of life. Moreover, these practices have paved the way for the integration of mind-body interventions in conventional medical settings, highlighting the importance of holistic approaches to health and healing.

While Autogenic Training and 'The Relaxation Response' have been lauded for their positive impact on stress management and mental health, some critics have raised concerns about the potential oversimplification of complex psychological issues and the reliance on self-directed techniques for addressing deeper emotional challenges. Skeptics also emphasize the need for a comprehensive approach to mental health that integrates these techniques with evidence-based therapies and treatments tailored to individual needs.

In conclusion, Autogenic Training and 'The Relaxation Response' represent notable contributions to the field of mind-body medicine, underscoring the profound effects of relaxation techniques on overall well-being. These practices continue to serve as valuable tools for cultivating inner peace, reducing stress, and fostering a deeper connection between the mind and body. As our understanding of the mind-body connection continues to evolve, the integration of these techniques into mainstream healthcare underscores the importance of incorporating holistic approaches to promote mental and physical health.

The pros, cons, criticism, legacy, and reading lists for Autogenic Training and 'The Relaxation Response':

Autogenic Training:

Pros:
- Offers a simple and accessible technique for inducing relaxation.
- Empowers individuals to develop self-regulation and stress management skills.
- May help alleviate symptoms of anxiety, insomnia, and certain stress-related disorders.
- Can be easily incorporated into daily routines and lifestyle practices.

Cons:
- Requires regular practice and dedication to yield significant results.
- May not be suitable for individuals with certain psychological or medical conditions without professional guidance.

310

- Effectiveness may vary depending on individual responsiveness and commitment to the practice.

Criticism:
- Some critics argue that Autogenic Training oversimplifies complex psychological issues and may not adequately address underlying emotional challenges.
- Skeptics emphasize the need for a more comprehensive approach to mental health that integrates Autogenic Training with evidence-based therapies.

Legacy:
- Autogenic Training has contributed to the advancement of mind-body medicine and the integration of relaxation techniques in stress management and holistic health practices.

Reading List:
1. "Autogenic Training: A Mind-Body Approach to the Treatment of Chronic Pain Syndrome and Stress-Related Disorders" by Wolfgang Luthe and J.H. Schultz
2. "The Comprehensive Guide to Autogenic Training" by J.H. Schultz

The Relaxation Response:

Pros:
- Provides a simple and effective method for inducing a state of deep relaxation.
- Can help reduce stress, anxiety, and promote overall well-being.
- Offers a practical tool for individuals to manage stress and cultivate mindfulness in daily life.

Cons:
- Requires consistent practice and commitment to experience lasting benefits.
- May not address underlying psychological or emotional issues that contribute to chronic stress or anxiety.

Criticism:
- Critics suggest that 'The Relaxation Response' may oversimplify the complexities of stress management and may not be sufficient for addressing more profound psychological challenges.
- Skeptics emphasize the need for a holistic approach that inte-

grates 'The Relaxation Response' with evidence-based therapies in clinical settings.

Legacy:
- 'The Relaxation Response' has significantly influenced the integration of mind-body practices in stress reduction programs, promoting a holistic understanding of the mind-body connection in health and wellness.

Reading List:
1. "The Relaxation Response" by Herbert Benson
2. "Beyond the Relaxation Response" by Herbert Benson

Understanding the pros, cons, criticisms, and legacies of Autogenic Training and 'The Relaxation Response' provides valuable insights into the benefits and limitations of these techniques, highlighting the importance of incorporating holistic approaches to stress management and overall well-being.

§

Skill Acquisition as a Path to Self-Actualization and Fulfillment

The entire point of this section is in the title.
Learn skills. Be happy.

From cooking to painting. From basket weaving, pottery, home repair, car repair, gardening or setting out into your parcel of land and homesteading. One of the key messages of the 70s was- get out and do it. Learn, Baby, Learn.

From 'The Whole Earth' to Infinity

"The Whole Earth Catalog" was a groundbreaking publication that provided a wealth of information and resources on various topics, including tools, self-sufficiency, alternative lifestyles, and environmentalism. It was known for its countercultural and holistic approach to living. If you're interested in books or publications similar in spirit or content, you might consider the following:

1. "The Last Whole Earth Catalog" (1971): This was the follow-up to the original catalog and continued to provide a diverse range of information and resources, including tools, books, and products relevant to the counterculture movement of the time.

2. "Shelter" by Lloyd Kahn: This book explores alternative and sustainable housing designs, DIY building techniques, and ideas for living off the grid. It aligns with the self-sufficiency and environmental themes of "The Whole Earth Catalog."

3. "Mother Earth News" Magazine: While not a book, this long-running magazine focuses on sustainable living, DIY projects, and self-reliance. It covers topics such as gardening, renewable energy, and homesteading.

4. "The Foxfire Book" Series: This series, based on the "Foxfire" magazine, offers a treasure trove of traditional Appalachian knowledge and skills, including folk wisdom, craft techniques, and stories from the region.

5. "The Self-Sufficient Life and How to Live It" by John Seymour: Similar to "The Whole Earth Catalog," this book provides a comprehensive guide to living a self-sufficient and sustainable lifestyle, covering everything from gardening to raising livestock.

6. One of the notable organic gardening magazines that gained prominence during the 1970s was "Organic Gardening & Farming." This magazine played a significant role in popularizing organic gardening practices and promoting environmentally friendly and sustainable agricultural methods. It provided information and resources to help individuals grow their own food organically and reduce their reliance on chemical pesticides and synthetic fertilizers.

"Organic Gardening & Farming" was originally founded in the 1940s but experienced significant growth and influence during the 1970s, aligning with the broader environmental and ecological awareness of the era. The magazine featured articles on topics such as composting, companion planting, natural pest control, and soil health. It aimed to educate readers about the benefits of organic gardening and how it could contribute to healthier, more sustainable lifestyles.

The magazine also played a role in advocating for organic farming practices on a larger scale and promoting awareness of issues related to the environment, conservation, and the impact of agriculture on the planet.

While "Organic Gardening & Farming" was one of the prominent magazines of its time, it's important to note that there were other regional and specialized publications related to organic gardening and sustainable agriculture during the 1970s, reflecting the growing interest in these topics among readers and communities.

7. "Gaia's Garden: A Guide to Home-Scale Permaculture" by Toby Hemenway: This book delves into permaculture principles and practices for designing sustainable and productive gardens and landscapes.

8. "The New Organic Grower" by Eliot Coleman: For those interested in organic gardening and sustainable agriculture, this book provides valuable insights into small-scale farming and market gardening.

9. "How to Be an Explorer of the World" by Keri Smith: While not directly related to self-sufficiency, this book encourages readers to be more observant, curious, and engaged with the world around them, aligning with the spirit of exploration and discovery found in "The Whole Earth Catalog."

These books and publications share some thematic similarities with "The Whole Earth Catalog," including a focus on self-sufficiency, sustainability, DIY culture, and alternative lifestyles. They can serve as valuable resources for those interested in living more consciously and in harmony with the environment.

Homesteading books published between 1829 and 1980 in the United States played a significant role in educating and inspiring individuals to pursue self-sufficiency and land ownership. Here are ten such books:

1. "The American Frugal Housewife" by Lydia Maria Child (1829): This influential book provided practical advice on household management, thrift, and self-sufficiency in the early 19th century.

2. "The Prairie Homestead" by Frank Patterson (1908): Written by a homesteader himself, this book offers insights into the challenges and rewards of homesteading on the American prairie.

3. "One Man's Wilderness: An Alaskan Odyssey" by Richard Proenneke (1973): The author's personal account of building a cabin and living a self-sufficient life in the Alaskan wilderness.

4. "The Woodland Homestead" by Brett McLeod (1979): Originally published as "Small-Scale Forest Farming," this book explores sustainable forestry and farming practices on homesteads.

5. "Rural Living in France" by W.D. Van Riper (1926): This book offers insights into rural living and homesteading in France but contains valuable lessons for aspiring homesteaders in the U.S.

6. "Homesteading: A Montana Family Album" by Pat Bean (1983): While published slightly beyond 1980, this book documents the experiences of a Montana homesteading family and their journey toward self-sufficiency.

7. "Little Heathens: Hard Times and High Spirits on an Iowa Farm During the Great Depression" by Mildred Armstrong Kalish (2007): Although published after 1980, this memoir provides a vivid account of life on an Iowa farm during the Great Depression.

8. "Living the Good Life" by Helen and Scott Nearing (1954): The Nearings' book chronicles their move to a homestead in Vermont and their commitment to a simple, self-sufficient life.

9. "The New Complete Book of Self-Sufficiency" by John Seymour (1976): Seymour's comprehensive guide covers a wide range of topics related to homesteading, self-sufficiency, and sustainable living.

10. "Pioneering Today" by Laura Ingalls Wilder (1932): The author of the beloved "Little House" series reflects on her experiences as a pioneer and homesteader in the late 19th century.

11. Ten Acres Enough: A Practical Experience, Showing How a Very Small Farm May Be Made to Keep a Very Large Family" by Edmund Morris is a classic homesteading book that provides valuable insights and guidance on self-sufficiency and farming on a ten-acre plot of land. Originally published in 1864, this book offers a historical perspective on homesteading practices in the 19th century and remains a valuable resource for those interested in small-scale farming and self-sufficiency.

Five books that complement "Ten Acres Enough" by Edmund Morris and provide additional insights into homesteading, self-sufficiency, and small-scale farming:

1. "The New Organic Grower" by Eliot Coleman: This modern classic explores organic farming techniques and practices for small-scale farmers, offering valuable guidance on sustainable agriculture.

2. "The Self-Sufficient Life and How to Live It" by John Seymour: John Seymour's book is a comprehensive guide to self-sufficiency, covering everything from gardening and animal husbandry to food preservation and building.

3. "The Backyard Homestead" by Carleen Madigan: Geared toward individuals with limited space, this book offers practical advice on how to maximize a small backyard for self-sufficiency through gardening, livestock, and more.

4. "The Resilient Farm and Homestead" by Ben Falk: Focusing on permaculture principles, this book provides insights into creating a resilient and self-sufficient homestead, emphasizing sustainability and regenerative practices.

5. "The Market Gardener" by Jean-Martin Fortier: This book is particularly useful for those interested in small-scale market gardening. It explores efficient and profitable techniques for growing vegetables on a small plot of land.

These books, combined with "Ten Acres Enough," offer a well-rounded collection of resources for anyone looking to embark on a journey of self-sufficiency, homesteading, and sustainable living. They cover a range of topics and provide valuable advice for both novice and experienced homesteaders.

Car Repair in the 70s

The 1970s marked a significant period in the rise of DIY (Do-It-Yourself) car repair, reflecting a growing cultural shift towards self-sufficiency, frugality, and hands-on technical skills. During this decade, various social, economic, and technological factors contributed to the increasing popularity of DIY car repair, leading to a widespread movement of individuals taking automotive maintenance and repair into their own hands.

Amidst the economic challenges and fuel crises of the 1970s, many car owners sought cost-effective solutions to maintain their vehicles and minimize repair expenses. The rising costs of professional auto repairs, coupled with the increasing complexity of automotive technology, prompted a greater interest in DIY car repair as a practical and budget-friendly alternative. Automotive enthusiasts, hobbyists, and mechanically inclined individuals found empowerment and satisfaction in learning how to troubleshoot and repair their cars, fostering a sense of independence and skill mastery.

The emergence of DIY car repair manuals and instructional resources further facilitated the democratization of automotive knowledge, enabling individuals to access step-by-step guides, troubleshooting tips, and comprehensive instructions for a wide range of car maintenance and repair tasks. Popular DIY publications, such as the "Chilton's Repair Manual" and the "Haynes Manual," became essential resources for car owners seeking to understand the intricacies of automotive systems and undertake repairs with confidence.

Moreover, the DIY car repair movement of the 1970s contributed to a broader culture of self-reliance and practical skill-building, encouraging individuals to take a proactive approach to maintaining and preserving their vehicles. Hands-on experiences with automotive repairs fostered a deeper understanding of mechanical principles and instilled a sense of pride and accomplishment among DIY enthusiasts, fostering a community of like-minded individuals dedicated to mastering the art of car maintenance.

While the rise of DIY car repair in the 1970s provided car owners with valuable opportunities to save money and develop practical skills, it also presented certain challenges and limitations. Complex automotive technologies and sophisticated engine systems introduced new complexities that necessitated specialized knowledge and equipment, making certain repairs and diagnostics increasingly challenging for non-professionals. Additionally, the proliferation of electronic components and computerized systems in modern vehicles has further heightened the demand for specialized expertise and diagnostic tools, creating a greater reliance on professional automotive services for intricate repairs and maintenance tasks.

In contemporary times, the legacy of the 1970s DIY car repair movement continues to resonate within the automotive community, fostering a culture of hands-on learning, skill-sharing, and technical empowerment. The availability of online resources, video tutorials, and user-friendly guides has further expanded the accessibility of DIY car repair knowledge, empowering a new generation of car enthusiasts and hobbyists to embrace the art of self-sufficiency and practical problem-solving in the realm of automotive maintenance and repair.

Pioneers of TV Skill Acquisition and the Good Life: Painting, Cooking, Building

The 1970s was a decade of transformation and self-discovery, marked by various movements and figures that encouraged individuals to embark on journeys of self-improvement. Let's explore how learning new skills became a pathway to a better, fuller, and more enriching life during this era.

Bob Ross

Bob Ross, beloved painter and host of the popular television show "The Joy of Painting," captivated audiences with his soothing voice, gentle demeanor, and signature artistic style. Born on October 29, 1942, in Daytona Beach, Florida, Bob Ross discovered his passion for painting at an early age. His journey as a painter and instructor led to the development of an iconic television program that inspired countless viewers to embrace their creativity and appreciate the beauty of nature.

"The Joy of Painting" first aired on PBS in 1983, running for over a decade and gaining a devoted following worldwide. Through his half-hour instructional episodes, Bob Ross shared his love for landscape painting, demonstrating simple techniques and encouraging viewers to explore their artistic abilities. His calm and encouraging demeanor, coupled with his trademark phrase "happy little trees," endeared him to audiences and transformed him into a cultural phenomenon.

Despite his success on television, Bob Ross remained dedicated to his art and the promotion of accessible painting techniques. He emphasized the therapeutic and meditative aspects of painting, emphasizing the importance of creativity as a means of self-expression and stress relief. Bob Ross's unique approach to teaching and his ability to make painting approachable and enjoyable for everyone contributed to the enduring legacy of his television show and artistic philosophy.

Bob Ross's impact extended far beyond his television program. His legacy continues to inspire artists, educators, and individuals seeking creative outlets for self-expression. The Bob Ross Inc. company, established to preserve and promote his artistic vision, continues to offer painting classes, instructional materials, and a range of art supplies. Additionally, the widespread availability of his episodes on various streaming platforms has introduced new generations to his timeless teachings and artistic techniques.

Bob Ross's enduring influence on popular culture is evident in the numerous references to his work in television, film, and internet memes. His positive spirit, coupled with his dedication to sharing the joy of painting, has left an indelible mark on the art world and the hearts of millions of fans around the globe. As an enduring symbol of artistic inspiration and creative expression, Bob Ross's legacy serves as a reminder of the transformative power of art and the enduring impact of a gentle and encouraging spirit.

TV Chefs in the 70s. U.S. & U.K.

TV chefs of the 1970s played a significant role in promoting the importance of learning new culinary skills as a pathway to happiness and personal fulfillment. These chefs, through their engaging television programs, not only showcased the art of cooking but also inspired audiences to embrace the joy of learning and mastering new skills in the kitchen. Their emphasis on accessible and practical cooking techniques encouraged viewers to explore the world of gastronomy, fostering a sense of empowerment and achievement through the acquisition of culinary knowledge.

In an era marked by social and cultural transformations, the presence of TV chefs provided a source of inspiration and guidance for individuals seeking to broaden their culinary horizons. These chefs highlighted the transformative power of hands-on learning, demonstrating that the process of acquiring new skills and knowledge could lead to a deeper sense of satisfaction and personal growth. By demystifying complex cooking methods and presenting cooking as an accessible and enjoyable activity, they instilled a sense of confidence and enthusiasm among audiences, encouraging them to embark on their own culinary journeys.

Furthermore, the TV chefs of the 1970s not only imparted practical cooking techniques but also emphasized the value of creativity and self-expression in the culinary arts. By encouraging experimentation and innovation in the kitchen, they fostered a spirit of exploration and discovery, promoting the idea that cooking could be a form of artistic expression and a source of joy and fulfillment. Their emphasis on the creative aspects of cooking inspired viewers to view the kitchen as a space for self-discovery and personal transformation, cultivating a sense of happiness and fulfillment through the act of cooking and sharing meals with others.

The enduring legacy of these pioneering TV chefs continues to underscore the significance of learning new skills as a means of fostering happiness and personal well-being. Their influence on popular culture and the culinary world serves as a testament to the transformative power of hands-on learning and the profound impact of embracing one's creativity and passion for cooking. As ambassadors of culinary education and advocates for the joy of learning, these TV chefs of the 1970s left an indelible mark on the hearts and kitchens of aspiring cooks and food enthusiasts, inspiring generations to discover happiness through the art of cooking and culinary exploration.

1. Graham Kerr: Known as "The Galloping Gourmet," Graham Kerr hosted a popular cooking show that emphasized entertaining and gourmet cooking techniques. With his energetic and engaging approach, he introduced viewers to a world of sophisticated and creative culinary delights.

2. Julia Child: Julia Child, a legendary figure in the culinary world, became renowned for introducing French cuisine to American audiences through her groundbreaking show "The French Chef." Her warm and enthusiastic personality, coupled with her passion for French cooking, made her an iconic figure in the culinary arts.

3. James Beard: A celebrated chef and culinary expert, James Beard made numerous television appearances during the 1970s, sharing his extensive knowledge and love for cooking with audiences. His dedication to promoting American culinary traditions and techniques cemented his legacy as a pioneering figure in the culinary world.

4. The Two Fat Ladies (Jennifer Paterson and Clarissa Dickson Wright): Known for their unapologetic love of indulgent cooking, Jennifer Paterson and Clarissa Dickson Wright brought humor and traditional British cooking to the screen. Their witty banter and passion for rich, hearty dishes endeared them to audiences worldwide.

5. Jeff Smith: Dubbed "The Frugal Gourmet," Jeff Smith hosted a cooking show that focused on affordable and accessible recipes, making him a popular figure in the 1970s and 1980s. His emphasis on simple yet flavorful dishes appealed to audiences looking to create delicious meals on a budget.

6. Madhur Jaffrey: Renowned for her expertise in Indian cuisine, Madhur Jaffrey also made appearances on television during the 1970s, sharing her rich knowledge of Indian cooking and culture with a broader audience. Her passion for authentic Indian flavors and cooking techniques inspired viewers to explore the vibrant world of Indian gastronomy.

7. Justin Wilson: The Cajun chef and humorist, Justin Wilson, gained popularity for his cooking show, where he showcased traditional Louisiana cooking and entertained audiences with his humorous anecdotes. His charming personality and dedication to preserving Cajun culinary traditions made him a beloved figure in the culinary world.

8. Martin Yan: One prominent Asian TV chef from the 1970s is Yan Can Cook, also known as Martin Yan. Martin Yan is a celebrated Chinese-American chef and television personality who gained widespread recognition for his popular cooking show "Yan Can Cook." Born in Guangzhou, China, Yan developed a passion for cooking at an early age and later immigrated to the

United States. His television show, which first aired in the late 1970s, showcased his expertise in Chinese cuisine and culinary techniques, introducing audiences to the rich and diverse flavors of Asian cooking.

Through his engaging and charismatic on-screen presence, Yan not only demonstrated the intricacies of Chinese culinary traditions but also promoted the accessibility of Asian cooking for a global audience. His ability to simplify complex cooking methods and his emphasis on the use of fresh ingredients resonated with viewers, inspiring them to explore the art of Chinese and Asian cuisine in their own kitchens. Yan's dynamic approach to cooking, coupled with his infectious enthusiasm for sharing his culinary knowledge, made him a beloved and influential figure in the culinary world, both in Asia and the Western world.

Yan's contributions to popularizing Asian cooking and culture on television during the 1970s paved the way for a greater appreciation of Asian gastronomy and culinary techniques on a global scale. His commitment to promoting the joy of cooking and the art of Asian cuisine continues to inspire chefs and food enthusiasts worldwide, fostering a deeper understanding and appreciation of the diverse culinary traditions that enrich the global food landscape. Yan's legacy as a pioneering Asian TV chef serves as a testament to the power of culinary education and cross-cultural culinary exchange, highlighting the enduring influence of Asian culinary traditions and the universal appeal of Asian cuisine.

Selected Reading List

1. Graham Kerr:
- "The Graham Kerr Cookbook" by Graham Kerr
- "Graham Kerr's Creative Choices Cookbook" by Graham Kerr

2. Julia Child:
- "Mastering the Art of French Cooking" by Julia Child
- "The Way to Cook" by Julia Child

3. James Beard:
- "James Beard's American Cookery" by James Beard
- "James Beard's Theory and Practice of Good Cooking"
    by James Beard

4. The Two Fat Ladies (Jennifer Paterson and Clarissa Dickson Wright):
- "Two Fat Ladies: Gastronomic Adventures" by Jennifer Paterson
    and Clarissa Dickson Wright
- "Two Fat Ladies: Full Throttle" by Jennifer Paterson and
    Clarissa Dickson Wright

5. Jeff Smith:
- "The Frugal Gourmet" by Jeff Smith
- "The Frugal Gourmet Cooks American" by Jeff Smith

6. Madhur Jaffrey:
- "Madhur Jaffrey's Quick & Easy Indian Cooking" by
    Madhur Jaffrey
- "Madhur Jaffrey's World Vegetarian: More Than 650 Meatless
    Recipes from Around the World" by Madhur Jaffrey

7. Justin Wilson:
- "Justin Wilson's Easy Cookin': 150 Rib-Tickling Recipes for Good
    Eating" by Justin Wilson
- "Justin Wilson's Cajun Humor" by Justin Wilson

8. Martin Yan:
- "Martin Yan's Feast: The Best of Yan Can Cook" by Martin Yan
- "Martin Yan's Chinatown Cooking: 200 Traditional Recipes
    from 11 Chinatowns Around the World" by Martin Yan

These selected books offer readers a diverse array of culinary
expertise, encompassing various cooking styles and traditions
from around the world.

Home Repair, Woodworking and Carpentry
TV Shows in the 70s

In the 1970s, there were several popular home repair and wood-working TV shows that provided valuable insights and instructions for DIY enthusiasts and woodworking aficionados. Here are a few notable shows from that era:

1. "This Old House" (1979):
"This Old House," a pioneering television series that first premiered in 1979, revolutionized the way audiences approached home improvement and renovation projects. Created by Russell Morash and produced by WGBH, the show quickly became a cornerstone of the home improvement genre, captivating viewers with its practical advice, expert guidance, and in-depth exploration of various renovation and construction endeavors. With its emphasis on historic preservation, craftsmanship, and the restoration of older homes, "This Old House" not only inspired a generation of DIY enthusiasts but also fostered a renewed appreciation for the beauty and heritage of vintage and historic properties.

The show's format, which followed a team of experts as they transformed dilapidated and aging homes into stunning, revitalized spaces, captured the imaginations of viewers and offered a firsthand look at the intricacies of home renovation and restoration. Through its engaging narratives and informative demonstrations, "This Old House" provided audiences with invaluable insights into the art of carpentry, plumbing, electrical work, and other essential aspects of home improvement, fostering a deeper understanding of the craftsmanship and attention to detail required in revitalizing older properties.

The series not only showcased the technical aspects of home renovation but also emphasized the historical significance and architectural integrity of each featured property. By highlighting the stories behind the homes and underscoring the importance of preserving their unique character and design, "This Old House" fostered a sense of cultural heritage and community stewardship among its viewers. The show's dedication to historical accuracy and its commitment to promoting sustainable and environmentally conscious renovation practices helped raise awareness about the value of preserving and maintaining older homes for future generations.

Furthermore, "This Old House" served as a source of inspiration and empowerment for homeowners and DIY enthusiasts, encouraging them to take an active role in the renovation and restoration of their own properties. The show's practical tips, step-by-step tutorials, and expert advice empowered viewers to tackle home improvement projects with confidence and provided them with the necessary tools and knowledge to transform their living spaces into functional, aesthetically pleasing, and historically rich environments.

The enduring legacy of "This Old House" continues to resonate with audiences, underscoring the importance of preserving architectural heritage, fostering community engagement, and promoting the values of craftsmanship and attention to detail in the realm of home improvement and renovation. As a trailblazing television series that redefined the concept of home renovation and restoration, "This Old House" remains a testament to the transformative power of revitalizing aging properties and the enduring significance of preserving the historical and cultural legacy of homes for generations to come.

2. "The Woodwright's Shop" (1979):
"The Woodwright's Shop," a beloved television series that first aired in 1979, offered viewers a captivating journey into the world of traditional woodworking and craftsmanship. Hosted by the charismatic and knowledgeable Roy Underhill, the show celebrated the art of hand-tool woodworking, emphasizing the timeless techniques and age-old methods employed by early American craftsmen. Through its engaging and educational format, "The Woodwright's Shop" not only entertained audiences but also served as a valuable platform for preserving and promoting the rich heritage of woodworking traditions.

The show's emphasis on hand-tool woodworking techniques, such as joinery, carving, and woodturning, provided viewers with a firsthand glimpse into the intricate and meticulous process of creating functional and artistic wooden objects. Roy Underhill's enthusiastic demonstrations and expert insights into the history

328

of woodworking not only showcased the practical applications of traditional tools but also underscored the importance of preserving the craftsmanship and ingenuity of earlier generations.

Beyond its educational value, "The Woodwright's Shop" fostered a sense of nostalgia and appreciation for the simplicity and artistry of handcrafted woodworking. The show's emphasis on the use of hand tools and manual techniques highlighted the meditative and tactile nature of woodworking, offering a refreshing alternative to the modern world's reliance on mechanized and automated processes.

"The Woodwright's Shop" served as a beacon for woodworking enthusiasts and artisans, inspiring a renewed interest in traditional woodworking methods and encouraging a new generation of craftsmen to embrace the artistry and timeless appeal of hand-tool woodworking. Roy Underhill's passion for preserving the legacy of woodworking and his commitment to promoting the art of craftsmanship helped solidify the show's place in the hearts of viewers and woodworking aficionados, leaving an enduring legacy that continues to celebrate the art, skill, and enduring beauty of traditional woodworking.

3. "The New Yankee Workshop" (1989): Although it began in the late 1980s, this show hosted by master carpenter Norm Abram, who first appeared in "this Old House" in 1979, continued into the 1990s. It featured detailed woodworking projects and provided step-by-step instructions on how to create various furniture pieces.

4. "The Woodshop" (1975-1987): Hosted by Andy Standing, "The Woodshop" was a British television program that introduced viewers to woodworking techniques and practical woodworking projects.

These TV shows from the 1970s and their successors in the following decades played a crucial role in educating viewers about home improvement, DIY projects, and woodworking. They continue to be celebrated for their contributions to the world of home improvement and woodworking knowledge.

"The Victory Garden"

"The Victory Garden," which premiered in 1975, was a groundbreaking television series that significantly contributed to the resurgence of interest in gardening and horticulture in the United States. Created by Russell Morash and produced by WGBH, the show played a pivotal role in promoting organic gardening practices, sustainable agriculture, and environmental stewardship. With its emphasis on practical gardening techniques, horticultural education, and the cultivation of diverse plant varieties, "The Victory Garden" became a source of inspiration and guidance for gardening enthusiasts across the nation.

The show's title, a nod to the World War II concept of victory gardens that promoted self-sufficiency and food production, reflected its mission to empower viewers to reconnect with the land and cultivate their own bountiful gardens. "The Victory Garden" provided a platform for expert horticulturists, garden designers, and botanists to share their knowledge and passion for gardening, offering viewers valuable insights into soil management, pest control, plant propagation, and seasonal gardening practices.

Through its engaging and informative episodes, "The Victory Garden" fostered a sense of environmental consciousness and promoted the principles of sustainable living. The show's advocacy for organic gardening methods and eco-friendly practices resonated with a growing movement of individuals seeking to embrace a more natural and holistic approach to gardening and land stewardship. "The Victory Garden" not only provided practical advice for cultivating vibrant and thriving gardens but also highlighted the importance of biodiversity, conservation, and the preservation of green spaces for future generations.

Furthermore, "The Victory Garden" served as a catalyst for community engagement and the sharing of gardening knowledge and expertise. The show inspired a sense of camaraderie and a shared passion for gardening among its viewers, fostering a nationwide network of gardening enthusiasts who were eager to exchange ideas, tips, and success stories. This sense of community and shared enthusiasm for gardening helped cultivate a deeper appreciation for the beauty and abundance of nature and reinforced the importance of fostering sustainable and environmentally conscious gardening practices.

As a pioneering television series that championed the values of organic gardening, sustainability, and environmental stewardship, "The Victory Garden" left an indelible mark on the gardening landscape of the 1970s and beyond. Its enduring legacy continues to inspire a new generation of gardeners to embrace the principles of ecological balance, biodiversity, and the transformative power of cultivating their own flourishing and sustainable gardens. "The Victory Garden" remains a testament to the enduring significance of gardening as a source of joy, nourishment, and environmental stewardship, fostering a deeper connection between individuals and the natural world.

100 Alternative and Complimentary Health Practices

1. Acupuncture
2. Chiropractic Care
3. Massage Therapy
4. Yoga
5. Meditation
6. Aromatherapy
7. Herbal Medicine
8. Tai Chi
9. Reiki
10. Naturopathy
11. Holistic Nutrition
12. Ayurveda
13. Traditional Chinese Medicine (TCM)
14. Craniosacral Therapy
15. Hypnotherapy
16. Sound Therapy
17. Reflexology
18. Biofeedback
19. Energy Healing
20. Cupping Therapy
21. Homeopathy
22. Biofield Therapies
23. Crystal Therapy
24. Art Therapy
25. Breathwork
26. Color Therapy
27. Earthing or Grounding
28. Qigong
29. Holographic Repatterning
30. Emotional Freedom Techniques (EFT)
31. Somatic Experiencing
32. Animal-Assisted Therapy
33. Floatation Therapy
34. Holotropic Breathwork
35. Traditional Indigenous Healing
36. Holographic Repatterning
37. Shamanic Healing
38. Bioresonance Therapy
39. Cymatics Therapy
40. Hakomi Therapy
41. Polarity Therapy
42. Theta Healing
43. Cymatics Therapy
44. Hakomi Therapy
45. Polarity Therapy
46. Theta Healing
47. Feldenkrais Method
48. Alexander Technique
49. Cranial Sacral Therapy
50. Rosen Method
51. Bach Flower Remedies
52. Orthomolecular Medicine
53. Traditional Thai Massage

54. Feng Shui
55. Biodynamic Craniosacral Therapy
56. Somatic Movement
57. Neuro-Linguistic Programming (NLP)
58. Vipassana Meditation
59. Mindfulness-Based Stress Reduction (MBSR)
60. Feldenkrais Method
61. Bates Method (Vision Therapy)
62. Gua Sha Therapy
63. Quantum Healing Hypnosis Technique (QHHT)
64. Rolfing Structural Integration
65. Kinesiology
66. Sensory Deprivation Tanks
67. Ortho-Bionomy
68. BodyTalk
69. Matrix Energetics
70. Somatic Experiencing
71. Zero Balancing
72. Jin Shin Jyutsu
73. Emotional Freedom Techniques (EFT)
74. Soul Retrieval
75. Holosync
76. Yuen Method
77. Vortex Healing
78. Thought Field Therapy (TFT)
79. Traditional Hawaiian Lomilomi Massage
80. Pilates
81. Biodanza
82. Nambudripad's Allergy Elimination Techniques (NAET)
83. SomaVeda Thai Yoga
84. Access Bars
85. Fusion Therapy
86. Couples Counseling
87. Gestalt Therapy
88. Biogeometry
89. Bowen Therapy
90. Core Energetics
91. Jin Shin Do Acupressure
92. Quantum Touch
93. Body Stress Release
94. Pulsed Electromagnetic Field (PEMF) Therapy
95. Visceral Manipulation
96. Phoenix Rising Yoga Therapy
97. Somatic Healing
98. Neuromuscular Therapy (NMT)
99. Kundalini Yoga
100. Transcendental Meditation (TM)

Beyond the Game: Sports as a Path to Self-Realization in the 1970s

In the 1970s, sports emerged as a powerful avenue for self-realization, personal growth, and social change. Amid a backdrop of cultural shifts and societal transformations, the world of sports served as a dynamic platform for individuals to explore their potential, express their identity, and transcend social boundaries. Athletes, both amateur and professional, harnessed the spirit of sportsmanship and competition to challenge conventional norms, redefine personal limitations, and inspire collective change.

During this transformative era, sports became a vehicle for empowerment and self-expression, enabling individuals to break through barriers and assert their unique identities. Athletes from diverse backgrounds and communities found solace and purpose in the pursuit of athletic excellence, using their prowess and achievements to defy stereotypes and pave the way for greater inclusivity and diversity in the realm of sports.

Moreover, the 1970s witnessed a surge in the recognition of women's sports and the growing advocacy for gender equality in athletic pursuits. Female athletes, through their remarkable achievements and unwavering determination, shattered gender stereotypes and catalyzed a paradigm shift in the perception of women's capabilities and contributions in the sports arena. Their triumphs not only elevated the status of women in sports but also ignited a global conversation about the importance of equal opportunities and representation in athletic competition.

In addition to promoting individual empowerment, sports in the 1970s became a catalyst for social change and community engagement. Athletes, through their activism and advocacy, leveraged their platforms to address pressing social issues, promote unity, and foster a sense of collective resilience and solidarity. Their commitment to social justice and equality transcended the boundaries of the playing field, sparking meaningful dialogue and mobilizing communities toward a shared vision of a more equitable and inclusive society.

The transformative power of sports in the 1970s extended beyond the realm of competition, serving as a catalyst for personal and societal transformation. Athletes, spectators, and communities alike embraced the values of perseverance, resilience, and teamwork, recognizing the transformative potential of sports as a pathway to self-realization, empowerment, and collective progress. The legacy of sports in the 1970s continues to inspire a new generation of athletes and advocates, highlighting the enduring impact of sports as a catalyst for personal growth, social change, and the pursuit of individual and collective excellence.

Suggested Reading

1. "The Inner Game of Tennis: The Classic Guide to the Mental Side of Peak Performance" by W. Timothy Gallwey (1974)
2. "The New Toughness Training for Sports: Mental, Emotional, and Physical Conditioning from One of the World's Premier Sports Psychologists" by James E. Loehr (1974)
3. "Sports Hypnosis in Practice: Scripts, Strategies, and Case Examples" by Joseph Tramontana (1977)
4. "Run to the Top: Arthur Lydiard's Masterful Guide to Running" by Arthur Lydiard and Garth Gilmour (1962)

Weightlifting in the 70s

These books from the 1960s and 1970s provide valuable insights into sports psychology, mental conditioning, and training techniques, offering readers a deeper understanding of the psychological aspects of athletic performance and personal development during that dynamic era.

In the 1970s, weightlifting culture embraced a newfound emphasis on health and wellness, promoting the benefits of regular exercise, strength training, and bodybuilding as essential components of a holistic approach to physical fitness. Weightlifting enthusiasts and athletes championed the ideals of discipline, perseverance, and dedication, utilizing weightlifting as a means to cultivate mental resilience and fortitude alongside physical strength and endurance.

Furthermore, the 1970s witnessed the emergence of influential figures in the world of weightlifting and bodybuilding, whose achievements and contributions helped shape the cultural landscape of the sport. Renowned weightlifters and bodybuilders such as Arnold Schwarzenegger, Franco Columbu, and Lou Ferrigno captured the public's imagination, propelling weightlifting into the spotlight and popularizing the pursuit of a sculpted and muscular physique.

The culture of weightlifting in the 1970s not only fostered a sense of camaraderie and shared passion among enthusiasts but also inspired a new generation of individuals to embrace physical fitness as a transformative and empowering lifestyle choice. Weightlifting became a symbol of discipline, dedication, and the pursuit of excellence, embodying the values of perseverance and hard work that resonated with a broader audience seeking to achieve their personal fitness goals and aspirations.

Selected Reading List

1. "The New Encyclopedia of Modern Bodybuilding" by Arnold Schwarzenegger
2. "The Strongest Shall Survive: Strength Training for Football" by Bill Starr
3. "Super Squats: How to Gain 30 Pounds of Muscle in 6 Weeks" by Randall J. Strossen
4. "Keys to the Inner Universe" by Bill Pearl
5. "The Complete Keys to Progress" by John McCallum

These selected readings provide comprehensive insights into During the 1970s, the culture of weightlifting underwent a significant evolution, influenced by a growing interest in physical fitness, bodybuilding, and athletic performance. This era saw weightlifting transform from a niche activity to a mainstream pursuit, with a heightened focus on strength training, muscle development, and physical endurance. As weightlifting gained popularity, it began to transcend its traditional association with competitive sports, becoming a symbol of personal empowerment, physical prowess, and the pursuit of an idealized physique.

On Nature: Some Guides

Aristotle: Aristotle's philosophical insights highlighted the intrinsic relationship between human flourishing and the natural world. His emphasis on the concept of eudaimonia, or human flourishing, incorporated the idea of living in accordance with nature's inherent principles. Aristotle's ethical framework emphasized the importance of cultivating a balanced and virtuous life, grounded in a harmonious coexistence with the natural environment.

Benjamin Franklin: Franklin, known for his pragmatic approach, emphasized the importance of harmony with nature. He recognized the interconnectedness of humans and the environment, advocating for responsible stewardship of natural resources. Franklin's appreciation for the balance between human progress and environmental preservation underscored the significance of ecological consciousness in fostering a sustainable and harmonious society.

Ralph Waldo Emerson: Emerson's transcendentalist philosophy celebrated the spiritual interconnectedness between humanity and nature. His writings underscored the transformative power of nature in fostering self-discovery, spiritual awakening, and a deeper connection to the natural world. Emerson's advocacy for embracing the inherent beauty and spiritual significance of nature emphasized the role of environmental interconnectedness in nurturing personal fulfillment and spiritual enlightenment.

Buckminster Fuller: Buckminster Fuller, a renowned architect, inventor, and futurist, expressed a profound reverence for nature and its intricate systems. Fuller's vision of nature extended beyond its aesthetic and biological aspects, encompassing a holistic understanding of the interconnectedness and interdependence of all living organisms and the environment. He emphasized the essential role of nature as a source of inspiration and knowledge, advocating for a harmonious integration of human innovation and technological advancement with the inherent principles of the natural world.

Fuller viewed nature as a complex and dynamic system, characterized by a delicate balance that sustains life and enables the perpetuation of the Earth's ecosystems. He recognized the intricate web of relationships within nature, emphasizing the importance of understanding and respecting the regenerative capacity of the planet's resources. Fuller's appreciation for the resilience and adaptability of natural systems guided his innovative approach to sustainable design and technology, inspiring the development of environmentally conscious solutions that harmonize with the Earth's natural processes.

Stewart Brand: Brand, a prominent environmentalist and founder of the 'Whole Earth Catalog', emphasized the importance of ecological awareness and sustainable living. His advocacy for a holistic approach to environmentalism encouraged individuals to cultivate a sense of connectedness with the natural world and to prioritize ecological preservation and responsible resource management. Brand's vision of ecological interconnectedness highlighted the imperative of environmental stewardship in promoting global sustainability and long-term well-being.

Collectively, the perspectives of these thinkers underscore the intrinsic connection between human happiness, ecological consciousness, and a harmonious relationship with the natural world. Their insights highlight the significance of embracing environmental interconnectedness and fostering a sense of stewardship for the preservation of nature, contributing to a holistic understanding of the interconnected relationship between human well-being and the environment.

Harmony with Nature: Ecology and the 1970s Self-Help Movement

In the backdrop of the 1970s, an era characterized by a growing consciousness of environmental concerns and a fervent pursuit of personal development, the intertwining concepts of harmony with nature and ecology assumed a profound significance within the burgeoning self-help movement. This period witnessed a collective awakening to the intricate relationship between human well-being and the natural environment, prompting a holistic reevaluation of the interdependence between personal growth and the ecological balance of the planet.

The increasing emphasis on ecological consciousness during the 1970s found a natural alliance with the principles espoused by the self-help movement. This partnership forged an intricate web of interconnected beliefs and practices that emphasized the imperative of living in harmony with nature as a fundamental pillar of personal well-being and spiritual fulfillment. Individuals sought to weave an intimate connection with the natural world into the fabric of their daily lives, recognizing the intrinsic value of environmental stewardship as a conduit for inner peace, holistic growth, and a deeper understanding of the self.

The 1970s marked a critical juncture in the history of environmental awareness, as the devastating impact of industrialization and unchecked human activity on the Earth's delicate ecosystems became increasingly apparent. Amidst the burgeoning environmental movement, the self-help industry positioned itself as a catalyst for personal transformation, advocating for a comprehensive approach to well-being that encompassed ecological mindfulness, sustainable living, and a deep reverence for the natural world. Self-help literature and programs offered a diverse array of techniques and practices that encouraged individuals to cultivate a profound sense of environmental responsibility, nurturing a deeper connection with the Earth and fostering a sense of kinship with all living beings.

Moreover, the ethos of the 1970s self-help movement extended beyond individual spiritual growth and psychological well-being, encompassing a collective vision of societal transformation rooted in the principles of ecological harmony. Individuals were encouraged to embrace a lifestyle that honored the Earth's intrinsic beauty and resilience, fostering a culture of environmental stewardship, and advocating for sustainable practices that preserved the planet's natural resources for future generations. The integration of ecological principles into the fabric of the self-help movement underscored a shared commitment to fostering a harmonious relationship between human civilization and the natural environment, signaling a paradigm shift in the collective consciousness of society.

As the decade progressed, the symbiotic relationship between personal well-being and ecological consciousness continued to evolve, prompting a profound reevaluation of the interconnectedness between the human experience and the natural world. The self-help movement, in collaboration with the burgeoning environmental movement, fostered a culture of mindfulness and introspection that transcended individual growth, inspiring a collective reimagining of humanity's role as custodians of the Earth. Individuals were encouraged to embrace practices that celebrated the sanctity of nature, promoting a deeper understanding of the intricate web of life and the delicate balance that sustained the planet's diverse ecosystems.

The integration of ecological consciousness into the narrative of personal growth and self-help during the 1970s not only redefined the parameters of holistic well-being but also underscored the profound implications of environmental stewardship for the preservation of the planet and the collective welfare of humanity. Individuals were inspired to embrace a lifestyle that embodied the principles of ecological mindfulness, cultivating a profound sense of connectedness with the natural world and fostering a renewed commitment to sustainable living practices. This holistic approach to well-being and environmental consciousness laid the groundwork for a transformative cultural shift, heralding a new era of environmental awareness, personal growth, and collective responsibility for the preservation of the Earth's precious ecosystems.Eco-Spirituality,

The Eco-Self Connection: Eco-Spirituality, Eco-Psychology, and Interconnectedness.

Eco-psychology, a field that emerged in the late 20th century, represents a holistic approach to psychology that emphasizes the interconnectedness between human well-being and the natural environment. It delves into the intricate relationship between the human psyche and the ecological systems in which individuals are deeply embedded. Eco-psychology posits that a healthy connection with nature is essential for human psychological and emotional health, fostering a sense of interconnectedness that is vital for personal and environmental well-being. The discipline draws from various psychological theories, environmental studies, and spiritual practices to elucidate the profound interdependence between human mental health and the health of the planet.

In the realm of eco-psychology, several key figures have contributed to the development and popularization of this interdisciplinary field. One such figure is Theodore Roszak, whose seminal work "The Voice of the Earth: An Exploration of Ecopsychology" (1992) laid the foundation for the conceptual framework of eco-psychology. Roszak emphasized the need for a psychological shift that acknowledges the significance of nature in nurturing human well-being and advocates for a deeper connection with the natural world.

Another prominent figure is Joanna Macy, whose work in the area of deep ecology and environmental activism has significantly influenced eco-psychology. Her book "Coming Back to Life: Practices to Reconnect Our Lives, Our World" (1998), co-authored with Molly Young Brown, highlights the transformative power of reconnecting with nature and emphasizes the role of eco-psychology in fostering environmental consciousness and emotional healing.

Furthermore, the contributions of David Abram, author of "The Spell of the Sensuous: Perception and Language in a More-Than-Human World" (1996), have been instrumental in exploring the intersection between human perception, language, and the

344

natural environment. Abram's work delves into the sensory experience of nature and the ways in which human consciousness is shaped by the environment, underscoring the critical role of eco-psychology in cultivating a deeper understanding of the interconnectedness between humans and the natural world.

The emergence of eco-psychology has paved the way for a comprehensive understanding of the psychological, emotional, and spiritual dimensions of human-nature interconnectedness. By emphasizing the reciprocal relationship between human well-being and environmental health, eco-psychology has inspired a profound reevaluation of the human place within the natural world. Its interdisciplinary approach, drawing from psychology, ecology, and spirituality, continues to foster a deeper appreciation for the symbiotic relationship between human consciousness and the intricate web of life, advocating for a harmonious coexistence that promotes the well-being of both individuals and the planet.

Contemporary Echoes

1. Mary Gomes M.D., Ph.D.: A pioneer in the field of eco-psychology, Mary Gomes has focused her research on the psychological benefits of nature immersion and the therapeutic effects of eco-therapy. Her works, including "Healing with Nature: Mindfulness and Somatic Practices" (2009), have contributed to the integration of nature-based practices into therapeutic interventions, emphasizing the healing potential of nature in addressing psychological distress and promoting emotional well-being.

2. Chellis Glendinning, Ph.D.: As a psychotherapist and eco-activist, Chellis Glendinning has been instrumental in advocating for the recognition of the psychological impact of environmental degradation and the importance of re-establishing a profound connection with the natural world. Her book "My Name is Chellis and I'm in Recovery from Western Civilization" (1994) delves into the psychological implications of modern Western society's disconnection from nature and underscores the role of eco-psychology in fostering ecological consciousness and personal transformation.

3. Craig Chalquist, Ph.D.: A depth psychologist and ecotherapist, Craig Chalquist has focused his research on the intersection of psychology, mythology, and environmental studies. His work "Terrapsychology: Reengaging the Soul of Place" (2007) explores the psychological significance of the natural environment and emphasizes the importance of ecological awareness in nurturing a sense of place-based identity and environmental stewardship.

These key figures, alongside the previously mentioned thought leaders, have collectively enriched the field of eco-psychology, contributing to a deeper understanding of the profound interdependence between human well-being, mental health, and the ecological balance of the planet. Their collective efforts have not only advanced the theoretical foundations of eco-psychology but have also inspired practical applications that promote the integration of nature-based practices into psychological interventions and holistic well-being approaches.

Holistic Living and Environmentalism: Vegetarianism, Aware Living, and Sustainability

The global shift toward vegetarianism and sustainable living has gained significant traction in recent years, reflecting an increasing awareness of the interconnectedness between dietary choices, environmental sustainability, and conscious living. Vegetarianism, as a dietary practice, advocates for the exclusion of meat and, in some cases, animal by-products from one's diet, with a focus on plant-based nutrition and ethical consumption. This conscious choice aligns with the principles of sustainability, emphasizing the importance of reducing one's ecological footprint and promoting the well-being of both individuals and the planet.

Aware living, an ethos rooted in mindfulness and conscious decision-making, complements the principles of vegetarianism and sustainability. It embodies a holistic approach to living that prioritizes ethical consumption, environmental stewardship, and the cultivation of a deep connection with the natural world. By fostering a heightened sense of awareness and responsibility, aware living encourages individuals to make informed choices that align with their values, promoting a lifestyle that respects the interconnectedness between human well-being and the health of the environment.

The concept of sustainability, central to the discourse of vegetarianism and aware living, emphasizes the imperative of preserving natural resources and promoting ecological balance. Sustainable living practices underscore the significance of reducing waste, conserving energy, and adopting eco-friendly alternatives, contributing to the mitigation of environmental degradation and the promotion of long-term planetary health. By embracing sustainable living principles, individuals not only contribute to the preservation of the Earth's ecosystems but also actively participate in the collective endeavor to create a more sustainable and resilient future for generations to come.

As the world grapples with the challenges posed by climate change and global environmental degradation, the integration of vegetarianism, aware living, and sustainability into mainstream consciousness has become increasingly vital. This triad of interconnected principles fosters a collective consciousness that acknowledges the profound impact of dietary choices and lifestyle practices on the health of the planet. By embracing vegetarianism as a dietary choice, cultivating aware living as a guiding ethos, and prioritizing sustainability as a foundational principle, individuals and communities can contribute to a more sustainable and harmonious coexistence with the natural world, paving the way for a healthier and more resilient global ecosystem.

Vegetarianism

Vegetarianism, a dietary practice characterized by the exclusion of meat and animal products from one's diet, has a rich and diverse history that spans cultures and civilizations across the globe. While vegetarianism has gained considerable attention in recent decades, its roots can be traced back to ancient civilizations, where the consumption of plant-based diets was prevalent among various communities and religious groups.

The origins of vegetarianism can be identified in ancient Indian and Greek cultures, where philosophical and religious teachings advocated for the ethical and spiritual benefits of abstaining from meat consumption. In India, the practice of vegetarianism found its roots in the ancient Vedic texts, such as the Rigveda and Upanishads, which emphasized the principles of ahimsa (non-violence) and advocated for a compassionate lifestyle that revered all living beings. This ethical foundation laid the groundwork for the development of vegetarian dietary practices among various Indian communities.

In ancient Greece, influential philosophers such as Pythagoras and his followers promoted the virtues of a plant-based diet, attributing spiritual and ethical significance to the consumption of vegetarian food. Their teachings emphasized the interconnectedness between human morality and dietary choices, fostering a philosophical framework that championed the values of compassion, temperance, and ethical conduct.

Throughout the centuries, vegetarianism continued to be embraced by diverse religious and philosophical movements, including Jainism, Buddhism, and certain sects of Christianity, each emphasizing the spiritual and ethical dimensions of abstaining from meat consumption. The dissemination of these teachings and beliefs facilitated the spread of vegetarian dietary practices across different regions, contributing to the establishment of vegetarian communities and the development of culinary traditions centered around plant-based cuisine.

The modern resurgence of vegetarianism gained momentum in the 18th and 19th centuries, driven by the efforts of various social reformers, health advocates, and ethical philosophers who championed the benefits of vegetarian diets for human health, animal welfare, and environmental sustainability. Influential figures such as Sylvester Graham and John Harvey Kellogg promoted vegetarianism as a means to attain physical and moral purity, advocating for the adoption of plant-based diets as a pathway to personal and societal well-being.

By the early 20th century, vegetarianism had evolved into a global phenomenon, with vegetarian communities and organizations emerging in various parts of the world. The establishment of vegetarian societies and the proliferation of vegetarian literature and cookbooks facilitated the dissemination of vegetarian ideals and practices, contributing to the growing popularity of plant-based diets among individuals seeking to embrace a lifestyle centered around compassion, ethical values, and holistic well-being.

As the world approached the 1980s, vegetarianism had become a dynamic and multifaceted movement, encompassing a spectrum of dietary practices, ethical beliefs, and cultural traditions that celebrated the virtues of plant-based nutrition and sustainable living. The historical trajectory of vegetarianism reflected the enduring legacy of ancient wisdom, ethical teachings, and social reform movements that continue to inspire individuals and communities to embrace a compassionate and sustainable approach to dietary choices and lifestyle practices.

Several famous individuals embraced vegetarianism prior to 1979, advocating for the ethical, health, and environmental benefits associated with a plant-based diet. Some of these notable figures include:

1. Leonardo da Vinci - The acclaimed Italian polymath and Renaissance artist.
2. George Bernard Shaw - The renowned Irish playwright and critic.
3. Mohandas Karamchand Gandhi - The influential leader of the Indian independence movement.
4. Albert Schweitzer - The esteemed German-French theologian, philosopher, and physician.
5. Franz Kafka - The celebrated Czech writer known for his surreal and existential works.
6. Upton Sinclair - The American author and activist, famous for his novel "The Jungle."
7. Rabindranath Tagore - The revered Indian poet, philosopher, and Nobel laureate.
8. H.G. Wells - The prominent English writer, best known for his science fiction works.

9. Henry David Thoreau - The American transcendentalist philosopher and author of "Walden."
10. Nikola Tesla - The visionary inventor and electrical engineer.

These individuals, among others, paved the way for the promotion of vegetarianism and the advocacy of its associated values long before the close of the 1970s, leaving a lasting legacy that continues to inspire individuals to adopt plant-based lifestyles for personal and global well-being.

Benefits and Risks of Being a Vegetarian

A vegetarian diet, when well-planned, can offer various health benefits and contribute to overall well-being. Some of the advantages of a vegetarian diet include:

1. Lower risk of chronic diseases: Studies suggest that a vegetarian diet can reduce the risk of certain chronic illnesses such as heart disease, hypertension, type 2 diabetes, and certain cancers.

2. Weight management: Vegetarian diets, particularly those rich in whole foods, fruits, vegetables, and legumes, can contribute to healthy weight management and help prevent obesity.

3. Improved digestion: Plant-based diets are typically high in fiber, which can promote healthy digestion and reduce the risk of constipation and other digestive issues.

4. Lower cholesterol levels: Vegetarian diets are often associated with lower levels of LDL cholesterol, contributing to better heart health and a reduced risk of cardiovascular diseases.

5. Environmental sustainability: Plant-based diets generally have a lower environmental impact compared to diets that include large amounts of meat, contributing to reduced carbon footprint and conservation of resources.

However, it's important to note that a poorly planned vegetarian diet may pose certain risks and deficiencies, such as:

1. Nutrient deficiencies: Without careful planning, vegetarians may be at risk of deficiencies in essential nutrients such as vitamin B12, iron, calcium, zinc, and omega-3 fatty acids. This can lead to issues such as anemia, bone health problems, and impaired immune function.

2. Potential for processed foods: Some individuals may rely heavily on processed vegetarian foods that are high in added sugars, unhealthy fats, and sodium, which can contribute to various health issues, including obesity and heart disease.

3. Limited food options: In certain social and cultural contexts, individuals following a vegetarian diet may face limited options, leading to potential nutrient imbalances and dietary monotony.

To mitigate these risks, individuals should ensure that their vegetarian diet is well-balanced, diversified, and includes a variety of nutrient-dense plant-based foods to meet their nutritional needs. Consulting with a healthcare provider or a registered dietitian can be beneficial in creating a well-rounded vegetarian meal plan that meets all necessary nutritional requirements.

'Vegetarian Times'

Vegetarian Times is a popular American magazine founded in 1974 by Paul Obis. It focuses on vegetarian cuisine, health, and ethical living. The magazine offers a variety of vegetarian recipes, nutritional advice, and articles on the benefits of plant-based diets. It has been a significant resource for individuals interested in vegetarian and plant-based lifestyles, promoting the values of sustainable, cruelty-free food choices and highlighting the creativity and diversity of vegetarian cooking.

Three Ancient Vegetarian Recipes

1. Ancient Roman Lentil Soup

Ancient Roman Lentil Soup is a traditional dish that has its origins rooted in the culinary practices of ancient Rome. This hearty and nourishing soup embodies the essence of ancient Roman cuisine, known for its simplicity and emphasis on wholesome, rustic flavors. Made primarily with staple ingredients such as lentils, vegetables, and aromatic herbs, this soup reflects the culinary ingenuity of ancient Roman cooks who skillfully combined basic elements to create a satisfying and flavorful dish.

The soup typically features tender lentils that have been simmered to perfection in a rich and savory vegetable broth, resulting in a robust and earthy base that forms the heart of the dish. Complemented by the natural sweetness of onions, the subtle warmth of garlic, and the delicate flavors of carrots and celery, the soup offers a delightful balance of textures and aromas that evoke a sense of comfort and warmth.

Infused with the essence of the Mediterranean, the Ancient Roman Lentil Soup is often seasoned with a hint of aromatic bay leaf, adding a subtle herbal nuance that enhances the overall depth of the flavors. The finishing touch of a drizzle of olive oil further enriches the soup, imparting a luscious mouthfeel and a hint of fruity richness that perfectly complements the earthy notes of the lentils and vegetables.

Characterized by its simplicity and wholesome ingredients, the Ancient Roman Lentil Soup serves as a testament to the ancient Romans' appreciation for nourishing and soulful cuisine that emphasizes the natural goodness of seasonal produce and basic culinary techniques. With its rustic charm and hearty appeal, this soup continues to resonate with modern palates, offering a timeless taste of ancient Roman gastronomy that celebrates the inherent beauty of simple, yet meticulously crafted, plant-based dishes.

Ingredients:
- 1 cup lentils
- 4 cups vegetable broth
- 1 onion, chopped
- 2 carrots, chopped
- 2 celery stalks, chopped
- 2 cloves garlic, minced
- 1 bay leaf
- Salt and pepper to taste
- Olive oil for drizzling

Directions:
1. Rinse the lentils thoroughly and set aside.
2. In a large pot, sauté the onion, carrots, celery, and garlic in olive oil until tender.
3. Add the lentils, vegetable broth, and bay leaf to the pot. Bring to a boil, then reduce to a simmer and cook until the lentils are soft and the flavors have melded, about 30-40 minutes.
4. Season with salt and pepper to taste. Drizzle with olive oil before serving.

2. Ancient Greek Stuffed Grape Leaves (Dolmades)

Ancient Greek Stuffed Grape Leaves, also known as Dolmades, represent a quintessential dish in ancient Greek culinary tradition, renowned for its intricate flavors and cultural significance. This delectable and aromatic dish exemplifies the art of ancient Greek cooking, showcasing a harmonious blend of fragrant herbs, delicate rice, and the exquisite taste of tender grape leaves, meticulously prepared and skillfully rolled into flavorful parcels of culinary delight.

Prepared with a filling of seasoned rice, pine nuts, and currants, the Dolmades offer a delightful medley of textures and flavors, combining the subtle nuttiness of pine nuts with the gentle sweetness of currants, creating a tantalizing balance that is both comforting and sophisticated. Enhanced by the fragrant essence of fresh dill and mint, the stuffing encapsulates the essence of the Mediterranean, infusing each bite with a refreshing herbal bouquet that lingers on the palate, reminiscent of the sun-kissed landscapes of ancient Greece.

The grape leaves, carefully selected and meticulously prepared, envelop the flavorful rice filling, imparting a subtle hint of their own unique tanginess to the dish. The tender and delicate texture of the grape leaves offers a satisfying contrast to the robustness of the rice filling, creating a delightful interplay of flavors and textures that exemplifies the artful craftsmanship of ancient Greek culinary tradition.

Elevated by a drizzle of olive oil and a touch of lemon juice, the Ancient Greek Stuffed Grape Leaves exude the essence of the Mediterranean diet, showcasing the region's reverence for wholesome and aromatic ingredients that celebrate the bountiful produce of the land. With its exquisite blend of flavors and its cultural significance deeply rooted in the ancient heritage of Greece, the Dolmades continue to embody the rich culinary legacy of the Mediterranean, offering a timeless and beloved delicacy that pays homage to the artistry of ancient Greek gastronomy.

Ingredients:
- 1 cup uncooked rice
- 1/4 cup pine nuts
- 1/4 cup currants
- 1/4 cup fresh dill, chopped
- 1/4 cup fresh mint, chopped
- 1/4 cup olive oil
- 1/4 cup lemon juice
- 1/2 teaspoon ground cinnamon
- Salt and pepper to taste
- 20-30 grape leaves (fresh or preserved)

Directions:
1. In a bowl, mix together the rice, pine nuts, currants, dill, mint, olive oil, lemon juice, cinnamon, salt, and pepper.

2. Place a grape leaf flat on a surface, shiny side down. Place a spoonful of the rice mixture in the center of the leaf and fold the sides over the filling. Roll tightly.

3. Repeat with the remaining grape leaves and filling.

4. Place the stuffed grape leaves in a pot, seam side down, and add enough water to cover them. Simmer for 30-40 minutes, or until the rice is cooked.

3. Ancient Egyptian Ful Medames

Ancient Egyptian Ful Medames is a traditional dish that dates back centuries, representing a cornerstone of Egyptian culinary heritage. This hearty and flavorsome dish reflects the essence of ancient Egyptian gastronomy, celebrated for its simplicity, wholesome ingredients, and rich, earthy flavors that pay homage to the fertile lands along the Nile River. Ful Medames epitomizes the ancient Egyptians' reverence for nourishing and nutrient-dense ingredients that sustained their communities and embodied the essence of their cultural identity.

This dish is centered around the humble fava bean, a staple legume that has been cultivated in the region for millennia. The fava beans are cooked to a tender consistency and then mashed, creating a luscious and hearty base that forms the foundation of the dish. Infused with the pungent aroma of garlic and the subtle richness of olive oil, the Ful Medames captivates the senses with its rustic and comforting appeal, evoking a connection to the ancient Egyptian way of life.

Seasoned with a touch of ground cumin that imparts a warm and earthy note, the Ful Medames embodies the ancient Egyptians' appreciation for the aromatic spices that added depth and complexity to their cuisine. Served with a garnish of fresh parsley that enhances its visual appeal and provides a burst of freshness, this dish offers a delightful juxtaposition of textures and flavors, showcasing the ancient Egyptians' adeptness at combining simple ingredients to create a dish that is both nourishing and satisfying.

Elevated by a drizzle of lemon juice that adds a subtle tangy accent, the Ful Medames embodies the time-honored culinary wisdom of ancient Egyptian culture, reflecting their resourcefulness and respect for the abundant gifts of the Nile River Valley. With its wholesome and unpretentious character, the Ful Medames serves as a testament to the ancient Egyptians' profound connection to the land and their enduring legacy of culinary ingenuity that continues to captivate the hearts and palates of generations to come.

Ingredients:
- 2 cups cooked fava beans
- 2 cloves garlic, minced
- 1/4 cup olive oil
- 2 tablespoons lemon juice
- 1 teaspoon ground cumin
- Salt and pepper to taste
- Chopped parsley for garnish

Directions:
1. In a bowl, mash the cooked fava beans with a fork or a potato masher.

2. Add the minced garlic, olive oil, lemon juice, cumin, salt, and pepper. Mix well.

3. Serve the mixture in a bowl, drizzle with additional olive oil if desired, and garnish with chopped parsley. Enjoy with flatbread or pita.

1970s Lentil Loaf

A 70s-style Lentil Loaf captures the essence of the era's health-conscious and plant-based culinary movement, embodying a wholesome and nutritious approach to vegetarian cooking that gained prominence during that time. This comforting and hearty dish exemplifies the 1970s' focus on natural and unprocessed ingredients, showcasing the versatility of lentils as a key component in creating a satisfying and flavorful plant-based alternative to traditional meatloaf.

The lentil loaf is crafted using cooked lentils as the foundation, providing a robust and earthy base that forms the heart of the dish. Complemented by the aromatic notes of sautéed onions and garlic, the lentils create a rich and savory flavor profile that reflects the era's emphasis on hearty and nourishing vegetarian fare. The addition of grated carrots and finely chopped celery lends a delightful textural contrast, infusing the loaf with a vibrant medley of colors and flavors that evoke a sense of rustic charm and home-cooked goodness.

Blending seamlessly with the lentils and vegetables, the binding agents of eggs and breadcrumbs serve to create a cohesive and moist texture, ensuring that the loaf holds its shape while offering a satisfying and hearty bite. Seasoned with a hint of soy sauce and tomato paste that adds a savory umami depth, the lentil loaf encapsulates the essence of the 1970s' penchant for wholesome and balanced flavors that catered to the era's growing interest in vegetarian and health-conscious dining.

Baked to a golden brown finish, the lentil loaf embodies the comforting and familiar essence of classic home-cooked meals that were celebrated during the 1970s. With its nourishing and satisfying appeal, the lentil loaf pays homage to the era's culinary innovation and commitment to plant-based cooking, offering a wholesome and flavorful dish that continues to resonate with contemporary palates and a renewed appreciation for the enduring legacy of 1970s-style vegetarian cuisine.

Ingredients:

- 1 cup dried lentils
- 3 cups vegetable broth
- 1 onion, finely chopped
- 2 cloves garlic, minced
- 1 carrot, grated
- 1 celery stalk, finely chopped
- 1 tablespoon soy sauce
- 1 tablespoon tomato paste
- 1 teaspoon dried thyme
- 1 teaspoon dried oregano
- 1 cup breadcrumbs
- 2 eggs, beaten
- Salt and pepper to taste
- Olive oil for greasing

Instructions:

1. Preheat your oven to 375°F (190°C).
2. Rinse the lentils thoroughly and combine them with the vegetable broth in a saucepan. Bring to a boil, then reduce the heat and simmer for about 20-25 minutes, or until the lentils are tender and most of the liquid has been absorbed.
3. In a separate pan, sauté the onion, garlic, carrot, and celery until they are soft and fragrant.
4. In a large mixing bowl, combine the cooked lentils, sautéed vegetables, soy sauce, tomato paste, dried thyme, dried oregano, breadcrumbs, and beaten eggs. Mix well until all the ingredients are thoroughly combined. Add salt and pepper to taste.
5. Grease a loaf pan with olive oil and transfer the lentil mixture into the pan, pressing it down evenly.
6. Bake for 40-45 minutes or until the top is golden brown and the loaf is firm.
7. Allow the lentil loaf to cool for a few minutes before slicing. Serve with your favorite vegetarian gravy and a side of roasted vegetables for a wholesome 1970s-inspired meal. Enjoy!

Aware Living and Sustainability

Aware Living in the 1970s encapsulated a cultural shift towards holistic well-being, mindfulness, and conscious living. Amidst the backdrop of social change and a growing emphasis on personal development, the concept of aware living gained traction as individuals sought to foster a deeper connection with themselves, others, and the natural world. Emphasizing self-awareness, empathy, and introspection, this movement promoted a mindful approach to everyday life, encouraging individuals to cultivate a heightened sense of consciousness and a profound understanding of their interconnectedness with the environment and society.

During the 1970s, various practices such as meditation, yoga, and holistic healing gained popularity, serving as foundational pillars of aware living. These practices aimed to foster a sense of inner peace, emotional balance, and spiritual harmony, offering individuals the tools to navigate the complexities of modern life with a greater sense of clarity and purpose. The era witnessed an increased awareness of the mind-body connection and the importance of nurturing one's mental, emotional, and physical well-being, leading to a widespread adoption of mindful practices and lifestyle choices that prioritized personal growth, self-reflection, and a conscious engagement with the world around them.

The concept of 'sustainability' emerged as a pivotal paradigm in the 1970s, rooted in the recognition of the finite nature of Earth's resources and the pressing need for responsible stewardship of the environment. Key figures instrumental in popularizing this concept include:

1. Rachel Carson: Known for her groundbreaking book "Silent Spring" (1962), Carson's work highlighted the detrimental effects of pesticides on the environment, inspiring a generation of environmentalists and paving the way for the sustainability movement.

2. The Club of Rome: A group of scientists, economists, and industrialists who published the influential report "The Limits to Growth" (1972), warning of the consequences of unchecked economic and population growth on the planet's resources.

3. E.F. Schumacher: Notable for his book "Small Is Beautiful: A Study of Economics As If People Mattered" (1973), Schumacher advocated for a sustainable, human-scale approach to economics that prioritized environmental conservation and social well-being.

'Sustainability' in this context refers to the capacity to meet present needs without compromising the ability of future generations to meet their own needs. It embodies a holistic approach to development that integrates environmental, social, and economic considerations, aiming to strike a balance between human well-being and ecological integrity.

Criticism of the sustainability movement often centers around the challenges of implementing sustainable practices within existing economic and political frameworks, as well as the potential conflicts between short-term economic interests and long-term environmental conservation goals. Additionally, critics argue that the notion of sustainability can be vague and difficult to quantify, leading to challenges in policy implementation and measurement.

Key works that contributed to the discourse on sustainability include Donella Meadows' "Thinking in Systems: A Primer" (1972), which introduced systems thinking as a tool for understanding complex environmental issues, and the United Nations' "Our Common Future" (1987), also known as the Brundtland Report, which popularized the concept of sustainable development on an international scale, emphasizing the interconnectedness of environmental and social challenges. These works laid the foundation for the modern sustainability movement, shaping policies and practices that continue to guide global efforts toward a more sustainable and equitable future.

Critics of deindustrialization have raised several concerns regarding its potential impacts on economies, societies, and the workforce. Some of the key criticisms include:

1. Job Losses: Deindustrialization can lead to significant job losses in traditional manufacturing sectors, impacting the livelihoods of workers and communities that rely on these industries for employment and economic stability.

2. Economic Disparities: Critics argue that deindustrialization can widen economic disparities, as the loss of manufacturing jobs may disproportionately affect certain regions and communities, leading to social and economic marginalization.

3. Global Competition: The shift of manufacturing to countries with lower labor costs and less stringent environmental regulations has been criticized for promoting a race to the bottom, where workers in developing countries may face exploitative working conditions and environmental degradation.

4. Skills Mismatch: The transition from industrial to service-based economies may require workers to acquire new skills and competencies, posing challenges for those who lack access to education and training opportunities.

5. National Security: Some critics argue that heavy reliance on imports for essential goods, resulting from deindustrialization, may pose risks to national security and sovereignty, particularly during times of geopolitical tension or global crises.

6. Loss of Innovation: Deindustrialization has been criticized for potentially leading to a decline in innovation and technological advancements, as manufacturing hubs often serve as centers for research, development, and technological progress.

Addressing these criticisms requires comprehensive policy measures that prioritize workforce retraining and education, support for affected communities, and the promotion of sustainable and inclusive economic growth. Balancing the need for economic competitiveness with the protection of workers' rights and environmental sustainability remains a key challenge in the ongoing discourse surrounding deindustrialization.

Additionally, conflating pollution with industrial activity can lead to a misunderstanding of the complex relationship between economic development and environmental sustainability. This oversimplification may give rise to several dangers and challenges, including:

1. Stifling Innovation: Overgeneralizing industrial activity as inherently polluting may discourage investment in clean technologies and sustainable manufacturing practices, hindering the development of eco-friendly solutions and impeding progress toward a more sustainable future.

2. Economic Stagnation: Viewing all industrial sectors as environmentally harmful may lead to the stigmatization of manufacturing, potentially resulting in reduced investment, job losses, and economic stagnation, particularly in communities that rely on industrial activities for livelihoods and economic growth.

3. Neglecting Positive Environmental Practices: Focusing solely on the negative impacts of industrial activity may overshadow the positive strides made by many industries in implementing eco-friendly initiatives, such as adopting renewable energy sources, reducing waste, and implementing green technologies to minimize their environmental footprint.

4. Ineffective Policy Solutions: Conflating pollution with all industrial activities may result in the implementation of overly broad or misdirected environmental policies that fail to address the specific sources and types of pollution effectively, potentially leading to regulatory inefficiencies and unintended consequences for both the economy and the environment.

5. Global Economic Imbalances: Misinterpreting industrial activity as synonymous with environmental harm may contribute to the transfer of manufacturing to countries with lower environmental standards, exacerbating global environmental imbalances and promoting unsustainable practices in the long run.

To address these dangers, it is crucial to adopt a nuanced approach that acknowledges the diverse environmental practices within different industrial sectors. Encouraging collaboration between industry stakeholders, policymakers, and environmental experts can facilitate the development of targeted and effective strategies that promote sustainable industrial practices while mitigating the adverse effects of pollution on the environment and human health.

William Morris and E.F. Schumacher

William Morris and E.F. Schumacher shared a vision of a sustainable polity rooted in principles of social justice, environmental conservation, and the promotion of human well-being. Both figures advocated for an alternative economic and social framework that prioritized the needs of communities and emphasized the importance of sustainable practices in fostering a more equitable and harmonious society.

William Morris, a prominent figure in the British Arts and Crafts Movement, envisioned a society where individuals could engage in meaningful and fulfilling work, surrounded by well-crafted and environmentally conscious goods. His emphasis on the integration of art, craftsmanship, and nature into everyday life reflected his belief in the transformative power of aesthetically pleasing and sustainable environments, serving as a catalyst for social change and communal harmony.

E.F. Schumacher, known for his influential work "Small Is Beautiful: A Study of Economics As If People Mattered" (1973), advocated for an economics that prioritized human well-being over endless growth and consumption. Schumacher emphasized the importance of human-scale technologies and decentralized, community-based economic structures that promoted self-reliance and environmental stewardship. He promoted the concept of "Buddhist economics," which emphasized the interconnectedness of human prosperity, environmental sustainability, and spiritual fulfillment.

Both Morris and Schumacher underscored the importance of a sustainable polity that nurtured a sense of community, fostered ecological balance, and promoted the values of craftsmanship, ethical production, and social responsibility. Their visions continue to inspire contemporary movements that seek to address pressing environmental and social challenges, advocating for the integration of sustainable practices into the fabric of governance, economics, and everyday life, with a focus on promoting human dignity, environmental stewardship, and the well-being of present and future generations.

In envisioning a sustainable polity, William Morris and E.F. Schumacher advocated for economic structures that emphasized localized production, community engagement, and environmental stewardship, with a focus on fostering self-reliance, social equity, and ecological balance. While their specific approaches varied, their visions shared common themes that emphasized the importance of sustainable living practices and the integration of ethical and holistic principles into all aspects of society.

For both Morris and Schumacher, the primary source of food would likely be rooted in decentralized agricultural practices, with an emphasis on organic farming, permaculture, and community-supported agriculture. They would promote the cultivation of diverse crops and the use of sustainable farming techniques to ensure food security and environmental resilience.

In terms of sanitation, they would likely advocate for eco-friendly waste management systems, promoting the use of composting, recycling, and decentralized wastewater treatment methods to minimize environmental impact and conserve natural resources.

For energy, both would prioritize renewable and decentralized energy sources, such as solar, wind, and hydroelectric power, to reduce reliance on fossil fuels and mitigate the ecological footprint of energy production. They would encourage the development of community-owned energy cooperatives and the implementation of energy-efficient technologies to promote sustainability and resilience.

Regarding employment, education, and public safety, Morris and Schumacher would emphasize the importance of local craftsmanship, vocational training, and community-led initiatives to create meaningful employment opportunities and foster a sense of collective responsibility. They would advocate for the development of holistic educational programs that integrate practical skills training, environmental awareness, and social ethics to empower individuals and communities to actively participate in the sustainable development of their societies. They would promote community policing and collaborative safety measures that prioritize the well-being and security of all community members, fostering a sense of shared responsibility and mutual support.

Overall, their economic structures would reflect a commitment to social and environmental justice, encouraging a symbiotic relationship between human activities and the natural world, with an overarching goal of fostering resilient, self-sustaining, and equitable communities that prioritize the well-being of both present and future generations. There are a lot of strong objections and arguments to a lot of their assumptions, but they were influential in the 70s.

Nature's Wisdom: Exploring the Deep Ecology Movement

Deep ecology is a philosophical and environmental movement that advocates for the intrinsic value of all living beings and emphasizes the interconnectedness of humans with the natural world. It promotes a holistic approach to environmental issues and advocates for fundamental changes in human attitudes and behaviors toward nature. Some key figures associated with the development of deep ecology include:

1. Arne Næss (1912-2009): A Norwegian philosopher, Arne Næss is credited with coining the term "deep ecology." He emphasized the importance of self-realization and the ecological self, arguing that humans should recognize their interconnectedness with all forms of life. Næss advocated for a biocentric outlook that prioritized the well-being of the entire ecosystem over human-centric perspectives.

2. George Sessions (born 1930): An American environmental philosopher and disciple of Arne Næss, George Sessions contributed to the development of deep ecology through his work on ecophilosophy and environmental ethics. He co-authored the widely recognized and influential text "Deep Ecology for the 21st Century" (1995), which expanded the principles of deep ecology and their implications for contemporary environmentalism.

3. Joanna Macy (born 1929): An American environmental activist, scholar, and Buddhist practitioner, Joanna Macy has played a pivotal role in integrating deep ecology principles with the practice of engaged Buddhism. She is known for her work in environmental education and the promotion of eco-philosophy, emphasizing the interconnectedness of all life and the need for collective action to address global ecological challenges.

4. Bill Devall (1938-2009): An American sociologist and environmental activist, Bill Devall contributed significantly to the articulation and promotion of deep ecology principles, advocating for a paradigm shift in human consciousness and social structures

to foster a more sustainable and ecologically harmonious society. He co-authored the influential book "Deep Ecology: Living as if Nature Mattered" (1985), which explored the ethical and philosophical foundations of deep ecology.

These key figures, among others, have shaped the evolution of deep ecology as a prominent ecological and philosophical movement, inspiring a broader recognition of the interconnectedness of all life and the importance of fostering a more harmonious and sustainable relationship between humans and the natural world.

In addition to the key figures previously mentioned, several other prominent thinkers have contributed to the development and evolution of the deep ecology movement. Some notable deep ecology thinkers include:

1. Gary Snyder (born 1930): An American poet, environmentalist, and advocate for bioregionalism, Gary Snyder has integrated deep ecological principles into his literary works, emphasizing the importance of reconnecting with the natural world and promoting sustainable living practices.

2. Dolores LaChapelle (1926-2007): An American ski mountaineer, author, and deep ecologist, Dolores LaChapelle emphasized the spiritual and cultural dimensions of deep ecology, advocating for a reevaluation of human relationships with the natural environment and the recognition of nature's intrinsic value.

3. John Seed (born 1949): An Australian environmental activist and deep ecologist, John Seed is known for his work in promoting environmental awareness and activism through the practice of "ecosophy," which combines ecological principles with spiritual and philosophical perspectives, fostering a deeper connection with the natural world.

4. Vandana Shiva (born 1952): An Indian scholar, environmental activist, and ecofeminist, Vandana Shiva has contributed significantly to the discourse on deep ecology by highlighting the importance of biodiversity conservation, sustainable agriculture, and the protection of indigenous knowledge systems, advocating for a more holistic and inclusive approach to environmentalism.

These thinkers have expanded the scope of deep ecology, incorporating diverse perspectives and interdisciplinary approaches to address complex environmental challenges and promote a more harmonious relationship between humans and the natural world.

Suggested Reading

1. Arne Næss:
- "The Shallow and the Deep, Long-Range Ecology Movement: A Summary" (1973)
- "Deep Ecology" (1986)
- "Ecology, Community and Lifestyle: Outline of an Ecosophy" (1989)

2. George Sessions:
- "Deep Ecology for the 21st Century" (1995)
- "Ecological Sensibility and Its Relevance to the Human Mind" (1997)

3. Joanna Macy:
- "Despair and Personal Power in the Nuclear Age" (1983)
- "Thinking Like a Mountain: Towards a Council of All Beings" (1986)
- "World as Lover, World as Self" (2007)

4. Bill Devall:
- "Deep Ecology: Living as if Nature Mattered" (1985)
- "Simple in Means, Rich in Ends: Practicing Deep Ecology" (1999)

5. Gary Snyder:
- "The Practice of the Wild" (1990)
- "Turtle Island" (1974)
- "The Real Work: Interviews and Talks, 1964-1979" (1980)

6. Dolores LaChapelle:
- "Sacred Land, Sacred Sex: Rapture of the Deep" (1993)
- "Earth Wisdom" (1997)

7. John Seed:
- "Thinking Like a Mountain: Towards a Council of All Beings" (1986)
- "Thinking Like a Forest: Conversations with John Seed" (2013)

8. Vandana Shiva
Vandana Shiva is an eminent Indian scholar, environmental activist, and ecofeminist known for her profound contributions to the fields of sustainable agriculture, biodiversity conservation, and social justice. Throughout her career, she has been a vocal advocate for the rights of farmers, women, and indigenous communities, promoting a holistic and inclusive approach to environmentalism and sustainability.

Born on November 5, 1952, in Dehradun, India, Shiva earned her Ph.D. in philosophy from the University of Western Ontario, Canada. She later shifted her focus to interdisciplinary research, exploring the interconnectedness of ecological and social systems and the impact of globalization on local communities and ecosystems.

Shiva's work has centered on the preservation of traditional farming practices, the protection of biodiversity, and the promotion of sustainable agriculture. She has been a staunch critic of corporate control over seeds and agricultural resources, advocating for seed sovereignty and the rights of small-scale farmers against the dominance of industrial agriculture and genetically modified organisms.

As the founder of Navdanya, an organization that promotes seed conservation and organic farming, Shiva has been instrumental in establishing community seed banks and promoting agroecology as a sustainable and resilient alternative to conventional industrial farming practices. Her efforts have contributed to the revitalization of indigenous seed varieties and the empowerment of local farming communities across India and beyond.

Shiva's influential works, including "Staying Alive: Women, Ecology, and Survival in India" (1988) and "Biopiracy: The Plunder of Nature and Knowledge" (1997), have brought attention to the intersections of gender, ecology, and social justice, highlighting the importance of recognizing the vital role of women in sustainable development and environmental stewardship.

Her environmental activism and advocacy for biodiversity conservation and social equity have earned her numerous accolades, including the Right Livelihood Award (1993) and the Sydney Peace Prize (2010). Shiva's lifelong dedication to promoting sustainable agriculture, social justice, and grassroots activism has left an indelible mark on the global environmental movement, inspiring countless individuals and communities to strive for a more just, equitable, and ecologically sustainable world.
  - "Staying Alive: Women, Ecology, and Survival in India" (1988)
  - "Biopiracy: The Plunder of Nature and Knowledge" (1997)
  - "Earth Democracy: Justice, Sustainability, and Peace" (2005)

This reading list provides a comprehensive overview of the influential works and contributions of the eight deep ecology thinkers, offering valuable insights into the philosophical, ethical, and practical dimensions of the deep ecology movement and its implications for contemporary environmentalism and sustainability.

Criticism of Deep Ecology

Critics of deep ecology have raised several concerns regarding its philosophical premises and practical implications. Some key criticisms include:

1. Anthropocentrism Debate: Critics argue that deep ecology's rejection of anthropocentrism can neglect the legitimate interests and well-being of human communities, potentially leading to the devaluation of human life and welfare in environmental decision-making.

2. Biocentric Extremism: Some critics view deep ecology's advocacy for biocentrism as extreme and impractical, challenging the notion of giving equal moral consideration to all living beings and ecosystems, and emphasizing the complexities of implementing biocentric principles in real-world environmental policies.

3. Social Justice Concerns: Critics point out that deep ecology's emphasis on wilderness preservation and ecological integrity may overlook the social and economic impacts on marginalized communities, potentially exacerbating social inequalities and environmental injustices.

4. Technological Skepticism: Deep ecology's skepticism toward technological advancements and industrial progress has been criticized for disregarding the potential of technology to contribute to sustainable solutions and environmental conservation, overlooking the role of innovation in addressing complex environmental challenges.

5. Cultural Insensitivity: Some critics argue that deep ecology's universalist approach may neglect the cultural diversity and traditional ecological knowledge of indigenous communities, potentially undermining their rights and interests in natural resource management and conservation efforts.

Addressing these criticisms requires a nuanced understanding of the complexities of environmental ethics and sustainable development, emphasizing the importance of balancing ecological concerns with social justice, cultural sensitivity, and technological innovation. Integrating diverse perspectives and engaging in interdisciplinary dialogue can foster a more holistic and inclusive approach to environmentalism that acknowledges the interconnectedness of ecological, social, and cultural dynamics in shaping a more sustainable and equitable future.

Mindful Eco-Self: 'The Tao of Physics' and Fritjof Capra's Influence

"The Tao of Physics," authored by Fritjof Capra in 1975, stands as a groundbreaking exploration of the intersection between modern physics and Eastern mysticism, illuminating profound parallels between the principles of quantum mechanics and the philosophical tenets of ancient Eastern philosophies, particularly Taoism and Buddhism. Capra's work not only redefined the discourse on the nature of reality and the interconnectedness of all things but also exerted a significant influence on the intellectual landscape of the 1970s, particularly within the realms of ecology and self-help movements.

Capra's synthesis of Eastern spirituality and contemporary physics fostered a paradigm shift in the understanding of consciousness, interconnectedness, and the human relationship with the natural world. The book's overarching message of unity and interconnectedness resonated deeply with the burgeoning ecological consciousness of the 1970s, inspiring a new wave of environmental activism grounded in holistic and systemic approaches to addressing ecological challenges. Capra's emphasis on the interconnectedness of all life and the importance of balance and harmony reverberated within the emerging ecological movements, highlighting the need for a more holistic and sustainable approach to environmental stewardship.

Furthermore, Capra's insights into the interconnected nature of reality and consciousness had a profound impact on the burgeoning self-help and personal development movements of the 1970s. His exploration of the parallels between modern physics and Eastern mysticism offered a new perspective on human consciousness, self-awareness, and the transformative power of holistic approaches to personal growth and well-being. Capra's ideas inspired a shift in the self-help landscape, encouraging individuals to seek a deeper understanding of their place within the interconnected fabric of the universe and to cultivate a more holistic and integrated approach to personal and spiritual development.

"The Tao of Physics" not only bridged the gap between scientific inquiry and spiritual wisdom but also catalyzed a broader cultural shift toward holistic and ecological worldviews, emphasizing the interconnectedness of all life and the importance of balance, harmony, and self-awareness. Capra's profound influence on the ecology and self-help movements of the 1970s continues to resonate today, serving as a testament to the enduring significance of his pioneering work in fostering a more holistic and interconnected understanding of human consciousness, nature, and the universe.

Capra vs. Emerson

Fritjof Capra and Ralph Waldo Emerson, though belonging to different eras and intellectual contexts, share a common ground in their philosophical inquiries into the interconnectedness of human consciousness, nature, and the universe. While Emerson, a seminal figure of the American transcendentalist movement in the 19th century, emphasized the individual's connection with the natural world and the importance of self-reliance and intuition, Capra, a physicist and systems theorist in the 20th and 21st centuries, delved into the parallels between modern physics and Eastern mysticism, highlighting the interrelated nature of scientific principles and spiritual wisdom.

Emerson's emphasis on the individual's capacity for self-discovery and self-reliance reverberates within Capra's exploration of consciousness and interconnectedness, emphasizing the importance of self-awareness and holistic approaches to personal growth and well-being. Both thinkers underscore the significance of human consciousness in shaping one's understanding of the universe and in fostering a deeper connection with the natural world.

However, while Emerson's focus lies predominantly within the realms of individual transcendence and intuitive insight, Capra extends his exploration to encompass the principles of modern physics, offering a scientific foundation for the interconnectedness of all life and the holistic nature of the universe. Capra's work, particularly "The Tao of Physics," serves

376

as a bridge between scientific inquiry and spiritual wisdom, highlighting the parallels between Eastern mysticism and contemporary physics and contributing to a more holistic understanding of the interconnected fabric of the universe.

Ultimately, both Capra and Emerson have left indelible marks on the intellectual landscape, inspiring a deeper appreciation for the interconnectedness of human consciousness, nature, and the cosmos. Their works continue to resonate within contemporary discourses on consciousness, spirituality, and the ecological interconnectedness of all life, underscoring the enduring significance of their contributions to the exploration of the human experience and its relationship with the broader universe.

Capra vs. Bateson

Fritjof Capra and Gregory Bateson, two influential thinkers of the 20th century, shared an interest in the intersection of science, philosophy, and the interconnectedness of systems. While they approached their inquiries from distinct disciplinary backgrounds, their work converged on the exploration of the interconnected nature of reality and the interdependence of living systems.

Fritjof Capra, a physicist and systems theorist, examined the parallels between modern physics and Eastern mysticism, highlighting the interconnectedness of all life and the importance of balance and harmony in the universe. His work, exemplified by "The Tao of Physics," emphasized the holistic nature of reality and its resonance with Eastern philosophical traditions, fostering a deeper understanding of the interconnected fabric of the universe.

Gregory Bateson, a renowned anthropologist, social scientist, and cyberneticist, focused on the interconnectedness of ecological and social systems, emphasizing the role of communication and feedback mechanisms in shaping human behavior and ecological dynamics. His seminal work, "Steps to an Ecology of Mind," emphasized the interconnected nature of living systems and the importance of understanding the broader context in which complex interactions take place, highlighting the profound interdependence between human society and the natural world.

While Capra's work drew upon the principles of modern physics and Eastern philosophy to explore the interconnectedness of consciousness and nature, Bateson's interdisciplinary approach integrated anthropology, cybernetics, and systems theory to illuminate the complex relationships between human behavior and ecological processes. Both thinkers contributed significantly to the understanding of systems thinking and the interconnected nature of life, inspiring a more holistic and integrated approach to addressing ecological, social, and philosophical challenges in the contemporary world.

Suggested Reading by Capra

Fritjof Capra is renowned for his insightful works on the interconnectedness of science, philosophy, and spirituality. Some of his key works and related books include:

1. "The Tao of Physics: An Exploration of the Parallels between Modern Physics and Eastern Mysticism" (1975) - This seminal work examines the intersections between quantum physics and Eastern philosophy, emphasizing the interconnected nature of the universe and the significance of consciousness in shaping our understanding of reality.

2. "The Turning Point: Science, Society, and the Rising Culture" (1982) - In this book, Capra delves into the implications of systems thinking and holistic approaches to science, addressing the interconnected challenges of sustainability, societal change, and human well-being within the context of modern civilization.

3. "The Web of Life: A New Scientific Understanding of Living Systems" (1996) - Capra explores the intricacies of living systems and the principles of complexity and network theory, highlighting the interconnectedness of ecological and social systems and the importance of a holistic understanding of life and its interrelated dynamics.

Suggested reading list related to Fritjof Capra's work:

1. "The Dancing Wu Li Masters: An Overview of the New Physics" by Gary Zukav - "The Dancing Wu Li Masters' presents a compelling exploration of the fundamental concepts of modern physics, elucidating complex scientific principles in a comprehensible and engaging manner. Through an accessible narrative, Zukav introduces readers to the profound insights of quantum mechanics, relativity, and particle physics, inviting them to contemplate the profound implications of these scientific discoveries on our understanding of reality and consciousness.

By skillfully weaving together scientific explanations and philosophical reflections, Zukav demystifies the enigmatic realm of physics, offering readers a captivating journey into the nature of the universe and the intricacies of human perception. With a blend of insightful anecdotes, historical context, and thought-provoking analyses, "The Dancing Wu Li Masters" serves as a gateway to the world of modern physics, inviting readers to ponder the interconnectedness of the physical world and the spiritual dimensions of existence. This seminal work not only illuminates the complexities of quantum theory but also invites readers to contemplate the profound connections between science, consciousness, and the fundamental nature of reality.

2. "The Hidden Connections: Integrating the Biological, Cognitive, and Social Dimensions of Life into a Science of Sustainability" by Fritjof Capra - This book further expands on Capra's exploration of the interconnectedness of all life and the implications for creating a sustainable and resilient future for humanity and the planet.

3. "The Systems View of Life: A Unifying Vision" by Fritjof Capra and Pier Luigi Luisi - This collaborative work offers a comprehensive exploration of the systems perspective in understanding life, consciousness, and sustainability, emphasizing the interconnected nature of living systems and the significance of systems thinking in addressing complex global challenges.

Part VII: The Anachronistic Paperback Rack

A few select books that capture the spirit, even if they were not all published in the 1970s.

"Feel the Fear and Do It Anyway"

"Feel the Fear and Do It Anyway" by Susan Jeffers, published in 1987, holds a significant place in the realm of self-help literature, extending the spirit of the self-improvement movement that gained momentum in the 1970s. Jeffers' book serves as a powerful guide for individuals seeking to overcome self-doubt and embrace a life of resilience and courage, reflecting the broader societal shift towards personal growth and empowerment during this period.

Emphasizing the inevitability of fear in the human experience, Jeffers encourages readers to reframe their perspectives on fear, recognizing it as a catalyst for personal development rather than a barrier to success. Her work resonated with the ethos of the 1970s self-help movement, which championed the transformative potential of self-awareness and personal agency. By advocating for the importance of confronting inner obstacles and cultivating a positive mindset, Jeffers' book aligns with the movement's core principles of individual empowerment and emotional resilience.

Through the integration of practical exercises, motivational insights, and empowering narratives, "Feel the Fear and Do It Anyway" serves as a beacon of encouragement for those navigating the complexities of self-doubt and anxiety. By fostering a culture of proactive self-improvement and mental fortitude, Jeffers' work embodies the spirit of personal growth that characterized the self-help landscape of the 1970s, inspiring readers to embrace their fears, pursue their aspirations, and chart a path towards a more empowered and fulfilling life.

"Looking Out for #1"

The 1970s in the United States were characterized by a complex interplay of cultural upheavals and a shifting social landscape, catalyzed by the aftermath of the civil rights movement, the Vietnam War, and the rise of countercultural movements. Against this backdrop, the emergence of the self-help book "Looking Out for #1" by Robert Ringer in 1977 marked a distinct cultural moment that reflected the prevalent zeitgeist of individualism, self-interest, and personal empowerment.

Ringer's work resonated deeply with a society grappling with the effects of economic instability and disillusionment with traditional social structures. The book's emphasis on self-reliance, assertiveness, and strategic thinking appealed to individuals navigating an increasingly competitive and unpredictable job market, fostering a cultural climate that prioritized personal success and material achievement as symbols of self-worth and validation.

Furthermore, "Looking Out for #1" intersected with the broader literary landscape of the 1970s, which saw the rise of self-help and motivational literature that advocated for personal agency and emotional resilience. Authors like Nathaniel Branden, with "The Psychology of Self-Esteem" (1970), and M. Scott Peck, with "The Road Less Traveled" (1978), contributed to the cultural discourse on personal growth and self-actualization, echoing the prevalent theme of individual empowerment and self-improvement that permeated the societal consciousness of the era.

Psychologically, Ringer's emphasis on the pursuit of self-interest and personal success reflected the collective desire for autonomy and self-fulfillment in a time of social and economic uncertainty. It tapped into the human psyche's inclination toward self-preservation and the pursuit of personal gain as a means of asserting control in the face of external challenges and societal changes.

While critiqued for its promotion of individualistic values potentially at odds with communal well-being, Ringer's work highlighted the cultural undercurrents that shaped the 1970s, underscoring the significance of personal agency and material success as cultural touchstones in an era marked by profound social and economic transformations. Its cultural impact and psychological resonance underscored the role of self-help literature in capturing and reflecting the collective aspirations, anxieties, and ambitions of a generation navigating a rapidly evolving socio-cultural landscape.

"A Whack on the Side of the Head"

"A Whack on the Side of the Head" by Roger von Oech, although published in the 1980s, is deeply rooted in the foundational principles and intellectual currents of the 1970s self-help movement. The 1970s witnessed a cultural shift towards personal growth, individual empowerment, and the exploration of alternative modes of thinking, which laid the groundwork for the creative and innovative perspectives championed by von Oech in his book.

The book's emphasis on fostering a playful and flexible mindset toward problem-solving echoes the broader cultural emphasis of the 1970s on the importance of self-discovery, creativity, and holistic personal development. Von Oech's approach aligns with the psychological theories and self-help strategies popularized during this period, emphasizing the significance of self-actualization, creative expression, and the pursuit of personal fulfillment.

Moreover, the 1970s witnessed a surge in the popularity of self-help literature that advocated for unconventional approaches to achieving success and personal growth. Authors such as Abraham Maslow, with his work on self-actualization and humanistic psychology, and Mihaly Csikszentmihalyi, with his exploration of the concept of flow, contributed to the cultural discourse on the importance of creativity, innovation, and holistic well-being, laying the groundwork for von Oech's ideas on nurturing creative thinking and problem-solving.

By building upon the intellectual currents of the 1970s, "A Whack on the Side of the Head" extends the ethos of personal growth and empowerment into the realm of creative expression and innovative thinking. It encapsulates the era's emphasis on embracing alternative perspectives, challenging conventional wisdom, and fostering a mindset of curiosity and exploration, reflecting the broader cultural climate that emphasized the value of individual agency and creative self-expression as pathways to personal fulfillment and success.

"Awareness"

"Awareness" by Anthony de Mello, first published in 1990, stands as a profound and introspective exploration of spiritual wisdom and self-discovery. De Mello's book transcends traditional notions of self-help, offering readers a transformative journey into the realms of mindfulness, inner peace, and spiritual enlightenment. Through a blend of insightful parables, meditative reflections, and practical exercises, the book invites readers to cultivate a deeper awareness of themselves and the world around them, fostering a path toward greater personal growth and spiritual awakening.

At its core, "Awareness" encourages readers to transcend the limitations of ego-driven consciousness and embrace a state of profound self-awareness and inner stillness. De Mello's teachings draw upon a rich tapestry of Eastern and Western spiritual traditions, weaving together elements of mindfulness, contemplative prayer, and psychological insight to guide readers toward a deeper understanding of the nature of human consciousness and the interconnectedness of all life.

By emphasizing the transformative power of self-awareness and inner silence, "Awareness" serves as a beacon of guidance for individuals seeking to embark on a journey of self-discovery and spiritual awakening. De Mello's poignant narratives and philosophical reflections inspire readers to transcend the confines of conditioned thinking and embrace a more mindful and compassionate way of being, fostering a profound sense of inner peace and interconnectedness with the world.

Despite its post-1970s publication date, "Awareness" resonates with the broader cultural legacy of the 1970s self-help movement, which emphasized the importance of introspection, spiritual growth, and the pursuit of inner peace and emotional well-being. De Mello's work builds upon the foundational principles of self-awareness and mindfulness popularized during the 1970s, serving as a testament to the enduring significance of personal introspection and spiritual enlightenment as transformative pathways to a more fulfilling and purposeful life.

"Zen in the Art of Archery"

"Zen in the Art of Archery" by Eugen Herrigel, published in 1948, gained considerable attention in the 1970s due to the cultural and intellectual climate that embraced Eastern philosophy and mindfulness practices. The book's exploration of the spiritual dimensions of archery, combined with its profound insights into Zen Buddhism, struck a chord with a generation grappling with the complexities of modern life and seeking alternative paths to personal fulfillment and inner peace.

During the 1970s, there was a growing fascination with Eastern spirituality and philosophical traditions in the West, fueled in part by the countercultural movements that sought to challenge traditional social norms and spiritual conventions. Herrigel's work, with its profound exploration of the interconnectedness of mind, body, and spirit in the practice of archery, resonated with the broader cultural shift towards mindfulness, meditation, and the pursuit of spiritual enlightenment as means of achieving inner balance and personal growth.

Furthermore, the book's emphasis on the importance of intuitive awareness and the cultivation of mental stillness through the practice of archery mirrored the broader cultural ethos of the 1970s, which valued introspection, self-awareness, and the pursuit of alternative paths to self-realization. Herrigel's insights into the transformative power of Zen philosophy and the art of archery provided readers with a unique perspective on the significance of mindfulness and spiritual discipline as transformative tools for achieving a sense of inner harmony and well-being.

In essence, "Zen in the Art of Archery" became a significant cultural touchstone in the 1970s, reflecting the era's broader preoccupation with Eastern spiritual practices, the pursuit of mindfulness, and the search for alternative pathways to personal fulfillment and spiritual enlightenment. Its resonance within the cultural milieu of the time underscores its enduring relevance as a testament to the transformative power of Zen philosophy and the art of archery in fostering a deeper understanding of the self and the interconnected nature of all existence.

"Mastery: The Keys to Success and Long-Term Fulfillment"

George Leonard's "Mastery: The Keys to Success and Long-Term Fulfillment," published in 1991, stands as a timeless guide to personal growth and the pursuit of excellence. Leonard's legacy is deeply rooted in his profound insights into the principles of mastery and the importance of perseverance, dedication, and continuous learning in achieving long-term success and fulfillment. His work continues to inspire countless individuals to embrace a mindset of resilience and commitment in their quest for personal and professional development.

Leonard's enduring legacy lies in his emphasis on the significance of practice, patience, and self-discipline as essential components of the mastery journey. By advocating for a holistic approach to personal growth that values progress over perfection, Leonard's work encourages readers to cultivate a resilient mindset that embraces challenges as opportunities for growth and self-improvement.

Furthermore, Leonard's exploration of the concept of mastery resonates with the broader cultural legacy of the 1970s self-help movement, which emphasized the importance of self-awareness, personal agency, and the pursuit of excellence as pathways to personal fulfillment and success. His emphasis on the transformative power of perseverance and dedication aligns with the ethos of personal growth and self-actualization that characterized the cultural landscape of the 1970s, underscoring the enduring significance of his contributions to the field of personal development.

Leonard's legacy extends beyond the realm of personal growth and development, serving as a source of inspiration for individuals across various domains, including education, sports, and professional training. His insights into the dynamics of mastery continue to influence contemporary discourses on skill acquisition, performance enhancement, and the cultivation of resilience and excellence in various fields of endeavor.

In essence, George Leonard's enduring legacy rests on his unwavering commitment to promoting the values of perseverance, resilience, and continuous learning as essential cornerstones of personal and professional growth. His work serves as a testament to the transformative power of dedication and practice in fostering a lifelong journey of mastery and self-fulfillment.

Part VIII: Bestsellers and Their Impact

In the world of self-help literature, certain books have achieved the status of blockbusters, revolutionizing the way people perceive and navigate their lives. Among these, 'Your Erroneous Zones' by Wayne Dyer and 'I'm OK - You're OK' by Thomas Harris stand out as timeless classics. Both books delve into the complexities of human psychology, offering profound insights and practical advice on how to lead a more fulfilling and authentic life. This essay aims to explore the fundamental ideas presented in these self-help blockbusters and their impact on the field of personal development.

'Your Erroneous Zones' by Wayne Dyer

Published in 1976, 'Your Erroneous Zones' catapulted Wayne Dyer into the limelight as a renowned self-help author. The book is centered around the idea that individuals can take control of their lives by identifying and eliminating self-destructive thought patterns and behaviors. Dyer introduces the concept of 'erroneous zones,' which are negative beliefs and habits that hinder personal growth and happiness. He emphasizes the significance of self-awareness and the power of choice in transforming one's life.

Dyer's book encourages readers to break free from societal conditioning and take responsibility for their actions, thoughts, and emotions. He advocates for the importance of self-love, emphasizing that individuals must prioritize their well-being and pursue their authentic desires. Dyer's motivational approach resonates with readers, offering practical steps to overcome self-imposed limitations and cultivate a positive mindset.

Biography of Wayne Dyer:

Wayne Dyer (1940-2015) was an American self-help author and motivational speaker who gained international recognition for his influential work in the field of personal development. Born in Detroit, Michigan, Dyer overcame significant challenges in his

early life, including a difficult childhood and strained family relationships. His experiences shaped his perspective on self-improvement and inspired him to dedicate his career to helping others
realize their potential and achieve personal fulfillment.

Dyer earned his doctorate in educational counseling from Wayne
State University and subsequently began his career as a counselor
and educator. He initially gained prominence through his lectures
and books, with 'Your Erroneous Zones' (1976) serving as his
breakthrough work. Throughout his prolific career, Dyer authored
over 40 books, many of which became bestsellers and garnered
a global following. He frequently appeared on television and
conducted numerous public speaking engagements, captivating
audiences with his charismatic and engaging style.

Dyer's teachings emphasized the power of positive thinking,
self-empowerment, and spiritual growth. He blended psychological concepts with elements of spirituality, advocating for the
importance of mindfulness, gratitude, and personal responsibility. His profound impact on the self-help industry earned him
a reputation as one of the most influential figures in the field,
inspiring millions to pursue a path of self-discovery and inner
transformation.

Criticism of his work:

Despite his widespread popularity and positive impact on many
individuals, Wayne Dyer's work has also faced certain criticisms.
Some critics have argued that his emphasis on the power of positive thinking and the law of attraction oversimplifies the complexities of life, potentially leading to unrealistic expectations and
disillusionment for those unable to achieve immediate results.
Additionally, some psychologists have raised concerns about the
lack of empirical evidence supporting some of the claims made in
his books, suggesting that his approach may lack scientific rigor.

Furthermore, Dyer has been criticized for the commercialization
of spirituality, with some asserting that his incorporation of spiritual concepts into a marketable self-help brand could dilute the
authenticity of spiritual teachings. Critics have also questioned

the originality of some of his ideas, asserting that certain concepts presented in his work were not entirely novel but rather repackaged versions of existing philosophies and teachings.

Despite these criticisms, Wayne Dyer's legacy continues to resonate with many individuals who have found solace and inspiration in his motivational messages. While acknowledging the valid criticisms, it is important to recognize the positive impact he had on the lives of numerous individuals seeking guidance and transformation.

'I'm OK - You're OK' by Thomas Harris

In 'I'm OK - You're OK,' Thomas Harris introduces the concept of Transactional Analysis (TA), which serves as a framework for understanding human behavior and communication. Published in 1967, the book focuses on the dynamics of interpersonal relationships and the role of ego states in shaping individuals' interactions with others. Harris categorizes these ego states into Parent, Adult, and Child, providing readers with insights into how these states influence communication patterns and emotional responses.

Harris's book emphasizes the significance of recognizing one's ego state and understanding the impact it has on interactions with others. By promoting the 'I'm OK - You're OK' mindset, he encourages individuals to foster healthy relationships based on mutual respect and understanding. Harris's work has been instrumental in promoting effective communication and conflict resolution, offering practical techniques for improving interpersonal dynamics and promoting emotional well-being.

Impact on Personal Development

Both 'Your Erroneous Zones' and 'I'm OK - You're OK' have had a profound impact on the field of personal development. These blockbusters have inspired countless individuals to embark on a journey of self-discovery and self-improvement. They have provided readers with valuable tools and strategies for overcoming self-limiting beliefs, enhancing self-esteem, and fostering healthier relationships.

Furthermore, these books have laid the groundwork for a deeper understanding of human psychology and behavior, contributing to the evolution of various therapeutic approaches and counseling techniques. They have empowered individuals to take charge of their emotional well-being and develop a more positive outlook on life.

Conclusion

In conclusion, 'Your Erroneous Zones' by Wayne Dyer and 'I'm OK - You're OK' by Thomas Harris have left an indelible mark on the self-help genre, serving as beacons of guidance and inspiration for individuals seeking personal growth and transformation. Through their innovative insights and practical advice, these books have instilled a sense of empowerment and self-awareness, encouraging readers to embrace their true potential and lead more fulfilling lives. The enduring influence of these self-help blockbusters continues to resonate with audiences worldwide, underscoring the timeless relevance of their profound messages.

Biography of Thomas Harris:

Thomas Harris (1910-1995) was an American psychiatrist and author known for his groundbreaking work in the field of Transactional Analysis (TA). Born in Texas, Harris earned his medical degree from the University of Arkansas and went on to specialize in psychiatry. His interest in understanding human behavior and communication led him to develop the concept of ego states and Transactional Analysis, which he later popularized in his influential book, 'I'm OK - You're OK' (1967).
Harris's work in Transactional Analysis revolutionized the field of psychotherapy, providing a comprehensive framework for analyzing interpersonal relationships and communication patterns. He played a pivotal role in advancing the understanding of psychological dynamics and promoting healthier interactions between individuals. Harris's contributions to the field of psychiatry have had a

lasting impact, shaping therapeutic practices and influencing the way professionals approach counseling and psychoanalysis.

Criticism of his work:

While Thomas Harris's work in Transactional Analysis was widely acclaimed, some critics have raised concerns about the oversimplification of complex psychological phenomena in 'I'm OK - You're OK.' They argue that Harris's model, although effective in many contexts, may not fully encapsulate the intricacies of human behavior and emotions. Some psychologists have suggested that an over-reliance on the TA framework could potentially overlook the deeper underlying issues that contribute to psychological distress and interpersonal conflicts.

Additionally, some critics have contended that Harris's work may lack the empirical evidence necessary to support certain claims made in 'I'm OK - You're OK,' prompting discussions about the need for further research to validate the effectiveness of Transactional Analysis as a therapeutic approach.

Legacy and Reasons to Read His Work Today:

Thomas Harris's legacy lies in his significant contributions to the field of psychiatry, particularly through his development and popularization of Transactional Analysis. His groundbreaking ideas have shaped the way psychologists and counselors approach the understanding of human behavior and interpersonal dynamics. Harris's work continues to serve as a foundational framework for professionals in the field of psychotherapy, guiding therapeutic interventions and promoting effective communication strategies.

Today, readers can benefit from studying Harris's work to gain a comprehensive understanding of Transactional Analysis and its practical applications in improving interpersonal relationships and communication. 'I'm OK - You're OK' remains relevant for individuals seeking insights into their own behaviors and thought patterns, as well as for professionals interested in enhancing their therapeutic techniques and counseling approaches. Despite the criticisms, Harris's contributions have left a lasting impact on the field of psychology, making his work a valuable resource for those interested in personal development and improving their interactions with others.

Cultivating Self-Esteem: Exploring Nathaniel Branden's 'The Psychology of Self-Esteem'

Nathaniel Branden's seminal work, 'The Psychology of Self-Esteem,' published in 1969, serves as a foundational piece in the exploration of self-esteem and its profound impact on personal growth and well-being. Through his groundbreaking insights and innovative perspectives, Branden revolutionized the field of self-help and psychology, emphasizing the crucial role of self-esteem in shaping individuals' perceptions of themselves and their capabilities. This essay delves into the fundamental concepts presented in 'The Psychology of Self-Esteem' and highlights the significance of cultivating a healthy sense of self-worth for achieving personal fulfillment and success.

Understanding Self-Esteem

Nathaniel Branden defines self-esteem as the disposition to experience oneself as competent to cope with the basic challenges of life and as worthy of happiness. He emphasizes that self-esteem is not a fixed trait but a dynamic, evolving aspect of one's psychological makeup, shaped by various internal and external factors. Branden's work underscores the multifaceted nature of self-esteem, linking it to emotional well-being, resilience, and the ability to pursue meaningful goals.

Cultivating Self-Esteem

Branden introduces the concept of self-responsibility, emphasizing the importance of taking ownership of one's thoughts, feelings, and actions. He advocates for the development of self-awareness and introspection, encouraging individuals to confront their insecurities and fears in order to foster personal growth. Branden underscores the significance of setting realistic goals and striving for continuous self-improvement as essential components of building and maintaining healthy self-esteem.

Furthermore, Branden addresses the impact of external influences, such as societal expectations and cultural norms, on individuals' self-esteem. He emphasizes the need to challenge limiting beliefs and cultural conditioning, encouraging readers to embrace their unique identity and pursue authentic self-expression. Branden's work promotes the idea that self-acceptance and self-assertiveness are integral to fostering a robust sense of self-worth and confidence.

Impact and Legacy

Nathaniel Branden's 'The Psychology of Self-Esteem' has had a profound impact on the field of psychology and self-help literature. His pioneering insights have influenced countless individuals seeking to understand the intricacies of self-esteem and its transformative power. Branden's emphasis on the importance of self-acceptance and self-responsibility has resonated with readers, inspiring them to embark on a journey of self-discovery and personal empowerment.

Moreover, Branden's work has significantly shaped therapeutic approaches and counseling techniques, highlighting the crucial role of self-esteem in promoting emotional well-being and psychological resilience. His legacy continues to influence contemporary discussions on self-esteem, fostering a greater understanding of the psychological mechanisms that contribute to individuals' sense of self-worth and confidence.

Conclusion

Nathaniel Branden's 'The Psychology of Self-Esteem' remains a timeless masterpiece that continues to offer valuable insights into the intricate dynamics of self-worth and personal development. Through his profound understanding of human psychology and the complexities of self-esteem, Branden has paved the way for individuals to cultivate a healthier and more positive relationship with themselves. His work serves as a beacon of guidance, encouraging readers to embrace their innate potential and strive for a more fulfilling and authentic life.

Being With Ayn Rand

Ayn Rand (1905-1982) was a Russian-American writer and philosopher known for her influential works of fiction and philosophy. She developed a philosophical system called Objectivism, which emphasized individualism, rational self-interest, and the pursuit of one's own happiness as the moral purpose of life. Her novels, including "The Fountainhead" and "Atlas Shrugged," promoted her philosophical ideas and continue to be widely read and debated. Rand's emphasis on capitalism, reason, and individualism has sparked both admiration and criticism, making her a polarizing figure in the realms of literature and philosophy.

Nathaniel Branden, known for his work on self-esteem, had a complex relationship with the influential philosopher Ayn Rand. The criticism surrounding Branden and his connection to Rand largely stems from their personal and professional relationship, as well as their philosophical differences.

Criticism:

1. Personal Relationship: Branden's romantic involvement with Ayn Rand, who was his mentor and an influential figure in his intellectual development, has raised questions about the nature of their association. Their affair, along with its eventual dissolution, led to a publicized rift that affected the Objectivist movement they were both involved in.

2. Alleged Deception: Some critics have accused Branden of ethical misconduct and deceit within the Objectivist movement, leading to a tarnished reputation in the eyes of some of Rand's followers. The controversies surrounding the dissolution of his relationship with Rand have fueled skepticism regarding his character and credibility.

3. Departure from Objectivism: Branden's eventual departure from the strict tenets of Objectivism, the philosophical system developed by Ayn Rand, led to further criticism. His evolving perspectives on psychology and his exploration of areas beyond Rand's philosophical framework have been seen as a deviation from the principles he once espoused.

Relationship to Ayn Rand:

1. Influence on Objectivism: Nathaniel Branden played a significant role in popularizing Ayn Rand's philosophy of Objectivism through his writing and public speaking. He co-founded the Nathaniel Branden Institute to promote Objectivist ideas, contributing to the movement's growth and dissemination.

2. Psychological Applications: Branden's work on self-esteem, which was influenced by his association with Ayn Rand, integrated psychological concepts with Objectivist philosophy. His emphasis on the importance of self-esteem and self-responsibility resonated with some of the core principles of Objectivism, albeit with an expanded psychological perspective.

3. Philosophical Divergence: Despite his early adherence to Rand's Objectivist philosophy, Branden eventually developed his own theories in the field of psychology, delving into areas beyond the scope of Objectivism. This divergence led to a divergence between the two thinkers, culminating in a publicized break that shaped their respective legacies.

In summary, Nathaniel Branden's criticism and relationship to Ayn Rand are intertwined with the complexities of their personal and intellectual connections. While his contributions to Objectivism were significant, his divergence from the strict confines of Rand's philosophy and the controversies surrounding their relationship have left a complex legacy that continues to be a subject of debate and scrutiny within philosophical and psychological circles.

The Alchemy of Personal Change: Exploring 'The Road Less Traveled' by M. Scott Peck

M. Scott Peck's 'The Road Less Traveled,' published in 1978, remains a transformative guide that has influenced generations with its profound insights on personal growth and spiritual development. With a unique blend of psychology and spirituality, Peck invites readers to embark on a transformative journey of self-discovery, emphasizing the significance of embracing personal responsibility, discipline, and love as fundamental catalysts for personal change. This essay delves into the key themes presented in 'The Road Less Traveled' and highlights the transformative power of embracing personal challenges and fostering spiritual growth.

Embracing Personal Responsibility

At the heart of 'The Road Less Traveled' lies the idea of embracing personal responsibility as the cornerstone of personal development. Peck underscores the significance of accepting life's challenges and confronting one's own shortcomings with courage and humility. He encourages readers to recognize the importance of self-discipline and the willingness to make difficult choices as essential components of personal growth.

Cultivating Spiritual Growth

Peck's work delves into the transformative power of spirituality, emphasizing the role of love, grace, and spiritual discipline in fostering inner harmony and emotional well-being. He presents spiritual growth as an ongoing process that requires conscious effort and dedication, advocating for the integration of spiritual principles into daily life to attain a deeper sense of purpose and fulfillment.

The Alchemy of Personal Change

'The Road Less Traveled' serves as a guide for individuals seeking to embark on a path of personal transformation and self-realization. Peck's emphasis on the alchemical process of personal change underscores the transformative power of self-awareness and introspection, guiding readers toward a deeper understanding of themselves and their place in the world. His approach encourages individuals to embrace life's complexities and uncertainties, viewing challenges as opportunities for spiritual and emotional evolution.

Impact and Legacy

M. Scott Peck's 'The Road Less Traveled' has had a profound impact on the field of personal development and spiritual growth. His innovative blend of psychology and spirituality has resonated with readers worldwide, inspiring them to confront their inner struggles and cultivate a more profound sense of self-awareness and empathy. Peck's work continues to serve as a source of guidance and inspiration, fostering a greater understanding of the transformative power of personal change and spiritual evolution.

Conclusion

'The Road Less Traveled' by M. Scott Peck stands as a timeless masterpiece, offering valuable insights into the transformative journey of personal change and spiritual growth. Through his profound understanding of psychology and spirituality, Peck invites readers to embark on a path of self-discovery and inner transformation, emphasizing the importance of embracing personal responsibility and spiritual discipline. His work continues to inspire individuals to confront life's challenges with resilience and compassion, guiding them toward a more fulfilling and meaningful existence.

Criticism

Criticism of M. Scott Peck's 'The Road Less Traveled' has emerged from various perspectives, with some scholars and critics raising concerns about the book's theoretical underpinnings, philosophical implications, and practical applications. While the work has resonated with many readers, it has also faced scrutiny on several fronts.

1. Simplistic Solutions: Critics have argued that Peck's advice and solutions for personal growth and spiritual development may oversimplify complex psychological and existential issues. Some believe that the book's emphasis on self-discipline and personal responsibility could be perceived as overly prescriptive, neglecting the nuanced nature of individual experiences and the multifaceted challenges that individuals face in their personal journeys.

2. Lack of Empirical Basis: Some psychologists and scholars have questioned the empirical evidence supporting Peck's claims and methodologies. The book's integration of psychological concepts with spiritual principles has been criticized for its lack of scientific rigor and empirical validation, raising doubts about the effectiveness of the proposed techniques and strategies for personal transformation.

3. Ethical and Cultural Considerations: **Critics have also raised eth**ical concerns about certain aspects of Peck's advice, particularly regarding his views on discipline and love. Some have questioned the potential cultural biases and assumptions underlying his recommendations, suggesting that they may not be universally applicable or suitable for individuals from diverse backgrounds and belief systems.

4. Philosophical Implications: Peck's incorporation of spiritual concepts and the integration of psychology and spirituality have sparked philosophical debates. Critics have questioned the compatibility of his spiritual framework with established religious and philosophical traditions, raising concerns about the potential misinterpretation or misapplication of spiritual principles within a psychological context.

5. Commercialization of Self-Help: Some critics have raised concerns about the commercialization of self-help literature, including 'The Road Less Traveled,' highlighting the potential commodification of personal growth and spiritual development. They argue that the mass-market appeal of self-help books may prioritize profit over genuine personal transformation, potentially diluting the authenticity and depth of the philosophical and psychological insights presented.

While 'The Road Less Traveled' has garnered widespread acclaim for its inspirational and motivational content, these criticisms highlight the importance of critically evaluating self-help literature and acknowledging the complexities inherent in personal growth and spiritual development. Addressing these criticisms may lead to a more nuanced understanding of the challenges individuals face in their pursuit of personal transformation and spiritual fulfillment.

The Intersection of Pro-Sex Advocacy and Early Feminism: An Analysis of 'The Joy of Sex' by Alex Comfort and 'The Feminine Mystique' by Betty Friedan

The 1960s witnessed a significant societal shift in perspectives on sexuality and women's rights, reflected in the groundbreaking works of 'The Joy of Sex' by Alex Comfort and 'The Feminine Mystique' by Betty Friedan. These influential books not only shaped conversations surrounding sexual liberation and gender equality but also left a lasting imprint on popular culture. This essay delves into the convergence of pro-sex attitudes and early feminist ideals presented in these works, exploring the reception by the public and their profound impact on subsequent authors and societal attitudes.

'The Joy of Sex' by Alex Comfort

Dr. Alex Comfort, a British physician, published 'The Joy of Sex' in 1972. Drawing on his medical expertise, Comfort crafted a comprehensive guide that challenged societal taboos surrounding sexuality. He advocated for open communication and celebrated sexual intimacy, promoting a healthier and more positive approach to human sexuality. His work aimed to dismantle the prevailing stigma and shame attached to sexual expression, fostering a more inclusive and informed discourse on sexual practices and preferences.

Reception of 'The Joy of Sex' by the public was initially met with both enthusiasm and controversy. While some celebrated its progressive approach, others criticized its perceived deviation from traditional moral standards. However, its impact was undeniable, sparking a cultural shift toward more open and honest discussions about sexual health and pleasure. 'The Joy of Sex' influenced subsequent authors in the field of sexual education and popular culture, contributing to the broader sexual liberation movement of the 1970s and beyond.

'Feminine Mystique' by Betty Friedan

Betty Friedan, an American writer and feminist activist, published 'The Feminine Mystique' in 1963. Considered a foundational text of the early feminist movement, Friedan's book challenged the prevailing notion that a woman's sole fulfillment came through domestic roles. With scholarly rigor and personal insight, Friedan advocated for women's autonomy, education, and participation in the workforce. 'The Feminine Mystique' ignited a passionate discourse on gender equality and inspired women to demand equal rights and opportunities.

The public reception of 'The Feminine Mystique' was overwhelmingly positive, sparking conversations and debates that reverberated across the nation. Friedan's work not only influenced subsequent feminist literature but also catalyzed the women's rights movement, leading to significant strides in legislative and societal changes. It inspired a generation of women to challenge societal norms and assert their place in the realms of politics, education, and the workforce.

Impact on Popular Culture and Other Authors

'The Joy of Sex' and 'The Feminine Mystique' left an indelible mark on popular culture and subsequent literary endeavors. Comfort's work inspired a wave of sexual liberation literature and educational resources, contributing to a more open and informed cultural dialogue on human sexuality. Friedan's seminal text, on the other hand, inspired a host of feminist writers and activists, fostering a legacy of female empowerment and advocacy for gender equality.

These works influenced a plethora of subsequent authors, fueling a literary movement that continued to challenge societal norms and advocate for personal and social liberation. They also contributed to a broader cultural shift, empowering individuals to embrace their sexuality and assert their rights in both public and private spheres. Their profound impact on popular culture and subsequent literary works underscores their enduring relevance and legacy in the realms of sexuality, feminism, and social progress.

Critics of 'Joy'

'The Joy of Sex' by Alex Comfort, despite its groundbreaking approach to sexual education and openness, has faced several criticisms both at the time of its publication and in subsequent years. Some of the key criticisms include:

1. Traditional Moral Standards: At the time of its release in 1972, the book faced significant backlash from conservative and traditionalist circles who viewed its frank discussion of sexual intimacy as a departure from established moral values. Some critics argued that the book promoted a permissive attitude toward sexuality that undermined traditional family structures and values.

2. Gender Dynamics: Critics have highlighted the book's portrayal of gender dynamics as potentially reinforcing traditional gender stereotypes. Some argued that the book's illustrations and descriptions perpetuated a more passive role for women in sexual relationships, which conflicted with the evolving feminist discourse of the time.

3. Lack of Diversity: Some critics have pointed out the book's limitations in addressing the diverse experiences and orientations within human sexuality. 'The Joy of Sex' primarily focused on heterosexual relationships, potentially neglecting the experiences and needs of individuals with different sexual orientations and preferences.

4. Evolving Views on Consent: With the evolution of discussions around consent and sexual ethics, some critics have raised concerns about the book's portrayal of sexual encounters. Some argue that certain sections of the book could be interpreted as promoting sexual behaviors without a clear emphasis on the importance of mutual consent and respect in intimate relationships.

5. Impact on Sexual Expectations: Critics have also raised concerns about the potential impact of 'The Joy of Sex' on shaping unrealistic expectations regarding sexual performance and experiences. Some have argued that the book's emphasis on sexual techniques and pleasure might contribute to creating unrealistic standards that could affect individuals' self-esteem and intimate relationships.

While 'The Joy of Sex' remains a significant and influential work in the field of sexual education, these criticisms reflect the ongoing discourse and evolving societal expectations surrounding sexual ethics, gender dynamics, and the portrayal of intimacy in literature and popular culture.

Critics of "Feminine Mystique'

Betty Friedan, while celebrated for her influential work in the feminist movement, has faced criticism from various quarters regarding both her work and her persona. Some of the key criticisms are as follows:

1. Exclusivity: Some critics have argued that Friedan's work, particularly 'The Feminine Mystique,' did not adequately address the experiences of women from marginalized communities, including women of color and those from lower socioeconomic backgrounds. Critics have highlighted the book's focus on the experiences of white, middle-class women, suggesting that it overlooked the unique challenges faced by women from diverse backgrounds.

2. Essentialism: Some feminist scholars have criticized Friedan for essentializing gender roles, perpetuating the notion that all

404

women are inherently predisposed to certain domestic roles and responsibilities. Critics argue that her emphasis on women's participation in the workforce may have inadvertently reinforced gender stereotypes and neglected the diversity of women's aspirations and choices.

3. Exclusion of LGBTQ+ Voices: Friedan's work has also been criticized for its limited acknowledgment of the experiences of LGBTQ+ individuals. Some critics argue that her focus on conventional heterosexual relationships may have excluded the voices and experiences of individuals from the LGBTQ+ community, contributing to a lack of inclusivity within the broader feminist discourse.

4. Leadership Style: Some accounts of Friedan's leadership within the feminist movement have drawn criticism for her allegedly confrontational and exclusionary approach. Some critics have suggested that her leadership style may have alienated certain factions within the movement, leading to internal divisions and ideological conflicts that affected the unity and effectiveness of the feminist cause.

Despite these criticisms, it is essential to acknowledge Friedan's pivotal role in sparking critical discussions on gender equality and women's rights. While her work and persona have faced scrutiny, her contributions to the feminist movement remain integral to the broader narrative of women's empowerment and social progress. It is crucial to engage with her work critically, recognizing its historical significance while also acknowledging the need for inclusivity and diversity within feminist discourse.

Suggested Reading

Here is a reading list that includes books related to 'The Joy of Sex' by Alex Comfort and 'The Feminine Mystique' by Betty Friedan, along with works inspired by and critical of these seminal texts:

Books Related to 'The Joy of Sex':

1. 'The New Joy of Sex' by Alex Comfort and Susan Quilliam (2008) - An updated edition of the classic guide that provides contemporary insights into sexual intimacy and relationships.

2. 'The Guide to Getting It On!' by Paul Joannides (2018) - A comprehensive and inclusive guide that explores various aspects of human sexuality and intimacy.

3. 'Sex at Dawn: How We Mate, Why We Stray, and What It Means for Modern Relationships' by Christopher Ryan and Cacilda Jethá (2010) - A thought-provoking exploration of human sexuality and the implications of evolutionary psychology on modern relationships.

Books Inspired by 'The Joy of Sex':

1. 'The Joy of Gay Sex' by Charles Silverstein and Felice Picano (1993) - A groundbreaking guide that addresses sexual health and relationships within the LGBTQ+ community.

2. 'The Lesbian Sex Book' by Wendy Caster (1997) - An insightful exploration of lesbian sexuality and relationships, offering practical advice and empowering narratives.

3. 'The Joy of Sexus: Lust, Love, and Longing in the Ancient World' by Vicki León (2013) - A captivating historical exploration of sexuality in ancient civilizations, offering a unique perspective on human desire and intimacy.

Books Critical of 'The Joy of Sex':

1. 'Intercourse' by Andrea Dworkin (1987) - A critical analysis of the portrayal of sex and power dynamics in contemporary culture, challenging traditional narratives of sexual relationships.

2. 'The Sexual Liberals and the Attack on Feminism' by Dorchen Leidholdt and Janice G. Raymond (1990) - A critical examination of the impact of sexual liberation on feminist movements, highlighting the complexities of sexual politics and gender dynamics.

Books Related to 'The Feminine Mystique':

1. 'The Second Sex' by Simone de Beauvoir (1949) - Simone de Beauvoir's groundbreaking work 'The Second Sex' (1949) is a foundational text in the realm of feminist philosophy. It critically examines the cultural and social construction of gender roles, delving into the ways in which women have been historically marginalized and oppressed. De Beauvoir's work challenges the deeply ingrained patriarchal norms and advocates for the liberation and empowerment of women, emphasizing the importance of women's agency and autonomy in a male-dominated society.

While de Beauvoir's intellectual contributions have been widely recognized and lauded, her personal life has been the subject of scrutiny, particularly her long-term relationship with Jean-Paul Sartre. Some scholars have raised concerns about the nature of their relationship, highlighting instances of emotional complexity and, at times, alleged emotional abuse. Discussions about the dynamics of their partnership have prompted critical reflections on power dynamics and gender relations, emphasizing the complexities inherent in their personal and professional interactions.

It is crucial to approach discussions about the personal lives of individuals with empathy and respect, acknowledging that complex relationships can involve intricate dynamics that may not be fully captured by public narratives. While de Beauvoir's work has had a profound impact on feminist discourse and existential philosophy, her personal experiences remain a subject of debate and critical examination within scholarly and intellectual circles.

2. 'Feminism Is for Everybody: Passionate Politics' by bell hooks (2000) - A comprehensive exploration of feminist theory and activism, emphasizing the intersectionality of gender, race, and class in the pursuit of social justice.

3. 'The Beauty Myth' by Naomi Wolf (1990) - Naomi Wolf's 'The Beauty Myth' (1990) is a thought-provoking exploration of societal beauty standards and their impact on women's self-perception and empowerment. In this groundbreaking work, Wolf critiques the pervasive cultural narrative that dictates narrow and unrealistic ideals of beauty, arguing that these standards serve as a mechanism of social control, perpetuating gender inequality and limiting women's personal and professional advancement.

Wolf examines the ways in which the beauty industry and media promote unattainable beauty ideals, perpetuating a cycle of self-doubt and insecurity among women. She highlights the damaging consequences of this 'beauty myth,' ranging from body dissatisfaction and disordered eating to the pervasive objectification of women in various spheres of life. By exposing the ways in which these beauty standards are constructed and reinforced, Wolf calls for a collective awakening to the systemic injustices perpetuated by the beauty industry and media.

Furthermore, 'The Beauty Myth' advocates for a more inclusive and authentic understanding of beauty that celebrates diversity and rejects the notion of a singular, unattainable standard. Wolf encourages women to reclaim their agency and challenge the societal pressures to conform to narrow beauty norms, fostering a sense of empowerment and self-acceptance that transcends conventional beauty standards.

The impact of 'The Beauty Myth' has been far-reaching, sparking critical discussions about the intersection of gender, beauty, and power dynamics in contemporary society. Wolf's work continues to inspire individuals to question and challenge societal norms, fostering a more inclusive and equitable understanding of beauty that embraces authenticity and diversity. 'The Beauty Myth' remains a seminal text that invites readers to critically examine the ways in which beauty standards shape our perceptions and experiences, urging us to redefine beauty on our terms.

Books Inspired by 'The Feminine Mystique':

1. 'Lean In: Women, Work, and the Will to Lead' by Sheryl Sandberg (2013) - A compelling call to action for women to pursue leadership roles and challenge systemic barriers in the workplace.

2. 'Backlash: The Undeclared War Against American Women' by Susan Faludi (1991) - A comprehensive analysis of the backlash against the feminist movement and the persistent challenges faced by women in contemporary society.

3. 'The Feminine Mystique at 50: The Women's Movement and the Continuing Dilemma of Work-Life Balance' edited by Sheila Tobias and Mariko Lin Chang (2013) - A collection of essays that reflects on the enduring relevance of 'The Feminine Mystique' and the ongoing challenges in achieving work-life balance for women.

Books Critical of 'The Feminine Mystique':

'The Feminine Mistake: Are We Giving Up Too Much?' by Leslie Bennetts (2007) - Leslie Bennetts' 'The Feminine Mistake: Are We Giving Up Too Much?' (2007) is a thought-provoking exploration of the complexities and challenges faced by women in balancing their careers and personal lives. In this incisive work, Bennetts critically examines the societal pressures and expectations that often compel women to prioritize traditional domestic roles over their professional aspirations, potentially leading to a loss of financial independence and personal fulfillment.

Bennetts argues that the societal narrative emphasizing the primacy of motherhood and caregiving can hinder women's progress in the workforce, perpetuating gender disparities and limiting women's economic opportunities. She highlights the risks associated with prioritizing domestic responsibilities at the expense of career advancement, emphasizing the potential long-term financial consequences for women who choose to opt out of the workforce or scale back their professional pursuits.

'The Feminine Mistake' serves as a call to action, urging women to reconsider the societal pressures that may compel them to compromise their professional aspirations and financial independence. Bennetts advocates for a more comprehensive and equitable understanding of work-life balance that encourages women to pursue their career goals while also prioritizing their personal and familial needs.

The impact of 'The Feminine Mistake' has sparked critical conversations about gender equality, work-life balance, and the challenges faced by women in achieving both professional success and personal fulfillment. Bennetts' work continues to inspire individuals to challenge traditional gender norms and advocate for a more inclusive and supportive societal framework that values women's contributions in both the professional and personal spheres.

'The Feminine Mistake' remains a pertinent and insightful contribution to the ongoing discourse on women's empowerment and the need for a more equitable and accommodating approach to work and family life. Bennetts' work encourages readers to question the societal expectations placed on women and to advocate for a more balanced and fulfilling approach to their personal and professional endeavors.

2. 'The Trouble with Feminism: Gender, Dissent and Anti-Feminism in the 21st Century' by Lynne Segal (2013) - A critical analysis of contemporary feminist movements and the challenges posed by anti-feminist rhetoric in the modern era.

Fitness and Wellness: 'The Complete Book of Running' by Jim Fixx, 'Stretching' by Bob Anderson, and 'The New High-Intensity Training' by Ellington Darden

The 1970s witnessed a period of significant growth and diversity in the realm of fitness and wellness, marked by a burgeoning cultural shift towards prioritizing physical health and exercise. This era saw the rise of influential works such as 'The Complete Book of Running' by Jim Fixx, 'Stretching' by Bob Anderson, and 'The New High-Intensity Training' by Ellington Darden. These books not only fueled a surge in public interest in physical fitness but also laid the groundwork for lasting cultural effects that continue to shape contemporary attitudes towards exercise, health, and holistic well-being.

'The Complete Book of Running' by Jim Fixx

Published in 1977, 'The Complete Book of Running' played a pivotal role in popularizing running as a form of exercise and promoting the idea of regular physical activity for overall well-being. Fixx's book emphasized the physical and mental benefits of running, highlighting its capacity to improve cardiovascular health, alleviate stress, and foster a sense of personal achievement. His work spurred a nationwide running movement, encouraging individuals to embrace a more active and health-conscious lifestyle.

'Stretching' by Bob Anderson

Bob Anderson's 'Stretching,' first published in 1980, became a seminal guide for individuals seeking to improve flexibility and prevent injuries through targeted stretching exercises. Anderson's comprehensive approach to stretching not only promoted physical well-being but also emphasized the importance of incorporating stretching routines into daily fitness regimens. His work contributed to a broader understanding of the significance of flexibility and mobility in maintaining overall physical health and performance.

'The New High-Intensity Training' by Ellington Darden

Published in 1984, 'The New High-Intensity Training' by Ellington Darden revolutionized the fitness industry by advocating for a more efficient and intense approach to strength training. Darden's work popularized the concept of high-intensity workouts that prioritize brief, concentrated exercises over prolonged, traditional training methods. His book prompted a paradigm shift in the fitness world, encouraging individuals to maximize workout efficiency and achieve optimal results through focused and challenging training routines.

Lasting Cultural Effects

The 1970s fitness boom and the influential works of Fixx, Anderson, and Darden had a lasting impact on cultural attitudes towards physical fitness and wellness. The emphasis on regular exercise, flexibility, and high-intensity training fostered a more holistic understanding of health that transcended mere physical appearance. This cultural shift instilled a sense of personal responsibility for individual well-being, encouraging people to prioritize exercise and holistic self-care as integral components of a healthy lifestyle.

Moreover, the fitness boom of the 1970s paved the way for the development of a vibrant fitness industry that continues to thrive today. It led to the establishment of fitness centers, the introduction of innovative workout equipment, and the emergence of diverse fitness trends that cater to individuals' evolving health and wellness needs. The cultural effects of this transformative period continue to resonate, emphasizing the enduring importance of physical activity and holistic well-being in contemporary society.

Suggested Reading

Certainly, here is a list of suggested readings from the 1950s to the present day that explore the connection between fitness and happiness:

1. 'Younger Next Year: Live Strong, Fit, Sexy, and Smart—Until You're 80 and Beyond' by Chris Crowley and Henry S. Lodge (2004) - This book offers practical advice on how to maintain physical fitness and overall well-being as one ages, emphasizing the profound impact of exercise on longevity and happiness.

2. 'Born to Run: A Hidden Tribe, Superathletes, and the Greatest Race the World Has Never Seen' by Christopher McDougall (2009) - McDougall's exploration of the art of running and its effects on physical and mental well-being provides insights into the joy and fulfillment that can be derived from engaging in the act of running.

3. 'The Happiness Project: Or, Why I Spent a Year Trying to Sing in the Morning, Clean My Closets, Fight Right, Read Aristotle, and Generally Have More Fun' by Gretchen Rubin (2009) - Although not exclusively focused on fitness, this book delves into the pursuit of happiness through various lifestyle changes, including the incorporation of physical activity and exercise routines.

4. 'Becoming Ageless: The Four Secrets to Looking and Feeling Younger Than Ever' by Strauss Zelnick (2018) - Zelnick's book explores the intersection of fitness, nutrition, and overall wellness, offering insights into the ways in which maintaining physical fitness can contribute to a sense of vitality and happiness.

5. 'The Joy of Movement: How Exercise Helps Us Find Happiness, Hope, Connection, and Courage' by Kelly McGonigal (2019) - McGonigal's exploration of the profound psychological and emotional benefits of exercise emphasizes the power of movement in fostering happiness, connection, and overall well-being.

These books offer diverse perspectives on the connection between fitness and happiness, emphasizing the potential of physical activity in promoting holistic well-being and a sense of fulfillment. They provide valuable insights into the ways in which exercise and wellness practices can contribute to a more joyful and purposeful life.

Looking the Part: "Dress for Success" by John T. Molloy, and 'The Total Look: The Complete Style Guide for Every Woman' by Mary Quant

In both personal and professional spheres, the way we present ourselves plays a crucial role in how we are perceived and, consequently, in our levels of confidence and success. John T. Molloy's "Dress for Success" and Mary Quant's "The Total Look: The Complete Style Guide for Every Woman" are two pivotal works that delve into the profound impact of personal style and attire choices. These influential pieces provide comprehensive insights into the transformative nature of clothing and appearance, highlighting the intricate connections between outer appearance, self-confidence, and societal perceptions.

"Dress for Success" by John T. Molloy:

Originally published in 1975, "Dress for Success" by John T. Molloy swiftly became a guiding light in the realm of professional attire. Molloy's work delves deep into the intricacies of dressing for the corporate world, offering readers meticulous guidance on how to leverage their wardrobe as a powerful tool for success. Through his precise analysis of clothing choices and their implications, Molloy emphasizes the significance of dressing appropriately to convey competence, credibility, and authority in the workplace. His detailed insights and pragmatic advice have left an indelible mark on how individuals approach their attire in professional settings, underscoring the profound impact of dressing well as an essential component of career progression and self-assurance.

"The Total Look: The Complete Style Guide for Every Woman" by Mary Quant:

In 1967, fashion revolutionary Mary Quant released "The Total Look," a seminal work that reshaped women's approach to fashion and personal style. Quant's book transcended conventional fashion norms, encouraging women to embrace their uniqueness and creativity through their clothing choices. By advocating for a holistic approach to personal style that encompasses clothing, accessories, and grooming, Quant empowered women to utilize fashion as a conduit for self-expression and self-assuredness. Her work underscored the importance of cultivating an authentic style that reflects one's personality, challenging conventional ideals of beauty and fashion in the process.

The Lasting Impact:

The combined influence of Molloy's "Dress for Success" and Quant's "The Total Look" extends far beyond the realms of fashion and professional attire. These works have significantly contributed to the broader narrative surrounding self-presentation, emphasizing the transformative potential of clothing in shaping perceptions and fostering self-confidence. They have inspired individuals to view fashion as a means of self-expression, urging them to utilize clothing as a tool for asserting their identities and communicating their values and aspirations. The enduring legacies of these works serve as enduring reminders of the profound connection between personal style and self-empowerment, highlighting the timeless axiom that how one presents oneself to the world can greatly influence one's journey toward success and self-fulfillment.

Suggested Reading

Alongside "Dress for Success" by John T. Molloy and "The Total Look: The Complete Style Guide for Every Woman" by Mary Quant, several other influential books have contributed to the discourse on personal presentation and fashion. Some notable titles include:

1. "The Official Preppy Handbook" by Lisa Birnbach (1980) - This satirical guide offers a humorous yet insightful examination of the preppy subculture, providing readers with an entertaining exploration of preppy fashion, lifestyle, and etiquette.

2. "The Little Black Book of Style" by Nina Garcia (2007) - In this style guide, Nina Garcia, renowned fashion director and former

"Project Runway" judge, provides readers with practical advice on cultivating a personal sense of style and mastering the art of dressing for various occasions.

3. "The Wardrobe Wakeup: Your Guide to Looking Fabulous at Any Age" by Lois Joy Johnson (2012) - Johnson's book offers a comprehensive guide to revamping one's wardrobe and personal style at any stage of life, emphasizing the importance of embracing fashion as a means of self-expression and confidence-building.

4. "Deluxe: How Luxury Lost Its Luster" by Dana Thomas (2007) - Thomas' critical examination of the luxury fashion industry offers readers insights into the evolving landscape of high-end fashion, shedding light on the cultural and societal implications of luxury branding and consumption.

5. "The Curated Closet: A Simple System for Discovering Your Personal Style and Building Your Dream Wardrobe" by Anuschka Rees (2016) - Rees' book provides a practical approach to cultivating a personalized wardrobe, emphasizing the significance of mindful consumption and conscious clothing choices in achieving a cohesive and authentic personal style.

By exploring these diverse works, readers can gain a comprehensive understanding of the multifaceted nature of personal style and its broader implications in the realms of fashion, culture, and self-expression. Each book contributes unique insights and perspectives, offering readers practical guidance and critical reflections on the transformative power of clothing and personal presentation.

Navigating Unconventional Paths to Success: Insights from
'The Lazy Man's Way to Riches' by Joe Karbo and
'The Magic of Believing' by Claude M. Bristol

In the pursuit of success, unconventional paths often yield
profound insights into the interplay between mindset and
practicality. 'The Lazy Man's Way to Riches' by Joe Karbo and
'The Magic of Believing' by Claude M. Bristol exemplify the
transformative potential of unorthodox approaches, emphasizing
the significance of cultivating the right mindset and employing
practical strategies in achieving personal and professional
fulfillment. These works challenge traditional notions of success,
offering readers alternative perspectives on realizing their
aspirations through unconventional yet pragmatic means.

'The Lazy Man's Way to Riches' by Joe Karbo:
Joe Karbo (1913–1980) was an American author and entrepreneur
known for his influential contributions to the self-help and
success literature, particularly in the realm of New Thought and
positive thinking in the United States. His renowned publication,
'The Lazy Man's Way to Riches,' released in 1973, challenged
conventional beliefs about achieving success and presented an
innovative perspective on attaining financial prosperity through
unconventional means. Karbo's emphasis on practical strategies
and the power of mindset resonated deeply with the principles of
New Thought and the burgeoning movement of positive thinking
that had gained traction in the U.S. during the 20th century.

In comparison to the foundational concepts of New Thought,
which emphasize the transformative power of the mind in
shaping one's reality and experiences, Karbo's 'The Lazy Man's
Way to Riches' provided readers with a practical framework for
harnessing the potential of positive thinking in the pursuit of
financial success. Aligning with the core tenets of New Thought
philosophy, Karbo advocated for the strategic application of
mindset and practicality in achieving personal and financial
fulfillment, encouraging readers to cultivate a constructive and
empowered outlook on their endeavors.

Furthermore, Karbo's work intersected with the evolving discourse on positive thinking in the U.S., reflecting a departure from traditional narratives about wealth accumulation and success. In tandem with the principles of positive thinking, Karbo's emphasis on the significance of efficient decision-making and proactive goal-setting underscored the transformative potential of adopting an optimistic and goal-oriented mindset. His work not only resonated with the ethos of positive thinking but also contributed to the expanding repertoire of literature on personal development, offering readers a refreshing perspective on the interconnectedness of mindset, practicality, and success.

Ultimately, Joe Karbo's engagement with the principles of New Thought and positive thinking exemplifies the dynamic evolution of the self-help and success literature in the U.S. His work not only reflects the influence of these philosophical movements but also contributes to their continued legacy, emphasizing the profound impact of mindset and practical strategies in achieving personal and financial prosperity. Karbo's legacy stands as a testament to the enduring relevance of New Thought and positive thinking in shaping the trajectory of personal development literature and empowering individuals to pursue their aspirations with optimism and determination.

The reception of Joe Karbo's 'The Lazy Man's Way to Riches' upon its publication in 1973 was a mixed bag, eliciting both praise and criticism from readers and critics alike. While many individuals lauded Karbo's unconventional approach to achieving financial success and his emphasis on practical strategies, others raised concerns about the potential implications of promoting a "lazy" or effortless path to prosperity.

Supporters of the book commended Karbo for his practical and streamlined approach, emphasizing that his work provided a refreshing alternative to the traditional narratives surrounding hard work and perseverance. They appreciated his insights into maximizing efficiency and minimizing unnecessary effort, considering his strategies as valuable tools for navigating the complexities of wealth accumulation and financial management. Karbo's practical advice resonated with readers seeking innovative and non-conventional methods for achieving success, earning him a dedicated following among those who embraced his teachings.

However, critics of 'The Lazy Man's Way to Riches' expressed apprehensions about the potential misinterpretation of Karbo's message. They argued that the title and premise of the book might inadvertently promote a passive or complacent attitude toward success, undermining the value of diligence and hard work. Some critics cautioned that the notion of a "lazy" approach to wealth accumulation could foster unrealistic expectations among readers, leading them to overlook the importance of dedication, perseverance, and disciplined effort in achieving their goals. Furthermore, some skeptics questioned the feasibility of implementing Karbo's strategies in various industries and highlighted potential pitfalls associated with adopting an overly simplistic or reductionist approach to financial success.

Despite the criticism, 'The Lazy Man's Way to Riches' sparked meaningful discussions about the dynamics of success and the role of practicality in achieving prosperity. While some praised Karbo for challenging conventional norms, others called for a balanced perspective that acknowledges the significance of both strategic thinking and hard work. The diverse reception of Karbo's work underscored the complexities of navigating the realms of personal development and financial empowerment, highlighting the need for a nuanced understanding of success that integrates practicality with a strong work ethic.

'The Magic of Believing' by Claude M. Bristol:
In 'The Magic of Believing,' Claude M. Bristol explores the transformative power of belief and its profound influence on one's journey to success. Bristol's work delves into the intricate relationship between mindset and manifestation, emphasizing the pivotal role of belief in realizing one's goals and aspirations. By underscoring the significance of cultivating a positive and unwavering belief in one's capabilities, Bristol offers readers a transformative framework for harnessing the power of the mind to manifest success. His book serves as a guide for fostering a resilient and empowered mindset, illustrating the impact of self-

420

belief in navigating the complexities of personal and professional endeavors.

Claude M. Bristol's 'The Magic of Believing' is intricately woven into the tapestry of New Thought and positive thinking, aligning closely with the foundational principles of these philosophical movements. Bristol's work, akin to the tenets of New Thought, underscores the transformative power of belief and the influence of mindset on shaping one's reality and experiences. By emphasizing the significance of cultivating a positive and unwavering belief in one's capabilities, Bristol's book resonates with the core ideals of New Thought and its exploration of the interconnectedness of consciousness and manifestation.

In comparison to contemporary success literature, such as the works of Tony Robbins, Bristol's 'The Magic of Believing' offers readers a foundational understanding of the power of belief as a catalyst for personal and professional growth. While Robbins's writings delve into various aspects of self-improvement and success, Bristol's focus on the transformative potential of belief aligns closely with Robbins's emphasis on the significance of mindset in achieving one's aspirations.

Moreover, when juxtaposed with the philosophical insights of renowned figures like Ralph Waldo Emerson and Benjamin Franklin, Bristol's work complements their emphasis on self-reliance, individualism, and the power of thought in shaping one's destiny. Bristol's exploration of belief as a catalyst for success converges with Emerson's and Franklin's advocacy for self-trust, perseverance, and the pursuit of personal growth, collectively contributing to the evolving discourse on self-empowerment and human potential.

Additionally, 'The Magic of Believing' shares thematic affinities with Shakti Gawain's 'Creative Visualization,' which emphasizes the transformative potential of harnessing the mind's creative power to manifest one's desires. Bristol's work, along with Gawain's, underscores the transformative impact of visualization and belief in shaping one's reality, aligning closely with the contemporary exploration of the interplay between consciousness, intention, and manifestation.

In summary, Claude M. Bristol's 'The Magic of Believing' intertwines seamlessly with the philosophical underpinnings of New Thought and positive thinking, resonating with contemporary success literature and the enduring wisdom of influential figures such as Tony Robbins, Ralph Waldo Emerson, and Shakti Gawain. Its exploration of the transformative power of belief serves as a testament to the enduring legacy of these philosophical movements, encouraging readers to embrace the profound potential of their thoughts and beliefs in shaping their journey to personal and professional fulfillment.

Criticism of 'The Magic of Believing' by Claude M. Bristol primarily revolves around the potential oversimplification of the complex dynamics involved in achieving success. While Bristol's emphasis on the transformative power of belief resonated with many readers, some critics argued that his work tended to downplay the significance of practical action and external factors in the pursuit of one's goals. They contended that Bristol's focus on the power of belief might inadvertently foster an overly idealistic or deterministic perspective, leading individuals to overlook the essential role of diligent effort and external circumstances in the realization of their aspirations.

Furthermore, some skeptics raised concerns about the potential implications of an excessive reliance on the principles of positive thinking, cautioning that an exclusive focus on the power of belief could lead to an underestimation of the challenges and obstacles inherent in the path to success. Critics suggested that Bristol's work might promote a sense of complacency or unrealistic optimism, potentially deterring individuals from acknowledging the complexities and uncertainties of the journey toward their goals.

Moreover, some scholars and commentators within the field of psychology expressed reservations about the potential misinterpretation of Bristol's ideas, highlighting the need for a comprehensive understanding of the psychological and environmental factors that contribute to personal achievement. They underscored the importance of incorporating a balanced approach that integrates positive thinking with practical action and a nuanced understanding of the complexities of human behavior and motivation.

Despite these criticisms, 'The Magic of Believing' continues to resonate with readers seeking inspiration and guidance in their pursuit of personal and professional fulfillment. While acknowledging the potential limitations of an exclusive focus on the power of belief, Bristol's work remains a testament to the enduring appeal of positive thinking and the transformative impact of a resilient and empowered mindset in navigating the challenges of life and realizing one's aspirations.

Conclusion:
'The Lazy Man's Way to Riches' by Joe Karbo and 'The Magic of Believing' by Claude M. Bristol illuminate the unexplored dimensions of success, challenging conventional wisdom and advocating for a holistic approach that integrates mindset and practicality. These works emphasize the transformative potential of unconventional paths, urging readers to embrace innovative strategies and belief systems in their pursuit of personal and professional fulfillment. By highlighting the symbiotic relationship between mindset and practicality, Karbo and Bristol encourage individuals to adopt a nuanced and adaptive approach to achieving success, underscoring the timeless adage that the journey to success is as much about mindset as it is about practical action.

Part IX: The Limits of the Self

Cultural Shifts and Social Realities: The Me Decade, The Third Great Awakening, and Cultural Fragmentation in the 1970s

The 1970s in the United States witnessed a confluence of cultural shifts and social realities that left an indelible mark on the nation's collective consciousness. From the emergence of the "Me Decade" and the spiritual fervor of the Third Great Awakening to the persistent undercurrents of cultural fragmentation, this transformative era reflected a dynamic interplay between individualism, spirituality, and societal disintegration. These defining trends not only shaped the cultural landscape of the decade but also laid the groundwork for a nuanced understanding of the complexities and contradictions inherent in American society during this period of rapid change and transformation.

The 'Me' Decade:

Coined by writer Tom Wolfe, the term "Me Decade" encapsulated the growing emphasis on self-exploration and individualism that characterized the cultural ethos of the 1970s. The decade witnessed a notable shift in societal attitudes, with an increased focus on personal fulfillment, self-expression, and the pursuit of individual desires. The burgeoning self-help industry and the popularization of therapeutic practices underscored the growing preoccupation with self-discovery and self-actualization, reflecting a broader cultural shift towards prioritizing personal needs and aspirations over collective ideals.

The Third Great Awakening:

Simultaneously, the 1970s saw a resurgence of spiritual fervor and religious revivalism, often referred to as the Third Great Awakening. Amidst the backdrop of social and political upheaval, many Americans turned to spirituality and alternative belief systems in search of meaning and solace. This spiritual awakening manifested in various forms, including the rise of new religious movements, the popularity of Eastern philosophies and meditation practices, and the renewed interest in mystical and esoteric traditions. The Third Great Awakening offered a sense of communal belonging and spiritual transcendence, providing individuals with a framework for navigating the uncertainties and existential anxieties of the era.

Cultural Fragmentation:

Despite the prevalence of the "Me Decade" and the spiritual resurgence of the Third Great Awakening, the 1970s also witnessed deep-seated fissures within the cultural fabric of American society. The era was marked by profound social divisions, political polarization, and the erosion of collective values, leading to a sense of cultural fragmentation. The Vietnam War, the Watergate scandal, and the ongoing struggle for civil rights exacerbated existing societal tensions, contributing to a pervasive sense of disillusionment and distrust in established institutions. This cultural fragmentation fostered a climate of social upheaval and ideological discord, laying bare the underlying fractures within the American cultural landscape.

This complex interplay between the "Me Decade," the Third Great Awakening, and cultural fragmentation in the 1970s underscored the multifaceted nature of societal transformation and cultural evolution. While the era witnessed a heightened focus on individualism and spiritual exploration, it also grappled with the challenges of societal disintegration and political disillusionment. The legacy of these cultural shifts continues to reverberate in contemporary American society, serving as a poignant reminder of the enduring complexities and contradictions inherent in the pursuit of personal fulfillment, spiritual transcendence, and societal cohesion. Most of all, the 70's offered all sorts of new ways to be your 'authentic' self.

Demise of the Classical Education Structure

Classical education in the United States, before the changes of the 1960s and 1970s, was marked by a traditional pedagogical approach that focused on the study of classical languages, literature, history, and philosophy. This educational system aimed to foster a comprehensive understanding of the humanities, placing significant importance on the mastery of Latin and Greek, as well as the works of ancient scholars and philosophers.

The curriculum centered on the liberal arts, encompassing subjects such as rhetoric, logic, grammar, and arithmetic. Students were encouraged to engage with fundamental texts and notable works of literature, philosophy, and history, nurturing a deep appreciation for the cultural and intellectual heritage of Western civilization. The teachings of ancient philosophers, such as Plato and Aristotle, and classical authors like Homer, Virgil, and Cicero, were integral to the educational experience.

Additionally, classical education emphasized the development of moral character, aiming to instill virtues such as discipline, integrity, and critical thinking. The approach prioritized the cultivation of intellectual curiosity, rhetorical skill, and a holistic understanding of human experiences, thereby preparing students for careers in law, academia, and public service.

Overall, the classical education system in the U.S. before the changes of the 1960s and 1970s represented a structured and rigorous approach to learning, emphasizing enduring ideals of intellectual excellence, cultural heritage, and moral growth. It served as a fundamental pillar of American academia for generations, providing a strong foundation for a comprehensive understanding of the humanities and the lasting legacy of classical thought.

When researching this Book, I found the structure to be something I had not expected. Greek? Yes, the study of Latin and Greek was a significant part of the regular curriculum in many educational institutions in the United States before the 1960s. Classical languages were often considered essential components of a comprehensive education, especially in private schools, prestigious preparatory institutions, and higher education settings. The emphasis on Latin and Greek reflected the historical influence of classical education and the traditional focus on the liberal arts and humanities.

Students in these institutions were typically exposed to the study of Latin and Greek as part of their coursework, with a strong emphasis on grammar, syntax, and vocabulary. These languages were considered foundational to the study of literature, philosophy, and history, providing students with a deeper understanding of the origins of Western thought and culture. The mastery of Latin and Greek was often regarded as a mark of academic distinction and intellectual sophistication, and it was a prerequisite for pursuing advanced studies in fields such as law, medicine, and theology.

However, as educational priorities and approaches began to shift in the 1960s, there was a gradual decline in the emphasis placed on classical languages in mainstream educational institutions. Changes in curriculum design, evolving pedagogical philosophies, and a growing emphasis on contemporary subjects led to a diminishing role for Latin and Greek in the broader educational landscape. While some institutions continue to offer classical language courses as electives or specialized programs, the widespread inclusion of Latin and Greek in the regular curriculum has decreased significantly since the 1960s.

Surely not in public schools, then, right? Certainly, the Stuyvesant High School, located in New York City, is one example of a public school that has historically offered the study of Ancient Greek as part of its curriculum. Stuyvesant High School, renowned for its rigorous academic programs and emphasis on the humanities, has provided students with the opportunity to learn Ancient Greek as an elective or advanced language course. With a strong commitment to fostering a comprehensive understanding of classical languages and cultures, Stuyvesant High School has incorporated Ancient Greek into its curriculum, offering students the chance to engage with the rich literary and philosophical traditions of the ancient world. While the teaching of Ancient Greek in public schools has become less common over the years, institutions like Stuyvesant High School have continued to uphold the importance of classical languages in the context of a well-rounded and rigorous educational experience.

Before the educational and curriculum changes of the 1960s and 1970s, high school students in the United States were typically expected to be familiar with a range of classic literary works that formed the foundation of the standard curriculum. Some of the commonly assigned texts during this period included:

1. William Shakespeare's plays, such as "Romeo and Juliet," "Macbeth," and "Hamlet," which were often studied for their literary merit and cultural significance.

2. American literature classics like "The Adventures of Huckleberry Finn" by Mark Twain, "The Great Gatsby" by F. Scott Fitzgerald, and "The Catcher in the Rye" by J.D. Salinger, which offered insights into the American experience and societal values.

3. British literature masterpieces including novels like Charles Dickens' "Great Expectations" and "A Tale of Two Cities," as well as the poetry of John Keats, William Wordsworth, and other prominent Romantic and Victorian-era poets.

4. Ancient literature works, such as Homer's "The Odyssey" and "The Iliad," as well as classical plays by playwrights like Sophocles, Euripides, and Aristophanes, which provided students with a comprehensive understanding of the foundations of Western literary traditions.

5. Key works of world literature, including translations of ancient texts like "The Epic of Gilgamesh," and selections from authors such as Miguel de Cervantes, Leo Tolstoy, and Gustave Flaubert, which offered insights into diverse cultural and historical contexts.

These texts, among others, constituted the standard literary canon that high school students were typically expected to have read and analyzed as part of their English and literature curriculum before the educational reforms and curriculum changes of the 1960s and 1970s.

The shift away from the traditional literary canon began to gain momentum during the 1960s and 1970s, reflecting a broader societal and cultural movement toward inclusivity, diversity, and the reevaluation of established norms and values. Several factors contributed to the questioning and subsequent reconfiguration of the literary canon, including:

1. Social and Cultural Movements: The civil rights movement, the women's liberation movement, and the push for greater inclusivity and representation in various spheres of society prompted a reexamination of the traditional canon, which was criticized for its Eurocentrism and lack of diversity.

2. Postmodern Critique: The emergence of postmodernism and deconstructionist literary theories led to a critical reassessment of the notion of a fixed literary canon. Scholars and critics challenged the idea of a single, universal literary tradition, advocating for a more inclusive and pluralistic approach to literature that encompassed a broader range of voices and perspectives.

3. Cultural Relativism and Globalization: Increasing awareness of cultural relativism and the growing impact of globalization encouraged a more expansive view of literature that incorporated works from diverse cultural, ethnic, and linguistic backgrounds. The emphasis on multiculturalism and the recognition of non-Western literary traditions led to a reconsideration of the Western-centric canon.

4. Educational Reforms: The 1960s and 1970s witnessed significant educational reforms aimed at promoting a more holistic and inclusive approach to learning. Curricular changes sought to incorporate a broader range of literary texts that reflected the experiences and perspectives of marginalized communities, challenging the dominance of the traditional canon in educational settings.

As a result of these transformative social, cultural, and educational shifts, the notion of a fixed and exclusive literary canon gradually gave way to a more inclusive and diverse approach to literature that celebrated the richness and complexity of global literary traditions. The reevaluation of the canon reflected a broader commitment to recognizing the multiplicity of human experiences and fostering a more comprehensive understanding of the cultural, social, and historical contexts that shape literary production and reception.

And Colleges and Universities? They followed suit? Yes, Dear Reader, colleges and universities also experienced a notable shift away from the traditional focus on the 'classical Western canon' in their literature and humanities curricula. This transition occurred primarily during the latter half of the 20th century, with the 1960s and 1970s serving as a pivotal period for the reevaluation and expansion of the literary canon within higher education. While a range of factors contributed to this shift, including the influence of various intellectual and cultural movements, the emergence of Marxist literary criticism played a significant role in challenging the traditional canon and advocating for a more inclusive and socially aware approach to literary studies.

Prominent scholars and critics, influenced by Marxist theories of class struggle, cultural hegemony, and the critique of bourgeois culture, began to challenge the ideological underpinnings of the traditional canon. Figures such as Terry Eagleton, Raymond Williams, and Fredric Jameson, among others, played key roles in critiquing the traditional Western literary canon for its inherent biases and its perpetuation of dominant cultural and ideological narratives.

Additionally, the influence of postcolonial studies and the recognition of the colonial legacies inherent in the traditional canon further contributed to the push for diversification and inclusivity within literary curricula. Scholars like Edward Said and Gayatri Chakravorty Spivak emphasized the importance of decentering Western perspectives and integrating the voices and experiences of marginalized communities and non-Western cultures into the academic discourse.

The collective efforts of these scholars, alongside broader social and cultural movements advocating for greater representation and inclusivity, led to a paradigm shift within academic circles, prompting colleges and universities to reconsider the limitations of the traditional canon and the need for a more comprehensive and globally aware approach to literary education. This shift reflected a broader commitment to fostering critical engagement with diverse literary traditions and challenging the ideological foundations of the established literary canon.

Yes, the "Great Books" project, spearheaded by figures such as Mortimer J. Adler and institutions like St. John's College in Annapolis, Maryland, can be viewed as a response to the challenges posed by the shifting educational landscape and the critique of the traditional Western canon, including those influenced by Marxist and progressive ideologies. The initiative sought to uphold the importance of the Western intellectual tradition and promote the study of classic texts as a means of preserving the cultural and philosophical heritage of the West.

The "Great Books" movement emphasized the value of engaging with seminal works from the fields of philosophy, literature, history, and political science, advocating for the inclusion of these foundational texts in educational curricula. Institutions like St. John's College embraced a curriculum centered on the close study and critical analysis of classic texts, fostering a deep appreciation for the enduring ideas and intellectual contributions of Western civilization.

The project aimed to counter the perceived dilution of the Western canon and the growing emphasis on non-Western and non-traditional texts within educational settings. By championing the study of the "Great Books," Adler and proponents of the movement sought to reaffirm the significance of the Western intellectual tradition and its enduring relevance in contemporary education. They believed that a comprehensive understanding of the ideas and values embedded within these classic texts was vital for cultivating critical thinking, cultural literacy, and a deeper appreciation of the historical foundations of Western thought.

While the "Great Books" project did not directly position itself as an antagonistic response to the Marxist and progressive critique of the traditional canon, it did represent a concerted effort to uphold the intellectual legacy of the West and preserve the foundational texts that had shaped Western culture and civilization. The project aimed to foster a continued engagement with the timeless ideas and enduring philosophical inquiries that form the bedrock of the Western intellectual tradition.

The Cautionary Tale

The evolving socio-cultural landscape, marked by the challenges posed by the shifting educational paradigm, the decline of the manufacturing base, the prevalence of drug use, and the transformation of societal identities, undoubtedly left many individuals, particularly the youth, feeling disoriented and vulnerable to various ideological and cultural influences. The erosion of the traditional moorings associated with the 'Western canon' and the broader socio-economic changes of the time contributed to a sense of uncertainty and disillusionment, leaving many searching for a sense of purpose, belonging, and direction.

Amidst this backdrop, the allure of alternative ideologies, charismatic leaders, and radical movements, including both hokum and genuine intellectual pursuits, became increasingly appealing to a generation seeking meaning and belonging in a rapidly changing world. The proliferation of countercultural movements, the rise of alternative lifestyles, and the prevalence of drug use as a form of escapism reflected the broader societal disillusionment and the quest for alternative forms of consciousness and identity.

The presence of charismatic figures, gurus, and ideological influencers, including both genuine intellectuals and manipulative charlatans, further contributed to the vulnerability of young people searching for a sense of purpose and identity. The influence of Marxist professors and the propagation of radical ideologies within academic institutions also played a role in shaping the worldview of many individuals, offering alternative frameworks for understanding society, history, and culture.

The fragmentation of societal identities and the decline of traditional voluntary associations underscored the challenges of fostering a sense of community and shared purpose within a rapidly changing and increasingly individualistic society. As traditional social structures underwent transformation, many individuals found themselves navigating an uncertain and often fragmented social landscape, leading to a sense of alienation and disconnection from established norms and values.

Overall, the confluence of these complex socio-cultural changes created a fertile ground for the proliferation of diverse and often conflicting ideologies, leaving many individuals, particularly the youth, susceptible to the influence of both genuine intellectual pursuits and deceptive or manipulative forces seeking to exploit their search for meaning and identity.

What Do You Know?

Here are two lists, one from the 1950s and the other from 1979, reflecting the type of literature that college students might have been expected to be familiar with during those respective periods:

List from the 1950s:

1. William Shakespeare's "Hamlet" and "Macbeth"
2. Jane Austen's "Pride and Prejudice"
3. Fyodor Dostoevsky's "Crime and Punishment"
4. Charles Dickens' "Great Expectations"
5. Nathaniel Hawthorne's "The Scarlet Letter"
6. Emily Brontë's "Wuthering Heights"
7. Mark Twain's "Adventures of Huckleberry Finn"
8. Leo Tolstoy's "War and Peace"
9. Henry David Thoreau's "Walden"
10. James Joyce's "Dubliners"

List from 1979:

1. Gabriel García Márquez's "One Hundred Years of Solitude"
2. Toni Morrison's "The Bluest Eye"
3. Thomas Pynchon's "Gravity's Rainbow"
4. Sylvia Plath's "The Bell Jar"
5. Ken Kesey's "One Flew Over the Cuckoo's Nest"
6. Saul Bellow's "Herzog"
7. Kurt Vonnegut's "Slaughterhouse-Five"

8. Chinua Achebe's "Things Fall Apart"
9. Alice Walker's "The Color Purple"
10. John Updike's "Rabbit Is Rich"

These lists reflect the evolving literary landscape and the shifting preferences in literature over the decades, highlighting the emergence of new voices and perspectives that contributed to the diversification of the literary canon during the mid-20th century and the late 1970s. They both seem to include works of depth that would contribute to fostering meaningful conversation about contemporary ideas and practical problems.

The Arguments of Calvino and Adler

Italo Calvino and Mortimer J. Adler, each in their own right, provided compelling arguments for the study of the great books, emphasizing the enduring significance and value of engaging with classic texts that have shaped the course of human thought and civilization.

Italo Calvino, the renowned Italian novelist and essayist, advocated for the study of the great books as a means of fostering a deeper understanding of the universal themes and narratives that transcend time and cultural boundaries. Calvino underscored the timeless relevance of these works, arguing that they provide valuable insights into the complexities of human nature, society, and the human condition. By engaging with the great books, readers can develop a heightened awareness of the interconnectedness of human experiences across different historical epochs and cultural contexts, fostering a more profound appreciation for the shared narratives that unite humanity.

On the other hand, Mortimer J. Adler, a prominent American philosopher and proponent of the "Great Books" movement, championed the study of classic texts as a fundamental pillar of liberal education. Adler emphasized the role of the great books in cultivating critical thinking, intellectual curiosity, and a comprehensive understanding of the Western intellectual tradition. He argued that these texts provide readers with the tools to grapple with fundamental questions about morality, justice, and the nature of existence, fostering a more holistic and enriching educational experience. By engaging with the great books, students are encouraged to develop a deeper appreciation for the enduring ideas and values that have shaped the foundations of Western thought and culture.

Both Calvino and Adler emphasized the importance of the great books in fostering a more comprehensive understanding of the human experience and the intellectual heritage of humanity. They highlighted the capacity of these texts to stimulate critical inquiry, cultural awareness, and a deeper engagement with the timeless ideas and values that continue to resonate with readers across generations and cultural backgrounds.

Suggested Reading

1. "The Closing of the American Mind: How Higher Education Has Failed Democracy and Impoverished the Souls of Today's Students" (1987) by Allan Bloom. In this work, Bloom criticizes the contemporary education system for its neglect of the traditional Western canon and argues for a return to the classics to revive a sense of intellectual and moral purpose.

2. "Tenured Radicals: How Politics Has Corrupted Higher Education" (1990) by Roger Kimball. Kimball examines the influence of political ideology in higher education and the erosion of the Western canon, arguing that the politicization of academia has led to a devaluation of traditional values and intellectual standards.

3. "Cultural Literacy: What Every American **Needs to Know" (1988) by E.D. Hirsch Jr.** Hirsch emphasizes the importance of a shared cultural knowledge base and the study of the Western canon in fostering cultural literacy and intellectual development, advocating for a curriculum that prioritizes the foundational texts and ideas of Western civilization.

4. "Dumbing Down Our Kids: Why American Children Feel Good About Themselves but Can't Read, Write, or Add" (1995) by Charles J. Sykes. Sykes critiques the educational system for its emphasis on self-esteem over academic rigor and its neglect of the traditional Western canon, suggesting that this trend has led to a decline in intellectual standards and critical thinking skills among students.

5. "Killing the Spirit: Higher Education in America" (1990) by Page Smith. "Killing the Spirit: Higher Education in America" is a critical examination of the state of higher education in the United States, written by Page Smith and published in 1990. In this work, Smith expresses concerns about the decline of intellectual rigor, critical thinking, and academic freedom within American colleges and universities. He argues that the increasing bureaucratization and commercialization of higher education have led to a devaluation of the liberal arts and the erosion of intellectual values that are essential for fostering a vibrant intellectual culture.

Smith contends that the emphasis on vocational training and specialized knowledge has come at the expense of a comprehensive and holistic education that encourages broad intellectual inquiry and cultural engagement. He critiques the instrumentalist approach to education that prioritizes job training over the development of critical thinking skills and a deep understanding of the humanities. Smith highlights the importance of the humanities in cultivating moral and ethical reasoning, fostering a sense of civic responsibility, and nurturing a well-rounded intellectual and cultural sensibility.

Furthermore, Smith raises concerns about the growing influence of corporate interests and market-driven ideologies within academic institutions, suggesting that this trend has contributed to the erosion of academic freedom and the suppression of dissenting voices within the academic community. He calls for a revitalization of the liberal arts and a renewed commitment to fostering intellectual curiosity, cultural literacy, and a critical engagement with the ideas and values that underpin the Western intellectual tradition.

"Killing the Spirit" serves as a poignant critique of the commercialization and bureaucratization of higher education, advocating for the preservation of the liberal arts and the cultivation of a vibrant intellectual culture that values critical inquiry, academic freedom, and the pursuit of knowledge for its own sake. Smith's work continues to resonate with contemporary debates about the role of higher education in cultivating a well-rounded and intellectually engaged citizenry.

These works, written at different points in the late 20th century, express a shared concern about the erosion of the Western canon and the perceived decline in intellectual rigor and cultural literacy within the contemporary educational landscape. The authors articulate various arguments in support of the enduring value of the Western canon, emphasizing the need to uphold the intellectual and cultural heritage of the West as a means of fostering critical thinking, cultural literacy, and a deeper understanding of the human experience.

Esalen and Black Mountain

There have indeed been several attempts to establish alternative educational institutions in the United States that prioritize skill acquisition, interdisciplinary learning, and a blend of traditional and non-traditional approaches to education. Two notable examples include Esalen Institute and Black Mountain College, both of which sought to create innovative learning environments that diverged from conventional academic models.

Esalen Institute, founded in 1962 in Big Sur, California, emphasized a holistic approach to education and personal development, focusing on the exploration of human potential, consciousness studies, and the integration of various philosophical and spiritual traditions. While not a traditional university in the conventional sense, Esalen served as a center for alternative education and the study of various disciplines,

438

including psychology, spirituality, and the arts, drawing inspiration from a diverse range of intellectual and cultural traditions.

Black Mountain College, active from 1933 to 1957 in North Carolina, was known for its experimental and interdisciplinary approach to education, emphasizing the integration of the arts, humanities, and sciences. The college provided a unique learning environment that fostered creative expression, collaboration, and intellectual exploration, with an emphasis on the importance of the arts in education and the cultivation of a community of artists, writers, and intellectuals.

While Esalen Institute and Black Mountain College are significant examples of alternative educational institutions in the United States, other experimental learning communities have emerged over the years, each with its own distinct approach to education and learning. These institutions have contributed to the broader conversation about the purpose and nature of education, emphasizing the value of interdisciplinary study, creative expression, and the cultivation of critical thinking skills within a supportive and innovative learning environment.

Deep Springs College and Evergreen State College

Deep Springs College, with its emphasis on a rigorous academic curriculum, student self-governance, and a strong focus on manual labor and community engagement, has represented a unique model of alternative education that reflects both conservative and progressive elements within the changing landscape of U.S. education. Founded in 1917, Deep Springs College remained relatively insulated from the immediate changes of the late 1960s. However, its emphasis on manual labor and community engagement aligns with conservative traditions of self-reliance, hard work, and a practical, experiential approach to learning. These values resonate with conservative sentiments that emphasize traditional virtues and practical skill acquisition over ideological or political activism.

On the other hand, Evergreen State College, established in 1967, emerged during the peak of the progressive educational reforms of the late 1960s. Evergreen State College's interdisciplinary approach, student-driven learning, and collaborative, team-taught courses exemplify the progressive ideals of student empowerment, experiential learning, and a focus on social justice and activism. The college's commitment to interdisciplinary studies and its emphasis on social and environmental issues align with the progressive movements of the era, advocating for a more inclusive and socially engaged approach to education.

Both Deep Springs College and Evergreen State College, in their distinct ways, reflect the broader ideological shifts within the U.S. educational structure/system during the late 1960s, representing different responses to the changing cultural and intellectual climate of the time. While Deep Springs adheres to conservative values of self-reliance and practical skill development, Evergreen State embodies the progressive ideals of student empowerment, interdisciplinary studies, and social engagement, highlighting the diversity of educational models that emerged in response to the changing educational landscape of the late 1960s and early 1970s.

Conclusion

I am really not certain a useful and lasting and sustainable solution to the problem of education has been reached in the U.S. I am just not convinced. Something that is a cross between a Great Books School meets- OTJ training from the The Appropriate Technology Library by Village Earth meets Outward Bound and a monastery that grows organic apples for cider, with a requirement for athletics and nutritional studies? I will work on it. For the moment, let's take a look at how people sought to escape in the 70s.

Escapism and Group Identity in the 70s

In the 1970s, like in many other decades, people engaged in various forms of escapism and group identity as a way to cope with the social, political, and cultural realities of the time. Here
440

are some notable forms of escapism and group identity during that decade:

1. Music and Concerts: The 1970s were a vibrant era for music, with the rise of genres like rock, disco, and punk. Music offered a means of escapism as people attended concerts and music festivals to immerse themselves in the sounds and cultures associated with their favorite bands. Iconic events like Woodstock in 1969 and the growth of stadium rock concerts in the '70s exemplified the communal aspect of music fandom.

2. Disco Culture: Disco music and dance clubs became immensely popular in the mid-to-late 1970s. Discotheques like Studio 54 in New York City provided a glamorous escape for those looking to dance, dress up, and indulge in a hedonistic lifestyle. Disco culture was closely tied to a sense of belonging and identity, often centered around the LGBTQ+ community and people of color.

3. Role-Playing and Fantasy: Role-playing games like Dungeons & Dragons (D&D) gained popularity in the 1970s. These games allowed players to escape into imaginary worlds, create characters, and embark on adventures. D&D and similar tabletop games fostered a sense of group identity among players who shared a love for fantasy and storytelling. This eventually morphed into board game nights replacing bowling alley nights, where groups of outcasts and misfits enter a small controllable 4-page garden of rules , or surround themselves with stacks of rulebooks or chits, each protecting them from IRL (in-real-life) decisions, so they can act out small simulacrum of imagined danger and conquest between bags of Dorritos, tepid movie references and juvenile body-oriented humour.

4. Cinema and Film: Movies were a significant source of escapism in the 1970s. The decade saw the release of iconic films like "Star Wars" (1977) and "Close Encounters of the Third Kind" (1977), which transported audiences to distant galaxies and otherworldly experiences. These films created fan communities and contributed to a sense of group identity among sci-fi enthusiasts.
5. Subcultures and Countercultures: The 1970s saw the continuation of various subcultures and countercultures that

had emerged in the 1960s. For example, the hippie counterculture persisted, with people seeking an alternative lifestyle based on peace, love, and communal living. The punk subculture also emerged in the mid-'70s, characterized by its rebellious attitude and DIY ethos, offering a sense of belonging to those who rejected mainstream norms.

6. Sports Fandom: The 1970s marked a significant turning point in the evolution of sports fandom, as it witnessed a surge in the popularity and commercialization of various athletic competitions, particularly in the United States. This era saw the rise of iconic sports figures, the expansion of televised sports coverage, and the emergence of dedicated fan communities, all of which contributed to the transformation of sports from a mere pastime to a cultural phenomenon.

During the 1970s, the world of sports underwent a profound transformation, with events like the 1972 Summer Olympics in Munich and the 1976 Summer Olympics in Montreal capturing global attention and igniting widespread enthusiasm for athletic competition. The achievements of legendary sports personalities such as Muhammad Ali, Pelé, and Björn Borg, among others, not only captivated audiences with their exceptional skills but also contributed to the establishment of a global sports culture that transcended national boundaries and united fans around the world.

Moreover, the 1970s witnessed the commercialization and marketing of sports on an unprecedented scale, with the establishment of lucrative sponsorship deals, endorsement contracts, and the rise of sports merchandising. The increased visibility of sports in the media, including the advent of televised sporting events and the proliferation of sports magazines and newspapers, further fueled the growth of sports fandom, allowing fans to closely follow their favorite athletes and teams and to engage in spirited discussions and debates about their performances and achievements.

The growing popularity of sports in the 1970s also fostered the development of dedicated fan communities, with supporters coming together to form fan clubs, attend live sporting events, and express their allegiance through various forms of fan paraphernalia and memorabilia. This era witnessed the emergence of a passionate and dedicated fan base that not only celebrated the triumphs and victories of their favorite teams and athletes but also formed an integral part of the cultural fabric, contributing to the creation of a vibrant and dynamic sports culture that continues to thrive in the contemporary world.

In sum, the rise of sports fandom in the 1970s can be attributed to a convergence of factors, including the global appeal of sports personalities, the commercialization of sports, and the growing engagement of fan communities. This era laid the foundation for the modern sports industry, shaping the way sports are consumed, celebrated, and cherished by millions of fans worldwide.

And, yes, the rise of sports fandom in the 1970s was accompanied by a corresponding increase in sports betting and gambling, leading to concerns about the prevalence of gambling addiction and its impact on individuals and communities. As sports gained heightened visibility and commercialization, the allure of wagering on sporting events became more prominent, with an increasing number of individuals participating in various forms of sports gambling, including betting on the outcomes of games, tournaments, and individual performances.

The widespread availability of sports betting opportunities, facilitated by the expansion of legalized gambling in some regions, as well as the emergence of underground betting networks, contributed to the normalization of sports gambling within mainstream culture. The accessibility and convenience of placing bets, coupled with the thrill of potentially winning substantial sums of money, led to a surge in the popularity of sports betting among sports enthusiasts and casual fans alike.

However, the rise in sports gambling also gave rise to significant concerns about the adverse consequences of gambling addiction, as individuals became increasingly susceptible to the allure of quick financial gains and the excitement of risk-taking. The potential for financial ruin, psychological distress, and the breakdown of personal relationships associated with gambling addiction underscored the need for greater awareness and intervention measures to address the social and psychological impacts of excessive sports betting.

Furthermore, the normalization of sports gambling in the 1970s and its close association with the culture of sports fandom contributed to a complex and nuanced relationship between sports, gambling, and the broader societal implications of addictive behavior. This phenomenon highlighted the importance of implementing responsible gambling practices, promoting awareness about the risks of gambling addiction, and establishing support systems for individuals struggling with compulsive gambling behaviors.

In response to the growing concerns about gambling addiction, various regulatory measures, educational campaigns, and support programs were introduced to promote responsible gambling practices and to provide resources for individuals and families affected by gambling-related issues. These initiatives aimed to foster a more balanced and informed approach to sports gambling, emphasizing the importance of responsible decision-making, risk management, and the promotion of healthy and sustainable sports engagement within the context of sports fandom.

7. Political Activism: While not a traditional form of escapism, political activism in the 1970s often involved forming groups and communities with like-minded individuals who shared common goals and values. Movements like the civil rights movement, women's liberation movement, and the environmental movement brought people together to fight for social and political change.

8. Fashion and Style Tribes: The 1970s saw the emergence of various fashion and style tribes, each with its distinct identity. From disco fashion with its glittery and glamorous attire to the punk rock style with its rebellious and DIY aesthetic, what people wore often reflected their sense of belonging to a particular group.

9. Drugs: The 1970s witnessed a significant rise in drug culture, fueled by the widespread availability and use of substances such as marijuana, cocaine, and heroin. This era marked a shift towards increased experimentation with recreational drugs, leading to social and cultural movements that shaped the music, art, and countercultural expressions of the decade.

10. Swinging and Sex Clubs: The 1970s saw the emergence of sex clubs, such as Plato's Retreat, and a growing popularity of swinging, as expressions of the era's sexual liberation and openness. These phenomena reflected a broader cultural shift towards sexual exploration, experimentation, and the challenging of traditional norms and values surrounding relationships and intimacy.

In summary, the 1970s were a dynamic period with diverse forms of escapism and group identity. Whether through music, subcultures, fantasy role-playing, or political activism, people found ways to connect with others who shared their interests and to momentarily escape the challenges of the era.

Regional Identities in the U.S. in The 70s

The 1970s in the United States witnessed a resurgence of regional identities, as various cultural, social, and political factors contributed to the revitalization of distinct regional narratives and identities across the country. Amidst the backdrop of social and cultural shifts, the decade saw a renewed emphasis on celebrating and preserving the unique cultural heritage and traditions of different regions, fostering a sense of pride and belonging among residents and communities.

One of the key catalysts for the resurgence of regional identities in the 1970s was the growing recognition and appreciation of cultural diversity and the importance of local traditions within the broader fabric of American society. This recognition prompted a reevaluation of the significance of regional customs, dialects, and folklore, encouraging communities to embrace and showcase their distinctive cultural expressions as a source of collective identity and community solidarity.

Additionally, the 1970s marked a period of socio-political mobilization and activism, with various grassroots movements and advocacy groups emerging to champion the interests and concerns of specific regions. These movements sought to address issues related to regional development, environmental conservation, and the preservation of local economies, advocating for policies that supported the unique needs and aspirations of different regions and their residents.

Furthermore, the popularization of regional literature, music, and art during the 1970s played a pivotal role in fostering a renewed sense of regional pride and identity. Artists and writers from various regions gained prominence for their works that celebrated local customs, landscapes, and narratives, contributing to the cultivation of a rich cultural tapestry that reflected the diversity and vibrancy of regional experiences across the United States.

The resurgence of regional identities in the 1970s underscored the significance of localism, community engagement, and the preservation of cultural heritage as integral components of the American identity. By highlighting the unique contributions of different regions to the country's cultural mosaic, this resurgence not only promoted a deeper understanding of the nation's diverse cultural heritage but also fostered a sense of interconnectedness and mutual appreciation among communities, contributing to the enrichment and diversification of the American cultural landscape.

Examples of Regionalism in the 70s

In the 1970s, New York City (NYC) experienced a cultural revival characterized by the emergence of the punk rock movement in downtown Manhattan. Iconic music venues such as CBGB became hubs for punk and new wave bands, fostering a distinctive urban subculture that celebrated DIY aesthetics, anti-establishment sentiments, and a raw, gritty style of artistic expression. This cultural resurgence in NYC reflected a sense of resilience and

446

creative energy within the city's diverse and dynamic urban landscape, solidifying its reputation as a global center for contemporary arts and music.

The New South, encompassing states such as Georgia, North Carolina, and Tennessee, underwent a transformation that emphasized economic diversification and a shift towards modernization. Cities like Atlanta experienced significant growth in the banking, finance, and telecommunications industries, fostering a burgeoning urban culture that embraced innovation, entrepreneurship, and a forward-looking mentality. This economic and cultural revitalization of the New South challenged traditional perceptions of the region as primarily agrarian, highlighting its emergence as a dynamic hub for business, technology, and cultural exchange.

California, particularly around Los Angeles, witnessed the flourishing of the film and entertainment industry, solidifying its reputation as the global epicenter of the movie business. The rise of Hollywood in the 1970s led to the production of groundbreaking films that reflected the cultural zeitgeist and social dynamics of the era, contributing to the emergence of a vibrant and influential film culture that shaped global cinematic trends. Additionally, the countercultural movements in San Francisco continued to thrive, fostering a bohemian spirit of creativity, activism, and alternative lifestyles that celebrated communal living, environmental consciousness, and progressive social values.

Texas experienced a surge in economic growth and urban development, particularly in cities like Houston and Dallas, driven by the expansion of the oil and energy sectors. The state's oil boom in the 1970s fueled unprecedented economic prosperity, leading to the construction of iconic skyscrapers, corporate headquarters, and luxury developments that transformed the urban landscapes of major Texas cities. This economic resurgence in Texas reinforced the state's reputation as a symbol of economic opportunity and entrepreneurial spirit, underscoring its significance as a key player in the nation's energy industry and global business markets.

447

The Culture of Narcissism

In classical mythology, Narcissus was a character known for
his exceptional beauty. According to the myth, Narcissus
was so enamored with his own reflection in a pool of water
that he became unable to leave it, eventually pining away and
transforming into the narcissus flower. This myth serves as
an allegory for excessive self-love, vanity, and a preoccupation
with one's own image or persona, which has come to define the
concept of narcissism in contemporary psychological discourse.
Today, narcissism is commonly understood as a personality trait
characterized by an inflated sense of self-importance, a constant
need for admiration and validation, and a lack of empathy for
others. Individuals exhibiting narcissistic traits often prioritize
their own needs and desires above those of others, seeking
attention and recognition to bolster their fragile self-esteem. They
may also display a disregard for the feelings and perspectives of
others, leading to difficulties in forming genuine and empathetic
relationships.

Warnings

While specific warnings against narcissism may not have been
explicitly articulated by all of the following thinkers, their
teachings and philosophies do offer insights that can be applied to
the understanding of narcissistic tendencies and their potential
consequences.

1. Franklin's emphasis on humility and the virtues of self-
improvement may be interpreted as a caution against excessive
self-centeredness and vanity. His emphasis on the importance
of self-discipline and the cultivation of virtuous character
underscores the need for individuals to prioritize self-awareness
and personal growth over self-aggrandizement and egoism.

2. Aristotle's ethical teachings, particularly his concept of
eudaimonia, emphasize the pursuit of a well-balanced and
virtuous life. Aristotle's emphasis on the cultivation of moral
character and the importance of practicing moderation and self-
awareness serves as a warning against the dangers of excessive

self-indulgence and ego-centric behavior that characterizes narcissism.

3. Emerson's transcendentalist philosophy encourages individuals to seek self-reliance and self-awareness, emphasizing the value of introspection and the cultivation of one's unique potential. His call for individuals to trust their inner voice and pursue authentic self-expression can be seen as a caution against the superficiality and self-absorption that often accompany narcissistic tendencies.

4. Deep ecology thinkers, including Arne Naess and George Sessions, promote an ecological worldview that emphasizes the interconnectedness of all living beings and the importance of cultivating a harmonious relationship with nature. Their emphasis on the value of ecological awareness and the need for a more holistic and sustainable approach to life serves as a reminder of the dangers of human-centered egotism and the imperative to prioritize the well-being of the planet and all its inhabitants over individualistic and exploitative pursuits.

While these thinkers may not have directly addressed narcissism, their teachings highlight the significance of humility, self-awareness, and a holistic understanding of the self in relation to others and the natural world, offering valuable insights into the potential pitfalls of narcissistic behavior and the importance of cultivating a more balanced and empathetic approach to life.

Narcissism in the 70s

The culture of narcissism in the 1970s is often associated with the emergence of a self-absorbed and individualistic ethos that permeated various aspects of American society, influencing social, cultural, and psychological trends during the decade. This cultural shift was characterized by an increased emphasis on self-expression, personal fulfillment, and the pursuit of immediate gratification, reflecting a broader societal preoccupation with the self and the cultivation of one's individual identity.

In the realm of popular culture, the 1970s witnessed the rise of celebrity culture and the glamorization of fame, wealth, and material success, fueling a fascination with celebrity lifestyles and the pursuit of lavish and hedonistic pleasures. The proliferation of mass media, including television, magazines, and film, played a pivotal role in promoting an image-driven culture that celebrated beauty, youth, and superficiality, contributing to the cultivation of a narcissistic preoccupation with external appearances and the pursuit of instant gratification.

Moreover, the countercultural movements of the 1960s, which emphasized collective activism, social change, and communal values, underwent a transformation in the 1970s, as the focus shifted towards individual autonomy, personal freedom, and the fulfillment of one's desires. This shift reflected a growing sense of disillusionment with traditional social structures and a desire for greater personal agency and self-determination, leading to the popularization of self-help literature, therapeutic practices, and psychological self-exploration that catered to the growing demand for self-improvement and self-realization.

The culture of narcissism in the 1970s also manifested in the realms of consumerism and advertising, with marketers capitalizing on the trend towards self-indulgence and instant gratification. Advertising campaigns promoted a culture of conspicuous consumption, encouraging individuals to define their identities and self-worth through the acquisition of material possessions and the pursuit of status symbols, contributing to the perpetuation of a shallow and image-driven consumer culture.

Overall, the culture of narcissism in the 1970s reflected a broader cultural shift towards individualism, self-expression, and the prioritization of personal desires and ambitions, marking a distinct departure from the collective ideals and communal values that characterized the preceding decade. While this cultural shift underscored the importance of self-expression and personal autonomy, it also raised concerns about the erosion of social cohesion, the cultivation of shallow and superficial values, and the potential consequences of excessive self-absorption and individualistic pursuits on the fabric of society.

Several writers and cultural critics of the 1970s took exception to the prevailing ethos of self-indulgence and individualism that permeated the culture of narcissism during the decade. These writers offered insightful critiques and alternative perspectives that challenged the superficiality and materialism of the era, advocating for a deeper understanding of human values, social responsibility, and the pursuit of authentic meaning and purpose.

One notable critic was Christopher Lasch, whose influential work "The Culture of Narcissism: American Life in an Age of Diminishing Expectations" (1979) provided a comprehensive analysis of the narcissistic tendencies embedded within American society. Lasch's critique of consumer culture, the decline of community values, and the erosion of social solidarity highlighted the adverse effects of the culture of narcissism on the collective well-being and moral fabric of society, emphasizing the importance of fostering genuine connections and meaningful relationships based on shared values and mutual respect.

Additionally, cultural critics such as Susan Sontag, in her essays and cultural analyses, offered incisive commentaries on the pitfalls of an image-driven society and the commodification of experience and identity. Sontag's exploration of the impact of mass media and consumer culture on individual consciousness and artistic expression highlighted the need for a more critical engagement with cultural representations and the cultivation of a more discerning and introspective approach to media consumption and self-perception.

Moreover, writers such as bell hooks and Gloria Steinem, through their feminist perspectives, critiqued the culture of narcissism by highlighting the ways in which gender dynamics and power structures influenced the construction of individual identities and societal norms. Their writings underscored the importance of challenging traditional gender roles, promoting social equality, and advocating for inclusive and empathetic forms of human interaction that prioritize mutual understanding, respect, and social justice.

During the 1970s, the culture of narcissism was characterized by a heightened emphasis on individualism, materialism, and self-centered pursuits. This cultural context provided fertile ground for various manifestations of narcissistic personalities to display themselves, exhibiting behaviors and attitudes that reflected an inflated sense of self-importance, a constant need for admiration, and a lack of empathy for others. Some examples of how narcissistic personality traits might have been displayed during the 1970s include:

1. Self-promotion in the entertainment industry: Some individuals within the entertainment industry during the 1970s may have exhibited narcissistic tendencies through their relentless self-promotion, attention-seeking behavior, and the cultivation of larger-than-life personas. Their focus on personal success and public adoration often overshadowed the collaborative nature of artistic endeavors, reinforcing a culture of self-aggrandizement and ego-centric performance.

2. Excessive materialism and conspicuous consumption: The culture of conspicuous consumption and the pursuit of material possessions in the 1970s provided an avenue for individuals with narcissistic tendencies to showcase their wealth, status, and social standing through lavish lifestyles, extravagant purchases, and the public display of luxury goods. Their preoccupation with external symbols of success often masked deeper insecurities and a persistent need for external validation and recognition.

3. Charismatic leadership and political grandstanding: Some political figures and charismatic leaders in the 1970s may have exhibited narcissistic traits through their charismatic personas, grandiose speeches, and self-assured demeanor. Their focus on personal power and influence often overshadowed the collective needs and aspirations of the communities they represented, contributing to a culture of authoritarianism, self-aggrandizement, and political polarization.

4. Celebrity culture and media attention: Within the context of the burgeoning celebrity culture of the 1970s, some public figures and influencers may have exhibited narcissistic behaviors through their relentless pursuit of media attention, sensationalist stunts, and calculated public relations maneuvers. Their craving for public adulation and continuous media exposure often overshadowed their contributions to meaningful discourse and social change, perpetuating a culture of superficiality and image-driven self-promotion.

5. Being a Bad Guru and Therapist: Gurus, for example, may be revered for their spiritual wisdom and guidance, but some may exploit their influence for personal gain or manipulate their followers for adoration and unquestioning loyalty, demonstrating narcissistic tendencies that exploit the vulnerability and trust of their followers.

Therapists, while dedicated to helping individuals navigate their emotional and psychological challenges, may occasionally exhibit traits of narcissism that manifest in an excessive need for recognition, an inability to empathize with their clients' experiences, or a tendency to prioritize their own perspectives over those of their patients.

How To Spot a Narcissist

Spotting a narcissist can be challenging, as they often possess charming and charismatic personalities that can initially mask their true intentions and behaviors. However, there are several signs and behaviors to look out for that might indicate the presence of narcissistic traits:

1. Excessive need for admiration: A narcissist often craves constant validation and attention from others, seeking praise and admiration to boost their fragile self-esteem.

2. Lack of empathy: Narcissists tend to have difficulty empathizing with others and may disregard the feelings and perspectives of those around them, focusing solely on their own needs and desires.

3. Sense of entitlement: They may demonstrate a sense of entitlement, believing that they deserve special treatment and privileges without regard for the needs or boundaries of others.

4. Manipulative behavior: Narcissists often manipulate and exploit others to achieve their own goals, using charm and charisma to control and influence those around them.

5. Grandiose self-image: They may boast about their accomplishments, exaggerate their talents or abilities, and present an inflated sense of their own importance and achievements.

6. Lack of accountability: Narcissists tend to deflect blame onto others, refusing to take responsibility for their actions and behaviors, even when at fault.

7. Difficulty handling criticism: Criticism is often met with defensiveness or hostility, as narcissists struggle to accept any form of negative feedback or perceived personal attacks.

8. Exploitative tendencies: They may exploit others for personal gain, taking advantage of people's goodwill, resources, or emotional support without offering reciprocity.

9. Preoccupation with fantasies of success, power, or ideal love: Narcissists often indulge in grandiose fantasies or illusions of unlimited success, power, beauty, or idealized love, fueling their sense of self-importance and specialness.

10. Intense reactions to perceived slights: Minor criticisms or perceived slights can trigger intense emotional reactions or outbursts from narcissists, leading to anger, defensiveness, or vengeful behavior.

While these behaviors may indicate narcissistic tendencies, it is important to avoid labeling someone as a narcissist based solely on these signs. A professional mental health evaluation can provide a more accurate assessment and diagnosis.

Suggested Reading

Here are some suggested readings that delve into the topics of narcissism, sociopathy, and how to navigate relationships with such individuals:

1. "The Sociopath Next Door: The Ruthless Versus the Rest of Us" by Martha Stout provides insights into identifying sociopathic behavior, highlighting common traits and behaviors exhibited by sociopaths in everyday life. It also offers guidance on protecting oneself from manipulative and exploitative individuals.

2. "Psychopath Free: Recovering from Emotionally Abusive Relationships With Narcissists, Sociopaths, and Other Toxic People" by Jackson MacKenzie offers a comprehensive guide to recognizing and recovering from relationships with narcissists and sociopaths. It provides practical strategies for establishing boundaries and regaining emotional well-being.

3. "Without Conscience: The Disturbing World of the Psychopaths Among Us" by Robert D. Hare delves into the psychology of psychopathy, offering an in-depth analysis of the traits and behaviors exhibited by individuals with psychopathic tendencies. It provides valuable insights into understanding and identifying psychopathic behavior in various contexts.

4. "The Machiavellians: Defenders of Freedom" by James Burnham examines the political philosophy of Machiavelli and its implications for understanding the dynamics of power, influence, and manipulation in human interactions. It offers a historical perspective on the strategies employed by individuals in positions of authority and the ways in which Machiavellian principles continue to shape contemporary political thought and practice.

These recommended readings can provide valuable insights into the nature of narcissistic and sociopathic behaviors, offering practical advice on how to recognize and address these traits in personal and professional relationships. Additionally, exploring the historical and philosophical dimensions of these topics, as highlighted in works like "The Machiavellians," can contribute to a deeper understanding of the underlying dynamics of power, manipulation, and interpersonal influence within social and political contexts.

The Culture of Hedonism in the 70s

Self-help movements, popularized by figures like Norman Vincent Peale and Dale Carnegie, encouraged individuals to prioritize their own well-being and success. The pursuit of personal happiness, whether through career achievements, self-improvement techniques, or material consumption, became a defining feature of the era. As with the narcissist, the hedonist really misunderstandings the basic idea of balance that was part of the earlier Thinkers and motivators.

Hedonism refers to a philosophical and ethical doctrine that prioritizes the pursuit of pleasure and the avoidance of pain as the highest good and ultimate goal in life. This pursuit of pleasure is often associated with immediate sensual gratification and the fulfillment of one's desires, without a significant emphasis on long-term consequences or moral considerations.

Before the 1970s, examples of hedonistic cultures can be found throughout history and across various societies. In ancient civilizations such as the Roman Empire and ancient Greece, the pursuit of pleasure and indulgence in lavish feasts, entertainment, and sensual experiences were often celebrated as symbols of wealth, power, and social status. These cultures emphasized the enjoyment of life's pleasures, including food, wine, music, and various forms of entertainment, as a means of achieving happiness and fulfillment.

During the Weimar Republic in Germany (1919-1933), a period known for its cultural effervescence and social experimentation, hedonism was a prominent feature of the cultural landscape. The vibrant nightlife in cities like Berlin exemplified a spirit of liberation and indulgence, as cabarets, nightclubs, and avant-garde performances flourished, promoting a culture of sexual liberation, artistic expression, and social defiance. The Weimar

Republic era witnessed a flourishing of artistic and cultural movements that challenged traditional values and social norms, reflecting a broader societal shift towards the celebration of pleasure, experimentation, and alternative lifestyles.

In these historical contexts, hedonism served as a form of cultural expression that challenged conventional moral codes and societal expectations, emphasizing the pursuit of pleasure and the celebration of immediate gratification as a means of asserting individual freedom and social rebellion. Despite its liberating and subversive qualities, hedonism also carried the risk of moral and existential decadence, reflecting the complex interplay between pleasure-seeking, self-indulgence, and the search for deeper meaning and fulfillment within the human experience.

The culture of hedonism that emerged in the 1970s reflected a societal shift towards the pursuit of pleasure, self-indulgence, and the rejection of traditional social constraints. This era witnessed a confluence of various cultural movements and trends that celebrated the liberation of personal expression, experimentation with mind-altering substances, and the embrace of alternative lifestyles.

1. Drug Culture: The 1970s saw a widespread acceptance and normalization of recreational drug use, particularly the widespread use of marijuana, cocaine, and hallucinogens. The countercultural movements of the 1960s laid the groundwork for the promotion of a psychedelic and drug-fueled lifestyle, contributing to the rise of a subculture that embraced the exploration of altered states of consciousness and the pursuit of euphoria through chemical means.

2. Disco Culture: The disco phenomenon of the 1970s became a symbol of hedonistic excess and uninhibited revelry, as nightclubs and discotheques became hubs for dance, music, and the celebration of sensual pleasures. The disco culture celebrated liberation, sexual freedom, and the expression of individual identity through music and dance, fostering a sense of community and collective celebration that transcended social boundaries and cultural norms.

The disco culture of the 1970s exemplified a vibrant expression of hedonism through its celebration of sensual pleasures, uninhibited self-expression, and a collective pursuit of joy and ecstasy. Here are some examples of how the disco culture embodied the ethos of hedonism:

2.1. Celebration of Dance and Sensuality: Disco clubs and dance floors became spaces for individuals to immerse themselves in the euphoria of music, movement, and sensual experiences. The pulsating beats, rhythmic melodies, and electrifying ambiance of disco music fueled a collective celebration of dance, sensuality, and physical expression, allowing participants to transcend social barriers and inhibitions in a liberating environment of self-expression and collective joy.

2.2. Fashion and Glamour: The disco culture was characterized by flamboyant fashion, glittering attire, and extravagant styles that emphasized self-expression, individual identity, and the cultivation of a glamorous persona. The flamboyant costumes, sequined outfits, and flashy accessories became symbols of self-confidence, allure, and a desire for attention and admiration, reflecting the culture of hedonism that celebrated the pursuit of aesthetic pleasure and visual extravagance.

2.3. Nightlife and Escapism: Disco clubs and nightlife venues provided an escape from the mundane realities of everyday life, offering participants an immersive experience of vibrant lights, pulsating music, and a sense of collective euphoria that transcended the boundaries of time and space. The allure of the disco culture lay in its promise of escapism, providing an opportunity for individuals to immerse themselves in a realm of fantasy, hedonistic indulgence, and sensory stimulation, free from the constraints of social norms and moral expectations.

2.4. Free Expression of Sexuality: The disco culture promoted a free and open expression of sexuality, challenging traditional norms and fostering an environment of sexual liberation and exploration. The disco scene embraced diverse forms of sexual expression and fluid identities, encouraging individuals to embrace their sensual desires, celebrate their bodies, and engage

458

in intimate connections that transcended conventional moral codes and societal taboos, embodying the spirit of hedonism that prioritized the pursuit of pleasure and self-gratification.

The disco culture of the 1970s, with its emphasis on dance, fashion, nightlife, and sexual liberation, embodied the hedonistic spirit of the era, offering a space for individuals to revel in the joy of the present moment, celebrate their individuality, and embrace the pursuit of immediate pleasure and sensory gratification.

While, I, as a person that did not live through the disco era, view it as tame and somewhat silly fun, it is important to recognize that the consequences of this hedonistic lifestyle were not always benign. Despite the exuberance and excitement associated with the disco scene, there were instances where serious personal and societal damage was linked to the culture of hedonism during this era.

2.5. Substance Abuse and Addiction: The prevalence of drug use and substance abuse within the disco culture often led to addiction, health complications, and even fatalities. The widespread availability and acceptance of recreational drugs within disco clubs and nightlife venues contributed to a culture of substance abuse that resulted in long-term physical and psychological harm for many individuals, highlighting the darker consequences of hedonistic indulgence and uninhibited revelry.

2.6. Unsafe Sexual Practices and STDs: The culture of sexual liberation and promiscuity within the disco scene often led to unsafe sexual practices and a higher risk of sexually transmitted diseases (STDs) among participants. The lack of sexual education, coupled with a casual attitude towards sexual encounters and the use of protection, contributed to the spread of STDs and other health risks, underscoring the potential dangers of unchecked hedonistic behavior and the neglect of responsible sexual practices.

2.7. Psychological Toll and Burnout: The relentless pursuit of pleasure and the incessant partying associated with the disco culture often took a psychological toll on individuals, leading to burnout, emotional exhaustion, and a sense of disillusionment with the transient nature of hedonistic indulgence. The temporary highs and euphoric experiences were frequently accompanied by feelings of emptiness, loneliness, and a lack of deeper fulfillment, revealing the hollowness of a lifestyle centered solely on immediate gratification and sensory stimulation.

2.8. Social Alienation and Isolation: The hedonistic culture of the disco era, while fostering a sense of community and collective celebration, also contributed to social alienation and the breakdown of meaningful interpersonal connections. The superficiality of many disco relationships, combined with the emphasis on external appearances and instant gratification, often led to a sense of disconnection and emotional detachment, highlighting the inherent limitations of a hedonistic lifestyle that prioritized pleasure over genuine intimacy and authentic human connection.

In this light, while the disco culture of the 1970s embodied a form of hedonism that celebrated liberation, self-expression, and sensory enjoyment, it also exposed individuals to serious personal risks and potential long-term consequences, underscoring the need for a more balanced and mindful approach to the pursuit of pleasure and self-gratification within the context of social and personal well-being.

Studio 54, one of the most iconic and influential disco clubs of the 1970s, was renowned for its extravagant parties, celebrity guests, and hedonistic atmosphere. While it became a symbol of the era's excess and liberation, it also served as a cautionary tale, reflecting the darker realities and consequences of the disco culture during that time. Several cautionary tales emerged from Studio 54 and other disco spots, highlighting the perils and risks associated with the unrestrained pursuit of pleasure and indulgence:

2.9. Excessive Drug Use and Addiction: Studio 54's notorious reputation for drug-fueled parties and hedonistic excess underscored the prevalent culture of substance abuse and addiction that permeated the disco scene. The club's atmosphere of uninhibited revelry and easy access to a wide array of recreational drugs contributed to a cycle of addiction and dependency among patrons, leading to severe health complications, personal crises, and even tragic overdoses.

2.10. Social Escapism and Disillusionment: The allure of Studio 54 as a sanctuary of escapism and sensory stimulation often masked deeper existential anxieties and a sense of disillusionment among its patrons. The temporary euphoria and artificial highs experienced within the club's walls often gave way to feelings of emptiness, alienation, and a lack of genuine connection, highlighting the inherent emptiness and hollowness of a lifestyle centered solely on hedonistic pursuits and immediate gratification.

2.11. Celebrity Downfalls and Public Excesses: The media's portrayal of Studio 54 as a playground for the rich and famous also revealed the pitfalls and public excesses of celebrity culture within the disco scene. The frequent scandals, legal troubles, and personal meltdowns of prominent figures associated with the club served as cautionary tales, illustrating the dangers of unchecked privilege, fame, and the temptations of a lifestyle characterized by indulgence, extravagance, and the relentless pursuit of public adoration and acclaim.

One notable anecdote that highlights the rampant drug use and downfall of celebrity at Studio 54 involves the club's co-owner, Steve Rubell. In 1978, Rubell and his business partner were arrested and charged with tax evasion, leading to the club's temporary closure. During the investigation, it was revealed that Rubell had kept detailed records of the club's finances, which included a separate ledger named "cash," where he recorded large sums of money made from various illicit activities, including drug sales.

This revelation underscored the extent of drug use and illegal activities that were prevalent within the confines of Studio 54 during its heyday. The club's reputation as a hotspot for indulgence and excess was further solidified by this exposé, shedding light on the pervasive culture of substance abuse and underground dealings that defined the disco scene of the

1970s. The anecdote served as a stark reminder of the darker realities that often accompanied the euphoria and escapism associated with the disco era, highlighting the inherent risks and consequences of unchecked hedonism and the disregard for legal and ethical boundaries.

In sum, Studio 54 and other disco clubs of the 1970s, while emblematic of a cultural moment characterized by liberation, self-expression, and sensual pleasure, also offered cautionary tales that highlighted the darker undercurrents and potential pitfalls of a lifestyle defined by excess, escapism, and the relentless pursuit of immediate gratification. These cautionary tales continue to serve as reminders of the need for balance, mindfulness, and responsible decision-making in the pursuit of personal fulfillment and social belonging.

3. Satanism and the Occult: During the 1970s, there was a resurgence of public interest in Satanism and the Occult, marked by various cultural phenomena and the prominence of certain individuals associated with these practices. This period saw a blend of sensationalized media coverage, countercultural movements, and public fascination with alternative spiritual beliefs, giving rise to a heightened awareness of occult symbolism and Satanic imagery in popular culture. Some notable personalities and anecdotes from this era include:

> **1. Anton LaVey and the Church of Satan:** Anton LaVey, the founder of the Church of Satan, gained significant attention during the 1970s for his provocative and controversial views on Satanic philosophy. His book, "The Satanic Bible," published in 1969, became a significant manifesto for the Satanic movement, advocating for individualism, self-indulgence, and the rejection of conventional religious morality. LaVey's persona and the theatrical rituals performed at the Church of Satan contributed to the widespread curiosity and apprehension surrounding Satanic practices during this time.

2. Manson Family Murders: The Manson Family murders in 1969, though preceding the 1970s, had a profound impact on the public's perception of Satanic cults and the dangers associated with extreme ideological beliefs. The brutal killings orchestrated by Charles Manson and his followers sent shockwaves through society, fueling fears of Satanic rituals and the manipulation of vulnerable individuals by charismatic and manipulative leaders, thereby contributing to a heightened cultural awareness of the darker aspects of fringe religious movements.

3. Occult Symbolism in Popular Culture: The 1970s witnessed a proliferation of occult symbolism and imagery in various forms of media, including literature, music, and film. Bands like Black Sabbath incorporated Satanic themes into their music, while films like "The Exorcist" (1973) and "Rosemary's Baby" (1968) explored themes of demonic possession and occult rituals, capitalizing on the public's fascination with the supernatural and the unknown. The use of occult symbolism in popular culture during this era reflected a broader cultural preoccupation with mysticism, alternative spiritual beliefs, and the allure of the forbidden and taboo.

4. Publicized Rituals and Alternative Spiritual Movements: Various publicized rituals and alternative spiritual movements emerged during the 1970s, contributing to a growing interest in New Age practices, Wicca, and other forms of esoteric knowledge. Public figures such as self-proclaimed witch Sybil Leek and the New Age advocate and philosopher, Timothy Leary, contributed to the popularization of alternative spiritual beliefs and practices, fostering a climate of experimentation and curiosity regarding non-traditional forms of spirituality and mystical experiences.

The 1970s marked a period of heightened fascination with Satanism and the Occult, characterized by a blend of sensationalized media coverage, countercultural movements, and public curiosity about alternative spiritual beliefs. The prominence of certain personalities and the prevalence of occult symbolism in popular culture contributed to a cultural climate that both sensationalized and demystified the mysteries and allure of the Satanic and the supernatural.

The fascination with Satanism and the Occult in the 1970s bore some resemblance to the cultural climate of the Weimar Republic in Germany (1919-1933), particularly in the context of the Weimar-era's exploration of alternative spiritual movements, subversive artistic expressions, and a general rejection of traditional religious and moral values. Both periods exhibited a fascination with the esoteric, the taboo, and the provocative, reflecting a broader societal shift towards the questioning of established norms and the embrace of alternative philosophies.

During the Weimar Republic, the cultural landscape was marked by a spirit of experimentation, decadence, and social rebellion, characterized by the emergence of avant-garde art movements, cabaret performances, and an open exploration of themes related to sexuality, spirituality, and the supernatural. The Weimar-era's preoccupation with the mystical, the occult, and the provocative mirrored the 1970s' cultural fascination with Satanism and alternative spiritual beliefs, emphasizing a shared interest in challenging conventional religious doctrines and exploring the boundaries of human experience.

Additionally, the Weimar Republic witnessed the rise of various fringe groups, including occult societies, mystical orders, and esoteric movements that advocated for a rejection of mainstream Christianity and a return to pre-Christian spiritual practices. These groups often espoused beliefs in the power of the supernatural, the influence of cosmic energies, and the embrace of mystical symbolism as a means of attaining spiritual enlightenment and personal liberation. The Weimar-era's exploration of the esoteric and the occult can be seen as a precursor to the 1970s' fascination with Satanism and alternative spiritual movements, both of which sought to challenge traditional religious dogma and promote a more individualistic and unorthodox approach to spirituality and self-expression.

In this way, the cultural echoes between the Weimar Republic and the 1970s reveal a shared interest in subverting established norms, questioning conventional morality, and exploring the boundaries of human consciousness, reflecting a broader cultural and societal search for alternative forms of meaning, identity, and spiritual fulfillment outside the confines of mainstream religious institutions and traditional moral frameworks. Both led to-

4. Burnout and Excess: The culture of hedonism in the 1970s also gave rise to a phenomenon of burnout and excess, as individuals engaged in relentless partying, substance abuse, and a pursuit of instant gratification that often led to physical and emotional exhaustion. The relentless pursuit of pleasure and self-indulgence often masked deeper existential anxieties and a sense of disillusionment with traditional societal norms, leading to a culture of escapism and temporary gratification that could ultimately result in feelings of emptiness and disconnection.

Overall, the culture of hedonism in the 1970s reflected a broader societal shift towards the celebration of individual freedom, self-expression, and the pursuit of immediate pleasure, contributing to a cultural landscape that embraced the exploration of alternative lifestyles, sensory experiences, and the rejection of conventional moral codes and social expectations.

Lack of Fulfillment

Paradoxically, the relentless pursuit of pleasure can lead to a lack of overall life satisfaction and fulfillment. Hedonism may result in a perpetual cycle of seeking happiness through external means rather than finding contentment from within.

The relentless pursuit of pleasure, while initially appealing, can lead to a lack of overall life satisfaction and fulfillment, as it often prioritizes immediate gratification over long-term well-being and genuine contentment. Here are some ways in which this pursuit may result in an ultimate sense of dissatisfaction:

1. Ephemeral Nature of Pleasure: The pursuit of fleeting and transient pleasures often fails to provide lasting satisfaction, leaving individuals yearning for more intense or novel experiences to replicate the initial euphoria. This perpetual cycle of seeking new sources of pleasure can lead to a sense of emptiness and disillusionment, as the temporary highs of indulgence give way to a deeper sense of dissatisfaction and emotional disconnection.

2. Neglect of Meaningful Connections: An excessive focus on hedonistic pursuits may lead individuals to neglect the cultivation of meaningful relationships and genuine human connections. The pursuit of pleasure often occurs at the expense of investing time and energy in fostering authentic bonds with others, resulting in a profound sense of loneliness and isolation that cannot be fulfilled by momentary gratification or self-indulgence.

3. Emotional Turmoil and Instability: The pursuit of pleasure without considering its emotional implications can result in heightened emotional turmoil and instability. Individuals may find themselves oscillating between periods of intense excitement and profound despondency, as the temporary highs of hedonistic experiences are often accompanied by subsequent periods of emotional lows and dissatisfaction. This emotional rollercoaster can contribute to a sense of overall dissatisfaction and a lack of emotional balance and stability.

4. Compromised Physical and Mental Health: The relentless pursuit of pleasure may also have detrimental effects on physical and mental well-being. Unhealthy indulgences, substance abuse, and risky behaviors often associated with hedonism can lead to long-term health complications, emotional distress, and a compromised sense of self-worth and self-respect. The physical and psychological toll of hedonistic excesses can contribute to a diminished quality of life and an overall sense of dissatisfaction and regret.

Ultimately, the pursuit of pleasure, when not balanced with a deeper sense of purpose, meaningful connections, and holistic well-being, can lead to a profound lack of overall life satisfaction and fulfillment. It is essential for individuals to cultivate a sense of self-awareness, emotional resilience, and a holistic understanding of personal fulfillment that extends beyond the immediacy of momentary pleasures, encouraging a more balanced and sustainable approach to happiness and well-being.

Perspectives from Notable Figures on the Pursuit of Endless Pleasure

1. Ralph Waldo Emerson: He might emphasize the importance of self-reliance, individual growth, and the pursuit of a purposeful life aligned with one's inner values and principles.

2. Aristotle: Aristotle might stress the significance of achieving eudaimonia, a state of flourishing and well-being that arises from virtuous living and the pursuit of meaningful goals.

3. Benjamin Franklin: Franklin might highlight the value of temperance, industry, and the cultivation of moral virtues as essential components of a fulfilling and purposeful life.

4. Tony Robbins: Robbins might underscore the significance of setting meaningful goals, maintaining a sense of contribution, and fostering a sense of fulfillment through personal growth and continuous improvement.

5. Stewart Brand: Brand might emphasize the importance of responsible stewardship of the environment and the promotion of sustainable practices as a source of long-term fulfillment and global well-being.

6. Gary Snyder: Snyder might advocate for a deep connection with nature, the pursuit of ecological harmony, and a reverence for the interconnectedness of all life as a pathway to personal and collective fulfillment.

7. Buckminster Fuller: Fuller might stress the significance of holistic design thinking, global problem-solving, and the pursuit of solutions that benefit humanity as a whole, encouraging individuals to find purpose in contributing to the betterment of society and the planet.

10 Things That Are Better Than
the Pursuit of Endless Pleasure

1. Meaningful Relationships: Cultivating deep and meaningful connections with others.

2. Personal Growth: Engaging in self-improvement and personal development.

3. Contributing to Society: Making a positive impact on the community and the world.

4. Emotional Resilience: Building emotional strength and resilience in the face of challenges.

5. Intellectual Stimulation: Pursuing knowledge, education, and intellectual curiosity.

6. Spiritual Fulfillment: Seeking spiritual growth and inner peace.

7. Physical Health: Prioritizing physical well-being and a healthy lifestyle.

8. Creative Expression: Nurturing creative pursuits and artistic expression.

9. Environmental Stewardship: Promoting sustainability and environmental consciousness.

10. Legacy Building: Leaving a meaningful and lasting legacy for future generations.

11. Dogs

My Advice? Set up and Take the Lodge Building Class I thought up in the Esalon section. Bring friends. Make friends. Make an interesting soup for lunch. Drink good coffee during and good wine after. And, build that thing. Contribute to a Living Museum that would last lifetimes. That's *one* Option.

Part X: Extras

1. Films

Fie movies from the 1970s that reflect the values, attitudes, and cultural shifts of that era:

1. "Easy Rider" (1969) - While technically from the late 1960s, this film encapsulates many of the countercultural and anti-establishment sentiments that continued into the early 1970s. It follows two bikers on a cross-country journey exploring freedom and nonconformity.

2. "Annie Hall" (1977) - Directed by Woody Allen, this romantic comedy explores relationships and self-discovery in a witty and unconventional way, reflecting the changing dynamics of love and commitment in the 1970s.

3. "One Flew Over the Cuckoo's Nest" (1975) - This film, based on the novel by Ken Kesey, critiques authority and conformity through the story of a man who feigns insanity to escape prison but ends up in a mental hospital.

4. "Harold and Maude" (1971) - This offbeat romantic comedy-drama tells the story of an unlikely romance between a young man obsessed with death and an elderly woman who embraces life and individualism.

5. "Network" (1976) - A satirical look at the media and corporate culture of the 1970s, this film explores the blurring of entertainment and news, the power of television, and the loss of personal privacy.

These movies capture the spirit of the 1970s by addressing themes of rebellion, individualism, counterculture, and societal change that were prevalent during that decade.

Five more non-obvious movie choices from the 1970s that reflect the era's values and cultural shifts:

1. "Two-Lane Blacktop" (1971) - A road movie that explores themes of aimlessness, detachment, and the search for meaning in a changing America.

2. "The Last Picture Show" (1971) - Set in a small, dying Texas town, this film portrays the disillusionment of a younger generation and the decline of traditional values in a rapidly evolving society.

3. "Five Easy Pieces" (1970) - Jack Nicholson stars in this character study that delves into issues of identity, class, and rebellion against societal norms.

4. "Walkabout" (1971) - This visually stunning film explores the clash of cultures and the isolation of the modern world through the story of a young girl and a young Aboriginal boy in the Australian outback.

5. "The Heartbreak Kid" (1972) - A dark comedy that critiques the pursuit of superficial relationships and personal gratification in the context of marriage and societal expectations.

These non-obvious choices offer a deeper exploration of the complex values and cultural changes that characterized the 1970s.

Five More? you have that much free time?

- "Sleeper" (1973)
- "Being There" (1979)
- "Where's Poppa?" (1970)
- "The Last Picture Show" (1971)
- "Holy Hell" (2016) - A documentary about The Family cult

2. Music

During the 1970s, the music scene experienced a remarkable and diverse range of styles and genres, reflecting the cultural dynamism and social changes of the era. This period was characterized by an unparalleled fusion of musical influences, a spirit of experimentation, and a cultural openness to new sounds and artistic expressions. Several key factors contributed to the vibrant diversity of musical styles during the 1970s:

1. Cultural Shifts and Social Activism: The 1970s marked a period of significant social and political change, with movements such as civil rights, women's liberation, and anti-war activism shaping the cultural landscape. This cultural upheaval fostered a spirit of rebellion and artistic experimentation, inspiring musicians to explore new themes, musical forms, and unconventional styles that reflected the spirit of social activism and cultural revolution.

2. Technological Advancements and Musical Innovation: The 1970s witnessed significant advancements in recording technology and musical instruments, enabling artists to experiment with new sounds, production techniques, and studio innovations. The emergence of synthesizers, electronic effects, and multi-track recording systems revolutionized the creative process, allowing musicians to push the boundaries of traditional genres and pioneer groundbreaking musical styles that were previously unimaginable.

3. Cross-Cultural Exchange and Global Influences: The 1970s saw an increased interconnectedness and exchange of cultural influences on a global scale. Musicians were inspired by a rich tapestry of international sounds, including African rhythms, Latin grooves, Eastern melodies, and Caribbean beats, leading to a vibrant fusion of world music elements within mainstream genres. This cross-pollination of musical traditions and global influences contributed to the diverse and eclectic soundscape of the 1970s.

4. Countercultural Movements and Alternative Music Scenes: The rise of countercultural movements, underground music scenes, and independent record labels provided a platform for diverse and experimental musical expressions that challenged mainstream conventions. Genres such as punk rock, disco, funk, reggae, and progressive rock emerged as prominent musical movements, each representing a unique cultural ethos and musical sensibility that contributed to the rich tapestry of 1970s music.

In contrast, the musical landscape of 2020, often reflects a more homogenized and commercialized industry, where streaming services, digital platforms, and algorithm-driven recommendations tend to promote popular trends and mainstream sounds (read: shite) over niche or experimental genres. The dominance of commercial interests, the digitalization of music production, and the centralization of streaming platforms have, to some extent, streamlined the diversity of musical styles, making it challenging for niche or unconventional genres to gain mainstream exposure and recognition. While artistic diversity continues to thrive in pockets of the music industry, the broader commercial landscape of 2020 often favors familiar and commercially viable sounds, leading to a more standardized and predictable musical environment in comparison to the groundbreaking diversity of the 1970s.

The Obvious List

1. Led Zeppelin - Stairway to Heaven
2. The Beatles - Let It Be
3. Eric Clapton - Layla
4. Yes - Roundabout
5. The Who - Baba O'Riley
6. Genesis - The Musical Box
7. George Harrison - My Sweet Lord
8. Ravi Shankar - Raga Jog
9. Steely Dan- Rolling in the Years
10. David Bowie - Changes
11. Pink Floyd - Comfortably Numb
12. Elton John - Rocket Man
13. Joni Mitchell - Big Yellow Taxi
14. Bob Dylan - Tangled Up in Blue
15. Fleetwood Mac - Go Your Own Way
16. Queen - Bohemian Rhapsody
17. Stevie Wonder - Superstition
18. The Rolling Stones - Angie
19. Cat Stevens - Wild World
20. Black Sabbath - Paranoid
21. Crosby, Stills, Nash & Young - Ohio
22. Bob Marley & The Wailers - No Woman, No Cry
23. Steely Dan - Reelin' In The Years
24. Lou Reed - Walk on the Wild Side
25. Jethro Tull - Aqualung
26. Santana - Black Magic Woman
27. T. Rex - Bang a Gong (Get It On)
28. Janis Joplin - Me and Bobby McGee
29. Supertramp - Breakfast in America
30. Elton John - Tiny Dancer

This playlist captures the diverse and dynamic nature of 1970s rock music, showcasing a wide array of musical styles, lyrical themes, and instrumental techniques that defined the era's rich and influential soundscape.

10 Deeper Cuts- For when you are trying to figure out why you listened to all of those idiots in the first place...

1. "Over the Hills and Far Away" by Led Zeppelin from the album "Houses of the Holy" (1973)

2. "Going for the One" by Yes from the album "Going for the One" (1977)

3. "Selling England by the Pound" by Genesis from the album "Selling England by the Pound" (1973)

4. "Larks' Tongues in Aspic, Part One" by King Crimson from the album "Larks' Tongues in Aspic" (1973)

5. "Calyx" by Hatfield and the North from the album "The Rotters' Club" (1975)

6."Golf Girl" by Caravan - A whimsical and melodic track that was released in 1971, featuring intricate instrumentation and a light-hearted atmosphere.

7."Nine Feet Underground" by Caravan - A sprawling and ambitious composition released in 1971 that exemplifies the progressive and experimental tendencies of the Canterbury scene.

8."L' Auberge du Sanglier" by Camel - This instrumental piece was released in 1973, showcasing the band's virtuosic musicianship and intricate musical arrangements.

9."The Drowned World" by Hatfield and the North - Released in 1975, this complex and dynamic track highlights the band's fusion of jazz and rock elements.

10."As Long as He Lies Perfectly Still" by Soft Machine - This multifaceted and experimental track was released in 1970, embodying the band's innovative approach to blending jazz and rock.

10 Smooth Jazz Cuts

Good for your relaxation response exercises. Smooth jazz emerged as a popular subgenre in the 1970s, incorporating elements of jazz, R&B, and pop to create a mellow and accessible sound. Some of the top smooth jazz tracks from the 1970s, including works by Grover Washington and Bob James, could include:

1. "Mister Magic" by Grover Washington Jr. (1975)

2. "Feel Like Makin' Love" by Bob James (1974)

3. "Just the Two of Us" by Grover Washington Jr. (1980) - Although released in 1980, this track carries the smooth jazz sound of the late 1970s.

4. "Angela" by Bob James (1978) - Known for its appearance as the theme for the TV show "Taxi."

5. "Black Frost" by Grover Washington Jr. (1975)

6. "Westchester Lady" by Bob James (1976)

7. "Winelight" by Grover Washington Jr. (1980) - Released in 1980 but reflects the smooth jazz style of the late 1970s.

8. "Nautilus" by Bob James (1974)

9. "Sausalito" by Grover Washington Jr. (1978)

10. "Touchdown" by Bob James (1978)

These tracks represent the smooth jazz sound of the 1970s, highlighting the fusion of jazz, R&B, and pop elements that defined the genre during that era.

3. Buffet

In the context of the 1970s, a buffet referred to a self-service meal where various dishes were laid out on a table or sideboard from which guests could serve themselves. It often included a wide variety of foods, such as appetizers, main courses, side dishes, and desserts. Buffets were commonly used for formal events, gatherings, and parties. For example, a popular buffet option during the 1970s might have consisted of dishes like beef Wellington, coq au vin, Waldorf salad, and baked Alaska served at an elegant dinner party.

Odd fact:
Plato's Retreat was a popular, infamous, and controversial swingers' club that operated in New York City during the 1970s. While there is limited information available about the specific items on the buffet at Plato's Retreat, it was known for its sexually liberated atmosphere and its wide array of amenities, which included a buffet for its guests.

The club was famous for its extravagant and hedonistic parties, where patrons engaged in various sexual activities in a permissive environment. However, details about the specific food offerings at Plato's Retreat during the 1970s are not extensively documented.

It's important to note that Plato's Retreat was ultimately closed down in the early 1980s due to legal and public health concerns. While it played a significant role in the sexual liberation movement of the 1970s, its notoriety stems from its unique and controversial approach to social and sexual interaction rather than its culinary offerings.

If you really think I am going to leave this section without some bizarre menu for an all-day seminar on the self-help revolution in the 70s, you would be wrong.

The Unconventional 1970s Casserole Buffet

We invite you to experience the unconventional and nostalgic flavors of the 1970s with our specially curated casserole-inspired buffet. Our culinary team has carefully crafted each dish to bring a touch of whimsy and sophistication to your dining experience. Enjoy the journey into the eccentricities of 1970s cuisine while savoring the comforting and delightful flavors of these unconventional classics.

Appetizers:

- Ham and Banana Casserole Bites with Creamy Sauce Drizzle
- Mini Tuna and Jell-O Salad Cups with a Dollop of Mayonnaise

Main Course Selections:

- Chicken and Waffles Casserole Squares
- Individual Jellied Shrimp and Rice Casseroles
- Liver and Onion Sliders with Caramelized Onion Relish
-Lentil Loaf

Accompaniments:

- Radish and Spinach Salad with Green Goddess
or Catalina Dressing
- Cornbread & Parker House Rolls with Whipped Butter
- Assorted Pickles and Relishes

Beverages:

Wheatgrass Juice | Herbal Teas
Tang |Birch Beer
Alfalfa Sprout Smoothies

Indulgent Dessert Spread:

- Pineapple Upside-Down Cake
- Watergate Salad
- Ambrosia Salad

4. Earth Shoes

Earth shoes, a prominent footwear brand of the 1970s, captured attention with their distinctive negative heel design, which positioned the heel lower than the toe. Launched in the early 1970s, Earth shoes gained popularity for their purported health benefits, including improved posture and reduced back strain. The brand's legacy extended beyond its unique design, influencing the direction of footwear design and contributing to the growing emphasis on ergonomically shaped shoes.

The popularity of Earth shoes in the 1970s coincided with a broader fashion trend centered around natural and organic materials, as well as a preference for comfort and non-traditional styles. These shoes became associated with the era's holistic lifestyle movement, embodying the era's focus on health and well-being. Advertisements for Earth shoes often highlighted their connection to the natural environment, promoting a sense of harmony between the wearer and the world around them.

Alongside Earth shoes, the 1970s witnessed the emergence of various unconventional footwear options. These included platform shoes, clogs, and mules, characterized by their bold and exaggerated designs. Reflecting the adventurous and experimental spirit of the decade, these shoes often featured vibrant colors, chunky heels, and innovative materials, representing a departure from conventional footwear norms.

vs. Dr. Scholl's

Earth shoes and Dr. Scholl's were two prominent footwear brands that gained popularity in the 1970s, each offering unique and innovative designs that appealed to the era's evolving fashion trends and growing interest in comfortable footwear. While Earth shoes were known for their distinctive negative heel design and their association with the holistic lifestyle movement, Dr. Scholl's became renowned for its focus on foot health and its range of orthopedic and ergonomic footwear products.

Earth shoes gained recognition for their unconventional design, which purportedly provided health benefits such as improved posture and reduced back strain. The brand's emphasis on natural materials and its connection to the era's environmental consciousness contributed to its appeal among consumers looking for both style and comfort.

On the other hand, Dr. Scholl's focused on providing foot care solutions, offering a wide range of orthopedic footwear designed to support and promote foot health. Dr. Scholl's products included insoles, sandals, and shoes that aimed to alleviate foot discomfort and provide enhanced support, catering to individuals seeking practical and therapeutic footwear options.

While Earth shoes and Dr. Scholl's targeted different aspects of the footwear market, they both left a lasting impact on the industry, influencing the development of future footwear designs and contributing to the evolving trends in comfort and wellness-oriented fashion.

Earth shoes are still being produced today. Despite their initial rise to popularity in the 1970s, the brand has continued to evolve and adapt to contemporary fashion trends and consumer preferences. Over the years, Earth shoes have undergone various redesigns and updates to incorporate modern styles and technologies while maintaining their focus on comfort and wellness.

In recent times, Earth shoes have continued to emphasize their original philosophy of providing footwear that supports a healthy and natural gait. They often incorporate features such as arch support, cushioned footbeds, and durable materials, appealing to individuals seeking both style and comfort in their footwear choices. Earth shoes have also expanded their product lines to include a wide range of casual and dress shoes, catering to diverse fashion preferences and lifestyles.

The enduring presence of Earth shoes in the contemporary footwear market highlights their ability to adapt and remain relevant in an ever-changing industry, demonstrating their lasting appeal to consumers looking for comfortable and stylish footwear options.

5. Jell-O

Jell-O, a popular gelatin dessert, enjoyed a significant and colorful presence in the culinary landscape of the 1970s. This iconic dessert, known for its vibrant colors and versatility, became a staple at dinner tables, potlucks, and social gatherings throughout the decade. Its widespread appeal during this era can be attributed to several factors, including its convenience, vibrant aesthetic, and association with the spirit of experimentation and innovation that characterized the 1970s.

One of the defining features of Jell-O in the 1970s was its kaleidoscope of colors and flavors, reflecting the exuberance and vibrancy of the era. From electric green to bright red and sunny yellow, Jell-O desserts adorned dining tables, bringing a playful and whimsical touch to meals and special occasions. These colorful gelatin molds often took on imaginative shapes, ranging from intricate layered designs to whimsical molds featuring fruits, vegetables, and other playful motifs. The creative possibilities offered by Jell-O inspired a wave of culinary experimentation, encouraging individuals to express their artistic inclinations through food.

Moreover, the convenience of Jell-O made it a popular choice for busy households and aspiring home cooks. Its simple preparation and quick setting time provided a hassle-free dessert option that could be easily customized with various ingredients, including fruits, nuts, and whipped cream. This convenience factor resonated with the changing lifestyles of the 1970s, as more individuals sought efficient and time-saving solutions in their everyday lives.

In addition to its appeal as a dessert, Jell-O also found its way into a variety of savory dishes, blurring the lines between sweet and savory flavors. Popular recipes of the time included Jell-O salads incorporating ingredients such as shredded carrots, canned fruits, and mayonnaise, resulting in a curious amalgamation of tastes and textures that both delighted and intrigued palates. These unconventional culinary creations added a playful twist to traditional meals and became emblematic of the spirit of culinary innovation prevalent during the 1970s.

As a symbol of the 1970s culinary culture, Jell-O encapsulated the era's spirit of creativity, convenience, and experimentation. Its vibrant presence on dining tables and in cookbooks served as a testament to the era's enthusiasm for imaginative and unconventional culinary experiences, leaving a colorful legacy that continues to evoke nostalgia and fond memories of a dynamic and innovative period in culinary history.

During the 1970s, Jell-O became a versatile ingredient, lending itself to a variety of creative and unconventional recipes.

Here are ten of the most memorable and oddball Jell-O recipes from that era:

1. Frosted Ribbon Salad: A layered Jell-O salad incorporating gelatin, whipped cream, and canned fruit, often topped with a creamy frosting.

2. Tuna and Vegetable Jell-O Salad: A savory gelatin salad featuring canned tuna, chopped vegetables, and mayonnaise, creating a curious blend of flavors and textures.

3. Jellied Tomato Refresher: A tomato-based gelatin dessert infused with herbs and spices, served as a refreshing and unusual summer treat.

4. Carrot and Jell-O Ring: A molded gelatin dish combining shredded carrots, lemon gelatin, and pineapple, often served as a colorful and quirky side dish.

5. Cottage Cheese and Jell-O Mold: A blend of cottage cheese and fruit-flavored gelatin, set in a mold to create a textured and creamy dessert option.

6. Layered Gelatin Cake: A multi-layered cake featuring alternating layers of colorful gelatin and whipped cream, providing a whimsical and visually appealing dessert option.

7. Jell-O Meat Loaf: A savory meatloaf incorporating lime gelatin, ground meat, and various seasonings, creating a surprisingly tangy and unconventional twist on a classic dish.

8. Jell-O and Vegetable Medley: A combination of assorted vegetables suspended in colorful gelatin, offering a playful and imaginative take on a traditional vegetable dish.

9. Jell-O Waldorf Salad: A sweet and fruity twist on the classic Waldorf salad, featuring gelatin, diced apples, celery, and walnuts, creating a unique blend of textures and flavors.

10. Jell-O Frosted Lemonade: A tangy and refreshing beverage made with lemon gelatin, lemonade, and soda water, offering a fizzy and unconventional take on a classic lemonade recipe.

Jellied Tomato Refresher Using Jell-O

Ingredients:

- 1 package (3 ounces) of Jell-O
         (any red flavor, such as strawberry or raspberry)
- 4 large ripe tomatoes
- 1 small onion, finely chopped
- 1 cup tomato juice
- 1 tablespoon sugar
- 1 tablespoon lemon juice
- Salt and pepper to taste
- Fresh herbs for garnish (optional)

Instructions:
1. Prepare the Jell-O according to the package instructions, using only 1 cup of hot water to dissolve the gelatin. Set it aside to cool slightly.
2. Peel the tomatoes by scoring a small "X" on the bottom of each tomato, then submerging them in boiling water for about 30 seconds. Afterward, transfer the tomatoes to an ice water bath, making the skins easy to peel.
3. Chop the peeled tomatoes into small pieces and set them aside.
4. In a saucepan, combine the tomato juice, sugar, and lemon juice. Heat the mixture over low heat, stirring until the sugar is dissolved.
5. Add the dissolved Jell-O to the tomato juice mixture and stir until well combined.6. Mix in the chopped tomatoes and finely chopped onion. Season with salt and pepper to taste.
7. Pour the entire mixture into a lightly greased mold or individual serving dishes.
8. Refrigerate the Jellied Tomato Refresher for at least 2-3 hours, or until it is firmly set.
9. Once set, carefully unmold the dish onto a serving plate. Garnish with fresh herbs if desired.

After the Party

The 1970s were marked by significant social experimentation, hedonism, and a growing acceptance of non-traditional or 'weird' ideas, which had a profound impact on the emerging dominant culture in the 1980s. The 'Me' decade of the 1970s was characterized by a general relaxation of social norms, an emphasis on individualism, and a rejection of traditional values. This era saw the rise of countercultural movements, increased experimentation with drugs, and the mainstreaming of alternative lifestyles and beliefs.

The social effects of the excessive experimentation and hedonism of the 1970s were viewed with concern by many in the 1980s. The 1980s marked a shift towards a more conservative and materialistic culture, with an emphasis on traditional values, individual responsibility, and economic success. The excesses of the 1970s were seen as contributing to social instability, moral decay, and a breakdown of traditional social institutions. The emerging dominant culture of the 1980s sought to restore a sense of order, discipline, and moral clarity, reacting against what was perceived as the moral relativism and social chaos of the previous decade.

The 1980s saw the rise of the conservative political movement, epitomized by figures like Ronald Reagan in the United States and Margaret Thatcher in the United Kingdom. This movement sought to roll back the perceived excesses of the 1970s and promote a return to traditional values and social norms. There was a renewed emphasis on family values, patriotism, and the importance of hard work and personal responsibility. Additionally, there was a renewed focus on law and order, as well as a conservative approach to social issues such as drug use and sexuality.

The cultural shift in the 1980s was also evident in popular culture, with a resurgence of mainstream, commercialized music, film, and television that often reflected more conservative values. This was a departure from the experimental and boundary-pushing art and music of the 1970s. The 1980s also witnessed the emergence of the "culture wars," as different segments of society clashed over issues such as censorship, family values, and the role of religion in public life.

The excessive experimentation, hedonism, and acceptance of 'weird' ideas in the 1970s were viewed by the emerging dominant culture in the 1980s as contributing to social instability and moral decay. The 1980s marked a shift towards a more conservative and traditional culture, emphasizing values such as individual responsibility, moral clarity, and social order. This cultural shift was reflected in politics, popular culture, and social attitudes, as the 1980s sought to restore a sense of stability and traditional values that were perceived to have been eroded during the previous decade.

In the 1980s, there was a discernible shift in attitudes towards alternative lifestyles, including those associated with the hippie movement of the 1960s and 1970s, as well as the burgeoning self-help industry. Several factors contributed to these shifting attitudes, including the conservative political and social climate of the time, a growing emphasis on individualism, and a desire for economic success.

1. Rejection of Countercultural Values: The 1980s saw a rejection of the countercultural values that had characterized the 1960s and 1970s. The emphasis on communal living, anti-establishment sentiments, and non-materialistic lifestyles that were associated with the hippie movement became increasingly out of sync with the dominant ethos of the 1980s, which placed a premium on material wealth and success.

2. Emphasis on Individualism and Material Success: The 1980s were marked by a strong focus on individualism and the pursuit of material success. This focus was reflected in the growing popularity of the "greed is good" mentality and the elevation of entrepreneurship and capitalism as aspirational ideals. In this context, the values of simplicity and communal living that were often associated with alternative lifestyles were viewed as incompatible with the pursuit of material wealth.

3. Self-Help and Personal Development: While the self-help industry continued to flourish in the 1980s, there was also a significant shift in the types of self-help messages that gained traction. Self-help literature increasingly emphasized strategies for achieving financial success and personal achievement, reflecting the broader cultural emphasis on individual success and material wealth. This shift marked a departure from the more holistic and

486

spiritually oriented self-help messages that were popular in the 1960s and 1970s.

4. Conservative Backlash: The conservative political and social climate of the 1980s contributed to a general skepticism towards alternative lifestyles and values that were perceived as countercultural or anti-establishment. This backlash was evident in the popular media, with depictions of hippies and alternative lifestyles often portrayed in a negative light or as relics of a bygone era.

5. Emphasis on Traditional Values: The 1980s saw a resurgence of traditional values, including an emphasis on family, patriotism, and conformity to societal norms. Alternative lifestyles were often viewed as a threat to these traditional values and were consequently marginalized or stigmatized in mainstream culture.

6. Analysis as a Religion: In the 1980s, there were significant critiques of psychoanalysis, stemming from the shifting cultural and intellectual climate of the time. While psychoanalysis had been a dominant force in the field of psychology for much of the 20th century, the 1980s saw the rise of alternative approaches and a growing skepticism towards some of the foundational principles of psychoanalytic theory. Some of the critiques that gained prominence during this period included:

> **1. Lack of Empirical Validation:** One of the key criticisms of psychoanalysis in the 1980s was its perceived lack of empirical validation. Many within the field of psychology argued that the concepts and techniques of psychoanalysis were not adequately supported by empirical evidence, leading to a call for a more scientifically rigorous approach to understanding and treating mental health issues.

> **2. Alternative Therapeutic Approaches:** The 1980s witnessed the growing popularity of alternative therapeutic approaches, such as cognitive-behavioral therapy (CBT) and humanistic psychology. These approaches offered more structured and goal-oriented methods for addressing psychological issues, in contrast to the more introspective and exploratory nature of psychoanalysis.

3. Cultural Shift Towards Pragmatism: The cultural and intellectual climate of the 1980s emphasized pragmatism and practicality, which led to a devaluation of some of the more abstract and theoretical aspects of psychoanalysis. The focus on measurable outcomes and concrete results in various fields, including psychology, contributed to a reevaluation of the utility and relevance of psychoanalytic concepts in contemporary practice.

4. Rise of Biological Psychiatry: The 1980s also saw a significant shift towards biological explanations for mental health disorders, with advancements in neuroscience and psychopharmacology gaining prominence. This shift led to a growing emphasis on the role of neurobiology and genetics in understanding and treating psychological issues, which, in turn, challenged some of the more psychodynamic and non-biological explanations put forth by psychoanalysis.

5. Sociopolitical Critiques: Some critics in the 1980s argued that psychoanalysis, with its emphasis on the individual psyche, neglected broader sociopolitical factors that contribute to mental health issues. These critiques highlighted the importance of considering social, cultural, and systemic influences on psychological well-being, advocating for a more holistic and contextual approach to understanding human behavior and mental health.

6. The Emperor's Clothing: There was significant evidence that led to a growing discomfort with some fields of psychology and psychiatry. The populace was forming a valid impression that psychiatry was requiring all the belief of a religious tradition, without possessing any of the intellectual or cultural traditions, fought over, and developed over, the course of centuries, to uphold their fanciful, and patent-able, assertions and bizarre foundational beliefs. Traditional Analysts, and Kinsey-esque and Reichen theoreticians who practiced beyond Good and Evil, where slowly being revealed as having one foot in the 'unconscious' and the other in advertising, self-promotion, manipulation, hero-worship, mind control, and propaganda, each the slightest degree away from the confirmed MKULTRA government testing on an unwilling populace, the personality-led cult figures of Jim Jones or Manson, and the snake-oil salesmen of the 19th century. It seemed infinitely preferable to bright men and women exiting the 70s to make money, stay away from hallucinogenic drugs and focus on becoming emotionally, physically and financially fit, all options the best of the 70s self-help revolution brought to the forefront of the minds of the general populace.

These critiques, along with broader cultural and scientific shifts, contributed to a reevaluation of the dominant position of psychoanalysis within the field of psychology in the 1980s, paving the way for the diversification and pluralism that characterized psychology in the later decades of the 20th century.

Overall, the 1980s marked a significant shift away from the communal and anti-establishment values of the 1960s and 1970s, towards an emphasis on individual success and material wealth. This is not to say cocaine and junk bond traders did not play a part in the NYC 80s zeitgeist, it is to say it was not as powerful a social force as the social experimentation in the 70s. This shift in values contributed to a general skepticism towards alternative lifestyles, including those associated with the hippie movement, as well as a narrowing of the focus of the self-help industry towards strategies for achieving financial success and personal achievement.

Aristotle and Franklin on the 80s

Considering the historical contexts and philosophical perspectives of Benjamin Franklin and Aristotle, it is important to note that they lived in vastly different times and cultural environments, which makes it challenging to speculate on their specific viewpoints regarding the return to conservative values in the 1980s. However, we can consider their broader philosophical principles and beliefs to provide potential insights:

1. Benjamin Franklin: As a key figure in the American Enlightenment, Franklin valued individual liberty, pragmatism, and a strong work ethic. He believed in the importance of personal responsibility and the pursuit of self-improvement. While Franklin was not an overtly political thinker, his writings suggest a preference for a moderate, pragmatic approach to governance. He might have viewed the return to conservative values in the 1980s through the lens of individual responsibility and the importance of maintaining a balanced approach to societal progress, with an emphasis on practicality and personal virtue.

2. Aristotle: A foundational figure in Western philosophy, Aristotle's ethical and political thought emphasized the importance of moderation, virtue, and the common good. He believed that the best form of government was one that promoted the flourishing of its citizens and cultivated virtuous character. Aristotle might have approached the return to conservative values in the 1980s with a critical eye, examining whether these values truly fostered human flourishing and the development of virtuous individuals, or whether they hindered progress and limited individual freedoms.

Both Franklin and Aristotle valued the importance of balance and moderation, and they emphasized the cultivation of individual excellence and societal well-being. They might have been critical of any societal or political movements that seemed to veer too far towards extreme positions, whether liberal or conservative, as they both advocated for a thoughtful and balanced approach to social and political life. Their perspectives would likely have emphasized the need for prudence and the careful consideration of the long-term consequences of societal shifts and changes in values.

The Recovery from Para-Rational Excess

If you were to choose a para-rational system of belief, it would be wise to choose one that, at the very least, does not cause harm to yourself, or your society.

The term "para-rational" refers to a concept that lies beyond or outside the boundaries of rational thought and empirical verification. In the context of non-verifiable belief systems sold as methods of 'self-help' in the 1970s, the term "para-rational" implies a departure from conventional rationality and scientific validation, often involving esoteric or mystical elements that are not easily subject to empirical scrutiny.

During the 1970s, there was a proliferation of various self-help movements and alternative belief systems that embraced para-rational concepts, often incorporating elements of spirituality, mysticism, and New Age philosophy. These belief systems typically emphasized subjective experiences, intuition, and personal transformation, placing less emphasis on empirical evidence or scientific validation.

The para-rational nature of these belief systems often appealed to individuals seeking alternative approaches to personal growth and well-being, especially those who were disillusioned with mainstream psychological and therapeutic methods. The emphasis on subjective experience and spiritual exploration allowed individuals to explore their inner worlds and seek personal meaning outside the confines of traditional rationality and scientific discourse.

However, the para-rational nature of these belief systems also raised concerns about the potential for exploitation and the dissemination of unfounded or unverifiable claims. The lack of empirical evidence to support the efficacy of these self-help methods led to criticisms regarding their scientific legitimacy and the potential for individuals to be misled or deceived by charismatic leaders promoting these belief systems.

Overall, the term "para-rational" highlights the existence of belief systems that fall outside the scope of conventional rationality and scientific validation, often emphasizing subjective experiences and spiritual exploration in the pursuit of personal growth and well-being.

We have the option of believing in numerology, phrenology, palmistry, astrology,alchemy, I Ching divination, Ancient astronaut theory, Flat Earth theory or Hollow Earth theory, and each one of them is less toxic, more benign, more interesting, more fun and more entertaining than the theories and/or worldviews of Freud, Skinner or Kinsey. They are all safer than prescribing drugs for depression when even The Guardian reports that there is "no clear evidence" that low serotonin levels are responsible for depression. Getting a hot stone treatment and taking a forest bath once a week would have probably done a lot better for an entire generation.

The oddball belief systems have often been criticized for lacking empirical evidence or scientific validity, but the same can be said of the 'established' systems that calcified into money-making machines that profited off of human suffering. Which really brings us back to the most valuable lessons from the 70s. And, those seem to be the Esalon moments. The Whole Earth Catalog insights. The Mother Earth News support. The fitness boom. The health food (when the ingredients match the claims, read "The Whole Soy Story: The Dark Side of America's Favorite Health Food" (2005) by Kaayla T. Daniel, Ph.D., CCN.). Which leads to the question-

What is Worth Keeping?

I am certain the list is a lot longer than this, but here is a solid initial go.

The 1970s self-help revolution introduced several enduring and invaluable lessons that have continued to shape personal growth and well-being. These lessons include:

1. Fitness and Wellness: The emphasis on physical health and wellness has fostered enduring practices promoting a healthy lifestyle and well-being.

2. Goal-Setting and Personal Development: The focus on goal-setting and personal development has provided individuals with tools for setting and achieving objectives, fostering a sense of accomplishment and progress.

3. Self-Esteem and Empowerment: The promotion of self-esteem and empowerment has encouraged individuals to recognize their self-worth, fostering confidence and a positive self-image.

4. Deep Ecology and Environmental Awareness: The increased awareness of environmental issues has inspired a greater understanding of ecological responsibility and sustainable living.

5. Self-Reliance and Skepticism of Authority: Encouraging self-reliance and skepticism towards authority has fostered critical thinking, independence, and the questioning of societal norms and power structures.

492

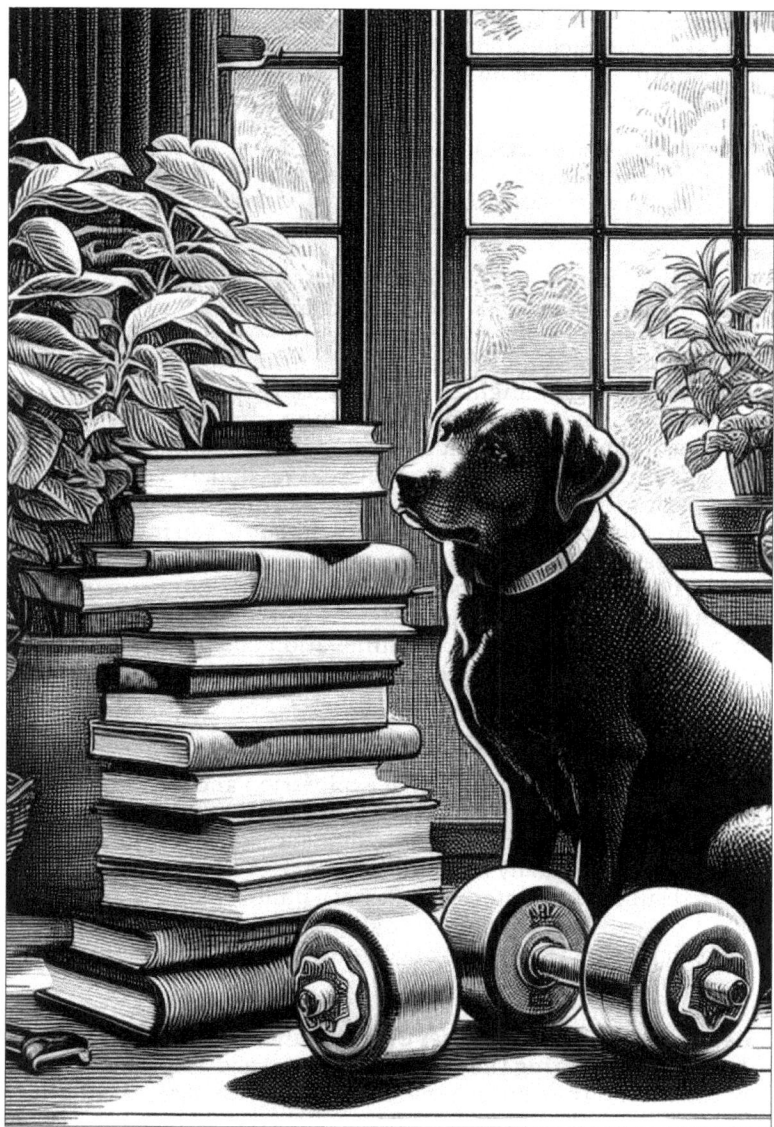

6. Learning New Skills: The encouragement of learning new skills has facilitated personal and professional growth, contributing to a lifelong pursuit of knowledge and self-improvement.

7. Respectful Interactions and Boundaries: Promoting respectful interactions and setting defined limits has enhanced interpersonal relationships, fostering understanding, empathy, and healthy boundaries.

8. Creative Thinking: The legacy of the 1970s self-help movement has had a profound impact on approaches to creative thinking, emphasizing the importance of fostering a mindset that encourages innovation, exploration, and open-mindedness. This movement highlighted the significance of embracing unconventional perspectives, nurturing a spirit of curiosity, and cultivating an environment that values experimentation and risk-taking in the pursuit of creative expression. It emphasized the integration of holistic practices, mindfulness, and diverse cultural influences, encouraging individuals to tap into their inner creativity and explore new avenues of self-expression. This legacy continues to underscore the importance of nurturing a conducive environment that supports and celebrates creative thinking, fostering a culture of innovation and personal growth that transcends traditional boundaries and fosters an appreciation for the power of imaginative exploration.

9. Renewed Wonder and Sense of the Sacred: During the 1970s, a cultural shift towards spiritual exploration and alternative belief systems fostered a renewed sense of wonder and a deeper connection to the sacred, as individuals sought to explore a more holistic and spiritually fulfilling approach to life. This period saw a resurgence of interest in Eastern philosophies, mystical traditions, and ecological spirituality, encouraging a broader appreciation for the interconnectedness **of all livi**ng beings and the natural world.

10. Ability to Embrace Other Cultures and Awareness of Other Perspectives. During the 1970s, there emerged a significant cultural trend that emphasized the importance of respecting and understanding other cultures, particularly those from the East, alongside a concurrent appreciation for the enduring wisdom and fundamental principles that have shaped Western civilization over centuries.

This cultural openness encouraged individuals to explore and integrate diverse perspectives and practices, recognizing the value of cross-cultural exchange and the enrichment it brings, while also reinforcing the significance of preserving the essential tenets and historical contributions of Western thought and heritage. This nuanced approach sought to bridge cultural divides, fostering a more inclusive and comprehensive worldview that celebrated the multiplicity of human experiences while upholding the core beliefs and values that form the bedrock of Western cultural identity. As long as one does not abandon the hard-fought and hard-win centuries of wisdom that their own culture provides to them as a foundation, a rock, a ballast in a not always pleasant storm of ideas and events, there is a lot to learn, share and enjoy.

These enduring lessons from the 1970s self-help movement have contributed to the cultivation of a holistic approach to personal growth, emphasizing physical, mental, and emotional well-being, as well as the development of strong interpersonal skills and social awareness.

Unlearning the Conventional: Challenges to the Education System 'Deschooling Society' by Ivan Illich and ' Teaching As a Conserving Activity' by Neil Postman

And, so much for the lessons. How do we communicate those lessons to the next generation? I have always thought of Illich and Postman as pointing a way (though I will be researching and writing about Black Mountain College in an upcoming Sentry Guide for 2024).

Ivan Illich's 'Deschooling Society' is a provocative critique of the modern education system, arguing that institutionalized schooling hinders genuine learning and perpetuates social inequalities. Illich contends that the traditional approach to education limits individual autonomy and creativity, promoting a one-size-fits-all model that fails to address the diverse needs and interests of learners. He advocates for the deinstitutionalization of education, emphasizing the importance of self-directed learning and the democratization of knowledge. Illich proposes alternative learning networks and community-based educational resources, aiming to empower individuals to take control of their own education and foster a culture of lifelong learning.

Neil Postman's 'Teaching as a Conserving Activity' complements Illich's critique by examining the cultural implications of the educational system. Postman emphasizes the need for educators to preserve and transmit cultural traditions and values, encouraging a critical evaluation of the content and purpose of education. He argues that the modern education system has become overly preoccupied with technological advancements and instrumental reasoning, neglecting the essential role of education in cultivating moral and civic virtues. Postman advocates for a return to a more humanistic and holistic approach to education, one that prioritizes the cultivation of ethical reasoning, critical thinking, and a deep understanding of cultural heritage.

Both Illich and Postman challenge the conventional education system by highlighting its limitations and proposing alternative approaches that prioritize individual agency, cultural preservation, and a holistic understanding of learning. They call for a reevaluation of the role of education in society, emphasizing the importance of nurturing a sense of intellectual curiosity, ethical awareness, and social responsibility. Their works underscore the need for a more nuanced and comprehensive approach to education that fosters a love of learning, critical inquiry, and a deeper engagement with the complexities of human experience. Through their thought-provoking insights, Illich and Postman inspire a broader conversation about the transformative potential of education in shaping a more just, informed, and culturally rich society.

Which really brings it down to the final classic of the 70s. One that perfectly illustrates how some thinkers made the leap from the venal and brutal, from the selfish and silly, from the fanatical and false into the realm of the utterly sublime.

The Secret Life of Plants: Bridging 70s Ecology and New Age Spirituality

"The Secret Life of Plants" is a groundbreaking book co-authored by Peter Tompkins and Christopher Bird, first published in 1973. The book delves into the intriguing and often controversial topic of plant consciousness and the mysterious ways in which plants interact with their environment and the living beings around them. It presents a wealth of research and anecdotal evidence suggesting that plants possess a form of awareness and sensitivity that transcends conventional scientific understanding.

Tompkins and Bird explore various scientific studies and anecdotal accounts that suggest plants may possess a level of consciousness and responsiveness to human emotions and intentions. The authors discuss topics such as plant perception, memory, and communication, highlighting experiments that demonstrate the ability of plants to react to external stimuli, including human thoughts and emotions. They also delve into the field of bioelectromagnetics, proposing that plants may have subtle energy fields that enable them to communicate and respond to their surroundings.

The book's exploration of plant consciousness and the interconnectedness of all living beings challenges conventional scientific paradigms and encourages readers to reconsider their relationship with the natural world. It raises thought-provoking questions about the nature of consciousness and the boundaries between the animate and inanimate realms, inviting readers to contemplate the profound implications of a living world that extends beyond the human experience.

Despite its controversial nature, "The Secret Life of Plants" has sparked a wider cultural conversation about the potential intelligence and sentience of the natural world, prompting a renewed appreciation for the interconnectedness of all living beings. The book continues to inspire further research and exploration into the mysteries of plant life, inviting readers to consider the intricate and enigmatic web of life that surrounds us and to cultivate a deeper sense of reverence and awe for the natural world.

Reception and Influence

Upon its publication, "The Secret Life of Plants" by Peter Tompkins and Christopher Bird had a notable impact on popular culture, sparking a widespread fascination with the mysteries and potential consciousness of the plant world. The book's exploration of plant perception and sensitivity resonated with a broad audience, leading to a cultural shift in the 1970s that saw a heightened interest in houseplants and botanical-themed establishments such as fern bars.

The book's intriguing revelations about plant communication and responsiveness captured the imagination of many, inspiring a newfound appreciation for the natural world and a desire to incorporate elements of nature into everyday living spaces. As a result, there was a surge in the popularity of houseplants and indoor gardening, with individuals seeking to cultivate greenery within their homes and offices, fostering a closer connection to nature and a sense of tranquility in urban environments.

Additionally, the concept of the fern bar, a type of stylish bar or restaurant adorned with an abundance of plants and greenery, gained popularity during this time, reflecting the cultural fascination with plant aesthetics and natural elements. Fern bars became trendy social spaces that provided a lush and inviting atmosphere, often adorned with various plant species to create a relaxed and natural ambiance for patrons.

Overall, "The Secret Life of Plants" contributed to a cultural reawakening of humanity's relationship with the natural world, inspiring a renewed appreciation for plant life and a desire to integrate elements of nature into everyday environments. Its impact on popular culture during the 1970s emphasized the enduring connection between humans and the natural world, fostering a greater awareness of the beauty and significance of plant life within contemporary urban lifestyles.

About the Authors

Peter Tompkins (1919–2007) was an American journalist and author known for his interest in the occult, alternative medicine, and environmentalism. He wrote several books on a range of esoteric subjects, including "The Secret Life of Plants," which became one of his most well-known works. Tompkins was also a war correspondent during World War II and later became a prominent investigative journalist, delving into various historical mysteries and alternative theories. He had a keen interest in the intersection of science, spirituality, and the natural world, which is reflected in his diverse body of work.

Christopher Bird (1928–1996) was a British author and journalist who shared Tompkins's passion for investigating alternative and esoteric subjects. He collaborated with Tompkins on "The Secret Life of Plants," contributing to the book's extensive research and writing. Bird's writing often explored unconventional topics, including parapsychology, alternative medicine, and the mysteries of the natural world. His work in collaboration with Tompkins helped bring the topic of plant consciousness and intelligence to a wider audience, sparking both controversy and curiosity about the hidden wonders of the natural world.

About the Documentary

"The Secret Life of Plants" is a documentary film directed by Walon Green, based on the book of the same name co-authored by Peter Tompkins and Christopher Bird. Released in 1979, the film explores the mysterious and fascinating world of plants, delving into their complex and often misunderstood nature. It delves into the largely unexplored realms of plant consciousness, perception, and their unique relationships with humans and the environment.

The documentary presents a series of experiments and observations that suggest plants may possess a form of awareness and responsiveness, challenging traditional scientific assumptions about the limits of plant life. It discusses topics such as plant communication, sensitivity to human emotions, and their alleged ability to react to external stimuli.

While the documentary was met with mixed reviews and some controversy, it contributed to a broader cultural conversation about the potential sentience and intelligence of the natural world, sparking both intrigue and skepticism among audiences. Despite the varied reception, "The Secret Life of Plants" remains a significant contribution to the exploration of plant consciousness and the interconnectedness of all living beings, inviting viewers to reconsider their relationship with the natural world and to contemplate the deeper mysteries of the plant kingdom.

About Stevie Wonder

Stevie Wonder was indeed involved in a project related to "The Secret Life of Plants," a documentary film directed by Walon Green and based on the book of the same name co-authored by Peter Tompkins and Christopher Bird. The documentary was released in 1979 and featured a soundtrack composed by Stevie Wonder. The soundtrack, also titled "Journey Through 'The Secret Life of Plants'," showcased Wonder's musical talents and his exploration of electronic and synthesizer-based sounds.

The album was experimental and innovative, reflecting Wonder's interest in pushing the boundaries of traditional R&B and soul music. While the documentary itself received mixed reviews and limited success, the soundtrack album was recognized for its ambitious and avant-garde approach, incorporating elements of ambient music and electronic experimentation. Despite the mixed reception at the time, the soundtrack has garnered a cult following over the years, appreciated for its unique sonic textures and its reflection of Wonder's musical versatility and creativity.

Stevie Wonder's involvement with "The Secret Life of Plants" marked a significant departure from his previous works, showcasing his willingness to explore new musical frontiers and experiment with unconventional sounds and themes. Though the project was not as commercially successful as some of his earlier albums, it stands as a testament to Wonder's artistic courage and his ongoing exploration of diverse musical genres and themes.

Finding the Sacred in *Chlorophytum comosum*

"The Secret Life of Plants" has left a lasting legacy in both scientific and popular culture, sparking ongoing discussions and research into the nature of plant consciousness and intelligence. While the book's claims have been met with skepticism from some scientific circles, its influence has extended beyond the realm of academic discourse, inspiring a deeper appreciation for the interconnectedness of all living beings and the mysteries of the natural world.

In popular culture, the book has contributed to a broader cultural consciousness about the importance of environmental conservation and the significance of fostering a more harmonious relationship with the natural world. It has encouraged a renewed reverence for the inherent intelligence and resilience of plant life, fostering a sense of wonder and respect for the intricate web of life that surrounds us.

"The Secret Life of Plants" has also inspired subsequent works in various media, including films, documentaries, and literature, that continue to explore the complexities of plant consciousness and the implications of these findings for our understanding of the natural world. Its legacy serves as a reminder of the ongoing quest to unravel the mysteries of the living world and to cultivate a deeper sense of ecological awareness and stewardship for the planet.

Suggested Reading

Here is a suggested reading list that includes books on Gaia theory and the interconnectedness of the natural world, along with works related to the theme of the secret life of plants:

1. "Gaia: A New Look at Life on Earth" by James Lovelock - A foundational work that introduces the Gaia hypothesis, proposing the Earth as a self-regulating, interconnected system.

2. "The Hidden Life of Trees: What They Feel, How They Communicate - Discoveries from a Secret World" by Peter Wohlleben - Explores the complex and interconnected life of trees, discussing their communication and social networks in forests.

3. "The Web of Life: A New Scientific Understanding of Living Systems" by Fritjof Capra - Examines the interconnectedness of living systems and the implications of this understanding for ecological sustainability and human well-being.

4. "Braiding Sweetgrass: Indigenous Wisdom, Scientific Knowledge, and the Teachings of Plants" by Robin Wall

Kimmerer - Blends indigenous wisdom with scientific knowledge, exploring the relationships between humans and the natural world.

5. "The Sixth Extinction: An Unnatural History" by Elizabeth Kolbert - Investigates the ongoing mass extinction event and its implications for the interconnected web of life on Earth.

6. "The Songs of Trees: Stories from Nature's Great Connectors" by David George Haskell - Explores the rich and complex relationships between trees and their environments, emphasizing the interconnectedness of all living beings in ecosystems.

7. "The Global Forest: Forty Ways Trees Can Save Us" by Diana Beresford-Kroeger - Discusses the vital role of trees in maintaining ecological balance and their significance for human health and well-being.

These books offer diverse perspectives on the interconnectedness of life on Earth, inviting readers to contemplate the intricate relationships between humans, nature, and the broader ecological systems that sustain life.

"Thanksgiving Prayer"
attributed to the Iroquois tradition.

It is often recited as a token of appreciation for the Earth's abundance and the interconnectedness of all living beings:

"We return thanks to our mother, the earth, which sustains us.

We return thanks to the rivers and streams, which supply us with water.

We return thanks to all herbs, which furnish medicines for the cure of our diseases.

We return thanks to the moon and stars, which have given to us their light when the sun was gone.

We return thanks to the sun, that has looked upon the earth with a beneficent eye.

Lastly, we return thanks to the Great Spirit, in whom is embodied all goodness, and who directs all things for the good of his children."

This prayer reflects the deep reverence for the natural world and the acknowledgment of the vital role that nature plays in sustaining life. It emphasizes the interconnectedness of all elements of the natural world and the essential balance that exists between humanity and the Earth.

"St. Patrick's Breastplate"
a traditional Celtic prayer

"St. Patrick's Breastplate" is a traditional Celtic prayer attributed to St. Patrick, the patron saint of Ireland. While it is not a direct thanksgiving to the Earth and the heavens, it reflects the deep spirituality and connection to nature characteristic of Celtic tradition. Here is an excerpt:

> "I bind unto myself today
> The power of Heaven, the light of the sun,
> The brightness of the moon,
> The splendour of fire,
> The flashing of lightning,
> The swiftness of wind,
> The depth of sea,
> The stability of earth,
> The compactness of rocks."

"Lines Composed a Few Miles above Tintern Abbey"
William Wordsworth

William Wordsworth, a prominent English Romantic poet, penned the renowned poem "Lines Composed a Few Miles above Tintern Abbey, On Revisiting the Banks of the Wye during a Tour, July 13, 1798." While not explicitly a prayer, it reflects on the beauty of nature and the spiritual connection to the natural world. Here is an excerpt that expresses gratitude to the Earth and the heavens:

"Nature never did betray
The heart that loved her; 'tis her privilege,
Through all the years of this our life, to lead
From joy to joy: for she can so inform
The mind that is within us, so impress
With quietness and beauty, and so feed
With lofty thoughts, that neither evil tongues,
Rash judgments, nor the sneers of selfish men,
Nor greetings where no kindness is, nor all
The dreary intercourse of daily life,
Shall e'er prevail against us, or disturb
Our cheerful faith, that all which we behold
Is full of blessings."

www.ingramcontent.com/pod-product-compliance
Lightning Source LLC
Chambersburg PA
CBHW070047030426
42335CB00016B/1827